The Ancient Secret of THE FLOWER OF LIFE

Volume 2

An edited transcript of
the Flower of Life Workshop
presented live to Mother Earth
from 1985 to 1994

Written and Updated by
Drunvalo Melchizedek

Book editor, Margaret Pinyan

Computer graphics originated by
Tim Stouse and Michael Tyree

ISBN 1-891824-21-X

Published by
Light Technology Publishing
P.O. Box 3540
Flagstaff, AZ 86336
(800) 450-0985

Printed by
SEDONA COLOR GRAPHICS
Sedona, AZ 86336

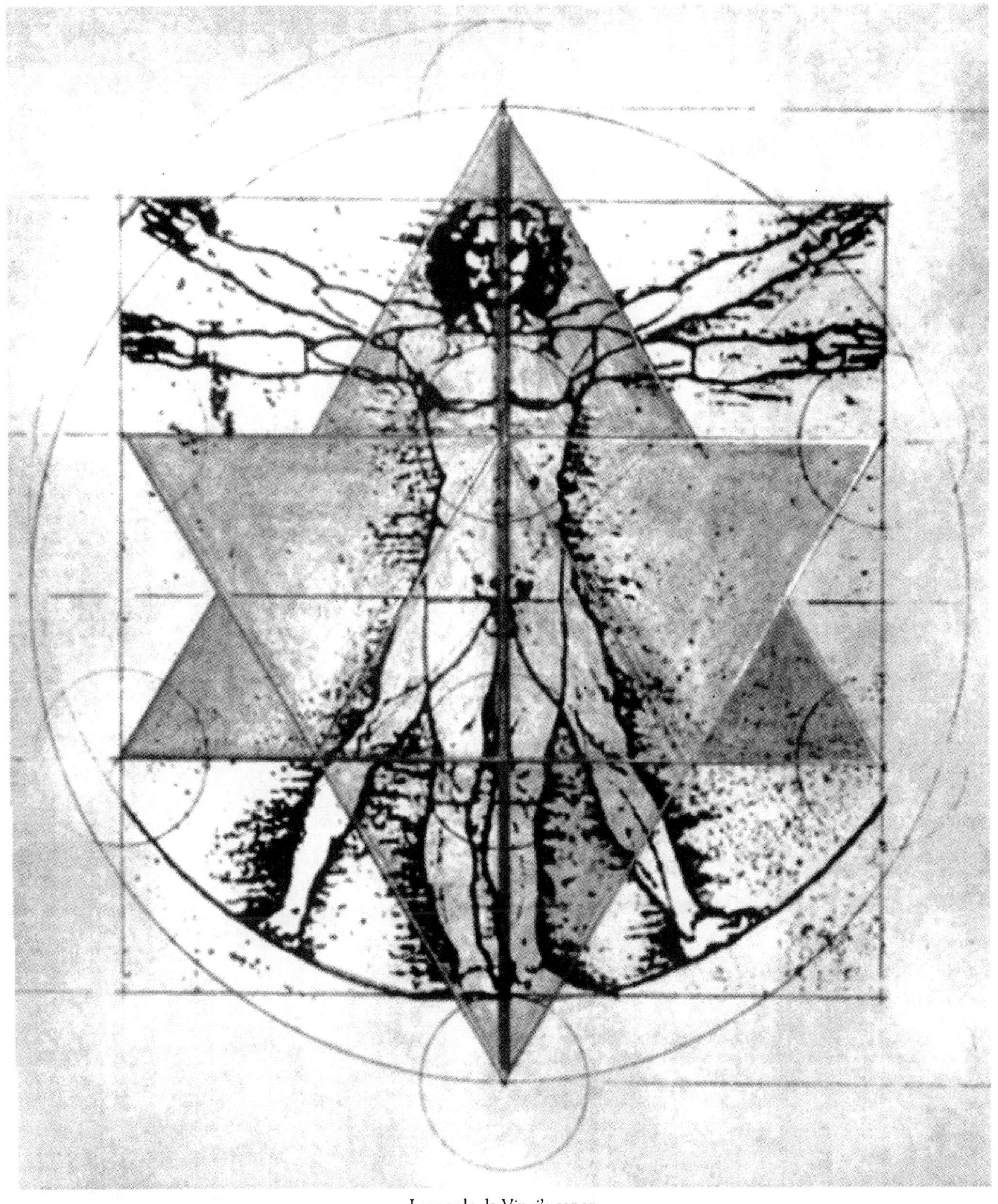

Leonardo da Vinci's canon
with Flower of Life sacred geometries.

Dedication

This book, volume 2, is dedicated to the child within you
and to all the new children as they emerge upon the face of the Earth
to bring us home into the higher light.

CONTENTS

Introduction xi

NINE Spirit and Sacred Geometry 225

The Third Informational System in the Fruit of Life 225

The Circles and Squares of Human Consciousness 225
Finding Near-Perfect Phi Ratios 226
The First and Third Levels of Consciousness 227
Locating the Second Level 228
Geometric Lenses to Interpret Reality 229
Superimposing the Fruit of Life 230
Lucie's Genius 230
Lucie's Ladder 231
Side Note: Sacred Geometry Is a Do-It-Yourself Project 233
A Snag in the Ladder 234

The Three Lenses 235

Square Roots and 3-4-5 Triangles 236
Leonardo's and CBS's Eye 237
Vitruvius' 10 by 12 238
10,000 Years to Figure Out 239

Vitruvius and the Great Pyramid 240

The Search for a 14 by 18 241
The Unknown Leonardo 242

A Great Synchronicity 245

Earth-Moon Proportions 246
Earth, Moon and Pyramid Proportions 248

Rooms in the Great Pyramid 248

More Rooms 250
The Initiation Process 250
Light Reflectors and Absorbers above the King's Chamber 251

Comparing the Levels of Consciousness 252

Catching the White Light 252
Proof of the Initiation Chamber 254
Catching the Dark Light 255
The Halls of Amenti and the Face of Jesus 256

Summary of the Initiation Process 256

TEN The Left Eye of Horus Mystery School 259
Egyptian Initiations 262
Crocodile Initiation at Kom Ombo 262
The Well under the Great Pyramid 267
The Tunnel beneath the Pyramid 268
The Hathors 278
Dendera 280
An Immaculate Conception 282
The World's Virgin Births 282
Parthenogenesis 283
Conception on a Different Dimension 284
Thoth's Genesis and Family Tree 285
An Earth Lineage Travels into Space 285
The Flower of Life Seen from the Feminine Side 287
Wheels on the Ceiling 292
The Geometry of the Egyptian Wheels 293

ELEVEN Ancient Influences on Our Modern World 297
The Heliacal Rising of Sirius 303
Virgo and Leo, Aquarius and Pisces 304
The Four Corners Implication 304
The Philadelphia Experiment 305

TWELVE The Mer-Ka-Ba, the Human Lightbody 309
The Geometries of the Human Chakra System 310
The Unfolded Egg of Life and the Musical Scale 311
The Human Chakras and the Musical Scale 314
The Wall with a Hidden Doorway 315
Ways to Find the Doorway 317
Chakras on Our Star Tetrahedrons 319
The Egyptian 13-Chakra System 320
Discovering the True Chakra Locations 321
A Body-Surface Chakra Map 322
A Different Movement on the Star Tetrahedron 323
The Five Spiraling Light Channels 324
Let There Be Light 324
Egyptian Sexual Energy and the Orgasm 330
The 64 Sexual/Personality Configurations 332
Instructions for the Orgasm 333
Beyond the Fifth Chakra 334
Through the Final Half Step 335
The Energy Fields around the Body 337
How to See Auras 338
The Rest of the Human Lightbody 340

THIRTEEN The Mer-Ka-Ba Geometries and Meditation 343

The Star Tetrahedron, Source of All Geometric Fields around the Body ... 344
Spherical Breathing and the Remembrance of the Mer-Ka-Ba ... 346
An Overview of the Meditation ... 347
Part 1: The First Six Breaths ... 347
Part 2: The Next Seven Breaths, Re-creating Spherical Breathing ... 350
Part 3: The Fourteenth Breath ... 352
Part 4: The Last Three Breaths, Creating the Vehicle of Ascension ... 353
Additional Information, and Problems That People Sometimes Experience ... 356
Minor Problems and Misunderstandings ... 359
The Acceleration of Spirit in Matter ... 360
An Overview of the Human Energy Field beyond the Mer-Ka-Ba ... 361

FOURTEEN The Mer-Ka-Ba and the Siddhis 367

Further Uses for the Mer-Ka-Ba ... 367
Meditation ... 368
Siddhis, or Psychic Powers ... 369
Programming Crystals ... 370
Mer-Ka-Ba Programs ... 371
Ways to Manifest Wine ... 371
The Gas Can ... 372
The Stack of Money ... 373
The Second Stack ... 374
Four Ways to Program the Mer-Ka-Ba ... 375
Male Programming ... 375
Female Programming ... 377
Both Programming ... 377
Neither Programming ... 377
The Surrogate Mer-Ka-Ba ... 378
Conclusion ... 378

FIFTEEN Love and Healing 379

Love Is Creation ... 379
"Heal Thyself" ... 382
Healing Others ... 384
A Final Message and a Story ... 390

SIXTEEN The Three Levels of the Self 393

The Lower Self—Mother Earth ... 396
The Higher Self—All That Is ... 399

From My Old Writings—Living as a Child 399
How Life Works When You're Connected with the Higher Self 401
Communicating with Everything Everywhere 403
Foretelling the Future 404
The Lessons of the Seven Angels 406
Testing the Reality of Your Connection with Your Higher Self 407

SEVENTEEN Duality Transcended **411**

Judging 411
The Lucifer Experiment: Duality 411
The Bright and Shining One 412
Creating a Dualistic Reality 414
Earth Humans as the Focus of the Experiment 417
Using the Intellect without Love 418
The Third, Integrated Way 419
The Sirian Experiment 419
My Three Days in Space 419
Technology Reconsidered 421
The History of the Sirian Experiment 422
August 7, 1972, and the Successful Aftermath 425
The Return of Free Will and Unexpected Positive Consequences 426

EIGHTEEN The Dimensional Shift **429**

The Great Change 429
An Overview of a Dimensional Shift 429
The First Signs 430
The Phase before the Shift 431
Five to Six Hours before the Shift 432
Synthetic Objects and Lucifer-Reality Thought Forms 433
Planetary Shifts 434
The Experience of an Actual Planetary Shift 435
Six Hours before the Shift 435
The Void—Three Days of Blackness 436
The New Birth 437
Your Thoughts and Survival 438
How to Prepare: The Secret of Everyday Life 440
This Unique Transition 442

NINETEEN The New Children **443**

The Current Growth of Knowledge 443
Human Mutations, Historical and Recent 445
DNA Changes in Blood Types 445
The Indigo Children 446
The Children of AIDS 448

The Bible Code and AIDS 449
The Superpsychic Children 450
The Fourth-Dimensional Shift and the Superkids 454
Life Is Great, an Epilogue 455
References 459
Index 463
Template for a Star Tetrahedron (see back of book)

INTRODUCTION

We meet again, together exploring the vastness of who we are, and again dreaming the same ancient secret that life is a beautiful mystery leading to wherever we envision.

Volume 2 contains the meditation instructions that were originally taught to me by the angels for entering the consciousness state called the Mer-Ka-Ba—in modern terms called the human lightbody. Our lightbody holds the possibility for the human potential to transcend into a new translation of the universe we find so familiar. Within a specific state of consciousness, all things can begin anew and life will change in ways that appear miraculous.

These words speak more of remembrance than of learning or teaching. You already know what is in these pages because it is written in every cell of your body, but it is also hidden deep inside your heart and your mind, where all that is really needed is just a simple nudge.

Out of the love that I have for you and all life everywhere, I offer these images and this vision to you so that they will be useful; so that they will bring you closer to the self-realization that Great Spirit is intimately and lovingly connected to your essence; and with the prayer that these words be the catalyst that opens the way for you into the higher worlds.

You and I live in a pivotal moment in Earth's history. The world is dramatically metamorphosing as computers and humans enter into a symbiotic relationship, giving Mother Earth two ways to see and interpret world events. She is using this new sight to alter and open the pathways into the higher worlds of light so that even a child can understand. Our Mother loves us so much.

We, her children, are now walking between the two worlds, our ordinary everyday life and a world that surpasses the dreams of even our oldest ancestors. With our Mother's love and our Father's help, we will find a way to heal the hearts of the people and transform this world back into unity consciousness once again.

May you enjoy what you are about to read, and may it truly be a blessing in your life.

In love and service,
Drunvalo

NINE

Spirit and Sacred Geometry

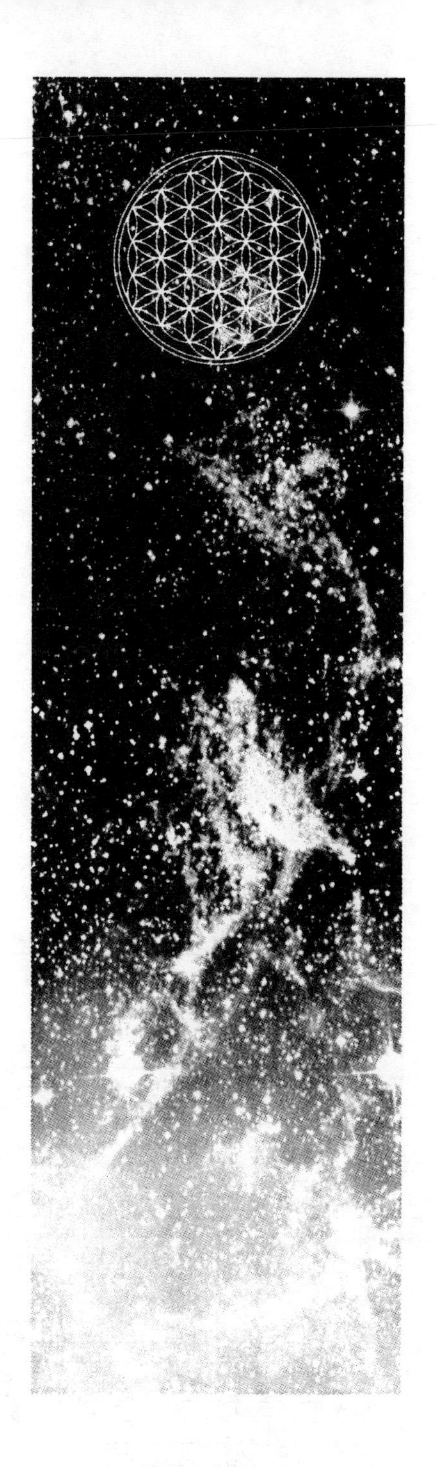

The Third Informational System in the Fruit of Life

What you are about to read is a subject outside most human thought. I ask you to read this with a little faith, and to carefully begin to see in a new way. It may not make sense until you are deep into the subject. It revolves around the idea that *all consciousness*, including human, *is solely based on sacred geometry*. Because it is, we can begin to see and understand where we have come from, where we are now and where we are going.

Remember that the Fruit of Life is the basis of all thirteen informational systems, and that it is by superimposing male straight lines in unique ways over the female circles of the Fruit of Life that these systems are created. In the first eight chapters we investigated two of these systems. The first system created Metatron's Cube, which generated the five Platonic solids. These forms created structure throughout the universe.

The second system, which we touched on lightly, was created by straight lines coming from the center of the Fruit of Life *and* concentric circles, thus creating the polar graph. This in turn created the star tetrahedron inscribed in a sphere, which is the basis of how vibration, sound, harmonics, music and matter are interrelated in all of creation.

The Circles and Squares of Human Consciousness

We will approach this third informational system indirectly. The source, the Fruit of Life, will reveal itself as we proceed. We'll call this new system *circles and squares of human consciousness*. It's what the Chinese called circling the square and squaring the circle.

According to Thoth, all levels of consciousness in the universe are integrated by a single image in sacred geometry. It is the key to time, space and dimension as well as consciousness itself. Thoth also said that even emotions and thoughts are based on sacred geometry, but that subject will have to wait until later in this book.

For each level of consciousness there is an associated geometry that completely defines how that specific level of consciousness will interpret the one Reality. Each level is a geometrical image or lens that spirit looks through to see the one Reality, resulting in a completely unique experience. Even the spiritual hierarchy of the universe is geometrical in its structure, copying nature.

According to Thoth, there are nine crystal balls beneath the Sphinx, one inside the other. Archaeologists and psychics have been searching for these crystal balls for a long time—it's an ancient legend. It is said that these crystal balls are somehow connected to the consciousness of the Earth and to the three levels of consciousness that humans are now experiencing.

Various seekers have searched for the nine spheres, spending a great deal of time and money, but according to Thoth, you don't need the crystal balls; you just need to draw nine concentric circles, because it's just as revealing. If they'd known it was geometry and consciousness they were seeking and not necessarily an object, the knowledge would have come easier.

According to Thoth, if you were to approach a planet you've never seen before and wanted to know the different levels of consciousness experienced on that planet, you would take some of the little beings on that planet and measure them, assuming you can get them to hold still long enough. From those measurements you can determine the square-and-circle sacred ratios connected with their bodies, and from this information determine their exact level of consciousness.

Other ratios, always derived from the cube, are used to determine the levels of consciousness in other than the human form, such as animals, insects and ETs, but in the case of humans, it's the circle and the square. By seeing if the square that fits around the body is bigger or littler than the circle that goes around the body, and by exactly how much, you can determine how they interpret the Reality and exactly what level of consciousness they're on. There are quicker ways, actually, but this way is fundamental to existence itself.

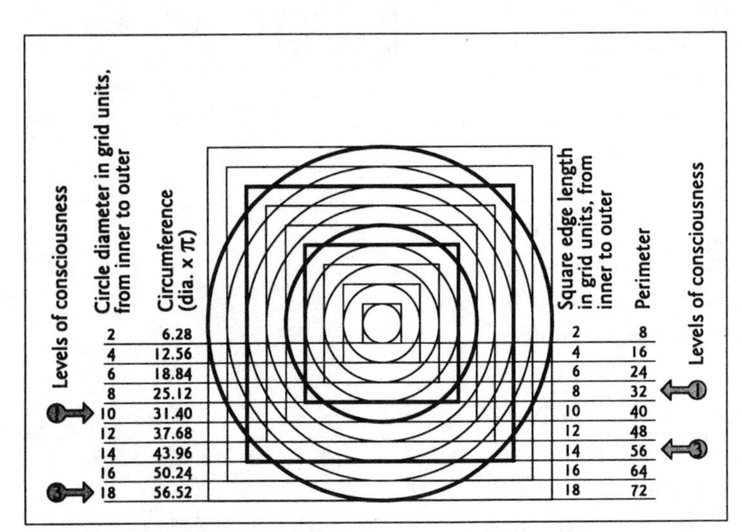

Fig. 9-1. Concentric circles and squares. The darker circles and squares are the pairs that approximate the phi ratio. They also locate the first and third levels of human consciousness. (One grid unit equals one *radius* of the center circle or *one-half side* of the square that surrounds it. One can see that the diameter of the center circle and one edge of its surrounding square are the same length.)

Thoth said to draw nine concentric circles and put a square around each one so that it fits perfectly (one side of the square and the diameter of the circle inside it will be equal), as in Figure 9-1. In this way you have equal male and female energies. Then see how the squares interact with the circles—how the male energy interacts with the female energy. The key, according to Thoth, is how closely the perimeter of the square and the circumference of the circle approximate the phi ratio. This is the key to human life.

Finding Near-Perfect Phi Ratios

Looking at the innermost square, no circles cross it; the same is true for the second square. The third square begins to penetrate the fourth circle, though it's obviously not a phi ratio. However, the fourth square penetrates the fifth circle in what *appears* to be a near-perfect phi ratio. Then it goes out of phi ratio again on the fifth and sixth squares. Then, unexpectedly, the seventh square penetrates the ninth circle again in what *appears* to be a near-perfect phi ratio—not *one* circle beyond, as it did on the fourth square and fifth circle, but *two* circles beyond. And it is even closer to the Golden Mean, the phi ratio of 1.6180339..., than the first one.

This is the beginning of a geometrical progression that could go on forever, a progression in which we humans are only the second possible step. (And we thought so highly of ourselves!) Using the full life of a human as the yardstick, in human history we are now at the level of consciousness represented by the development of the human zygote just after the completion of the first cell. Life in the universe is beyond anything we can image, yet we are a seed that contains the beginning as well as the end.

Coming back to the practical, you can measure these things without a measuring stick by calling the radius of the innermost circle one unit; thus the first circle and first square are two radii across. (This unit makes up an implied grid.) And when you expand to the fourth square, it will be 8 radii across. To know how many radii there are around all four sides of the square, you simply multiply by 4 to see that 32 radii compose the perimeter of the fourth square. We need to know the perimeter because when it equals or approximates the circumference of the circle, we have the phi ratio. (Check chapter 7.)

We wish to see if the fifth circle's circumference is equal to (or close to) the perimeter of the fourth square (32 radii), so we calculate its circumference by multiplying its diameter times pi (3.14). Since there are 10 units (radii) across the fifth circle, if you multiply that times pi (3.14), the circumference equals 31.40 radii. The square's perimeter is exactly 32, so they are very close; the circle is slightly smaller. According to Thoth, this represents the first time that human consciousness becomes self-aware.

Now let's calculate this for the seventh square and ninth circle. There are 14 radii across the seventh square; multiplying by 4 sides gives us 56 radii for the perimeter of the seventh square. The ninth circle has a diameter of 18 radii, and that times pi is 56.52. In this case the circle is slightly larger, whereas before, it was slightly smaller. If you keep making circles beyond the original nine, you'll see the same pattern: slightly larger, slightly smaller, slightly larger, slightly smaller—getting closer and closer to the perfection we noted on the Fibonacci sequence approaching the phi ratio [see chapter 8].

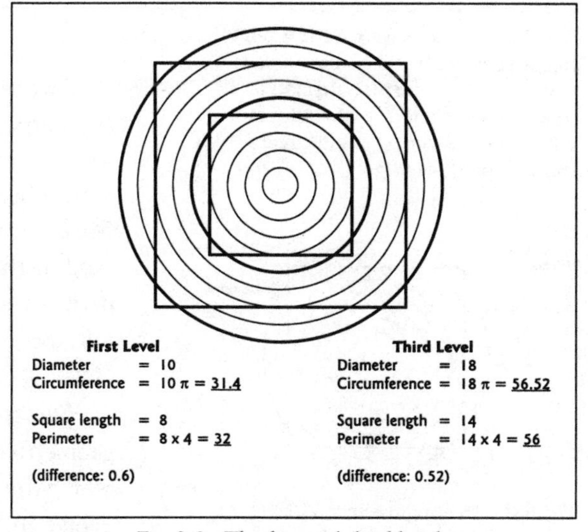

Fig. 9-2. The first and third levels of human consciousness, near-perfect phi ratios.

The First and Third Levels of Consciousness

In Figure 9-2 we are looking at the very beginning of consciousness in these first two phi-ratio places. This indicates that consciousness will probably continue forever to expand

and approximate the perfection of the phi ratio or the Golden Mean. So the fourth square relative to the fifth circle and the seventh square relative to the ninth circle form near-perfect phi ratios. Those happen to be, according to Thoth, the first and third levels of consciousness. They are very, very close to being harmonic consciousness, which makes them self-aware. Remember the nautilus shell (page 210)? In the beginning it was not even harmonically close, compared to several steps further down the geometrical path. It is the same here. But what happened to the second level of human consciousness?

According to Thoth, no one has ever figured out how to go from the first level, which is where the Aboriginals are, straight into the third level, which is Christ or unity consciousness. We needed to have a stepping stone or a bridge between the two—which is us, the second level. The question now is, where is our level of consciousness in this drawing?

5th square
6th circle
(second level)
7th square
9th circle
(third level)
4th square
5th circle
(first level)

Second Level
Diameter = 12
Circumference = $12\pi = 37.70$

Square length = 10
Perimeter = $10 \times 4 = 40$
(Difference: 2.3)

Fig. 9-3. The three geometric levels of human consciousness on Earth: square 4 and circle 5 = first (aboriginal) level; square 5 and circle 7 = second (present) level; and square 7 and circle 9 = third (Christ) level.

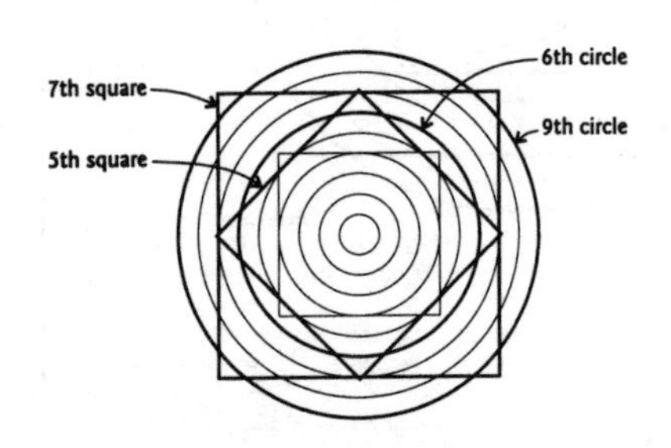

Fig. 9-4. Rotating the second-level square 45 degrees bridges the second and third levels of consciousness.

Locating the Second Level

There are two places where we (ordinary humanity) could be on this circle/square system: on the fifth or the sixth square relative to some other circle. There are only two squares between the first and third levels in Figure 9-1. From my way of seeing, I didn't know what difference it would make which square we were on, and Thoth wouldn't tell me. He just said, "It's the fifth square relative to the sixth circle" without explaining why. So for two or three years I was wondering why it was the fifth square relative to the sixth circle and not the sixth square relative to the seventh circle. Still he wouldn't tell me. He simply said, "You figure it out." It took me a long time to understand why. When I finally figured out why, Thoth simply gave me a nod, meaning I was correct. Here are the three levels of consciousness with the other nonharmonic squares removed [see Fig. 9-3].

If we rotate the square by 45 degrees [see Fig. 9-4] into a diamond, the secret purpose of our existence becomes apparent. In this view the rotated fifth square very closely approximates the location of the seventh square. It is not perfect because we are not harmonic ourselves, and we do not have a perfect Christ love, but we show the way to Christ consciousness by our human love. And further, we are still connected to the first level because our geometry perfectly touches the fourth circle of the first level of consciousness. We contain the Aboriginal consciousness perfectly, and we imperfectly contain the Christ love. This is what we are—a connecting bridge.

This is the key to why human consciousness is found in this particular geometric relationship and why it is necessary. Without our present way of seeing the one Reality, the first level of consciousness would never be able to evolve into the higher light. We are like a rock in the middle of a small stream. One jumps to it, but immediately continues on to the other side.

As you're going to see later in this chapter, this diamond view is the key to our second level of consciousness. You'll see this in the Great Pyramid and also in other works I'll be showing you. The square with the diamond inside is very important to humanity. Buckminster Fuller also thought it was very important. This form, when in 3D, is called the *cuboctahedron*. Bucky gave it a special name: the *vector equilibrium*. Bucky observed that the cuboctahedron has the amazing ability, through rotation, to become all five Platonic solids, giving a clue to its paramount position in sacred geometry. Why is it important to humanity? Because the square with the diamond inside it is connected to one of the primary reasons for human existence—the role of moving from Aboriginal, the first level of consciousness, to Christ consciousness, the third level.

When you measure the human geometries using this system, we humans are off by about three and a half radii. We're not even close to being harmonic. (You could measure this yourself if you wish.) We're a disharmonic consciousness, though we are necessary to complete life. So when life gets to where we are, it gets in and out as fast as possible, like jumping on the rock in the middle of the stream. Why? Because when we are disharmonic, we destroy anything and everything around us. If we stay there too long, our lack of wisdom will destroy even ourselves. If you look at the world's environment and our continual wars, you can understand. Yet we are essential to life.

Geometric Lenses to Interpret Reality

The next thing Thoth wanted me to do was look at these three different levels of consciousness geometrically so I could see what these geometrical lenses looked like. Remember, there's only one God, only one Reality. But there are lots of ways to interpret the Reality.

The innermost square (the fourth) in Figure 9-5 represents the first level; the middle square (the fifth) the second level; and the outer one (the seventh) the third level. I'm going to call the inner square an 8 by 10, meaning that it has eight radii per side and its relating circle (the fifth) has a diameter of ten. The middle square is 10 across and the sixth circle 12, so I'm calling it a 10 by 12. This is the middle or second level, which we exist on now. For the Christ-consciousness level, there are 14 radii across the square (the seventh) and 18 radii across the ninth circle, so we'll call that a 14 by 18. So we have an 8 by 10, a 10 by 12 and a 14 by 18.

Now, there's always a reason for everything in sacred geometry. Nothing—absolutely nothing—occurs without a reason. You might ask why, out of the whole spectrum of possibilities, did self-aware consciousness *begin* when the fourth square went into harmony with the fifth circle?

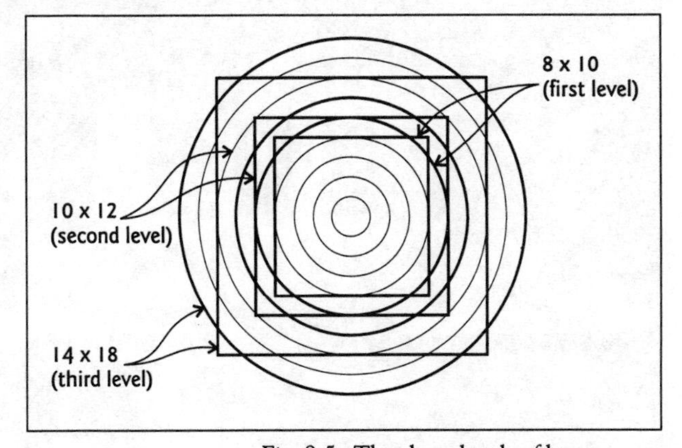

Fig. 9-5. The three levels of human consciousness in terms of units or radii in their circle-square pairs.

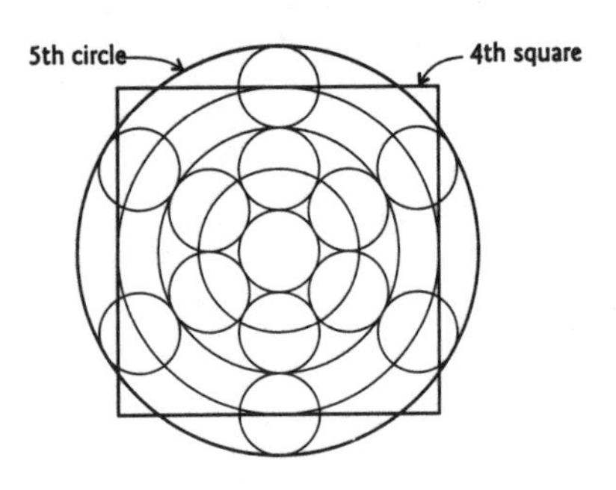

Fig. 9-6. Fruit of Life overlaid upon the first level of consciousness.

Superimposing the Fruit of Life

To understand why, let's try superimposing the Fruit of Life on this drawing of the first level of consciousness [see Fig. 9-6]. Look at that! It exactly fits the fourth square and the fifth circle, our 8 by 10! This center circle is the same as the center circle of the previous drawing, as are all five concentric circles here. This drawing shows only the fourth square, which forms a near-perfect phi ratio with the fifth circle, as we saw before.

Do you see the perfection of life? The Fruit of Life pattern was hidden beneath this pattern all along; they're precisely superimposed over one another. In a right-brain way, that's how to explain why consciousness first became self-aware between the fourth and the fifth circle—because that sacred image was hidden behind that part of the pattern. The Fruit of Life was completed at that precise moment and the phi ratio first appeared. When the phi ratio appeared, it was the first time that consciousness actually had a way to manifest.

Lucie's Genius

There's one more thing before we get into those three different images of consciousness. When I discovered that the concentric circles-and squares drawing could be superimposed perfectly over the Fruit of Life pattern, I wanted to see if anything had been written about it. At the time, I was sitting in my room listening to this man Thoth, whom nobody else could see but me, and he was telling me that the Egyptians perceived three different levels of human consciousness. I wanted to know if this idea existed in Egyptian history outside his account.

When I tried to find it in the writings, to my surprise, I did. At least I found it in the writings of Lucie Lamy, the stepdaughter of Schwaller de Lubicz. Nobody else I could find knew anything about this idea of three levels of human consciousness. Schwaller and Lucie understood deeply about Egypt's relationship to sacred geometry. Most Egyptologists didn't understand that *at all* until recently. In my estimation, after studying Lucie's work, she is one of the greatest people ever involved in sacred geometry. She has absolutely amazed me with her work. I always wanted to meet her, but I never did. She died a few years ago, about 1989 or so, in Abydos, Egypt. I want to show you something about Lucie Lamy so you can see what caliber of person she was.

Fig. 9-7. A side view of the temple at Karnak that Lucie put together.

This small temple [see Fig. 9-7] is inside the Karnak temple complex. Karnak is connected to the Temple of Luxor by a wide walkway about two miles long. It has human-headed sphinxes on both sides at the Luxor end, which gradually turn into sheep-headed sphinxes as it gets closer to Karnak. The Karnak temple complex is huge, and the pool where the ancient priests cleansed themselves would amaze you by its sheer size.

To give you a sense of the scale of this small temple, a person standing in front of it would come up to about the lower edge of the slanted windowsill. Before Lucie found the stones of this temple, they were literally just a big pile of rocks. The archaeologists knew that they belonged together because they were unique; there was nothing else around like them. But they didn't know what the building had looked like, so they left them in a big pile, hoping that someday someone would figure it out. Then they found another big pile of unique stones. They had no idea about them, either. What do you do with a bunch of broken-up stones? It's hard to say what the original building looked like, right?

But Lucie looked at the rocks, took some measurements, and then went home and drew plans that looked just like this photograph. She said, "That's what it's going to look like." And when they put it together, every single stone fit together and formed what you see there! She understood sacred geometry, and she had made the blueprint by examining the stones and measuring them. She put another building together in a similar way. I think that's really exceptional. The more I study this woman, the more I'm amazed by her.

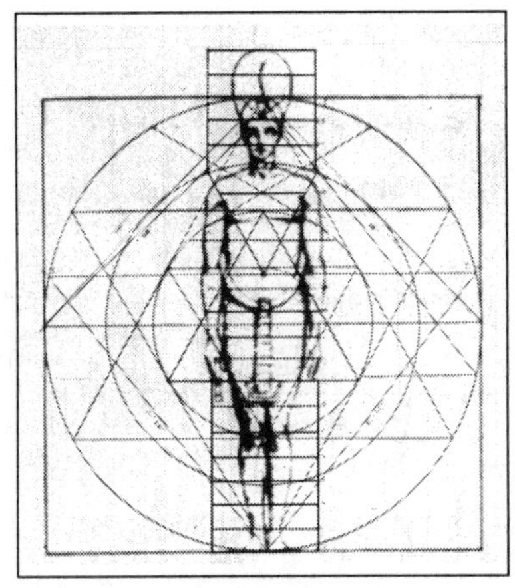

Fig. 9-8. Lucie Lamy's original drawing.

Lucie's Ladder

Before Lucie died, she put all her understanding of the Egyptians' knowledge of these three levels of consciousness into one drawing. She said this was the key to understanding Egypt's consciousness levels. Therefore I attempted to analyze what she was saying through her one drawing on this subject.

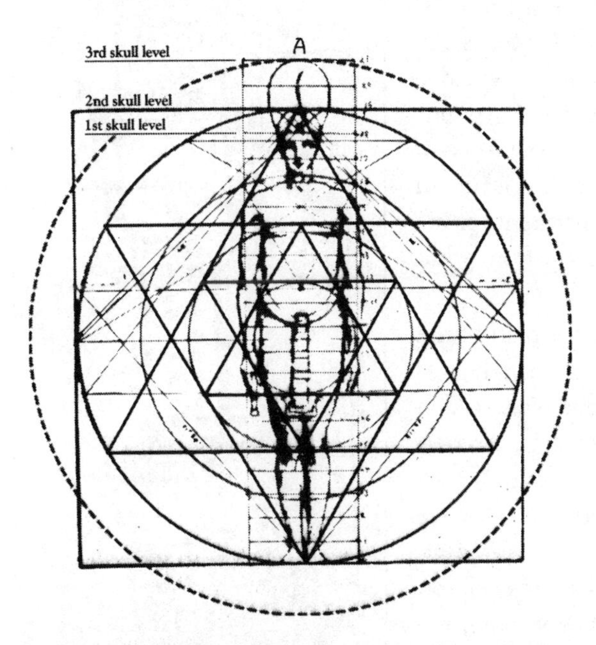

Fig. 9-9. Lucie's drawing with a new outer circle at the top of the head of the third level of consciousness and a small and large Star of David. The new circle's circumference matches the perimeter of the square.

This is her drawing [Fig. 9-8]. I redrew it in this next photo [Fig. 9-9] and later added the outer broken-line circle so I can show you something else. It was not copied clearly and had to be redrawn.

The first thing I noticed about her drawing was that there was a Star of David within a Star of David and a circle in

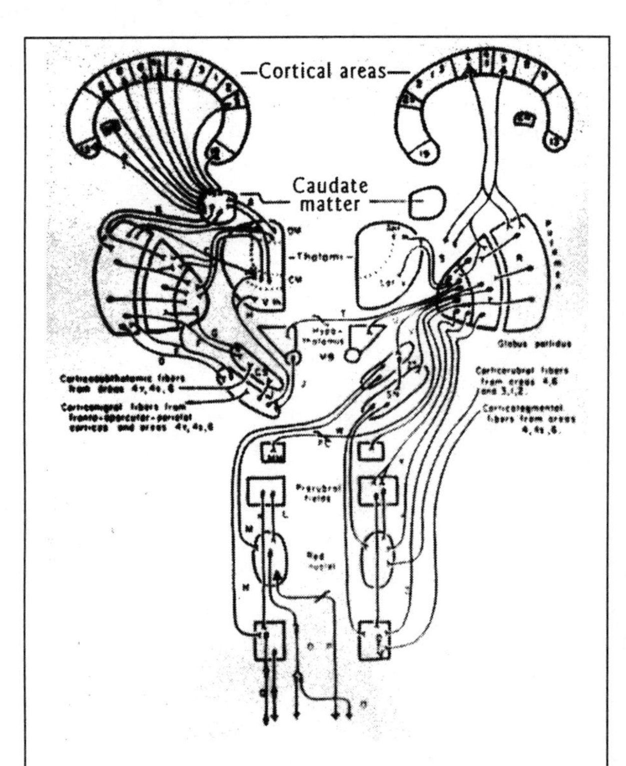

Schematic diagram of the computing centers and communications pathways of the extrapyramidal system in the human brain. Removal of the upper cortical areas, where conscious thinking takes place, has little effect on the circuit of information required for the equally complex computations needed for walking and maintaining equilibrium. The pathways show the routes of chemical reactions and electric-like impulses. (From *Brains, Behavior and Robotics* by James S. Albus, Byte Books, 1981.)

Fig. 9-10. Schematic of human brain showing that a lobotomy would not affect complex motor functions.

the middle. (We've seen that before in the Fruit of Life [see page 162] and we'll see it again shortly.) Also, there's a ladder going up the middle, from zero to 19 steps inside the square, then two more steps above, a total of 21.

According to Lucie, the numbers 18, 19 and 21 are directly connected to Egyptian thought concerning the three levels of consciousness. Eighteen symbolizes the Aboriginals, and she wrote that the ancient Egyptians believed that humans then didn't have the top half of the skull. Apparently the skull used to slope to the back. When we moved into the second level, we "added" a higher skull, and when we physically move into the third level, as we are about to do, we'll grow a huge skull that will extend to the phi-ratio point of the circle that would relate to the square—to 21. If you draw a phi-ratio circle around the square, indicated at point A, it exactly reaches the center of line 21. Therefore, each of the skull levels are actually contained in the geometry of this drawing, according to Lucie.

Figure 9-10 is a schematic of the human brain from *Brains, Behavior and Robotics* by James S. Albus. This shows that you can perform a lobotomy, removing the entire top half of the skull with everything in it, and it won't kill a person—which to me is astounding in itself. This is circumstantial evidence that what the Egyptians were saying was true: that the top half of our skull was added, that it is not an absolutely essential component for life and is something separate from what we used to be.

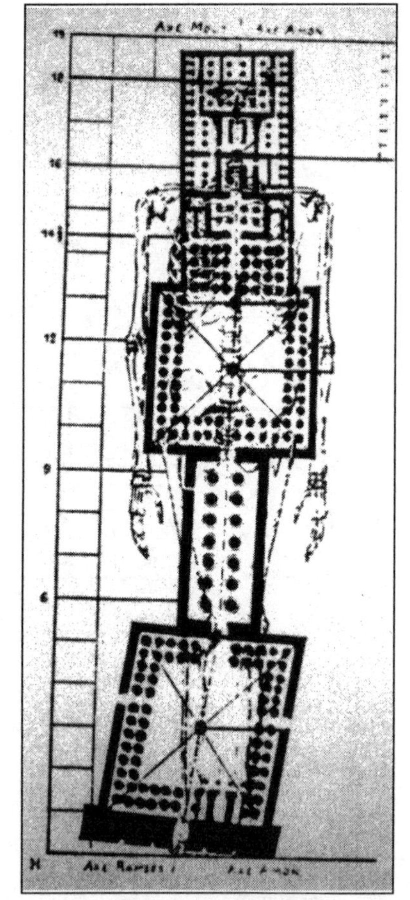

Fig. 9-11. Plan of the Temple of Luxor.

Figure 9-11 is the floor plan of the Temple of Luxor. This temple was dedicated to mankind and is also called the Temple of Man, which means *us*—not any man, not just any level of consciousness, but the second level we're on now. This plan is laid out in 19 divisions. You can see the human skeleton behind the drawing. Every room, everything in this drawing, was designed to represent all the various parts of the human being. Coming off from the feet was a long pathway that led several miles to the temple complex at Karnak.

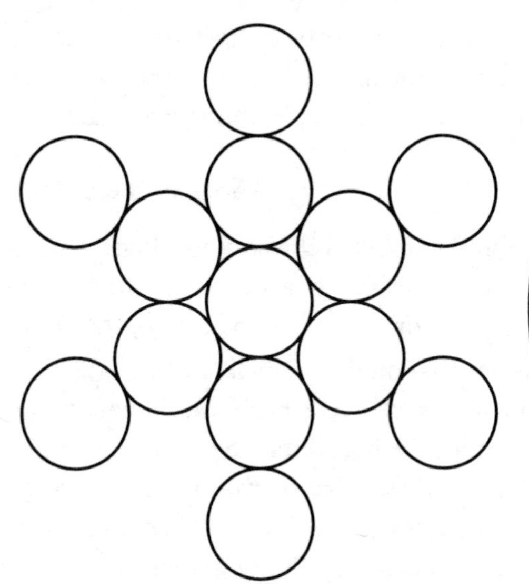

Fig. 9-12. The Fruit of Life.

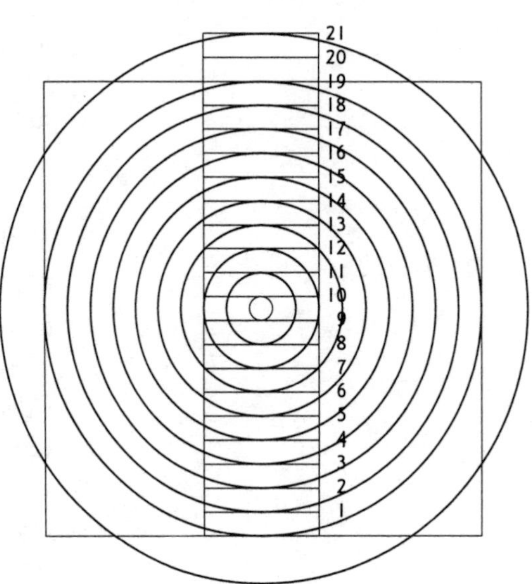

Fig. 9-13. Lucie's ladder, with concentric circles drawn to step 19 and again at step 21.

I had first noticed that the Fruit of Life [Fig. 9-12] was definitely contained in Lucie's drawing [Fig. 9-8]. This fact alone impresses me because I hadn't seen the Fruit of Life anywhere else in Egypt.

But I wanted to understand more about the ladder that goes to the top, to 19 and 21. I knew that a ladder like this is another way of making concentric circles, so I decided to study what Lucie was doing with this ladder. I began to redraw every one of her lines to see what she was trying to convey [Fig. 9-13]. So I took these two drawings [Figs. 9-12 and 9-13], which were obviously both out of her original drawing, and combined them. I reconstructed her drawing, superimposing the lines very accurately [Fig. 9-13a].

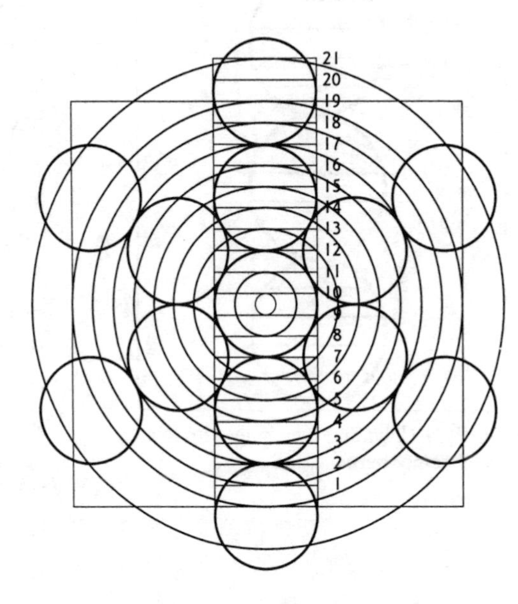

Fig. 9-13a. Lucie's basic geometry, with the temple plan and the Fruit of Life superimposed over it.

Side Note: Sacred Geometry Is a Do-It-Yourself Project

This might be the right time to take a little side trip and express something about sacred geometry that is very important to understand if you decide to become a student of the subject. When you sit in an audience and look at sacred geometry forms or read about it in this or any other book, receiving the information passively, you're absorbing a very small amount of the information coming off these drawings. However, if you were to sit down and *draw* them yourself, actually construct them, something happens to you, something far beyond what happens if you simply look at them. Anyone who has ever done this will tell you the same thing. This is one of the basic premises of the Masons. When you actually sit down and line things up and physically draw the lines, something seems to happen that is akin to a revelation. You draw the circle and you start understanding. Something happens inside. You start understanding on very, very deep levels why things are done the way they are. I believe there is no substitute for personally reconstructing these drawings.

I can *tell* you about how important this is, but what I've found is that few people actually take the time. It took me over twenty years to do these drawings, but it doesn't have to take you that long. For many of these drawings, I would spend two or three weeks in front of one, like a meditation, just gazing at the image. I might spend half a day and make only one line to fully understand the implications that line has for nature.

A Snag in the Ladder

Before I combined the two drawings, Figures 9-12 and 9-13, extracted from Lucie Lamy's original drawing, I started by drawing a concentric circle for every line on the ladder except 20, shown in Figure 9-13a.

Notice that on the original drawing [Fig. 9-8], the central circle was divided into exactly five horizontal components, or rungs on the ladder (don't count the horizontal line running through the middle of the circle). You can clearly see that on the original drawing. Therefore I assumed that the other circles of the Fruit of Life pattern would *also* be divided into exactly five components. Pretty straightforward. I did that. Here it is [Fig. 9-14], but only the top three vertical circles, leaving out the rest for simplicity's sake.

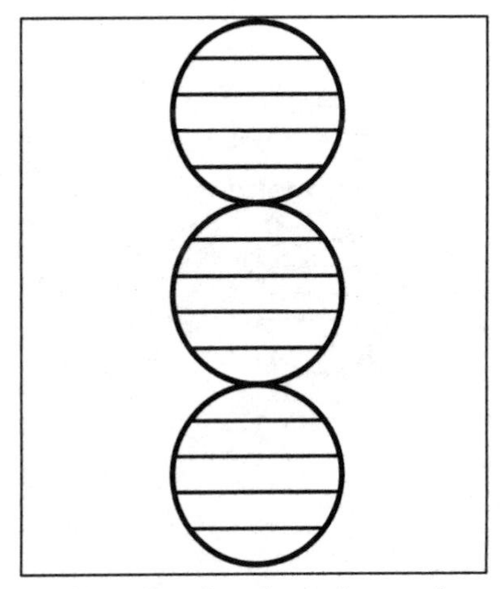

Fig. 9-14. Dividing the circles into five equal components.

Each circle has five equal components. The only problem is that it didn't fit, it didn't work. I couldn't believe it! I'd thought it was going to be a simple thing, and I would go on from there, but it didn't fit. It just simply didn't work geometrically. So I went back and checked the two drawings, thinking, *I can't be wrong here. There it is, plain as day.* But when I put them back together again, they still would not superimpose.

After many, many hours I went back and studied Lucie's original drawing again. There were definitely five divisions in the middle circle and seven divisions on either side of it. Then I got a special little instrument to measure the *size of the steps* of the ladder. I discovered that the seven divisions below and the seven divisions above the central circle were *smaller* than those *inside* the central circle! She had changed the sizes to make them fit! Lucie *knew* that we're on a disharmonic level of consciousness; she knew the ladder wouldn't fit without changing some of the measurements, but she wanted to put it all into one drawing. So she *made* it fit, knowing that if people would just study it, they would understand that the level she was drawing, with the 19 divisions, was a disharmonic level of consciousness.

It was subtle in a manner similar to Leonardo's canon of man, where he wrote in a mirror image on the top of his drawing so that you would have to hold up a mirror to read it. In the same way, the original drawing of Lucie's is the male aspect, and the female component of it is a mirror image. Many of the ancients were constantly changing things to hide knowledge. It's like a little game to hide what you don't want to be known by the outer world. When I realized that, I really began to understand that this is truly a disharmonic level of consciousness, and I knew then that the Egyptians also understood this. After that I began to spend a lot more time studying Lucie's drawings.

The Three Lenses

At this point, now that we know that the three levels of consciousness were known by the Egyptians, we'll go back to those three geometric drawings and study them carefully. They are the lenses that each level of human consciousness uses to interpret Reality: the 8 by 10, the 10 by 12 and the 14 by 18. We'll begin by drawing the 8 by10, the first level of consciousness.

Thoth showed me an ingenious way of constructing this drawing without measuring or calculations. You need only a straightedge and a compass. He showed me directly, saying that this would save me a lot of time [see instructions at bottom right for Fig. 9-15].

When the last step is completed, you have a grid of 64 small squares inside the large square, with *exactly one* additional grid square's width between the large square's perimeter and the large circle's circumference [Fig. 9-16]. The large square measures 8 grid squares across and the large circle measures 10 across—a perfect 8 by 10. And you didn't need a ruler to measure it!

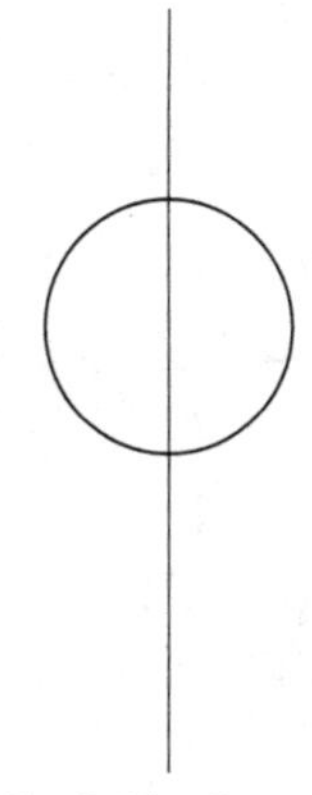

Fig. 9-15a. Step 1.

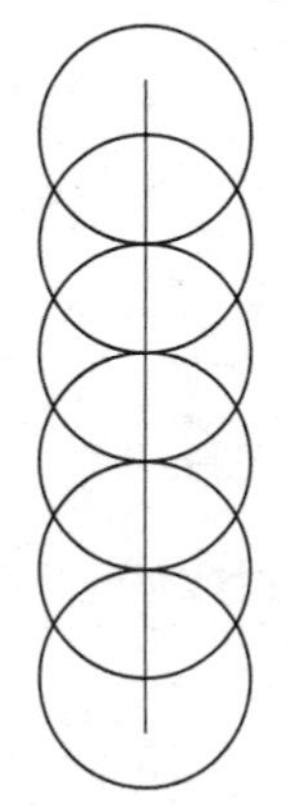

Fig. 9-15b. Step 2.

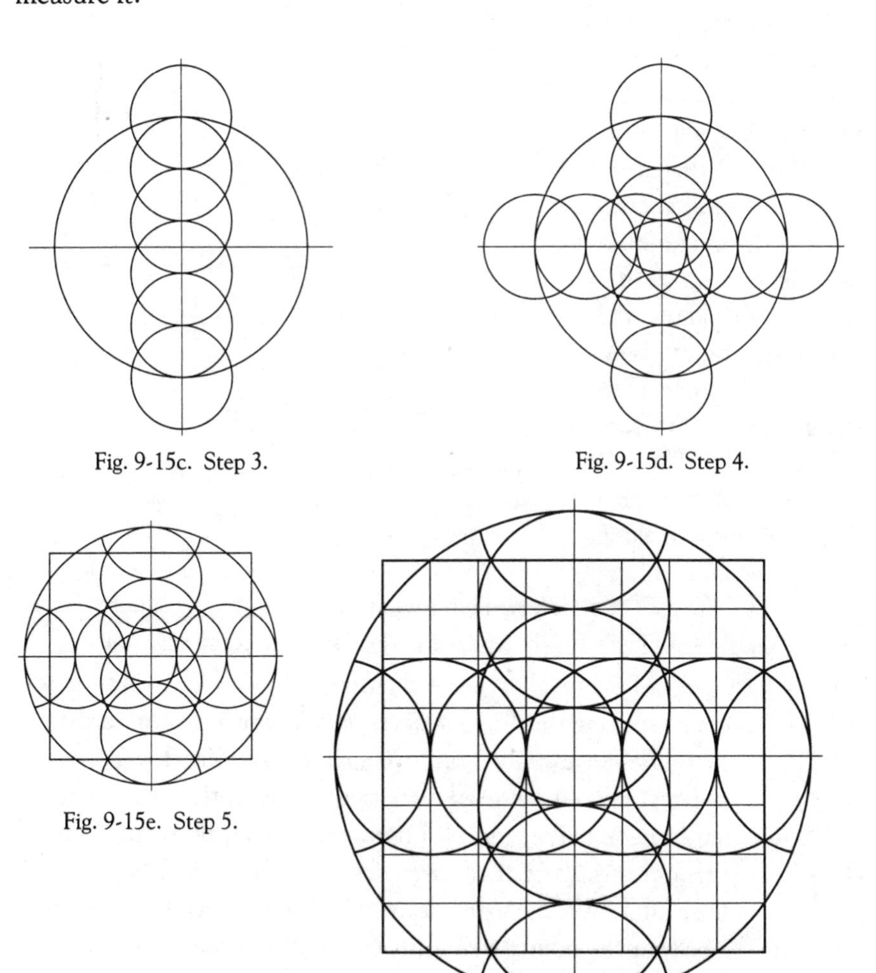

Fig. 9-15c. Step 3.

Fig. 9-15d. Step 4.

Fig. 9-15e. Step 5.

Fig. 9-16. Step 6: An 8-by-10 grid of the first level of consciousness.

1. Draw a vertical line, then draw a circle on the line [Fig. 9-15a].

2. Draw five more identical circles centered on the points where the vertical line crosses the circumference of the previous circle [Fig. 9-15b].

3. Draw a horizontal line through the points of the middle vesica piscis. Centered where the horizontal and vertical lines cross, draw a large circle around the four middle circles [Fig. 9-15c].

4. Draw the same size circle as in Fig. 9-15b centered over the horizontal line starting at the edge of the large circle. Create five more circles in the same manner as step 2, only horizontally [Fig. 9-15d].

5. Construct a phi-ratio square with sides passing through the long axes of the four outer vesica pisces.

6. Within the square, draw parallel lines through each tangent point (where circles touch but don't cross) and also through the long axes of each of the remaining vesica pisces [Fig. 9-16]. This gives you an 8-by-10 grid.

Square Roots and 3-4-5 Triangles

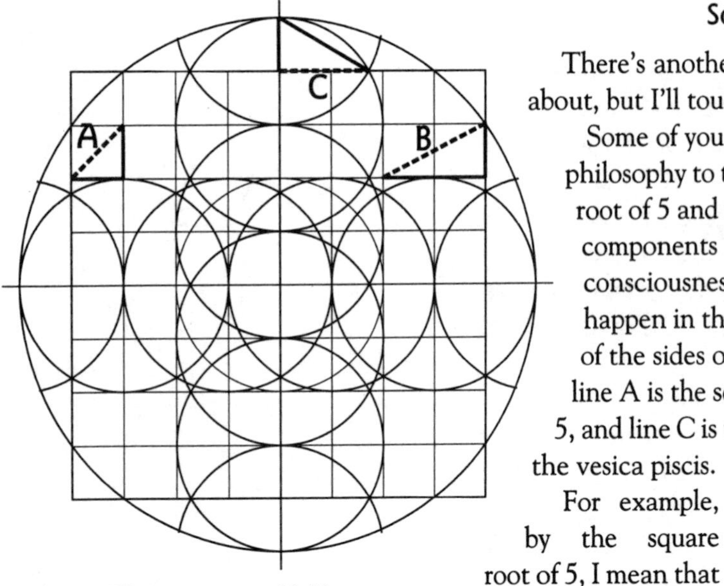

Fig. 9-17a. The square root of 2 (the triangle at A), the square root of 5* (the triangle at B) and the square root of 3 (the triangle at C).

Note: The Pythagorean theorem relates the hypotenuse of a triangle to its sides:

$h^2 = a^2 + b^2$ or $h = \sqrt{a^2 + b^2}$

where h is the hypotenuse and a and b represent the length of the sides.
*Thus when $a = 2$ and $b = 1$ (as in the triangle at B), $a^2 + b^2 = 5$, so $h = \sqrt{5}$.

There's another aspect of this 8-by-10 grid that I sometimes talk about, but I'll touch it lightly now.

Some of you may know that the Egyptians reduced their entire philosophy to the square root of 2, the square root of 3, the square root of 5 and the 3-4-5 triangle. It just so happens that all those components are in this drawing of the first level of consciousness, and it's extremely rare that such a thing would happen in the way it is occurring. In Figure 9-17a, if the length of the sides of the small squares is taken as 1, then the diagonal line A is the square root of 2; the diagonal B is the square root of 5, and line C is the square root of 3, from the equilateral triangle of the vesica piscis.

For example, by the square root of 5, I mean that if *four* grid squares are a unit (1) [Fig. 9-17b], then line D would be 1 and line E would be 2.

The Pythagorean rule states that the diagonal (hypotenuse) of a right triangle is derived by adding the squares of the two sides of a right triangle, then taking the square root of the result. Thus, $1^2 = 1$ and $2^2 = 4$; then $1 + 4 = 5$, making the diagonal the square root of 5 ($\sqrt{5}$). That's what they mean by the square root of 5. See Figure 9-17b, where four grid squares equal one unit.

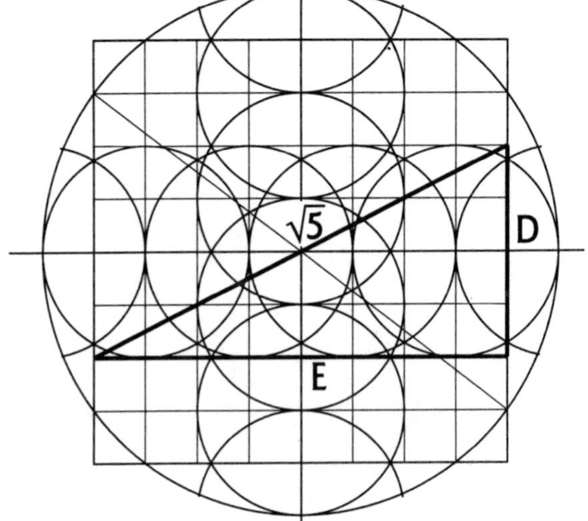

Fig. 9-17b. The square-root-of-five ($\sqrt{5}$) triangle shown another way, using *four* grid squares instead of one as equal to 1.0.

A 3-4-5 triangle is perfectly inscribed in Figure 9-17c. If you count the length of two squares as one unit for your yardstick, then line F is exactly 3 units (6 squares) and line E will be 4 (8 squares). Since these sides measure 3 and 4, then the diagonal *has* to be 5, making a 3-4-5 triangle. In fact, there are eight of them in this figure that are perfectly inscribed, whirling around the center. What is so rare is that the 3-4-5 triangles are inscribed *exactly* at the points where the circle crosses the square to form the phi ratio. These are amazing synchronicities that you wouldn't happen upon by pure coincidence. Now let's do this drawing a little differently.

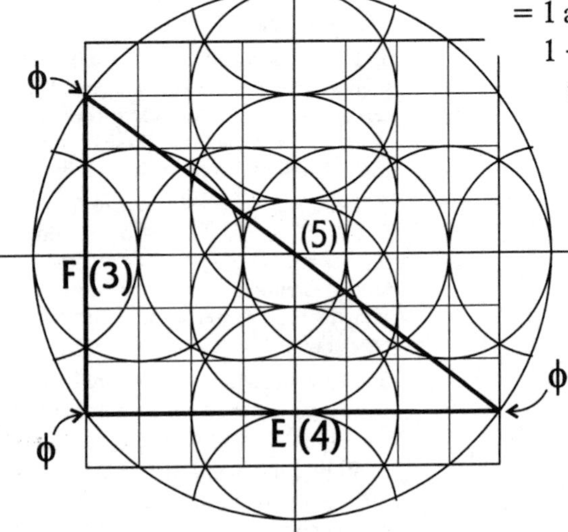

Fig. 9-17c. One of the eight 3-4-5 triangles inscribed in the circle in this grid. Here one unit is 2 grid-square lengths.

Leonardo's and CBS's Eye

We now superimpose two Fibonacci spirals, a female spiral (broken line) and a male spiral (solid line) [Fig. 9-18]. We saw a perfect reflection before [see Fig. 8-11]. The male spiral (A) touches the top of the "eye" and spirals up and around clockwise. The female spiral (B) passes through zero point (C), the center of the eye, then up and around counterclockwise. (This eye in the middle, by the way, happens to be the CBS eye, which makes me wonder who those guys were who designed their corporate image.) This eye is a lens, though Thoth sees it as an eye. It's the geometry through which the mind of the first level of consciousness interprets Reality. This drawing represents the Aboriginal level of consciousness with 42 + 2 chromosomes (the author regrets that he has lost the scientific reference paper from Australia to prove this fact). It's the first level of human consciousness on Earth, and it's the first time human consciousness becomes self-aware.

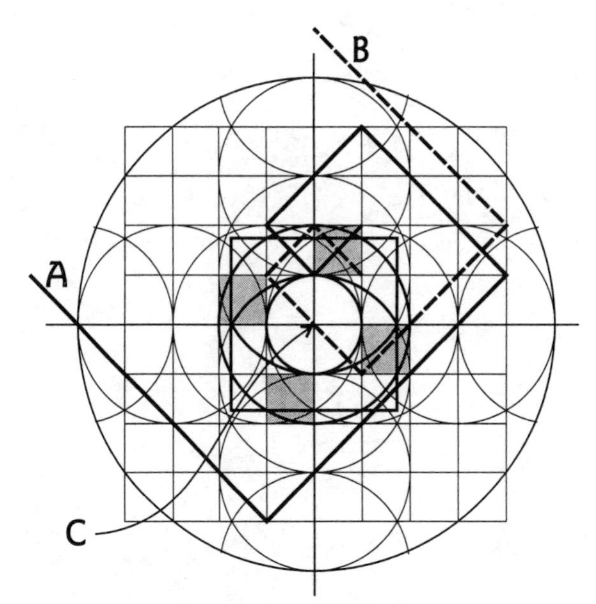

Fig. 9-18. A different perspective, showing the CBS eye in the center, at zero point (C).

Notice that this figure and the next two (out of Leonardo's canon, which we used before) have the same geometries [Figs. 9-19 and 9-20]. Both patterns have a 64-square grid and the same inner structure, although the circle and square are differently positioned in the Leonardo drawings. They're interrelated, making me wonder who Leonardo really was and what he was really studying!

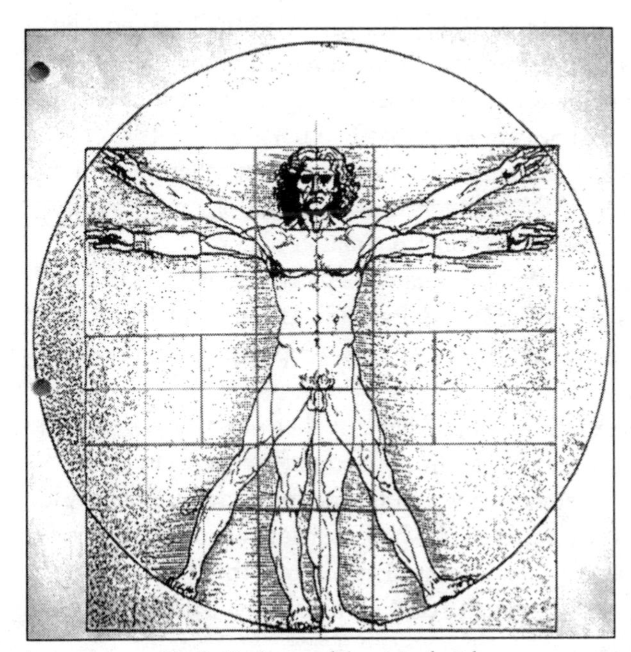

Fig. 9-19. Leonardo's original grid.

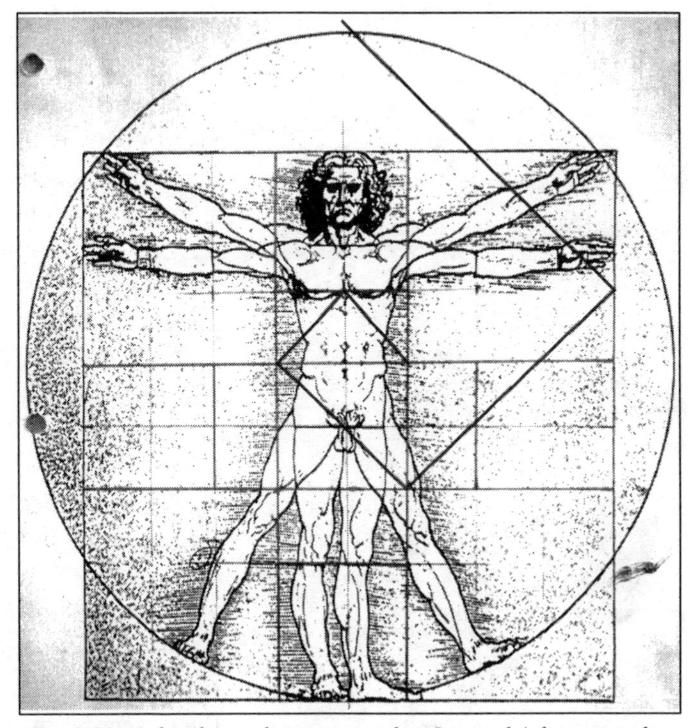

Fig. 9-20. A female spiral superimposed on Leonardo's human grid.

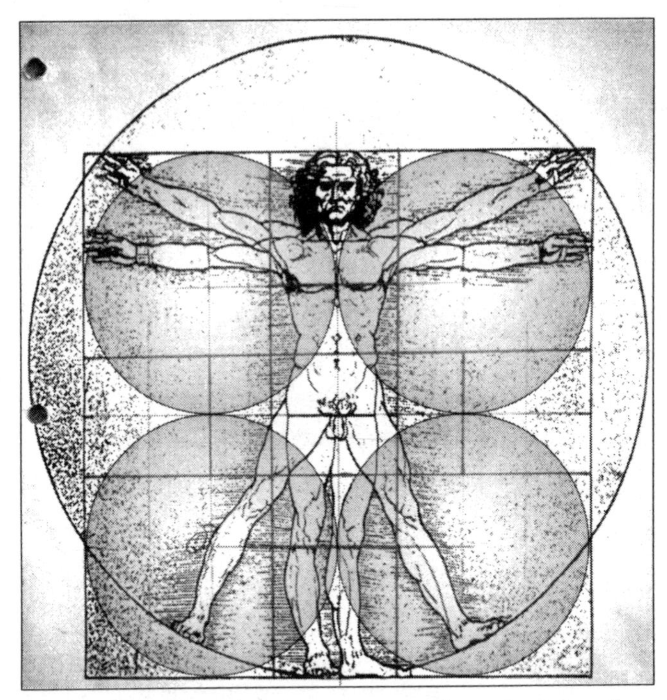

Fig. 9-21. The Leonardo canon superimposed over the eight-cell division (the other four cells hidden behind the visible four).

In Figure 9-21 you see the eight-cell division [see the Egg of Life in Fig. 7-26] and the human body underneath; you can begin to see the actual proportions of the adult human being contained in that eight-cell division. (Later in this chapter we will discuss in more detail the relationship between Leonardo's canon and the Egg of Life.) This also means that if Leonardo actually understood this information, if it wasn't just a coincidence, he was not talking about us, but about the first level of consciousness—the Aboriginals, the first peoples of the world. Of course, I don't *know* if he knew this or not, because this one piece of information is not enough to base that kind of judgment on.

Because Leonardo did create an 8 by 10 around his canon—and since there are lots of grid possibilities—this was enough for me to suspect that maybe he *did* understand these levels of consciousness based on geometry. So I began to search all of Leonardo's works to see if he had a human canon with a 10 by 12 or a 14 by 18. I searched and searched and looked and looked, but I couldn't find it. I mean I *really* looked, but after a while I gave up. Later, at another time when I was restudying Leonardo, I noticed that this drawing of the canon of man based on the 8 by 10 wasn't really Leonardo's work, because the proportions were drawn from his teacher, Vitruvius. Vitruvius actually lived about 1400 years before him, but Leonardo considered him his most important mentor.

Fig. 9-22. Four circles that will create the 8 by 10 grid.

Vitruvius' 10 by 12

Once I found out that this was really Vitruvius' proportions, I began to go through *his* works to see if I could find a 10 by 12 or a 14 by 18—and I did! I found a 10 by 12. This gave me two of the three levels of consciousness, which then made me suspect strongly that these men, Vitruvius and Leonardo, were following exactly the same line of thought that Thoth was teaching me. To top this off, Vitruvius was a Roman engineer whose writings, when revived and printed in the 1400s, were responsible for the architecture of some of the magnificent churches in Europe. Leonardo was a master mason.

If you draw *five* circles of the same diameter along the axes (as in Fig. 9-23) instead of four (as in Fig. 9-22) and draw lines through the lengths and conjunctions of all the vesica pisces, you come up with this grid of 100 squares—a 10 by 12.

You know that it's exactly a 10 by 12 because there are 10 squares across the big square and 12 squares across the diameter of the large circle. As we saw in Figure 9-16, the vesica pisces around the four sides are half inside and half outside the square, and because half the width of a vesica piscis determines the square sizes (you've drawn lines through the lengths of all 12 vesica pisces and parallel lines at all 10 conjunctions), you know you have the perfect ratios.

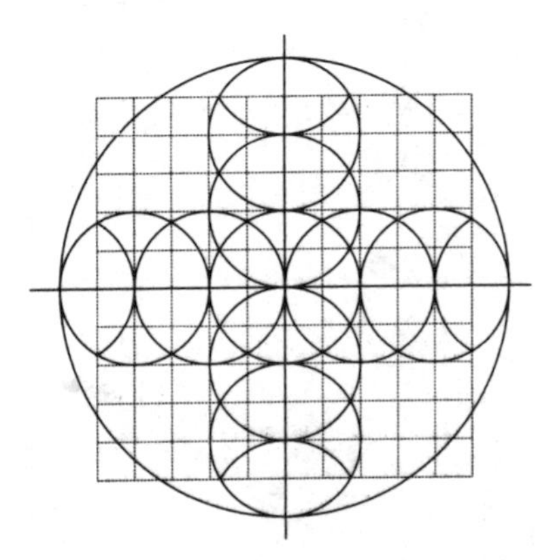

Fig. 9-23. The 10 by 12.

10,000 Years to Figure Out

However . . . when I started my (female-originating) Fibonacci spiral from the upper right corner of the central four squares (point A in Fig. 9-24), it didn't seem to be hitting in the right places as it did in the 8 by 10; it didn't seem to have synchronicity.

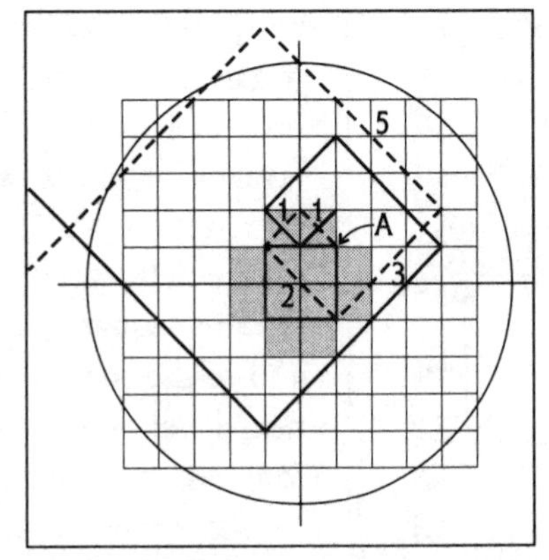

Fig. 9-24. Grid of consciousness level two; unsynchronized spiral. Here a unit is a diagonal of one grid square; you can follow the Fibonacci sequence.

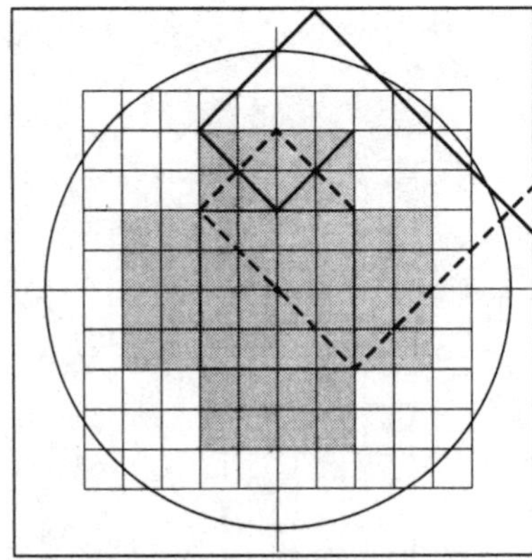

Fig. 9-24a. Grid of consciousness level two; synchronized spiral. Here a unit is a diagonal of two grid squares, so that only the first three numbers in the Fibonacci sequence are inside the grid. Can you find the difference in synchronicities between Fig. 9-24 and Fig. 9-24a, where there is an imbalance between the two in two ways? (The secret lies in the secret pyramid in Fig. 9-39.).

I remember that I was doing this while Thoth was watching. He watched me for a long time and then he said, "I think I'm just going to tell you this one." I said, "Well, I'll get it." He said, "No, I think I'll just tell you." I said, "How come?" He replied, "You probably won't get it for a while. It took us 10,000 years to figure this out, and I don't have the time."

This is what Thoth told me: For the first level of consciousness (8 by 10, Fig. 9-16), for those four grid squares in the middle, the number 1 we arrived at as our measuring stick was not 1. It was 1 *squared*—that was its actual value—and 1 squared equals 1. But how do you know the difference when you're looking at it? And when you come to the second level of consciousness, the 10 by 12, it's not 2, but 2 *squared*, which equals 4. So you have to take the diagonal of four squares as your unit of measure, which means it takes two diagonal lengths now instead of one to equal the 1 of our measuring stick [see Fig. 9-24a].

When you use this new measuring stick of two diagonals, then everything begins to move in synchrony again. I'm not going to tell you what this is about yet except that this is the second level of consciousness. This is us. And this drawing is the geometrical lens that we interpret the one Reality through.

Figure 9-25 is Vitruvius' canon, which is a 10 by 12. When you first look at it, it doesn't look like a 10 anything, because there are 30 squares on a side—900 squares in all. However, when you look carefully, you'll see a dot counting off every third square. And when you count from dot to dot, counting every three squares as one, you get exactly ten units on a side. So there are 100 bigger squares hidden within this grid.

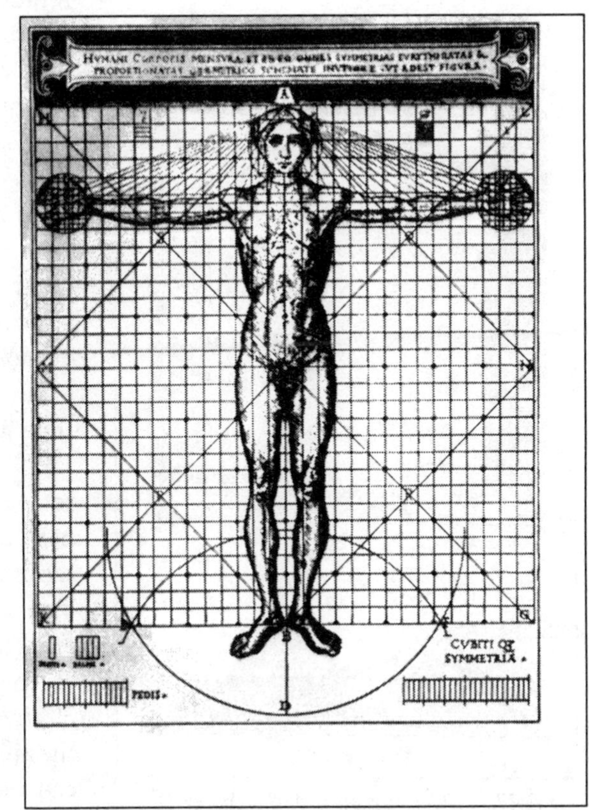

Fig. 9-25. Vitruvius' canon.

I believe that Vitruvius' canon is a 10 by 12, though it's difficult to prove that, since Vitruvius did not draw the phi-ratio circle. If he had, the circle would create a 10 by 12 for certain [see Fig. 9-26]. However, the other thing you see in the drawing is this diamond (apexes at A, B, M and N), which doesn't seem to fit anything. But this is also an indication of the second level of consciousness, referred to earlier in this chapter [see Fig. 9-4 and

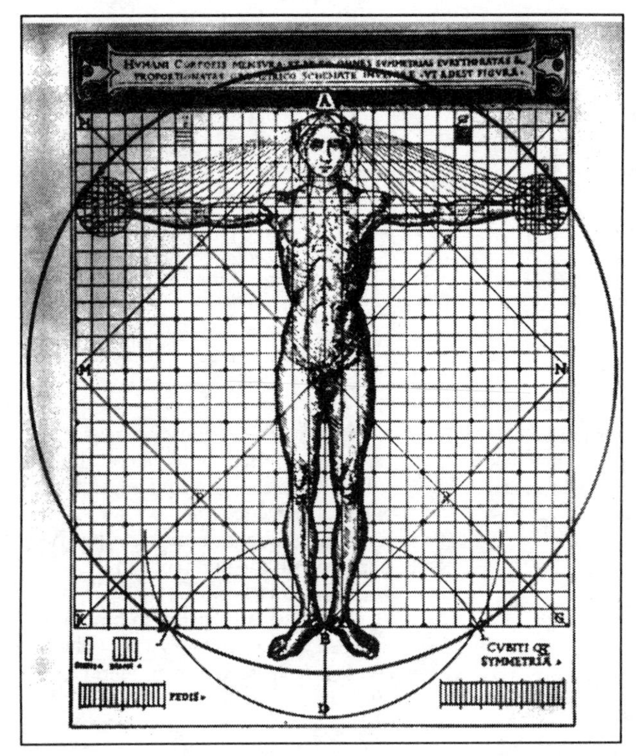

Fig. 9-26. New circle around Vitruvius' canon.

text] as the basis for the selection of the 10 by 12 in the first place. To me, the fact that Vitruvius drew this diamond over his canon is proof he understood that this was the second level of human consciousness.

Another thing about this canon is that inside each square delineated by the dots are nine little squares. Now, the nine-square pattern happens to be the key to the inner grid of the next level—Christ consciousness—because the next level doesn't use 1 squared or 2 squared—it uses 3 squared, and 3 squared equals 9. We have to take 9 squares to create the harmonics in the next level, which is the number of stones in the roof of the King's Chamber.

Vitruvius and the Great Pyramid

To say it again, Figure 9-26 shows the diamond shape around the second level of consciousness—the shape that ties the first and third levels of consciousness together. When we rotated the square of the second-level consciousness 45 degrees [see Fig. 9-4], it geometrically approximates where the Christ consciousness is and actually touches the seventh square of Christ consciousness. This square-and-diamond pattern is also found, subtly, in the plan of the Great Pyramid, which can be seen as further proof that the pyramid was meant to be used by the second level of consciousness to enter the third level.

If you cut the pyramid off at the floor level of the King's Chamber, the square on top [see Fig. 9-27] is exactly one-half the area of the base. The Egyptian government figured that one out. You don't need a measuring stick to see this. If you take the top square and rotate it 45 degrees as shown in Figure 9-28, its corners touch the base perimeter exactly. By drawing diagonals to connect opposite corners of the inner diamond-square, you make 8 equal triangles (four inside and four outside the diamond-square). Because the inner triangles are the same size as the outer ones (see the two darkened triangles), the area of the inner square is clearly exactly one-half the area of the base. You can see this without even calculating it.

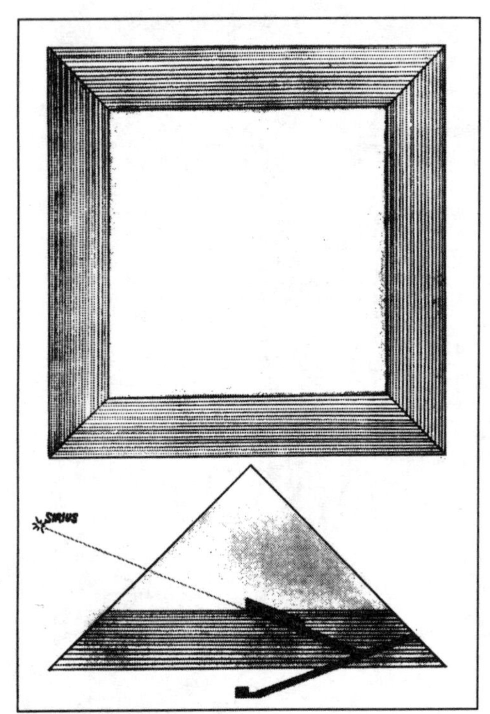

Fig. 9-27. Pyramid cut off at the level of the King's Chamber.

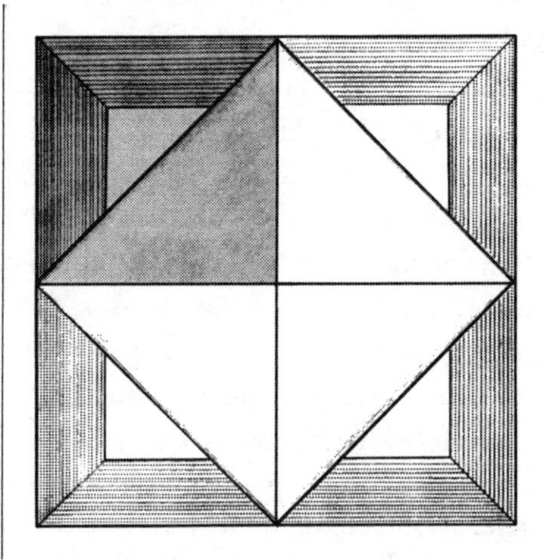

Fig. 9-28. Squares and diamonds that illustrate the fact that the "upper" square (see previous figure) has exactly half the area of the "lower" square base.

Fig. 9-29. Outer square with successive inner squares rotated by 45 degrees.

The King's Chamber—whose floor level determined the size of the upper square in both these figures—was built for us, for our level of consciousness, to go through the initiation into the next level of Christ consciousness. This becomes obvious as the information becomes known and understood.

In Figure 9-29 you can see the actual geometry of an outer square with successive inner squares of half the size rotated by 45 degrees. We could get into a deep discussion on the esoteric meaning of this geometrical progression, because the sacred square roots of 2 and 5 geometrically oscillate forever, but I believe you will understand on your own as we continue.

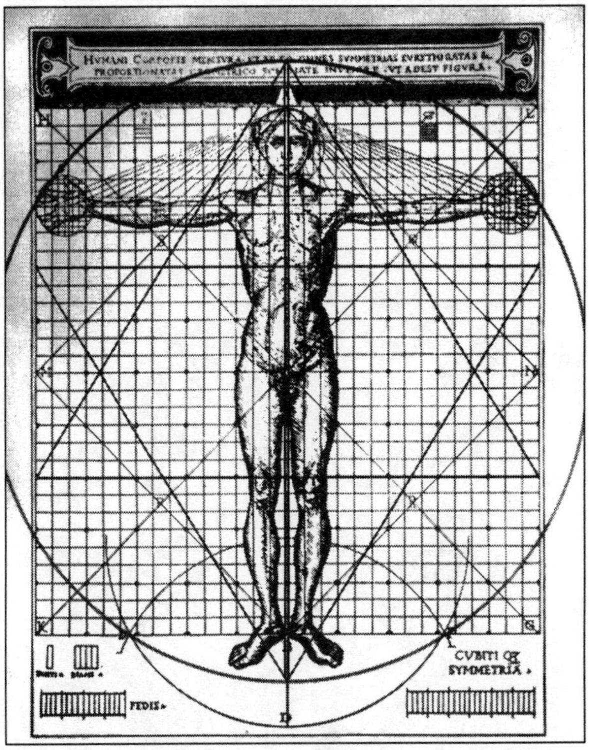

Fig. 9-30. Vitruvius' second level of consciousness. Added: the phi-ratio circle, the central prana tube and the star tetrahedrons that represent the basis of the Mer-Ka-Ba.

The Search for a 14 by 18

At this point I had drawings of two of the three levels of consciousness from the lineage of Leonardo and Vitruvius, and I was really excited. I started looking through everything I could find of Vitruvius, trying to find a 14 by 18. I looked and looked, then all of a sudden it dawned on me. The 14 by 18 is Christ consciousness. My logic said that if he did have such a drawing, it would be the most holy drawing he had, and it would probably be inside some gold container hidden deep under a sacred altar somewhere. It wouldn't be thrown around on a table and probably wouldn't emerge at all into public knowledge. I kept looking, but I've never found anything. I don't know if I ever will.

Figure 9-30 is the drawing of us, with added lines that are mine. It may become very important for you. In fact, it's so important to me that it is the frontispiece for the first eight chapters. It is of immediate importance because it shows the exact proportions of the star tetrahedron around your body; the tube running through the middle, which we will use for our breathing in the meditation that leads to the knowledge of the Mer-Ka-Ba, the human lightbody; and the phi-ratio circle. Figure 9-30a shows a sphere we haven't talked about yet—the sphere of consciousness that will develop around your universal heart chakra when you breathe in the ancient way. My prayer is that by the end of this book, this knowledge will have deep meaning for you and help you in your spiritual growth.

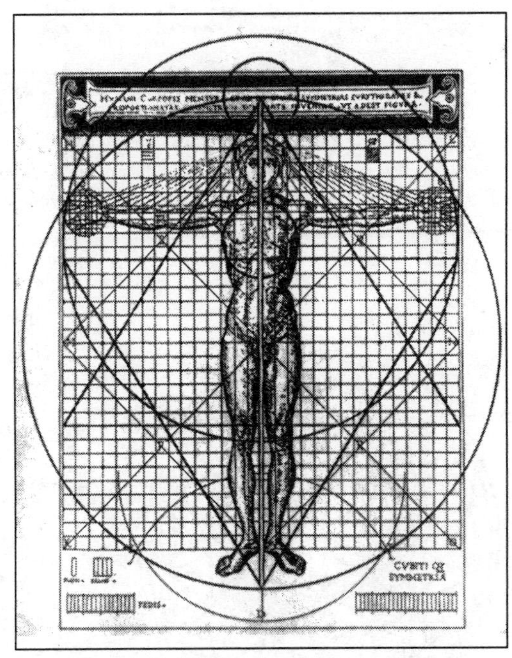

Fig. 9-30a. Added: the new sphere of consciousness centered at the heart chakra, which results from a different way of breathing.

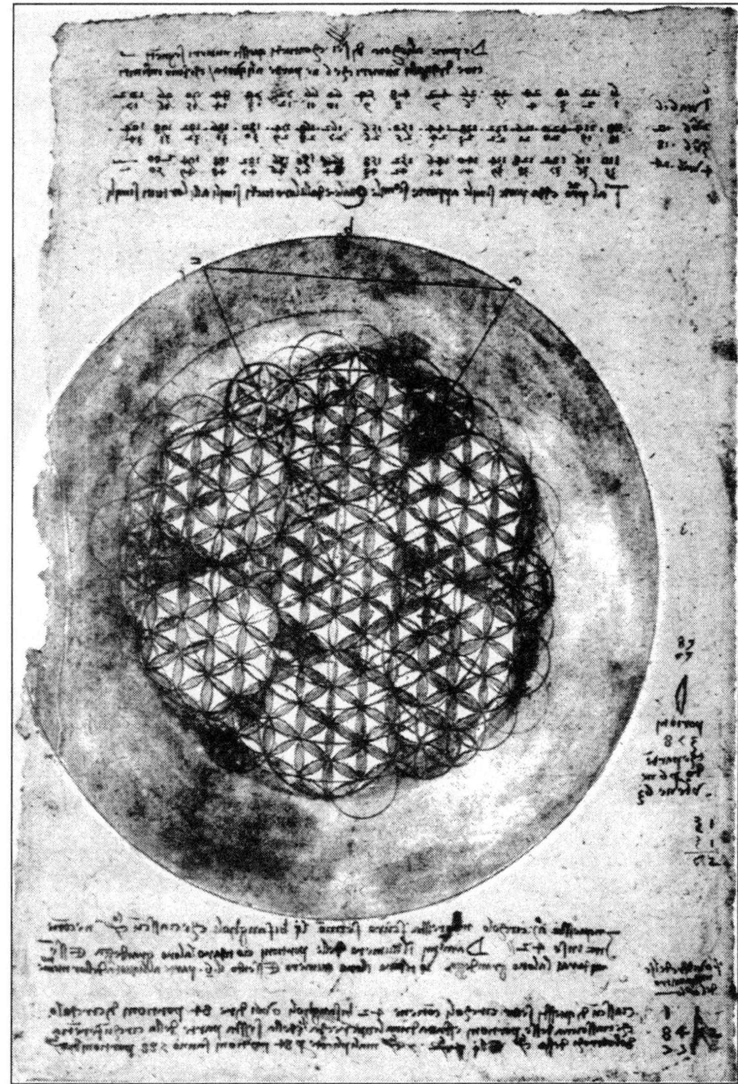

Fig. 9-31. Leonardo's Flower of Life. From *The Unknown Leonardo* (Ladislas Reti, ed., Abradale Press, Harry Abrams, Inc., Publishers, New York, 1990 edition).

Now I had two of the three pieces. I suspected strongly that Leonardo and Vitruvius were working along the same lines that Thoth was teaching me, but I still couldn't say absolutely. In my heart I was pretty sure, but it was still circumstantial evidence. Then one day I was in New York City; I had given a workshop there. I was sitting in the home of the woman who had sponsored this workshop and who had an excellent library. I noticed a book on Leonardo I had never seen before. It was called *The Unknown Leonardo*. It was composed of works by da Vinci that everybody considered unimportant. These sketches weren't included in the beautiful manuals because they were seen as just doodles and preliminary sketches.

As I leafed through this book I'd never seen before, I suddenly saw this [Fig. 9-31]. Leonardo had drawn the Flower of Life! And it wasn't just a doodle—he was actually calculating angles and studying and understanding the geometries associated with the Flower of Life.

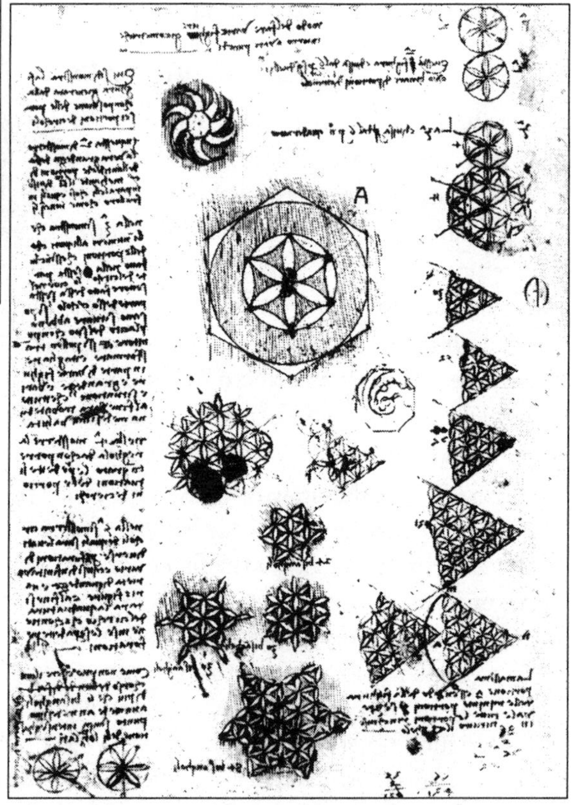

Fig. 9-32. More of Leonardo's Flower of Life sketches. A: the core of the Flower of Life. (From *The Unknown Leonardo*, page 64.)

Figure 9-32 is on another page of the book and shows how he drew various geometric patterns found in the Flower of Life. The flower design at point A is one of the keys you'll find all over the world—it's the central core of the Flower of Life. You'll find this image in churches, monasteries and places all over the planet, relating back to this core information about creation that we've forgotten.

He went on working with all the possible relationships and calculating angles he could find. As far as I know, Leonardo was the first person to figure all these ratios and apply them to physical inventions. He invented amazing things based on these ratios [Fig. 9-33a]—things such as the helicopter, which he first envisioned, and gear relationships as seen today in automobile transmissions. And they all came out of his drawings studying the Flower of Life! The editor of the book didn't recognize what all this was. He just said, "This is where his gear inventions came from." Leonardo went on and on, figuring as many ratios as possible. Here's another page of his work [Fig. 9-33b].

Now I can say quite confidently that Leonardo definitely was moving, or had already moved, in the same way geometrically that Thoth had taught me and I'm showing you. I believe Thoth's teachings and Leonardo's study were based on the same understanding of the Flower of Life.

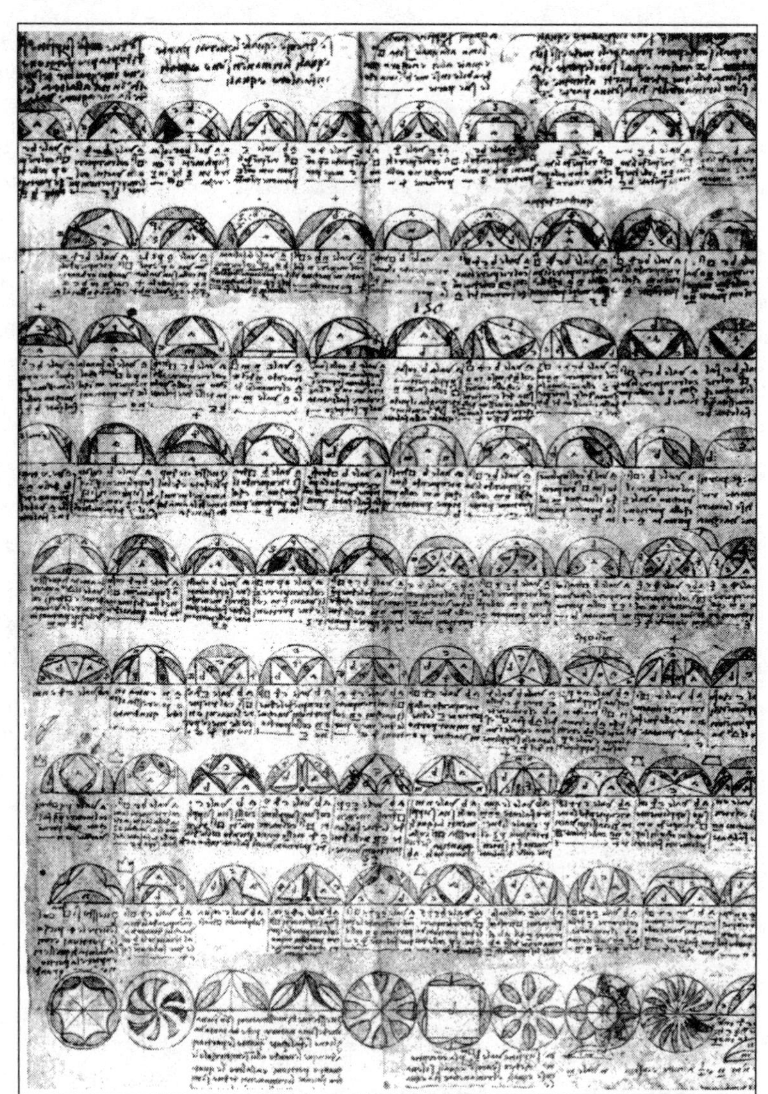

Fig. 9-33a. Leonardo's gear ratios applied to his inventions. (From *The Unknown Leonardo*, page 78.)

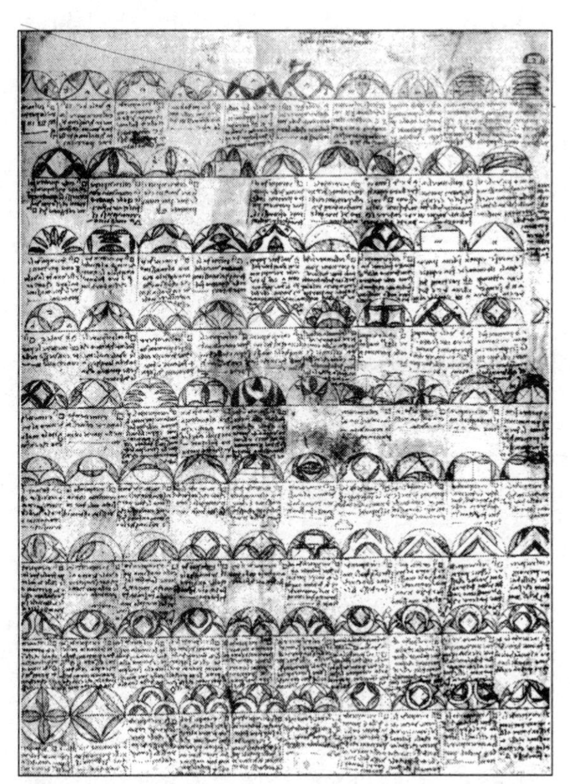

Fig. 9-33b. More ratios and proportions. (From *The Unknown Leonardo*, page 79.)

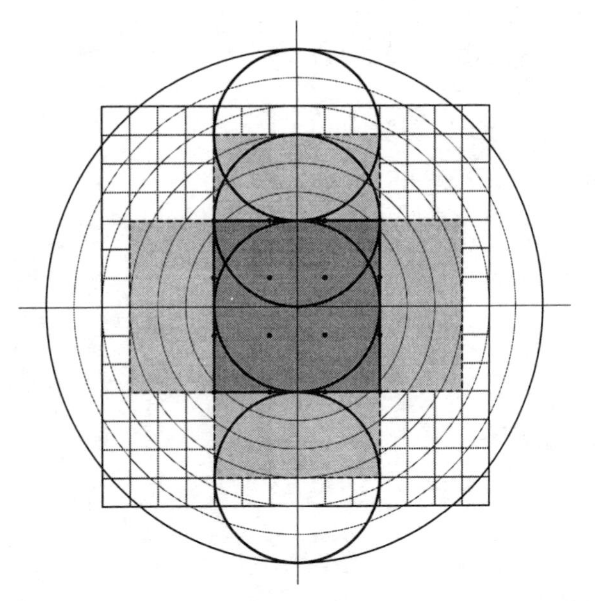

Fig. 9-34. The Christ consciousness; the 14 by 18 square-circle relationship of the third level of consciousness.

There is another famous man who was moving in the same manner—Pythagoras. When you work with sacred geometry and make the drawings—which forces you to know angles and geometrical proportions—you have to prove your actions. Every time I came up with something to prove, rather than going through all the trouble of actually creating the proof myself, I could find it in existing geometry books. And in almost every single case, the proof had come from Pythagoras.

Every proof that Pythagoras worked out—almost the whole spectrum of his school—was not just a random proof of some geometry. Each one was a living proof on the same path we're on right now. He *had* to prove each step in order to keep going. He couldn't just guess at something; he had to prove it, and he had to do it geometrically before continuing. After a while I got all of his drawings and proofs together because I knew I would need them. It had taken him his whole life to figure out these things, and of course I wanted to move faster.

So now we know that at least two of the great ones of the past, Leonardo da Vinci, one of the greatest men to ever live, and Pythagoras, the father of the modern world, both realized the significance of the Flower of Life and applied this knowledge to everyday life.

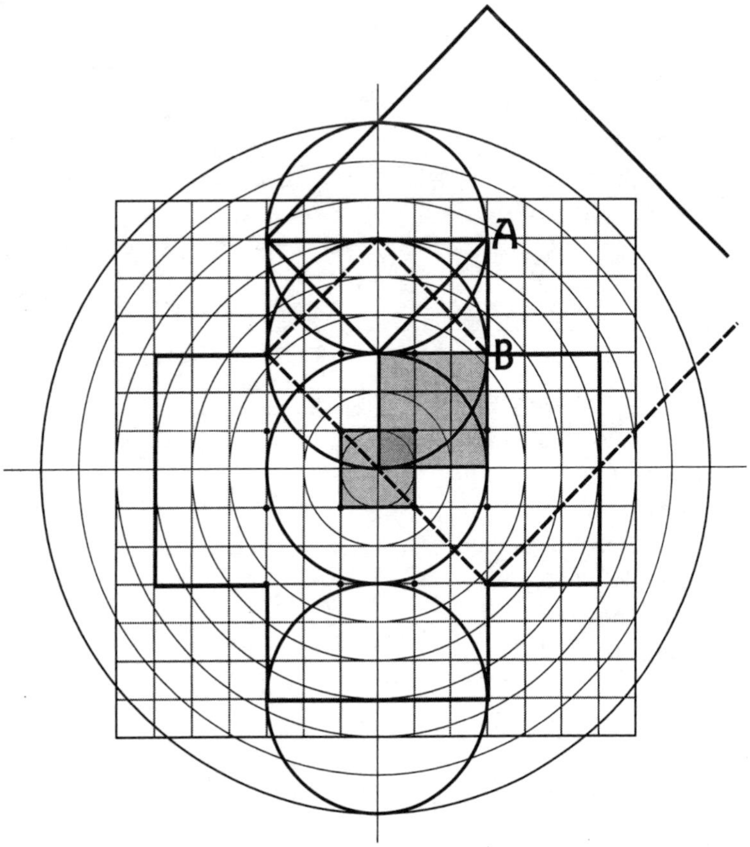

Let's examine the last geometrical drawing of consciousness, the 14 by 18, Christ consciousness [Fig. 9-34]. All you need is nine concentric circles as before, a square around the seventh circle, and you have the basic drawing of Christ consciousness—a 14 by 18. But when you come to the middle four squares, you cannot base them as 1 squared or 2 squared; you must use 3 squared as your basic unit. Three squared equals 9, so now you use nine squares as your basic unit to equal four center squares, and you draw a square around the nine as shown (shaded). Your measuring unit is now three diagonals. So the male-originating spiral [see Fig. 9-34a] would start at point A and go down, over and out, and the female spiral (broken line) would start at point B and go up, down, then precisely through the center or zero point and leave the grid. You have synchronicity happening again on this drawing, but only if you know to use three diagonals or nine squares (shaded), which was already in Vitruvius' drawing of the second

A
B

Fig. 9-34a. The Christ consciousness, 14 by 18, showing the basic unit (4 dark center squares) and the 3-square diagonal unit of the spiral (larger shaded square).

level of consciousness. This was his way of saying the same thing Thoth said: The second level of consciousness contains the basic information of the third level, Christ consciousness.

What is the synchronicity? Look how the female exactly passes through the female zero point and the male exactly passes over the center line and the outer circle. The same thing can be seen in Figure 9-24a. This is the key. In a few pages you will see what these points actually represent, the base and apex of the Great Pyramid.

A Great Synchronicity

Now I'm going to show you a series of drawings to illustrate a great synchronicity.

In Figure 9-35 you can see the original eight cells (shaded circles) surrounded by the inner surface of the zona pellucida [compare with Fig. 7-26]. (The other four cells are directly behind these four.) The outer circle forms the phi ratio with the square surrounding the human figure, and the adult human being fits the combined geometries perfectly. Even the star tetrahedron is there [Fig. 9-35a].

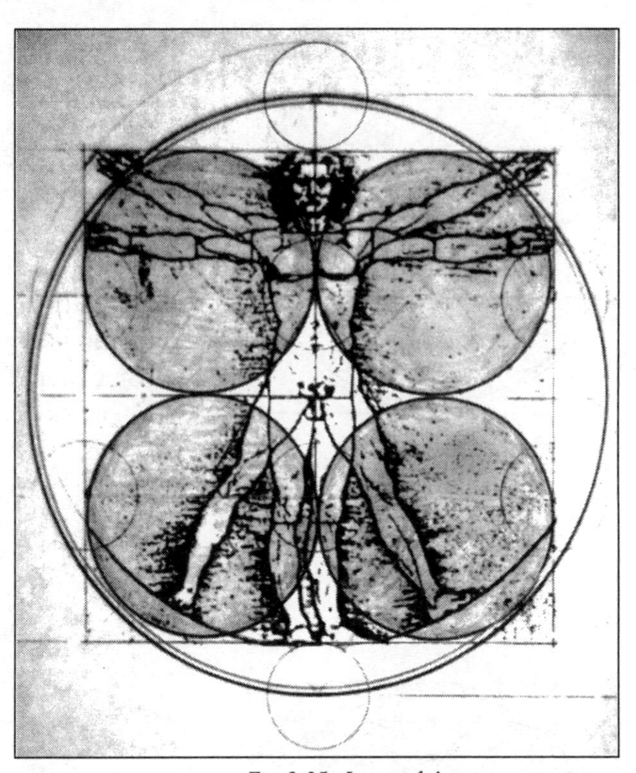

Fig. 9-35. Leonardo's canon superimposed over the eight original cells (shaded circles; four are behind the four you see).

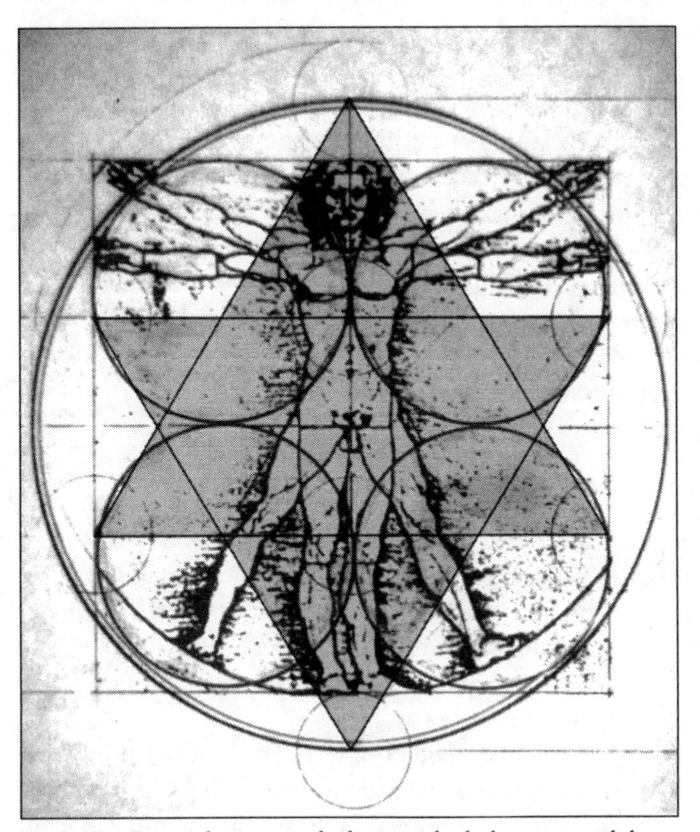

Fig. 9-35a. Fitting the star tetrahedron into both the canon and the original eight cells.

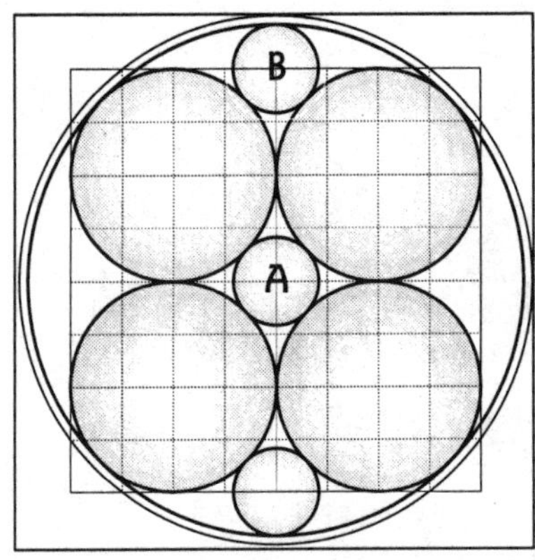

Fig. 9-36. The eight original cells without Leonardo's canon, adding three circles.

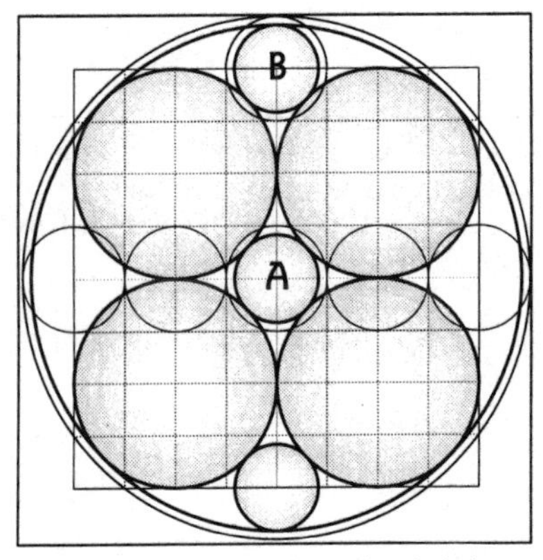

Fig. 9-36a. Showing how the slightly larger circle that fits into the grid square precisely fits *inside* the three-dimensional original cells and how this circle, on the *outside*, touches the outer surface of the zona pellucida.

If you were to draw three equal circles along the vertical axis [Fig. 9-36]—and they would fit perfectly because the star tetrahedron is divided into thirds—it would show that the original eight cells and the adult human being are interrelated. The microcosm is linked to the everyday world.

This is a two-dimensional drawing of the eight original cells. In a three-dimensional form, if you were to put a sphere in the middle that would pass through to the center—like a marble that would just fit between these spheres and enter the center—that sphere is represented by the circle at point A. If you take that same size circle and put it at the top (B), it would just touch the inner surface of the zona pellucida, showing you its location.

Then take the circle that fits *behind* the smaller central circle—the slightly larger one that fits into the 64-square grid [see Fig. 9-36a]. When you put this size circle at point B, it shows you the exact *outer* surface of the zone pellucida. So the smaller circle that fits through and the slightly larger one that fits perfectly inside are the keys to the inner and outer surface of the zona pellucida, and they indicate where these elements go in the phi ratio. My way to calculate this is the only way I know, though there may be others.

Now back to Leonardo's drawing superimposed over the original eight cells. On Figure 9-37 we superimpose over da Vinci's canon a different geometry that shows a further relationship to the macrocosm as well as the microcosm. Notice the large shaded sphere that fits perfectly around the human body from head to foot and also inside the square around the human body. Now notice the smaller shaded circle directly over the man's head. This small circle is created by putting the point of a compass on the top of the phi-ratio circle around the human body and extending the compass arm to the top of the human head. This same circle on Figure 9-35 would have a radius from the outer surface of the zona pellucida to the top of the head or the square. The smaller circle just touches the larger shaded circle. (As a side note, the center of the smaller circle is exactly where the thirteenth chakra is located.)

So what does all this mean?

Earth-Moon Proportions

Many people have claimed this next piece of information as their own, but none of them were the actual originators, because I found an even earlier person who was involved in this and was supposedly the originator. The earliest written work I can find is by Lawrence Blair [*Rhythms of Vision*], but he doesn't claim it; he says he got it from older works. I don't know who originally came up with this idea, but it's truly remarkable information, especially if you've never heard it before.

Consider: The size of the two shaded spheres on this drawing [Fig. 9-37] "happen" to have exactly the same ratio as that of the Earth and the Moon. This ratio is located in the human body and in the original eight cells of all life. In addition, not only do the spheres in this drawing possess the same relative sizes as the Earth and the Moon, but just as in this drawing, a square that would fit around the Earth and a circle that would pass through the center of the Moon (if the Moon were touching the Earth) would have a phi ratio. This can be proven, which also proves that the size of the Earth and the Moon are as stated.

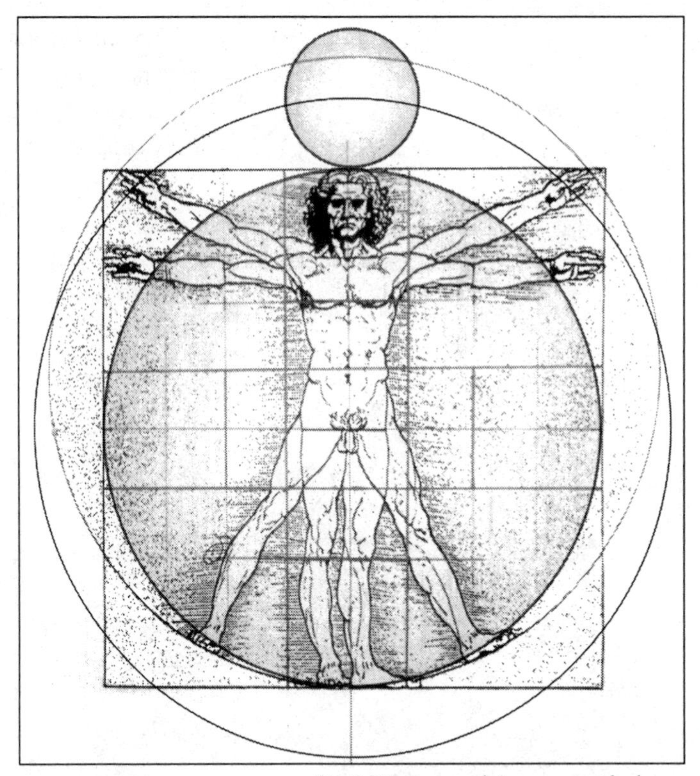

Fig. 9-37. Leonardo's canon with the square and the circle inside. The small shaded circle above the head is centered on the outer surface of the zona pellucida, which is the phi-ratio circle to the square.

To prove it, you have to know the diameter of the Earth, which is equal to one edge of a square that would fit around it, just like the same square that fits around the human body. Multiply that by 4 to find out how many miles it would take to go around the square. Once you determine that, you need to know how many miles go around the circle that would pass through the center of the Moon if the Moon were touching the Earth.

So let's look at this.

The average diameter of the Earth is 7920 miles. The average diameter of the Moon is 2160 miles. The perimeter of the square that would fit around the Earth equals the diameter of the Earth times 4, or 31,680 miles. To figure the miles in the circumference of the circle that passes through the center of the Moon, you need to know the diameter of the Earth and the radius of the Moon at both the top and the bottom of Figure 9-37—which is the diameter of both the Earth and the Moon—added together, times pi. If those numbers are the same or very close, then that would prove it. The circumference of the circle equals the diameter of the Earth (7920 miles) plus the diameter of the Moon (2160), which equals 10,080. If you multiply 10,080 times pi (3.1416), it is 31,667 miles [see Fig. 9-38]—*only 13 miles difference!* Considering that the ocean is 27 miles higher at the equator than it is anywhere else (the ocean is pulled outward in a 27-mile ridge), 13 miles is nothing. However, if you multiply 10,080 miles times 22/7 (a number often used to approximate pi), it comes out to the *exact same number* as the perimeter of the square—31,680 miles!

$$7920 \times 4 = 31{,}680$$
$$D = 7920 + 2160 = 10{,}080$$
$$10{,}080 \times \pi = 31{,}667$$

Fig. 9-38. Earth and Moon calculations.

Thus the size of the Earth is in harmonics with (in phi ratio to) the Moon, and these ratios are found in the proportions of our human energy fields and even in the very Egg of Life itself.

I spent weeks thinking about this paradox. The human energy field contains the size of the Earth we live on and the Moon that moves around her! It was like the thought about electrons traveling at 9/10 the speed of light. What does it signify? Does it mean that only certain sizes of planets are possible? And that there's no randomness at all, in any way? If our bodies are a measuring stick for the universe, does it mean that we contain within us, somehow or somewhere, all sizes of all possible planets? Does it mean the sizes of all suns are located in us somewhere?

This information has come up in a few books in recent times, but the authors pass over it like it's nothing. But it's not nothing; this is serious stuff. I'm still deeply amazed by the perfection of creation. This knowledge definitely supports the idea that "man is the measuring stick of the universe."

Earth, Moon and Pyramid Proportions

If this is not enough, check out what some of these other lines mean. If you were to draw a horizontal line through the center of the Earth to its circumference, then lines from those two points up to the center of the Moon, and from the center of the Moon a line back to the center of the Earth [Fig. 9-39, these are the *precise* proportions of the Great Pyramid in Egypt! That angle at A is 51 degrees 51 minutes, 24 seconds, exactly the same as that of the Great Pyramid [Figs. 9-40 and 41].

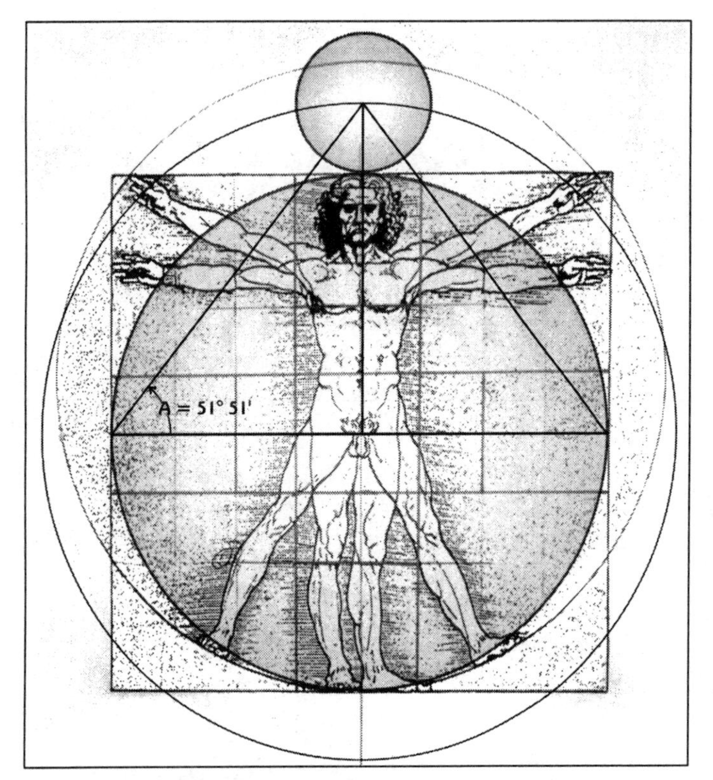

Fig. 9-39. Earth-Moon proportions. Angle A is the angle found in the Great Pyramid.

Thoth, when he was Hermes in Greece, says in *The Emerald Tablets* that he was the one who made the Great Pyramid, and that he did it from the proportions of the Earth. The above proof gives credence to his claim.

Since the Earth, the Moon (and the entire solar system), the physical human body and the Egg of Life are all related geometrically and the Great Pyramid ties them all together; and since we have these three different consciousness levels that happen to have pyramids inside each one, we can superimpose these drawings over the Great Pyramid and know what the rooms are all about and where they are located within the pyramid. The Great Pyramid is really the great map for the level of consciousness we are all on. No wonder why (why from a subconscious level) 18,000 people visit the Great Pyramid every day!

Rooms in the Great Pyramid

Until around 1990 almost everyone thought the Great Pyramid [see Fig. 9-41] contained only the King's Chamber (K), the Queen's Chamber (Q), the Grand Gallery (G), the Pit or Grotto (E)—which is a very strange place—and the Well (W) (called that because there was a "well" in the room). However, they've found four more rooms in just the last several years (since 1994). Three more rooms off three walls of the Queen's Chamber have been found. One room had nothing in it, another was filled from floor to ceiling with radioactive sand, and the third had nothing in it but a solid gold statue, which the Japanese allegedly removed. (Incidentally, the King's Chamber and Queen's Chamber don't have anything to do with male/female. The names were given to those rooms by the Muslims because the Muslims buried men under flat roofs and women under pitched roofs. It has nothing to do with kings and queens.)

This theft was followed by a silent alarm around the world. It caused the Egyptian Antiquities Minister to be fired and all the foreign archaeologists to be kicked out of the country during this crisis. There was a worldwide hunt for the gold statue, but they never found it, as far as I know, and they never found the people responsible. The statue is absolutely priceless. The solid gold alone would be worth a lot, but there's *no* amount of money that could match the value of the statue itself. The Japanese scientists were present when I was there in January 1990, and the statue was taken right after that.

Fig. 9-40. The Great Pyramid.

You see, the Japanese had made some instruments that could see into the Earth, and with these they found a brand-new room beneath the Sphinx. Through 60 feet of rock they could look into the room so well that they could see a coil of rope and a clay pot in a corner. They also found a tunnel leading from the room under the Sphinx to the Great Pyramid. This tunnel has been mentioned in many of the ancient writings, though the ancient writings say there are actually three tunnels.

The statue was located where the Japanese were investigating. According to my sources who were there, the Japanese imaged the gold statue inside the room next to the Queen's Chamber, then went to the Egyptian Minister of Antiquities and asked permission to remove it, but he refused them on every level. I think the Japanese thought there would be no problem. The entire Queen's Chamber was filled with their scaffolding at the time, and no one was allowed inside. So the Japanese had full access to this wall and the room behind it. About a month or so after they were denied permission, they gathered up their scaffolding and left the country. Only *after* they left Egypt did the Minister of Antiquities notice the new mortar in the bricks on the wall facing the hidden room where the gold statue was located, and realized what they (allegedly) had done. But it was too late. He got fired for it; it was quite a big deal.

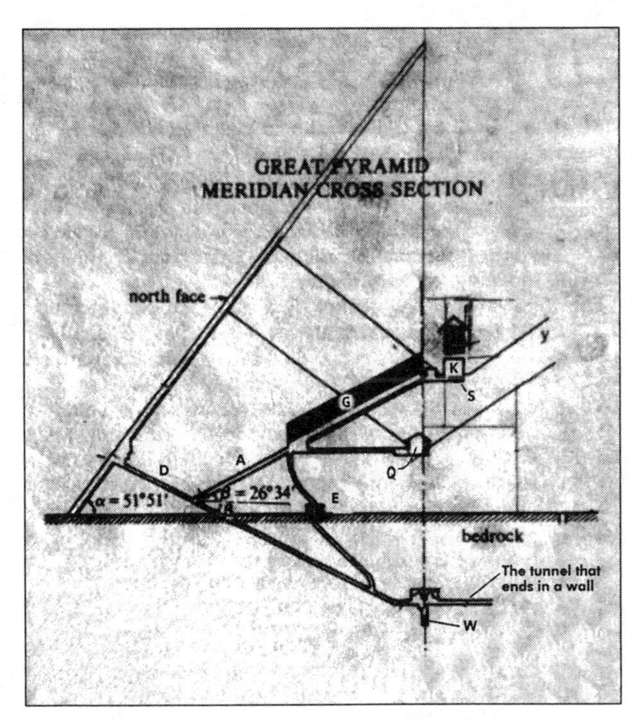

Fig. 9-41. Cross section of the Great Pyramid.

A: Ascending Passage
D: Descending Passage
E: excavation called the Pit
G: seven-corbeled Grand Gallery
K: King's Chamber
Q: Queen's Chamber
S: Sarcophagus
W: shaft called the Well

Update: About 300 or so years ago, Kepler believed that all the orbits of the planets in our solar system were based on the Platonic solids. He tried to prove this was true, but he could not because he had incorrect information for the planetary orbits. In modern times Englishman John Martineau has found the truth. Using computers, he input most of the known sacred geometry relationships and the precise information of the maximum, minimum and mean orbits of the planets as determined by NASA for the computer to compare. What he found is astounding.

It was found that simple sacred geometry determined the orbital relationships between the planets, and that *nothing* was random. Kepler was right, except that it was more than just the Platonic solids. John Martineau put all this new/old information into a book published in 1995, *A Book of Coincidence: New Perspectives on an Old Chestnut* [currently out of print, Wooden Books, Wales].

What is important to us is that all the sacred geometry relationships discovered by Martineau are found in the human energy field, the Mer-Ka-Ba. This means that not only is the relationship of the Earth and her moon found in the human energy field, but that of the entire solar system. It is becoming increasing clear that man is truly the measuring stick of the universe. ✧

More Rooms

They've recently found another room off the Queen's Chamber. There are two ventilation ducts about four to six inches in diameter that go upward out of the Queen's Chamber. A German researcher [Rudolf Gantenbrink] ran a little robot camera way up one of those ducts and found a doorway leading into another room.

The chamber at E is called the Pit; it's a really strange room. They usually won't let you into the Pit. If you've been there, it probably means you have friends in high places. It is just a big hole in the ground. Thoth never told me much about this room, so I can't tell you.

The three places Thoth *did* tell me about are the King's Chamber (toward the top), the Queen's Chamber (almost halfway up to the King's Chamber), and the Well (below ground level at the very bottom). I'll give you as much information about these three places as I can as they relate to the three levels of consciousness.

The Initiation Process

The initiation process of a person who moves from the second level of consciousness to the third begins in the Well. If you read *The Emerald Tablets*, it tells you that the initiation begins at the end of a tunnel that goes nowhere. It's a tunnel that seemingly has no purpose, and the Well is the only room we know of in the Pyramid that fits that description. This tunnel goes horizontally deep into the Earth about 80 to 100 feet and simply ends. The usual Egyptian archaeologist has no idea why the ancient Egyptians dug this tunnel. I've looked carefully at it, and it looks like when they were carving it out, they got to a certain place and decided, "Let's do something else," because the end is rough, like they simply decided to quit.

Now let's leave this tunnel for a while and look at the initiation process in the King's Chamber. First, the King's Chamber was made for you and me to move into Christ consciousness; this is its primary purpose. It's a room of initiation. I'm going to give you a concept of the particular technique the Egyptians used for resurrection. It was a rather synthetic way, because it required physical instruments and the knowledge of how to use them. We, you and I, are not going to be using this method at this time in history, but it is extremely educational to see how the Egyptians did it. Later I will tell you in detail what I believe humanity will be using to move into the third level of consciousness.

First we'll try to understand why these three rooms are placed where they are inside the Great Pyramid. This information will illuminate many questions you may have. The King's Chamber is not a Golden Mean rectangle, though you may have read that in several books. It's something a lot more interesting: It's a square-root-of-5 room—a perfect 1 by 2 by square-root-of-5 room. Remember the human body with that line down the middle and a diagonal, which were bisected at the center of the circle by a line that created a phi ratio [see Fig. 7-31]? Well, this room is like that. The floor plan is a perfect 1 by 2, and the height of the room is exactly one-half the diagonal of the floor.

See how the King's Chamber is off center in Figure 9-41? But it's off center in a very special way. When you enter it, having climbed the Grand Gallery and ducked to go through the tiny anteroom, the sarcophagus is off to your right. In its original placement, the exact center of the pyramid ran right through the sarcophagus, but it has been moved. The apex of the pyramid is shown at the top. You need to know this first.

Two initiations actually took place in the King's Chamber. The first one was in the sarcophagus. The second one, which usually happens many years later, sometimes even thousands of years later, happens precisely in the center of the room, marked by half the diagonal. There's a fourth-dimensional object you can't see physically that sits in the middle of the room. The room is made up of precisely 100 stones on the walls and ceiling. It was created for the second level of consciousness, and we have exactly 100 squares around our bodies geometrically.

Light Reflectors and Absorbers above the King's Chamber

Here's another aspect of this picture you need to see as we put the pieces of the puzzle together.

Figure 9-42 is a section drawing of the King's Chamber and the five layers above the room. The immediate ceiling of the King's Chamber is made of nine huge stones (remember that nine is the key to Christ consciousness), and over it is a series of stone layers, as shown in the drawing, with an air space between each layer. The usual explanation is that this was built to relieve the pressure on the flat roof of the King's Chamber so that it doesn't cave in. Well, it's true that it *does* that, but I don't believe that's the only reason for the layers. The standard explanation is that the Queen's Chamber doesn't need one of these pressure-relievers because it has a pitched roof. But there's at least one other room in the pyramid—the Well—without a pitched roof, and you could ask, why they didn't put one of these so-called pressure relievers over it, since it is beneath the Pyramid and has millions of tons more pressure? (There are two and a half million blocks in this pyramid, and their weight is tremendous.) So something else is obviously going on concerning these five spaces.

When you look carefully at those layers, it becomes pretty clear that they are more than just air space to relieve pressure. The bottom sides of the blocks are polished like glass. The top sides are totally irregular and covered with about a quarter inch of black foam. Yes, *foam!* It looks like somebody sprayed it on with a spray can. I don't know what it is, but that's what it looks like. When you think about it, you've got these mirrorlike surfaces facing downward and these irregular, foam-covered surfaces facing upward. It looks to me like it's designed to reflect energy coming from underneath and absorb energy coming from above. It's a separator, which we will explain in just a moment.

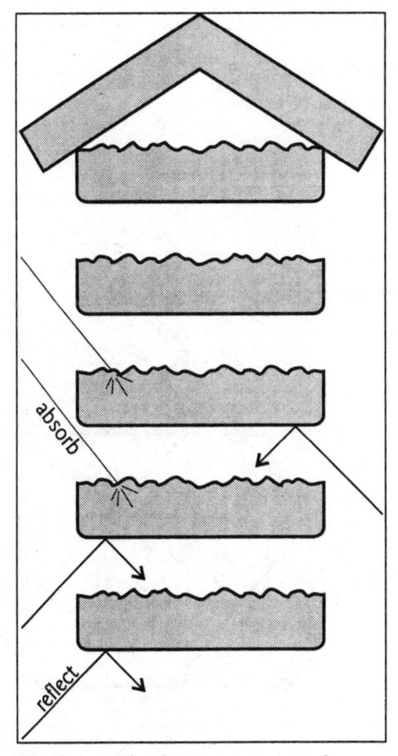

Fig. 9-42. The five open spaces above the King's Chamber.

It has still another function (almost everything the Egyptians did has more than one purpose): It's also a sound generator. When we look carefully at this room relative to the superimposed geometric images of human consciousness, this will become clear.

I want to repeat that this is Thoth's information, what he said to me. Most of this information is not written down anywhere.

Comparing the Levels of Consciousness

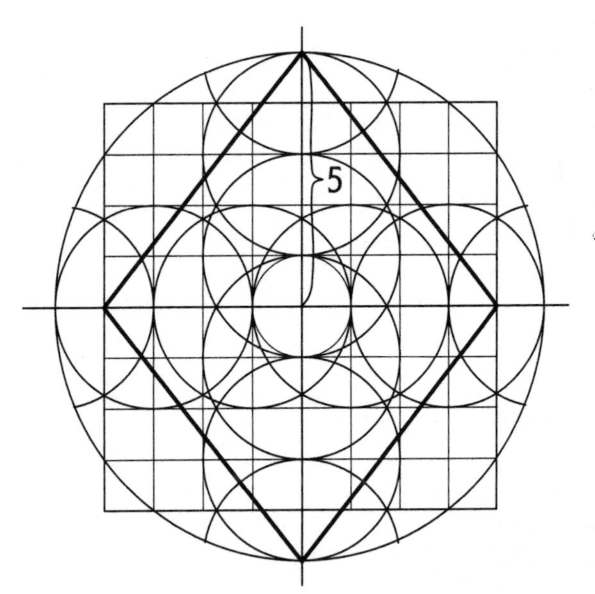

Fig. 9-43. Schematic of the first level of consciousness, 8 by 10.

The Great Pyramid is definitely not made for first-level Aboriginal types with 42 + 2 chromosomes. It has nothing to do with them. The Great Pyramid is primarily based on thirds, which synchronizes with our level and the Christ-consciousness level of consciousness, but not the first level.

Figure 9-43 is the drawing of the first level of consciousness, showing the pyramid. There are 5 grid units from its base to the apex; you see that the first level of consciousness is based on fifths, which is divisible only by 1 and 5.

Here's the second-level drawing with the pyramid [Fig. 9-44] and the 100-unit grid for this level of human consciousness. Counting from its base to the top are 6 units, divisible by 3.

The pyramid in the third-level drawing [Fig. 9-45] is 9 units high, also divisible by 3, and this is the Christ-consciousness level. The reason thirds were chosen as the basis for the Great Pyramid is because 3 is the common denominator between the two levels of consciousness connected to its ultimate purpose.

Catching the White Light

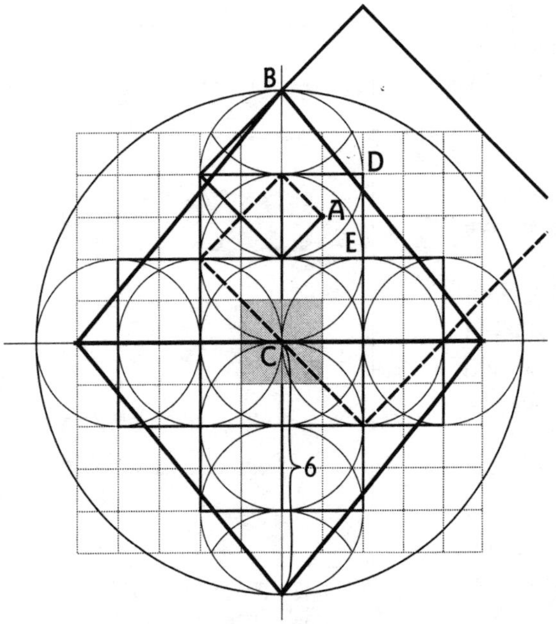

Fig. 9-44. Schematic of the second level of consciousness, 10 by 12, with a 100-unit grid. Dark-light spiral (broken line) goes through center (zero point) to the center of the Earth. White-light spiral (solid line) travels to the center of the galaxy.

Look at the second-level (10 by 12) drawing, Figure 9-44. Here you have the white-light energy [solid line] starting at point A and going down first, then spiraling around to exactly hit the apex of the pyramid at point B (if the capstone were there). And you have the dark-light energy [broken line], also starting at A but going up first, then spiraling around to pass through zero point, the center point of the base of the pyramid at C. According to Thoth, because of the placement of the Great Pyramid on the Earth connecting into the Earth's huge geometrical field—specifically the octahedral field of the Earth, which is equivalent to our own fields—and because of the pyramid's mass and the geometries used in it, the white-light energy field spirals upward and becomes extremely strong, stretching all the way out to the center of the galaxy. The dark-light energy comes in from above, spirals through zero point and connects with the center of the Earth. In this way the Great Pyramid connects the center of the Earth to the center of our galaxy.

Suppose you want to connect with only the white-light energy, get just that energy, and get it at its source. (In the Egyptian initiation this is necessary for experiencing Christ consciousness.) The white-light energy actually starts at point D and comes down one diagonal to cross the diagonal I've drawn starting at point A. And the dark-light spiral starts at point E and goes up across one square to meet *its* connection at point A. But if you start at points D and E, the energies will cross near their point of origin; the problem with that is that the energies tend to switch polarities.

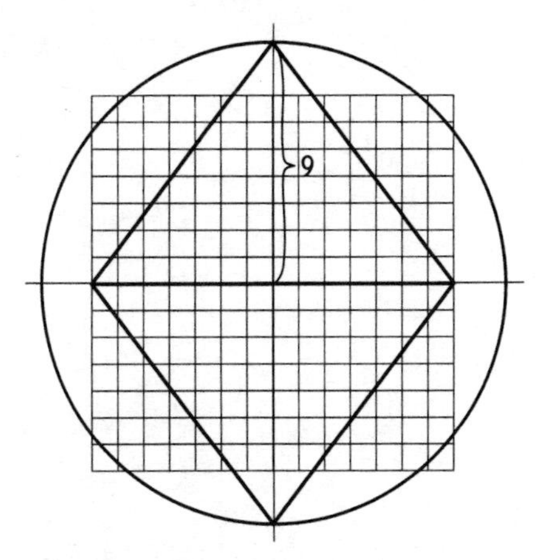

Fig. 9-45. Schematic of the third level of consciousness, 14 by 18.

Thoth tried to explain it to me. The female can come in and become the male, or the male can come in and become the female only when they are returning to the source, or beginning, and only at point A. The Egyptians wanted to use the white-light energy just after it crossed point A but *before* it made the 90-degree turn, which is precisely where the King's Chamber is located. But if they were to put the initiation room in that area, they would have another problem to solve, because just above that area is the black-light, or female, energy.

That's the reason for the separators, the five spaces above the King's Chamber. The spaces absorb the black-light energy coming from above and reflect the white-light energy coming from below. In this way they separate the two from each other. When you're lying in the sarcophagus, the male energy comes down, rises off the floor at a 45-degree angle and passes right through your head. That beam, about two inches in diameter, comes up through the back of your head and passes through your pineal gland, which is the hidden secret to all this work. (At the right time we will explain.)

Getting to this point in the Egyptian experience took twelve years of training in the Left Eye of Horus school and twelve years in the Right Eye of Horus. If they thought you were ready after twenty-four years, at the right time they would place you in that sarcophagus, put the lid on and leave you between two and a half to four days.

You would lie down in the sarcophagus, connect with that white-energy beam with your pineal gland, then (using your twenty-four years of training) you would go out on the spiral 1, 1, 2, 3, 5, 8, 13, making very specific turns, following the male straight-line, 90-degree energy (not the female curved energy, which cannot be followed), going *way* out to have the awesome experience of becoming all of creation—*synthetically* experiencing Christ consciousness.

After you'd been out in the cosmos for a few days, you would return. Because of your training, you knew you were supposed to return, and you would return by using the Fibonacci mathematics, which was the key to your being *able* to return.

According to Thoth, they did lose people occasionally. He said they lost about one out of every 200 initiates. When you're out there *being* the universe, it's so beautiful that the thought of coming back to Earth is not exactly the greatest thought in your mind. You don't really want to. It takes great discipline. When they trained you, the ancient Egyptians drilled this "returning" into your mind, because all you have to do is say no, and you remain there in that state of consciousness. If you do stay, then your body dies in the sarcophagus and you no longer live on Earth. But most of them did come back, because the reason for doing this in the first place was to evolve the human consciousness. If you did not come back, the Earth would not have that experience.

In the next chapter we will show how the Egyptians placed both the Fibonacci and Golden Mean spirals dramatically around the Great Pyramid. Why? Because they wanted you to know the important difference between these two mathematical relationships. Relating to what we just talked about with the dark and light energies, if the Egyptians went out on a Golden Mean spiral, they would never know where the beginning was, since a Golden Mean spiral has no beginning and no end. Therefore they would never know where their body was located relative to the universe. But because it's a Fibonacci spiral, they could count down, moving down the Fibonacci numbers such as 5, 3, 2, 1 and 1, locating their body exactly, then center into it. They would step out of this experience onto Earth inside the sarcophagus in the King's Chamber where their body was located. But they would be a completely altered person, never again the same, having had the direct experience of what it is like to be in Christ consciousness.

Proof of the Initiation Chamber

The fact that this is an initiation chamber and not a burial chamber is pretty obvious for two reasons. The first has to do with the mummification process used in Egypt. Throughout early Egyptian history—for every known king, queen, pharaoh, doctor, lawyer or other special person who was ever mummified—the process was carried out the same way. They had a ceremony, took out the organs and placed them in four clay jars, then wrapped the body, now in the process of mummification, and placed it in the sarcophagus, sealing the lid. Then they carried the sarcophagus and the four jars to wherever they were going to bury them.

There have been no known exceptions to this procedure that I am aware of; yet in the King's Chamber the sarcophagus is larger than the doorway. They couldn't have carried it into the room because they can't even get it out. It's one enormous piece of granite. It had to have been placed in the King's Chamber during the construction of the pyramid. That's the only reason it's still there—otherwise it would have been stolen a long time ago and put in the British Museum or somewhere. The lid's gone because it *could* be taken out, but they can't remove the sarcophagus.

The doorway into this chamber is small, and the tunnel you have to go through to get there is even smaller, smaller than the sarcophagus itself. It's clear that no one was buried in this sarcophagus. Further, a mummy was not found in this sarcophagus when the King's Chamber was first opened. This is circumstantial evidence, but it's pretty powerful.

The other indication that this is an initiation chamber is that there are air shafts going into it. If it were meant to be a tomb, they wouldn't need air ducts. Egyptian burial chambers are as airtight as possible to protect the mummy, and none have air ducts. But both the King's Chamber and the Queen's Chamber have them. Why? To make sure there is air circulating for the people who use the room for their ceremonies.

Here's another little piece of circumstantial evidence indicating what the King's Chamber was used for. When they first examined it, they noticed white powder inside the end of the sarcophagus facing the center of the pyramid, the very place where your head would be if you were being initiated as described above. They didn't know what it was, but they scooped it up and put it into a little glass vial, which is now sitting in the British Museum. Only recently did they figure out what it was. You see, when you are in meditation and you go into the theta state, the corpus callosum fully links the left and right brains and the pituitary gland begins to excrete a liquid through the forehead. When that liquid dries up, it becomes little white crystals, which flake off. That's what this was on the bottom of the sarcophagus in the King's Chamber. There was far more powder than a single person would produce. This probably meant that lots of people went through that initiation.

After you've returned to your body in the King's Chamber, they immediately take you down the Grand Gallery and into the Queen's Chamber. Thoth didn't describe exactly what they did there, but he said it was designed to stabilize you and your memory when you came back from that super cosmic experience so you wouldn't forget, wouldn't lose the experience. This was and still is the primary purpose of the Queen's Chamber.

Catching the Dark Light

The chamber below ground level called the Well is actually where initiation begins. Nobody I've studied in the conventional world knows why this room is there. But when you superimpose the cross section of the pyramid over the drawing of the second level of consciousness [see Fig. 9-44], you can see what it is.

Suppose you wanted to get only the *black*-light spiral, which is actually the beginning of the pyramid initiation. Logically, you would think you'd do it at the area *above* the King's Chamber (following the logic of its location—unless you know what's involved here. If you *did* do it in the higher area, you would have to go through zero point at the base, and going through the Great Void is not exactly desirable. There are too many variables in that state, according to Thoth. So they chose a place immediately after the energy beam left zero point, which is in the area of the tunnel.

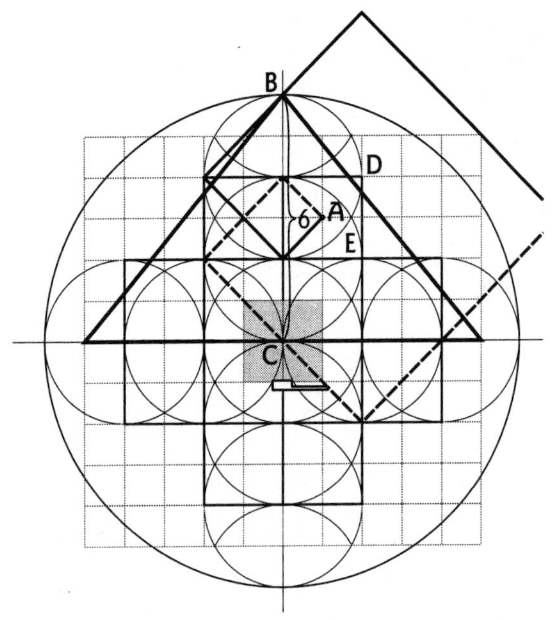

Fig. 9-46. The Great Pyramid, showing the black-light beam angling downward to cross the end of the tunnel below the pyramid.

Now, think about this for a moment. This drawing [Fig. 9-46] is not perfect, but if it were, you would see the black-light beam coming down at a 45-degree angle and actually crossing the end of this tunnel. The Egyptians continued to dig until they reached the dark-light beam, then they went about a foot farther and stopped. That beam is real, because I've been there and I've experienced it. If you lie down there, a powerful beam of energy comes in and locks onto you—and you *will* have an incredible experience.

The Halls of Amenti and the Face of Jesus

After the initiation process is completed in this tunnel, the initiates go through a training that teaches them how to go toward the center of the Earth to the Halls of Amenti, the womb of the Earth. This space is located about a thousand miles inside the Earth, not in the center. The Halls of Amenti is a space as vast as all of outer space. I've been there; some of you have heard me tell that story. And so have all Egyptian initiates, before they entered the King's Chamber to experience the third level of human consciousness.

There's another little fact about the Great Pyramid that has recently been discovered and it is very, very interesting. Leading into the Queen's Chamber, on the right-hand side way up high, they discovered something about three or four inches in size. You all probably know about the Shroud of Turin, on which is imprinted what some people suspect is the actual face of Jesus. Scientific analysis couldn't determine how the image of the face was put on the cloth, but it *has* shown that it was somehow created through an intense blast of heat. That's all they can say about it, at least from everything I've read. Leading into the Queen's Chamber, there's an image of a person on what looks like a photograph on stone, and they don't know how it was created. Scientific analysis indicates that it was made by an intense blast of heat. And the image appears to be the same face that's on the Shroud of Turin. It looks like the face of Jesus, if you accept that, and it leads into the Queen's Chamber, a chamber that was used to stabilize Christ consciousness.

Summary of the Initiation Process

First you go to the Well, to the initiation at the far end of the tunnel, and experience the dark-light energy that leads to the Halls of Amenti, or the womb of the Earth. Then you go to the King's Chamber, where you experience the white-light energy that gives the experience of being all of creation. Finally you go to the Queen's Chamber, where you are stabilized in the experience of creation so that you can return to everyday life to help others find their way. Then you wait a long time. At a certain moment, which could even be in a future life, you go back into the King's Chamber for the final initiation, which is a four- or five-minute ceremony that happens in the center of the room. In this ceremony an ankh is drawn on the third eye of the initiate to verify that you are still on the path and have stabilized over a long period of time. Those are the steps of initiation as described to me by Thoth.

What we have now seen is one of the major keys to knowledge in the universe: the geometry of the consciousness levels of human origins. We have only begun to explore this science. We have examined only the first three levels, but this knowledge gives us the understanding of where we have been, where we are now and where we are going. Without this understanding we could not know the basic blueprint and map to human consciousness.

TEN

The Left Eye of Horus Mystery School

There are three mystery schools in Egypt. The male school is the Right Eye of Horus. The female school is the Left Eye of Horus. And the third school is the child, the Middle or Third Eye of Horus, which is simply life—but the Egyptians considered life the most important school of all. From the Egyptian point of view, everything that happens in this life is a lesson, part of a school preparing for higher levels of existence, which the normal world calls death. Life is all about teaching and learning, and what we call everyday normal life has, to the Egyptians, a deep, secret meaning. This wall mural [Fig. 10-1] shows the right eye, the left eye and the middle eye. This mural is the symbol for not only all three schools, but also the meaning and purpose of life itself. The right eye is male, the left eye is

Fig. 10-1. Top center: Right eye, middle eye and left eye.

female and the middle eye is the child, the source of both the other two eyes, for we all begin life as a child.

The Left Eye of Horus, the feminine pathway, explores the human nature of emotions and feeling, both positive and negative, sexual energy and birthing, death, certain psychic energy, and everything that is not logical.

We've been looking at the male Right Eye Mystery School since chapter 5. Now I'd like to explore the other side of the brain, the feminine side. I'm probably not the best person to teach this subject since I am male, but I'm going to give it my best effort. What we are about to give to you is information that can help you today in life and ascension if you understand the subtle nature of what is discussed.

Fig. 10-2. Another wall mural of the three schools.

Figure 10-2 is another depiction of the different schools. You can see the two eyes with the sphere in the middle.

Figure 10-3 is a pyramid capstone that's now in the Cairo Museum. First of all, you Sitchin (see chapter 3) fans may remember that the symbol of the oval with the wings and the two cobras coming out of it is the symbol for Marduk, the tenth planet. Notice again the two eyes with the center component, symbolizing the three schools.

Another symbol for the Right Eye of Horus school is the ibis and the oval, shown underneath the right eye (left of center). To the left of those symbols is a name—a cartouche. And farther to the left you see the triangular symbol for the star Sirius and the ankh,

Fig. 10-3. Capstone from a pyramid.

Fig. 10-4. Isis, Osiris and the resurrection tools.

a symbol of eternal life. In the middle of that row of symbols is the egg of metamorphosis, representing the actual physical change that one goes through in life to reach immortality. Then going toward the right, another symbol for the Left Eye of Horus school is a flower stalk with a bee next to it. Then there's another cartouche, and farther to the right you see the star Sirius, eternal life and the snake, which represents kundalini energy.

Here you see Isis and Osiris [Fig. 10-4], and he's holding the tools of resurrection: from left to right, the hook, a 45-degree endpiece of the rod that has a tuning fork at the other end, and a flail. Isis has the ankh, and she's giving it to him from behind. According to Thoth, the only way you can initiate the ankh is from behind. If you initiate it from the front, it will destroy you. The ankh is *very* important, and we will be giving the sexual breathing instructions associated with the ankh later (all things at the right time).

The hook and the flail are actual tools, and these [Fig. 10-5] are King Tutankhamun's.

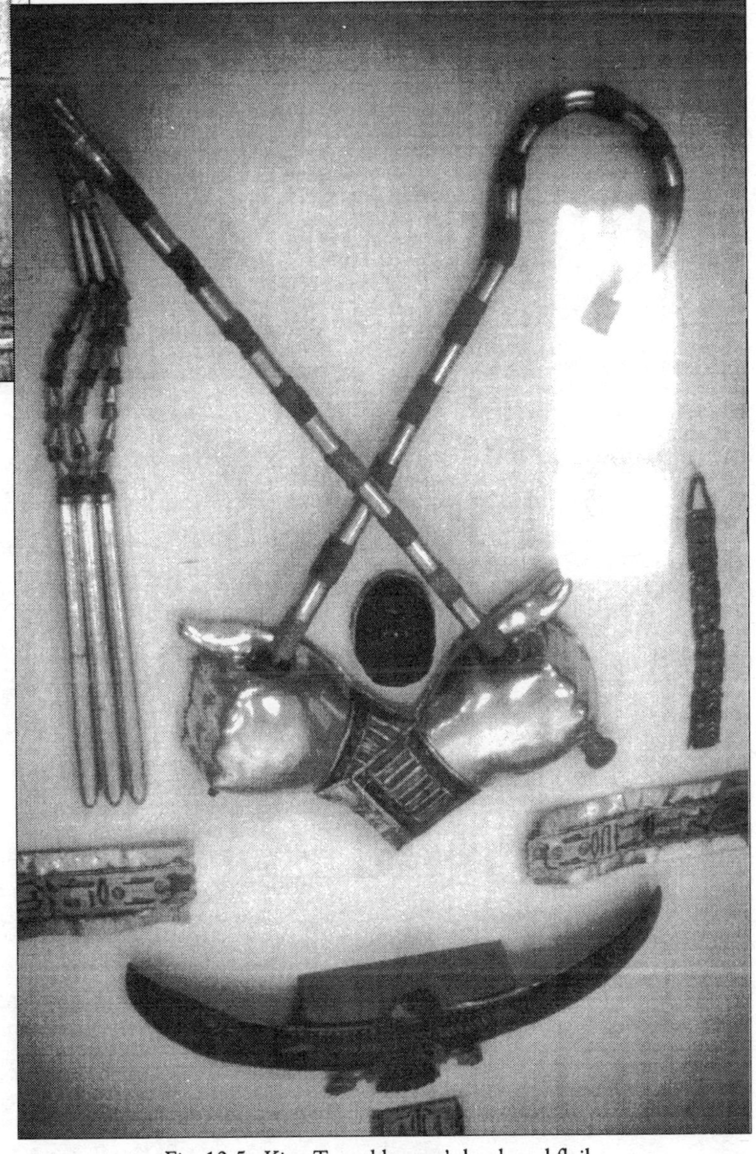

Fig. 10-5. King Tutankhamun's hook and flail.

Fig. 10-6. Isis, Horus and Osiris at Abu Simbel.

This mural is on a wall at Abu Simbel [Fig. 10-6], and you see the family here—Isis, Horus and Osiris. This is the only place I've seen in all of Egypt where they actually show the physical use of these tools of resurrection. I couldn't believe it when I saw it. Horus is holding the rod to the back of Osiris's head, right at the chakra point that is the primary doorway into the eighth chakra. The hook is not shown here, but they actually slide the hook up and down this main rod to tune it. Evidently they got it tuned just right without it. Here Osiris is holding his arm up and one finger is holding the tuning fork, which is an angled piece with which you can fine-tune your body to get the exact vibration running up your spine. As you can see, he has an erection. Sexual energy was and still is a paramount component in their concept of resurrection. The sexual energy was running up his spine. It was at the moment of orgasm that they were able to make this transition. This subject will require a book of its own because it is so complex, so we will not address the subject of Egyptian tantra fully at this time.

In Figure 10-7 you see Isis placing the ankh to Osiris' nose and mouth, showing that the ankh, or the key to eternal life, was linked to breath. Thus far the ankh is linked to both the sexual energy and to the breath.

In Figure 10-8 you see it again in another place. Instead of the usual sphere over the top of her head, you see the red oval of metamorphosis, meaning that she's giving him instructions about how to go through metamorphosis and about breathing, which is what you'll be receiving here. She's gently holding his hand, and she has a kind of Mona Lisa smile, a very gentle, loving smile, as she teaches him the breathing that will take him from ordinary consciousness into Christ consciousness.

Egyptian Initiations

Crocodile Initiation at Kom Ombo

In the feminine world of emotions and feelings, if they are not in balance within the initiate, this imbalance will stop us from evolving. Until the emotional balance is achieved, we can proceed on the path of enlightenment only a certain distance, then all will stop. For without love and compassion and a healthy emotional body, the mind will fool itself into thinking all is well. It will create the sensation that the initiate is reaching enlightenment when in truth he or she is not.

We are bringing the following ceremony to light because it is a perfect example of the importance that the Egyptians placed on overcoming fear, one of the negative emotions. Fear was and still is the primary force that stops a person from growing into the light. As we move into the higher worlds of light, we manifest our thoughts and feelings directly. This fact of nature becomes a tremendous problem, since we will almost always manifest our fears first. And in manifesting our fears in a new world, a new dimension of existence, we destroy ourselves and are forced to leave the higher worlds. Therefore, what all the ancient races have discovered, and what we are rediscovering now in modern times, is that in order to survive in the higher worlds, we must first overcome our fears here on Earth. To reach this goal, the Egyptians built special temples along the Nile.

Fig. 10-7. Isis offering ankh to Osiris.

Fig. 10-8. Another offering of the ankh.

Fig. 10-9. Temple at Kom Ombo.

Figure 10-9 is the temple at Kom Ombo. It represents the second chakra, the sexual chakra, of twelve chakras that run up the Nile—thirteen if you wish to count the Great Pyramid. Kom Ombo is the only temple that's dedicated to polarity, or duality, which is the basis of sexuality, and two gods are associated with it. In fact, it is the only temple dedicated to two gods in all of Egypt: Sobek, the crocodile god, and Horus. As you face the temple, the right half of this temple is dedicated to darkness and the left side to the light.

An interesting event recently happened in this temple—sort of a sign of the times. There was a major earthquake in Egypt in 1992, and Gregg Braden told me that he was sitting in this temple when the earthquake hit. Practically everything on the dark side fell, but the light side didn't lose a brick. As you will see in this work we do, the light is now stronger than the dark.

Fig. 10-10. Two left eyes.

The carving in Figure 10-10 is on the rear wall of that temple at Kom Ombo. Two left eyes of Horus show that this is the emotional-body school, the feminine school, and that it's really two schools dedicated to two gods. On the left you see the 45-degree rod of resurrection.

The first time I went there I took Katrina Raphaell, and the second time she took me. This was my second trip in 1990, and we went through a beautiful ceremony that Katrina had set up in Kom Ombo. For part of the ceremony we climbed down in a hole, and Figure 10-11 is a cross section of that hole.

A big granite slab comes down in the middle, allowing only a little space between the bottom of it and the ground. So we squeezed underneath the low part and came back out the other side. That was the physical part of this ceremony. Here's a photo of somebody going down into it [Fig.10-12].

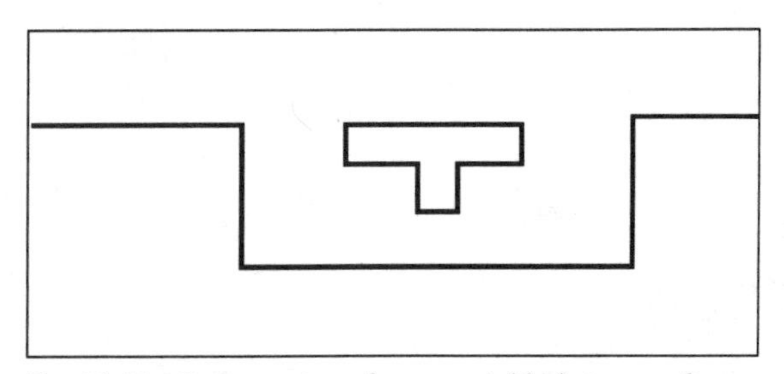

Fig. 10-11. Cross section of ceremonial hole in next figure.

But I could see that there must have been more to it than that in the ancient past. Katrina was working with a large group of people, so I mostly watched that day. I was conscious of Thoth's presence the whole time I was in Egypt, so I asked him, "Is that it?" He said, "No, there's more than that." So I asked, "Well, would you tell me?" He replied, "All right. This knowledge might be helpful to you."

Thoth told me to climb up high onto a wall at the back side of the temple and look back. So I climbed up on that wall, looked back and took this picture [Fig. 10-13]. The entrance to the ceremony hole was at point B, just off the picture. You can see the Nile in the background to the left of the large structure. The river ran along the front and the water from the Nile came right up into the temple. This was a temple where water and crocodiles were used in the teachings.

Fig. 10-12. Entrance to the ceremony hole. You can see the right hand and top of head of the man descending into it.

Fig. 10-12b. Shape of wedge at points A.

On the previous photo [Fig. 10-12], you can see the little wedge-shaped pegs at points A [Fig. 10-12b]. They use pieces of metal shaped like that to lock two stones together so that they don't move around during earthquakes; that makes it more stable. Those wedges actually hold walls in place at these points. Where the man is going down into the hole there used to be walls on both sides. When you are up high on the other side (where I took this picture), you can see the little wedge holes going all the way to the top at C. Walls at D and E had originally extended forward to where I took this picture, and you can see a secret hollow space in the middle. In this view from the back of the temple, the left side of this hollow center was the side of the "dark," and the right side was the side of the "light." If you were on either side of this wall, you wouldn't know there was a hollow place in the middle. It would be pretty hard to tell because you'd think that the other side of that wall was the other side of the temple.

At each of the temples in Egypt, they would create situations to force you to have experiences you would not normally bring on yourself, so that when you had similar experiences you would become stronger and less fearful. You would be put in extremely fearful situations to overcome your fears. That's what this secret hollow space was all about—an exercise to overcome fear, a specific kind of fear.

Fig. 10-13. What's left of the initiation site in Kom Ombo.

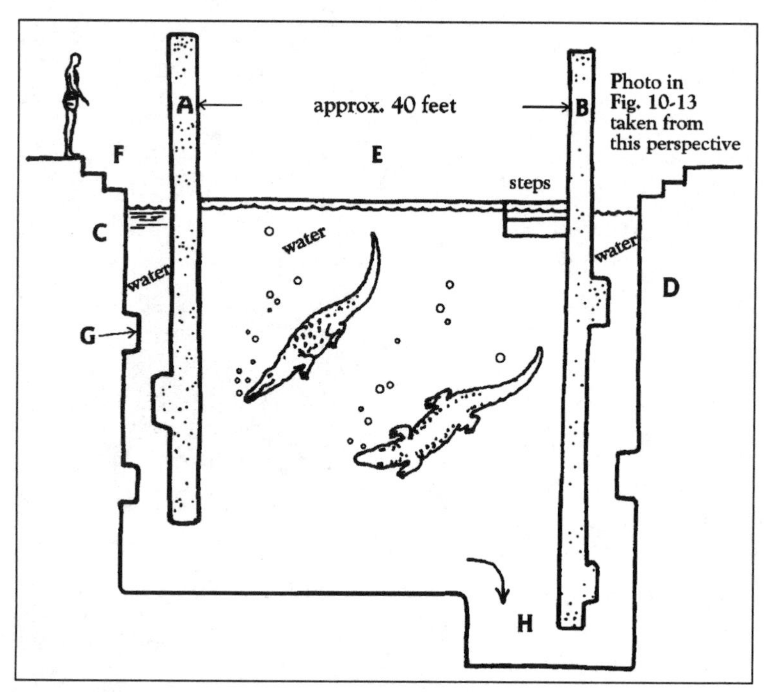

Fig. 10-14a. Crocodile pool used for initiatory experience.

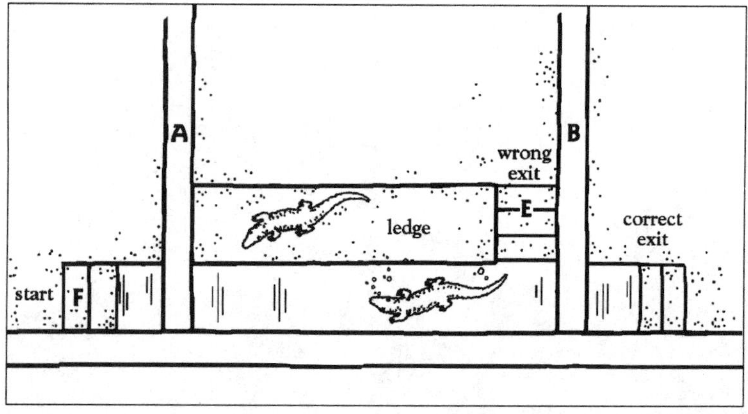

Fig. 10-14b. Top view of the crocodile pool.

That was more or less the function of the complex as Thoth explained it to me. Figure 10-14a is a section, viewed from the side, of the hollow place between the walls. The walls at A and B spanned the short distance to walls C and D, and this formed a sort of mazelike channel going from one visible opening to the other. Inside this channel was water—and crocodiles—maybe one lying on the ledge in the center, having a good ol' time waiting for some human to enter the water. Light came in through the opening at E.

Imagine yourself as a neophyte about to undertake this test. After much preparation and meditation, you would stand on the steps at F, look down and see a little square of water at your feet no bigger than about one square yard. You would not have any idea what was in the water or where it led to. Then you were told to go into the water and not come out the way you went in. You, the neophyte, had only one breath—and you had to be careful, because if you hurried to jump in without caution, you would hit the granite slab at point G. But your training would have taught you to be careful in all unknown situations. So at first you had to move around this granite slab. When you got to the bottom, which is about 20 feet deep and under wall A, you would emerge out of the darkness of the channel and look up toward the light. Then you would see the crocodiles. You can imagine the fear that would come up in such a situation. There was not much the initiate could do at this point except swim upward, squeeze by these fearful life forms and get out. That's what happened with almost everyone the first time around, according to Thoth.

What you didn't know was that these crocodiles were fully fed so they would not hurt you. But that hardly makes a difference to initiates down in that channel holding their breath and looking up at them. They didn't lose anybody to the crocs, but nevertheless . . .

When you, the initiate, stepped out of the water at E [see top view, Fig. 10-14b], you were told that you had just failed. Then you would have to go through more and more and more training. When your teachers thought you were ready, they would put you through this ceremony a second time. This time you knew about the crocodiles, that you had only one breath, and that the way out was *not* past the crocs toward the light. So you would go down to the bottom again, and at the moment of your greatest fear, when you could actually see the crocodiles, you had to search for another way out. The opening at H is where we went down and came up for Katrina's ceremony. So if you found the opening at H, you had to go farther down and under wall B before you could swim up and out another pitch-black channel, not knowing for sure that it was even the way out.

This was the kind of initiation the Egyptians performed in these schools —very calculated experiences. And these experiences were many and varied. This building had all kinds of special rooms designed to overcome fear. This temple also had a positive side, where they studied tantra—not just sexual pleasures, but understanding the sexual currents and other sexual energies and their relationship to resurrection. They also studied breathing and its relationship to all things that are human. The mundane ability to simply stay under water that long was quite a feat.

Now that we understand the importance of fear, I will talk about direct experience and the secret of the Well.

The Well under the Great Pyramid

The room in the Great Pyramid called the Well was closed off in about 1984 for safety reasons. They installed an iron door at the opening to the descending passage up at the main level, and kept a guard there for a long time. This was because many people had died in the Well, so many that they finally closed off the room to tourists. They had died of unbelievable things—for example, poisonous snakes and spiders that don't even *exist* in Egypt! The last incident happened just before they closed the Well. Some kind of poisonous gas appeared in the air and killed a group of people who were doing ceremony in the room. Nobody knows what it was.

This space has a very unusual nature, especially toward the end of the tunnel, where it ends at a wall. In this tunnel there is a connection between the third and the fourth dimensions. Whatever you think and feel *happens,* for real. If you've got any fears, they will become real. They will manifest and will not allow you to survive in the new world. If you are fearless, then you are free to manifest in the positive, which opens the door to the higher worlds. As you will see, this is the nature of the fourth dimension: whatever you think and feel happens.

This is why the Egyptian mystery schools took students through twelve years of training where they were faced with every fear known to man. Kom Ombo held only fears associated with the second chakra. Each chakra has its associated fears. They took initiates through every fear you can imagine, so that by the end of twelve years they were absolutely fearless because they had overcome all fear. All the mystery schools and training schools around the world did exactly the same thing in various ways.

The Incas were incredible. The things they did to get you into a fear state and then overcome it were unmentionable. In contrast to the Egyptians, they didn't care if they lost a high percentage of their people. They were intense. The Mayans did the same thing. Remember the Mayan ball games where two teams would practice all year long to play a game that was like basketball, but it is believed that the *winners* had their *heads* cut off? They believed it was an honor to die this way, but it was really all part of a higher-dimensional training program.

Another interesting thing that's happened many times down in the tunnel below the Pyramid is that people would lie down, close their eyes and have an awesome experience, then wake up in the sarcophagus *in the King's Chamber!* They'd ask, "How did *that* happen?" This has been written about many times, and the present-day Egyptians haven't a clue how this could take place. What happened was that the people who experience this phenomenon didn't have the right training, so they were pulled back along the black-light energy vortex, traveled through the Great Void and came to the beginning of the black-light vortex. Then they reversed polarities and went down the white-light spiral into the sarcophagus. It brought the whole being, body and all, right back through into this other reality.

There were many, many problems with people lying down in the sarcophagus in the King's Chamber and having experiences that were irrational by modern standards. For that reason they moved the sarcophagus a long time ago. They pulled it askew and pushed it back so it doesn't line up with the field at all. When you lie down in it now, you can't get your head in the beam. It's not even possible now. The Egyptians know. They understand; they're not dumb. And they've been there for a long, long time. Of course, they have a story about why the sarcophagus was moved, but they are silent about why they have not moved it back to its original position.

They understand about the sarcophagus, though they didn't understand about the tunnel beside the Well. So in 1984, after this group of people died down in the Well tunnel, they sealed the whole area off and wouldn't allow anyone else into it. When we went there in 1985 and explained to them that it was only the *end* of the tunnel where the problem was, they opened up the rest of the area to the public. Now it's open *except* for the tunnel. The entire area was closed off for a period of only about a year.

The Tunnel beneath the Great Pyramid

In the original Flower of Life workshop I used to tell stories each day, because it is one of the best methods I know to give and receive information. The story I am about to tell is my personal experience in the tunnel so that you can understand the nature of the initiation the Egyptians went through and the nature of the fourth dimension, which will become more and more important as this book unfolds. This happened exactly as I perceived it, and I hope this story opens an insight within you. You do not have to believe it. You can take it as just a story if you wish.

What follows has been edited because it is too long in its entirety, but the most important points have been retained.

In 1984 Thoth appeared to me and said that I was to prepare for an initiation in Egypt. He said it was necessary for me to go through this initiation in order to connect with the Earth's energies and move with the Earth's changes in the future. Thoth told me that for this initiation I had to arrive in Egypt without any help from myself. I could not buy a ticket or make any arrangements on my own. I also could not even tell anyone that I wanted to go to Egypt. Somehow the events in my life had to naturally take me there without any effort on my part. If they did, then the initiation would begin. If they did not, then the initiation would not happen. The beginning rules were simple.

About two weeks later I visited my sister, Nita Page, in California. I had not seen her in a very long time. She had just gotten back from China, so it seemed like a perfect chance to meet. Nita is always traveling. She has been to almost every major city and country in the world many times over. She loves to travel so much that she eventually bought a travel agency to blend her love with her job.

As I was sitting with her in her home, I was careful not to talk about what Thoth had requested of me. But without any words on my part, it just happened. It was late at night around 1:30 A.M. and we were talking about China. There was a book on her coffee table called *The Secret Teachings of All Ages* by Manley P. Hall. As she was talking, she casually flipped open the book to a page that showed the Great Pyramid, and the conversation changed to Egypt. After a while, she looked me in the eye and said, "You have never been to Egypt, have you?" I said no, and she said, "If you ever want to go, I will pay for everything. Just let me know."

I had to bite my tongue not to talk about what Thoth had requested of me, but I did. I did not say a word. I simply told her thanks, and that if I ever wanted to go, I would call her.

My sister had been to Egypt twenty-two times and had probably been to every temple in Egypt. I was glad she wanted to take me, but I didn't really know what this would mean in terms of the initiation. However, as soon as I arrived home, that same night Thoth appeared and told me that my sister *was* the way I would go to Egypt. I just sat there and listened to him. He then said that I was to call her in the morning and tell her that I wanted to go between January 10 to 19 in 1985. He said that this period was the only time this initiation could be given. Then he left. This was a day in early December 1984, which meant that we would have about a month to prepare.

The next morning I sat by my phone to call her, but I was feeling a little strange. When my sister had offered this trip and said that she would take me, I knew that what she really meant was someday, not immediately. So I sat by my phone thinking how I would ask her. I must have sat there for over twenty minutes before I finally got up the courage to call.

When she answered, I told her about Thoth and what he had asked of me. Then I told her we would have to leave in about a month. She immediately told me to hold on. She said it would not be possible for at least nine months, which was about what I expected her to say. Nita, as I said, ran a travel agency, and she was booked solid until the middle of September. She loved me and tried to soften to blow by saying that she was about to go to work, and she would check her schedule and call me in a few hours. When she hung up I assumed it was over, but I didn't understand it, since Thoth has never been wrong on anything, ever, and he had said, "This is how you will go to Egypt."

Shortly after, my sister called me back; she sounded strange. She said, "I am booked even longer than I remembered this morning. I am booked solid through October. But when I looked in the time period you gave me, there was not even one booking. It was completely blank! I am booked on the ninth and on the twenty-first, but nothing in between. Drunvalo, I believe that Thoth was right. We are supposed to go."

Not only that, Nita called me the next day to tell me further interesting news. She said, "When I phoned to buy the tickets for us at United Airlines, I talked to my friend in ticketing who does most of the ticketing for my travel agency, and when he found out that the tickets were for me and my brother, he gave them to me for free." To me, this just emphasized the perfection of this initiation. It truly was effortless.

Thoth then began to appear every day to teach me different information pertaining to the work I would need to do in Egypt. First he gave me an itinerary we were to follow. The order of which temples we would enter could not be broken for any reason. We had to visit them in this exact order or the initiation would not be completed.

Then he began to teach me to talk in Atlantean. There were certain phrases and statements that had to be spoken aloud in perfect Atlantean in order for this to work. Every day Thoth would come and instruct me how to say them. He would have me repeat them over and over until they were perfect for his ears. Then he would have me write them down phonetically in English so that I could remember them when I got to Egypt. In each temple I had certain words to say in Atlantean to begin the initiation.

Finally Thoth taught me how to work with fear. He taught me certain techniques to identify whether the fear was real or imaginary. He had me imagine electric-blue rings that would move up and down the outside of my body like hula hoops. If the fear was imaginary, the rings would move in one way, and if the fear was real, the rings would move in another way. I took this training very seriously. He told me my very life could depend on my knowing this meditation. I did as he said and studied everything he taught me as though my very existence depended on it.

As we came closer to the time we were to leave, other people became interested in this trip. Thoth knew before they even asked that they would want to go. He said it had been written down long ago. Finally there were five of us—myself and my sister, Katrina Raphaell and her husband Sananda Ra, and his brother Jake. I remember as we arrived in Egypt, we flew over the Giza complex and circled once. All five of us were like children waiting to go out and play, we were so excited.

We were met at the airport by Ahmed Fayhed, the most renowned Egyptian archaeologist in the world, next to his father Mohammed. Mohammed was famous all over Egypt, and both of them were good friends of my sister Nita. Ahmed led us out of the passport lines and took the stamp out of the hands of one of the officials, stamped our passports and immediately guided us out into the street and into a taxicab without anyone so much as asking us about our luggage. He took us to his home, which was more of an apartment building several stories high. His large family lived in different "apartments" in this building. From his home we looked straight into the eyes of the Sphinx.

Ahmed's father, Mohammed, was an interesting man. When he was a small child he had had a dream that there was a huge wooden boat next to the Great Pyramid. The next day he drew the boat, which included hieroglyphics. He also wrote down the exact location of the boat in his dream. Somehow the Egyptian officials saw this drawing and noticed that the hieroglyphics were real, so they drilled a hole in the location where the child said the boat would be. And it was really there!

The Egyptian government took the boat out of the ground but found that it was dismantled, so they tried to put it together. After two years of trying, they gave up. Then Mohammed had another dream. In this dream he saw the blueprints showing how to put the boat together. By now the Egyptian government listened to him. They took the blueprints and with them, the boat went together perfectly. They then built a special beautiful room next to the Great Pyramid to house the boat. It is still there today, and you can see it for yourself if you wish.

Mohammed found almost the entire buried city of Memphis by simply telling them exactly where to dig. He provided the Egyptians with a drawing of the building or temple before they dug it up, and he was right in every single detail.

The middle pyramid at Giza was also opened through Mohammed's psychic powers. The government asked him if it would be all right to open this pyramid. Mohammed meditated and finally said yes. The government said they would move only one block (out of over two million), so Mohammed meditated for five hours in front of this pyramid. He finally said, "Move that block." As it turned out, that was the exact block that hid the doorway, and the Egyptians entered the second pyramid for the first time. He is the father of Ahmed Fayhed, our guide and my sister's friend.

When we arrived at Ahmed's house, he gave us rooms and let us relax for a couple of hours. Then he met with my sister and me and asked us where we wanted to go. I gave him the itinerary that Thoth had given me. He looked at it and said, "This is no good. You have only ten days here, and the French train that goes to Luxor does not leave until 6:00 P.M. tomorrow tonight. You will lose almost two days. I feel we should go to Saqqara first, then immediately go to the Great Pyramid." This, of course, was exactly what Thoth said we could *not* do; he was emphatic that we must move exactly as the original itinerary indicated.

But Ahmed was even more emphatic that we *not* use this itinerary. Ahmed would not take no for an answer, and he set up everything for us to go into the Great Pyramid early the next morning. On top of that, he did not want us to go into the tunnel beside the room called the Well. It took a great deal of convincing him that we absolutely had to enter the tunnel. This was the primary reason for coming to Egypt. He told us how dangerous it was, that many people had died in that part of the pyramid, and that if we insisted on this part of the itinerary, he would not go there with us.

I didn't know what to do. Thoth said that we *had* to move according to his itinerary, and now it looked like we were not going to. I knew that if we didn't, the initiation would not happen. I decided to go to the Great Pyramid in the morning as Ahmed wanted, fully realizing that if I did, it would be all over.

The next morning I was sitting in Ahmed's living room along with the others in the group. We all had our little daypacks set up with everything we thought we might need, like flashlights, candles, water and so on. Finally the hour came for us to leave and Ahmed opened the front door and said, "Let's go." My sister went out and behind her were the other three members. I just stood there for a moment, then threw on my daypack and started to move toward the door.

Then something happened truly out of the blue. I felt absolutely perfectly healthy and happy that morning, but a little worried about this itinerary thing. As I took a step toward the door where Ahmed was waiting, I suddenly felt a wave of energy come over me. It stopped me in my tracks. Then a second very strong and powerful wave of energy went through my body. I couldn't figure out what was happening to me. Then these waves of energy came faster and faster. The next thing I knew, I had fallen to the floor and was throwing up. Every system in my body seemed to be breaking down before my eyes. Within ten to fifteen seconds, I was so sick I could hardly respond to my circumstances.

It's strange. When a person gets sick this fast, the spirit inside the body doesn't have time to get sick. I remember lying on the floor trying to figure out what was happening to me. It was almost like watching a movie of myself getting sick.

They carried me into a bedroom, where my condition quickly degenerated into total paralysis. I could not move any part of my body. It was an amazing experience. I lay there for about three hours, and it seemed that whatever it was, it was getting worse. There was not much anyone could do. The next thing I remember is waking up the next morning.

For most of the day I could do nothing but lie there. Finally around three in the afternoon I began to feel a little stronger. I tried to do the Mer-Ka-Ba meditation to heal myself, but at that time I didn't know how to do it lying on my side. I tried for a while, but to no avail. Finally I called Katrina and Sananda into the room and asked them to prop me up into a sitting position. They helped me to get into the familiar position for doing the meditation.

As soon as I got the prana flowing through my body again, I began to feel stronger. After only about thirty minutes, I was walking around the room—a little dizzy, but walking. Ahmed came into the room and saw me standing. He asked me if I was better, and I said yes, but I was still sick. He then reached into his pocket and pulled out the original itinerary and looked at it. He said that if I could travel in an hour and a half, we could get on the French train to Luxor. Then he said, "This should make you happy. We can now do your original itinerary as you planned."

I have always wondered if I made myself sick so that we could return to the original itinerary or if Thoth did it. Either way, the "sickness" was not normal. At least I have never felt anything like it in my entire life. So now, finally, the true initiation could begin. As I rode on the train to Luxor, the thoughts and feelings of the sickness kept trying to return, but I kept my pranic breathing going, filling my body with life-force energy, and by the time we reached Luxor the next morning, I was back to my old self again, excited for what might come.

We checked into a hotel in Luxor before we began the initiation at the first temple, the Temple of Luxor, the temple dedicated to man. Ahmed handed me my room key. It was room 444, the number of initiation into spirit. I knew then that everything was back on track and moving perfectly. In fact, all movements in Egypt flowed perfectly from then on. We arrived at each temple in the exact order that Thoth wanted. I had my little piece of paper so that I could remember the Atlantean words, and each ceremony was also performed in the manner that he wanted. Life flowed like the river Nile.

Finally, on January 17 we arrived back at Ahmed's house, ready to complete the final initiation in the tunnel. This had not been planned, as I had little control over the events in Egypt, but we went into the Great Pyramid on January 18, my birthday. In fact, the second time I went to Egypt, in 1990, I was following Katrina's plans, and I ended up in the Great Pyramid on my birthday again. I feel sure there is a cosmic reason for everything that happens.

We arrived on the seventeenth, but we couldn't get into the Great Pyramid until Ahmed received written permission from the government, which didn't come until late that night. So early in the morning of the eighteenth we headed for the tunnel.

When we arrived at the steel gate leading to the Well, Ahmed and his people stopped the flow of tourists at two points so the tourists could not see that we were going into this off-limits area. Realize that there were 18,000 people a day going into this pyramid, so it was like stopping cattle heading for their feed. The guard who let us in then said, "You have one hour and a half, exactly. Set your watch with your alarm. If you are not here on the dot, we will come and get you, and we will not be happy. Do not be late." Then he let us through, and as soon as we were out of sight, he let the tourists continue.

So here we were standing at the top of a long, sloping tunnel at an angle of 23 degrees, the same tilt as the Earth's axis, that led about 400 feet downward into an underground room.

None of us knew what to do. How do you move down a tunnel only about a yard high and a yard wide that slopes at a steep angle? You can't walk, you can't crawl. We laughed and thought maybe we could roll down. We had to remove our daypacks because they hit the ceiling of the tunnel, so we finally decided that we had to walk like a duck, with our daypacks in our laps. It seemed to work. Everyone else went first, and I was last.

As I proceeded down the tunnel, my mind was blank. I seemed to not be thinking but only observing. Then something happened that awoke me. There is a vibration in the Great Pyramid that is very deep and intensely masculine. It never seems to end. I was very aware of this vibration from the moment I entered the pyramid and I was concentrating on it as I descended. Suddenly I noticed these two red squares [see Fig. 10-15] embedded in the walls of the tunnel, one on each side. They were about two inches square. As I passed them, the vibration seemed to drop about one full octave, and at the same moment a feeling of fear went through me.

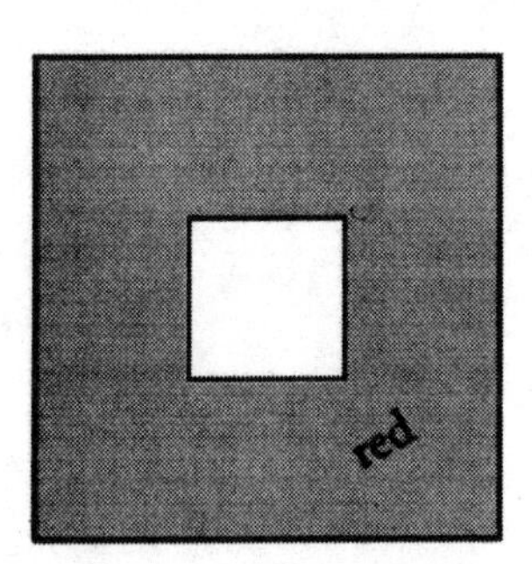

Fig. 10-15. The red square.

I was so involved with this vibration and this new feeling of fear (which is very unusual for me) that I forgot everything Thoth had taught me. He said that fear would be most important to overcome once I entered this space, but still I forgot everything. I was just reacting to my feelings.

As I proceeded deeper into the tunnel, I was simply feeling the fear, but then I came to another set of red squares. As I passed them, the vibration dropped another octave and the feeling of fear became even more intense. I started talking to myself. I asked, "What am I afraid of?" Then I heard a voice inside me say, "Well, you are afraid of poisonous snakes." I replied, "Yes, that is true, but there are no snakes in this tunnel." The inner voice said, "How can you be sure? There may be snakes in this tunnel."

As I arrived at the bottom, I was still having this internal dialogue and feeling this intense fear now over snakes. I mean, yes, I have a fear of snakes, but it isn't something that comes up very often in my life. Thoth seemed to be a million miles away. I forgot he existed. I forgot the electric-blue rings that could take the fear away. All that training for nothing.

We passed through the first room, which is seldom in any of the books on Egypt, into the main room where the tunnel we'd come to Egypt to visit branched off. There in the middle of the room was the "well" the room was named after. We looked into it, but it is filled with debris about 30 feet down. This room has no particular shape. It is totally female, with no straight lines. It looks more like a cave than a room. At last we were standing in front of the tiny tunnel that was the reason we came all this way.

An interesting side note: When I talked with Thoth about this area, he said that this room was not built by the Egyptians. It was so old that even he did not know who built it. He said that protecting this room was the primary reason why he placed the Great Pyramid in this exact location. He said it was the opening to the Halls of Amenti, the womb of the Earth and a fourth-dimensional space, one of the most important sites in the world.

Whenever I can, I check what Thoth says, which he encourages. Especially things that can easily be checked. So when I was with Ahmed on the French train going to Luxor, I had asked him about this room and who built it. He confirmed what Thoth had said, that it was not built by the Egyptians, and he didn't know who'd built it, either. Yet no book on Egypt that I am aware of speaks of this.

On with the story. This tunnel is very small. I'm not sure of the exact dimensions, but it is smaller than the one we came down in. The only way you can get inside this tunnel is by crawling on your belly. I believe it goes back into the Earth for about 80 to 100 feet, but people who are returning from there lately say that it goes back only about 25 feet. This cannot be, so the Egyptians have now probably sealed the tunnel. The floor was made of silica sand and was soft. The walls and the ceiling were covered with tiny quartz crystals and shone like diamonds. It was beautiful. When we pointed our flashlights inside, the light seemed to spiral, traveling just a few feet into the tunnel, then there was darkness. I have never seen anything like it.

One by one we each aimed our flashlights into the tunnel to assess the situation. After each person had done this, they all turned and looked at me and said, "You brought us here; you go first." I had no choice.

I tucked my daypack up against my chest and began to crawl, with my tiny flashlight pointing the way. Of course, I was still feeling the fear of snakes and was looking for them, hoping not to find them. After what seemed hours, I reached the end of the tunnel, with no sight of snakes. I breathed easier and relaxed. But then I noticed something—a small round hole near the right-hand side of the tunnel's end. It looked like a snake hole.

My fear jumped into high gear. I took my flashlight and pointed it into the hole to see if something was looking back. There wasn't. I didn't like it, but what could I do?

I shifted my attention to the immediate problem. It was then I realized that the Egyptian hieroglyphs that showed the way Osiris led initiates in this tunnel could not be performed in modern times because our bodies are bigger [see Fig. 10-16].

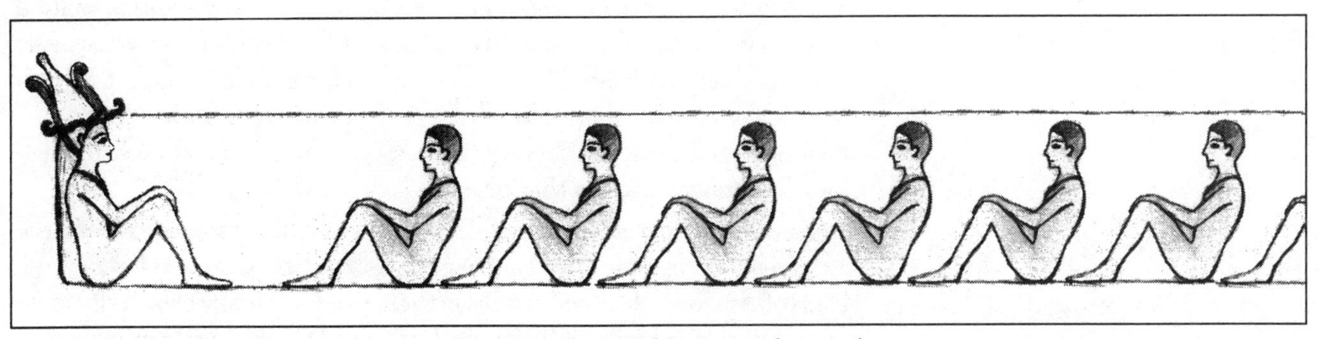

Fig. 10-16. Osiris and initiates in the tunnel.

According to the hieroglyphs, Osiris and his initiates sat. This was impossible for me, so I finally remembered Thoth again and asked him to come in. He told me to lie on my back with my head toward the end of the tunnel and for the rest of the group to do the same. I made this suggestion to the group, and they all complied.

As I lay there on my back, immediately several things happened. First I noticed overwhelmingly that this was the darkest place I had ever been. I held my hand up to my eyes, but it was so black that I couldn't even begin to see my hand. I do not believe that there was even one light photon in that space.

The next experience I had was the incredible sense of mass and gravity. I could feel the mountainous mass that was on top of me. It was like being buried alive. I had solid rock in every direction except out the tunnel, and that was clogged with human bodies. It was a very good thing that I am not claustrophobic. If I were, the fear of small, tight spaces would have ended the initiation for sure. Actually, for me this all felt great, no problem.

Thoth then came in very clearly and told me to begin my Mer-Ka-Ba meditation. I started to, but then the fear of snakes began to come back. I remembered that there was a tiny "snake" hole that was now just off to the left of my head behind me, but I couldn't see it. My imagination went wild. I could see snakes coming out of this hole and beginning to cover my body. It felt so real. I *knew* that if I continued with this fear, it *would* become real, and I would be covered with rattlesnakes. This knowing made it even worse. I knew this was how so many people had died in this tunnel. And *still* I forgot my training on fear that Thoth had taught me.

What I did was probably an American reaction. I grabbed my shirt like John Wayne and began to "talk sense" into myself. I said that I had come all the way to Egypt from America, and "so what if I died? Life would still go on." I told myself, "Get a hold of yourself. Forget the snakes and remember God" and "Even if my whole body is covered with snakes, I am going to continue."

Lucky for me, it worked, and I was able to shift my attention to completing the Mer-Ka-Ba meditation. The beautiful flying-saucer disk extended out to about 55 feet around my body, and a sense of well-being came over me. I completely forgot about the snakes. Although it did not occur to me at the time, not until I arrived home in America, it was interesting that I'd been unable to do the meditation lying down when I was sick a few days earlier, yet it happened naturally in this tunnel. I have thought about this; perhaps it was because there was almost no sense of up or down. It was like floating in outer space. Whatever the reason, thank God I was able to meditate lying on my back in that tunnel.

Thoth was now always in my field of view. He first requested of me the Atlantean words that would allow permission from the seven lords of the Halls of Amenti. He asked that I say these words with power, so I did as he said. There was a space after that. I can't really explain it, but it seemed like years went by. Thoth then asked me if I knew that when I had been in the Mer-Ka-Ba I'd been sending light out in all directions like the Sun. I told him, "Yes, I know that." He asked me again, "Do you *really* know?" I told him again that yes, I knew that. He then spoke a third time, saying, "If you really know, then open your eyes and see." I opened my eyes, and I could see in the tunnel. Everything was lit up with a soft glow, much like moonlight. It did not seem to come from a source. It was almost like the air was glowing.

Then my mind engaged, and I thought it was someone in the group with a light on. I leaned up on my elbows and looked down the tunnel at the other four initiates, but they were lying still with no flashlights turned on. I could see them clearly. I lay back and looked around; it was amazing. I could see perfectly every detail around me. I thought to myself that it was bright enough to read, then I closed my eyes again. Every so often I would open my eyes again, and the light was still there.

At one point when my eyes were closed, I asked Thoth what was next. He looked at me and said, "Isn't lighting up a tunnel enough?" What could I say? So for about one hour I lit up the tunnel and watched this incredible phenomenon. I remember that when my alarm went off to tell us to return to the top, I had my eyes closed. I opened my eyes, expecting the tunnel to be lit, but it was pitch black. That surprised me. The initiation was over.

We went to the top and the guards were there with the gate open. My sister went outside the pyramid, since she had been there so many times, but the rest of us became tourists and went into the King's Chamber and other rooms. We exchanged stories later, and it was clear that each person had a different experience—depending on what they needed, we assumed. My sister's story was extremely interesting to me. She talked about how she stood up in this little tunnel and was greeted by these very tall beings who took her into a special room for her initiation. Life is more than we know.

When I exited the pyramid, I could hardly believe my eyes. From the height of the doorway's location up the pyramid, I could see an enormous crowd that I estimated to be about 60 to 70 thousand people. As I looked closer, I realized that they were almost all children. Upon even closer examination, the children were from about five to twelve years old. There were very few adults. I don't know why they were there, but there they were.

As I looked down at the bottom step of the pyramid, I noticed that the children were holding hands in a line as far as I could see along one edge. I walked to the step just above them, around one of the adjacent sides, and the children were holding hands there, too. My curiosity was so great, I ended up walking around the entire Great Pyramid to see if it was true, and it was! The children were holding hands in a complete circle around the Great Pyramid. I even went to the second and the third pyramids to see if it was true there too, and it was. The children had circled all three pyramids while we were inside. I asked myself, What does this mean?

When I got back to my room at Ahmed's house, I went into meditation and brought the angels in. I asked them the question, "What do all those children mean?" They asked me if I remembered what they had said twelve years before. I didn't know what they were talking about, so I asked them to explain. They said that twelve years before, I had been asked to be the father of a child that they said had come from the Central Sun. They said that he would be the apex of a pyramid of millions of children who would come to Earth to help us during our transition into the next dimension. The angels said that these children would be almost like ordinary children until twelve years passed, then a quickening would begin and they would slowly emerge upon the face of the Earth as a force that could not be stopped. They said that these children were connected together by spirit, and at the right moment in history they would lead the way into the new world.

After the meditation, I calculated the years between my son Zachary's birth and that day. Zachary was born on January 10, 1972, and the day of this initiation was January 18, 1985. It had been thirteen years and one week. I had forgotten, but the children had not.

In the final chapter you will learn what science now knows about these children. You will see the great hope that is emerging on Earth from these beautiful beings from space, our children.

Remember, children are the Middle Eye of Horus; they are life itself.

The Hathors

The Hathors were the main or primary mentors within the Left Eye of Horus Mystery School. Though they were not from Earth, in the ancient days they were always here to assist us in unfolding our consciousness. They loved us dearly, and they still do. As our consciousness became more and more third-dimensional, we eventually could no longer see them or respond to their teachings. Only now, as we grow, are we beginning to see and communicate with them again.

Figure 10-17 is the likeness of a member of the Hathor race, a race of fourth-dimensional beings who come from Venus. You don't see them on the third-dimensional world of Venus, but if you tune to Venus on the fourth dimension, especially on the higher overtones, you'll find a vast culture there. They are the most intelligent consciousness in this solar system, and they function as the headquarters or central office for all life under our Sun. If you come into our solar system from the outside, you must check with Venus before proceeding.

The Hathors are beings of tremendous love. Their love is on a level of Christ consciousness. They use vocal sounds as their means of communicating and performing feats within their environment. They have amazing ears. They have almost no darkness to them at all; they're just light—pure, loving beings.

Hathors are very much like dolphins. Dolphins use sonar to do almost everything, and Hathors use their voices to do almost everything. We create machines to light or heat our houses, but the Hathors simply use sound through their voices.

There aren't many of these Hathor-face statues left because the Romans thought they were some sort of evil spirits and perpetrated great destruction upon their images. This carving is found in Memphis, and it's at the top of a 40-foot pillar, though the present ground level is just above the top of the pillar [what you see here is excavated]. They had recently discovered this temple when I was there in 1985.

Fig. 10-17. A Hathor.

The Hathors are about 10 to 16 feet tall, the same height as the Nefilim, mentioned in chapter 3. For a very, very long time they have helped people on Earth, almost always through their love and their incredible knowledge of sound. There's an initiation in Egypt where the sound of the ankh is created—this is one of the initiations in the Great Pyramid. It's a continuous sound that a Hathor makes, without stopping, for somewhere between half an hour to an hour. It is used primarily for healing the body or restoring balance in nature. It's like when we sound *Om* and have to breathe at the same time. The Hathors learned how to make a sound without stopping, breathing in through their nose, into their lungs and back out through their mouth continuously. Conducting this sound-of-the-ankh initiation ceremony was only one of the many things they would do for us to create balance. The Hathors were here on Earth helping mankind for thousands of years.

Breathing in and out at the same time and making a continuous sound without stopping is not unheard-of today. An Aborigine playing the didgeridoo uses circular breathing. He can make one tone nonstop for an hour by controlling the air flow into and out of his body. It's not that hard to learn, actually.

Fig. 10-18. Dendera and Katrina.

Dendera

Figure 10-18 shows you Dendera, and this temple was dedicated to the Hathors, the great mentors of the human race. There used to be Hathor faces on all those columns, but someone in the past tried to destroy them. There are huge pillars inside this temple that extend to the back of the temple. This temple is enormous; you can't *believe* the size of this place! It stretches back a quarter mile or so. (That's Katrina Raphaell in the foreground, by the way.)

Dendera has two primary places I would like to mention. Inside this temple you will find the astrological chart that I've referred to a couple of times. Here also you will find a room that I have seldom talked about because I have not personally seen it. If you enter the temple and turn right, beneath the front panel in the floor is a small room, as I understand it. In this room is something that is impossible by all of today's standards. There is a carving of the Earth from space, perfectly proportioned, with an extension cord coming out of the Earth that has a modern electrical plug on the end of it. Next to the plug is a wall outlet exactly like we have today. It is unplugged. How can this be? How could the Egyptians know that in the future the Earth would be electrified?

Let me tell you a story and show you the photo I promised in an earlier chapter. When I was in Abydos at the Seti the First Temple [Fig. 10-19a; see chapter 2] one of the guards who was working with me told me to wait until all the people were out of this area of the temple. He then told me to aim my camera and take a picture of a particular place on one of the ceiling beams. It was dark and I could not really see what I was photographing. It was not until I returned home and developed the picture that I could see what it was.

Fig. 10-19a. Seti the First Temple at Abydos.

This photo was also impossible by all known ideas of what the past, present and future means [see Fig. 10-19b]. As we talked about the "carved bands of time" on page 32, anything about 15 feet from the floor level were about the future. This photo shows a section about 40 feet from the floor level up against the ceiling.

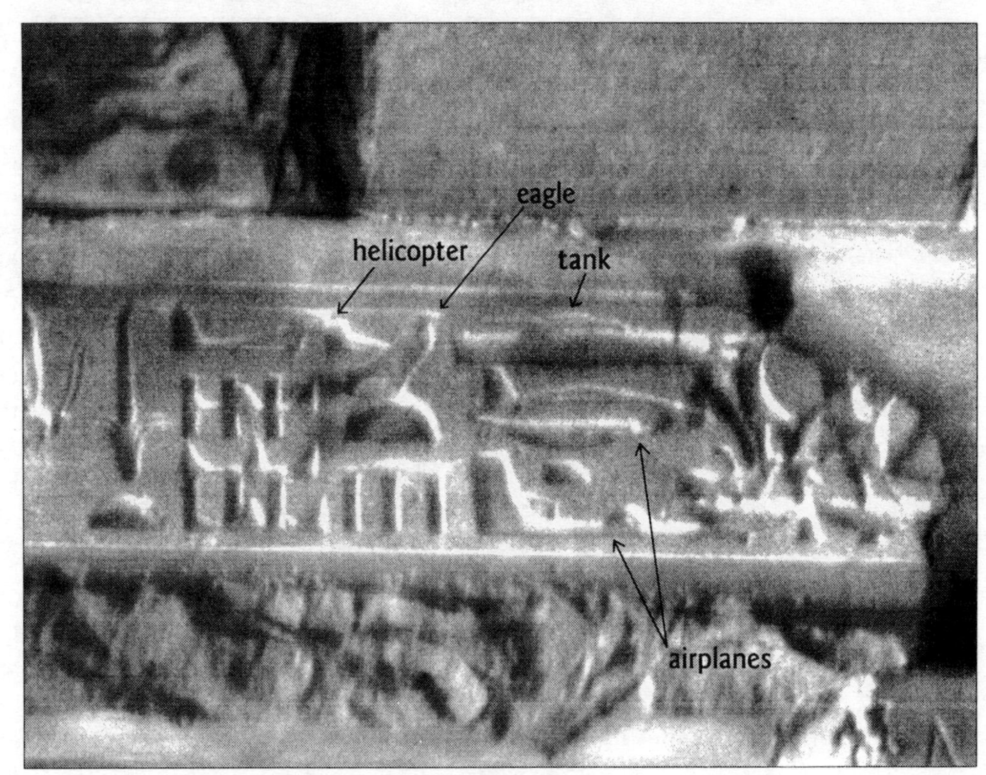

Fig. 10-19b. The carvings in Seti the First Temple at Abydos.

What is it? It is a picture of an attack helicopter with what looks like stacked oil barrels below and a half sphere with an eagle standing on top facing an armored tank. There appear to be two other kinds of airplanes facing the same direction. Facing this "enemy" is an armored tank. When I first showed this photo in 1986 it didn't make sense. But in 1991 there was a retired military officer in my workshop who identified the helicopter as a very specific U.S. military helicopter and said that the entire series of hieroglyphics fits the parameters of the Desert Storm war. This was the only war where this helicopter and tanks were present at the same time.

It is hard to say that the Egyptians could *not* see the future when they made these hieroglyphics thousands of years before the helicopter was even invented. Many people and Web sites around the world have been looking at this photo ever since I took it, and there is still no explanation.

This photo [Fig. 10-20] shows the top of a doorway to a small room up high in the back of the Temple of Dendera. In the center of the upper lintel stone is the symbol for Marduk, the planet of the giant Nefilim. Beneath that is a circle with the Left Eye of Horus inside, which is difficult to see here. And to its left is the hieroglyph for Thoth, who is pointing to the circle [see detail in Fig. 10-20a].

Beyond this portal and on the walls of the room is a beautiful rendition of the story of Isis and Osiris, which I retold in chapter 5, volume 1. I regret that the officials would not let me take photographs to show you. The story depicted on the wall is the basis of the Egyptian religion. In an extremely simplified form, it is told in this way.

Fig. 10-20. The lintel of the doorway to a room inside the Temple of Dendera. Top center is the symbol for the planet Marduk. Below it is the Left Eye of Horus in a circle, and to its left is the hieroglyph for Thoth. The room itself contains the story of Isis and Osiris in hieroglyphs.

An Immaculate Conception

Osiris and Set, and Isis and Nephthys, were brothers and sisters. Osiris married Isis and Set married Nephthys. At one point Set killed Osiris, put his body in a wooden casket and floated him down the Nile (really a river in Atlantis). Isis and Nephthys began to search the world to find Osiris' body. When they found it, they brought it back, but Set found out and cut Osiris' body into fourteen pieces. He sent the pieces all over the world to make sure Osiris would never return. Isis and Nephthys then searched for the pieces and found thirteen of them. The fourteenth was Osiris' phallus.

The story on the wall shows that the thirteen pieces were found and put together without the missing phallus. Then Thoth does some magic, the phallus comes alive and the creative energy flows through Osiris' body. It shows that Isis then turns into a hawk, flies through the air and comes down and wraps her wings around her husband's penis. Then she flies away, becoming pregnant. She has a hawk-headed baby, Horus, only he's not really hawk-headed—that's just the hieroglyph for his name. Horus then avenges his father's death and the pain that Set put Osiris through.

Thoth says that what they're depicting here is an immaculate conception, or virgin birth. Since the woman doesn't have to be a virgin, he called it immaculate conception. Thoth described the birth as an interdimensional one. Isis flew to Osiris interdimensionally; it was not a *physical* mating that took place.

Fig. 10-20a. Detail of circle at lower part of Fig. 10-21.

The World's Virgin Births

What I'm about to present to you is information I was told to tell you. I didn't know what to think about it myself for a long time, and you'll have to draw your own conclusions. I'm telling you what I now know to be true, but when they first told me this, I thought it was pure myth. Most people think it's pure myth, that the story about Mary and Joseph and the virgin birth could happen only to Jesus and couldn't possibly happen to the average person. But I've learned that there's hard evidence that immaculate conception is absolutely true and is a part of everyday life.

Many of the religious leaders and founders of the world's religions, like Krishna, for example, or Jesus, are said to have been born of a virgin birth—of a mother and father who did not physically mate. As I said, we think of that as something that couldn't possibly be true in everyday life. On levels of life on Earth other than human, virgin births occur every minute of the day all around us, all over the world, all the time. Insects, plants, trees, almost every level of life, use immaculate conception as one means of reproduction. I'll give you an example.

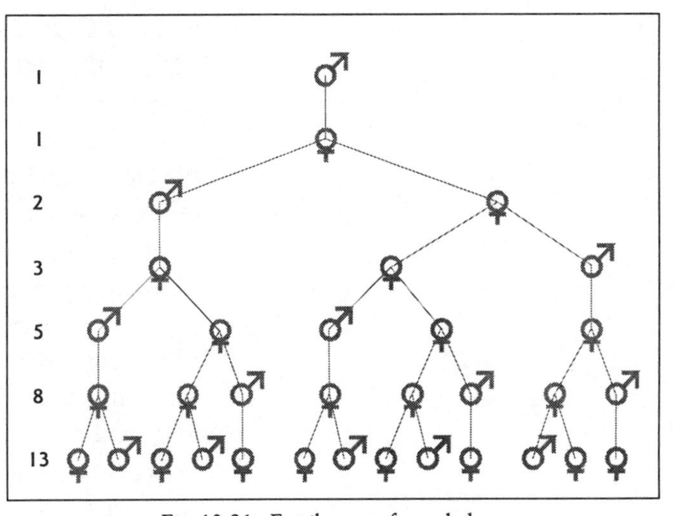

Fig. 10-21. Family tree of a male bee.

Figure 10-21 is the family tree of a male bee. A female bee can birth a male bee anytime she wants. She doesn't have to ask permission from the male and doesn't need a male to create a new male. She can just do it. If she wants to make a female bee, however, she must mate with a male. In this family tree, the male needs only a mother, but the female needs both father and mother. Any bee father needs only a mother, and the generations follow in this particular way. The column of numbers at the left of the figure show the number of members at each level of this family tree. When you look at these numbers, you'll see the sequence 1, 1, 2, 3, 5, 8 and 13—the Fibonacci sequence—unfolding here.

This indicates that immaculate conception—or at least this one—is based on a Fibonacci sequence. But if people mate in the normal way, what sequence is that? First there's the baby, then the two parents, the four grandparents, the eight great grandparents—1, 2, 4, 8, 16, 32, the binary sequence. These two birth processes emulate the two primary sequences of life; the Fibonacci sequence is female and the binary sequence is male. So according to this theory, immaculate conception is female and physical copulation is male.

Parthenogenesis

Figure 10-22 is a photo of a gecko, a little lizardlike being [the clipping, from the Tacoma, Washington, *Morning News Tribune* on January 15, 1993, comments on an article in the then-current issue of *Science*]. These geckos live in the Pacific islands, and this particular one is called the mourning gecko. They are about three inches long and are *only* female. There are no male mourning geckos—ever—on the planet, only female ones. The entire culture of mourning geckos are exclusively female, yet they keep having babies without any males around. The article says that they're all female, and they reproduce asexually by laying and hatching eggs without male help. How do they do that?

A12 The Morning News Tribune, Friday, Jan. 15, 1993

Associated Press

Gecko lizards were part of a competitiveness study.

Lizards with big appetites force smaller cousins to move outside

The Associated Press

LOS ANGELES — Scientists staged wars between lizards inside old hangars in Hawaii to learn why sexually reproducing geckos have pushed their asexual rivals out of urban homes throughout the South Pacific.

The answer: Sexual lizards are bigger and hog the dinner table.

Without overt aggressive action, the bigger wall-climbing, insect-eating lizards simply scare the smaller reptiles away from houses where tasty insects congregate around light bulbs, ecologists said in today's issue of the journal Science.

"Ecologists like me would like to be able to predict which ecosystems are more susceptible to invaders from outside, which are more resistant and why," said Ted Case, a co-author of the study and biology chairman at the University of California, San Diego.

The new study "is one of the best examples so far of the way and the rate at which an invader can displace a resident competitor," Case said Thursday during a phone interview from San Diego.

For thousands of years, people in the Pacific islands have shared their homes with mourning geckos, which enter houses through small openings and are virtually impossible to keep out. Mourning geckos are about 3 inches long. All are female. They reproduce asexually by laying and hatching eggs without male help.

Since World War II, 3.5- to 4-inch-long house geckos — a different species native to the Philippines and Indonesia — have displaced mourning geckos in urban homes as they hitchhiked on planes and boats to Fiji, Samoa, Tahiti and Hawaii.

House geckos come in male and female varieties. They reproduce sexually through copulation. They have pushed the mourning geckos into rural communities and forests far from bright city lights.

Fig. 10-22. Gecko in the news; an exclusively female species. Perhaps some readers can do more research on this subject.

Peter C. Hoppe and Karl Illmenser announced in 1977 the successful birth at the Jackson Laboratory in Bar Harbor, Maine, of seven "single-parent mice." The process was called parthenogenesis or virgin birth. However, "immaculate conception" would be a more accurate term, since the female does not have to be a virgin. In other words, they were able to take mice and, without a male, induce conception. How did they do that?

I had the good fortune to have a doctor in one of my workshops who had researched parthenogenesis and who had accomplished it in *human beings*. I was able to sit down and talk with him about it. According to this doctor, all a scientist needs to do is simply break the zona pellucida with a little pin. As soon as that happens, mitosis begins and soon a baby is born. It seems that breaking the surface is all that's necessary!

As I stated on page 189, the male does not necessarily contribute 50 percent of the chromosomes in a conception, which was always thought to be true. The female can contribute anywhere from 50 to 100 percent. Science has definitely established this as a fact. They've also found out something new about genes. Scientists had always thought that the function of each gene was fixed, that a certain gene did a certain thing. But now they've found that *that's* not true, either. A specific gene will do something totally different, depending on whether it comes from the mother or father. This has thrown another curve ball into the understanding of biology.

Since 1977, researchers have tried breaking the surface of the egg of all kinds of living forms. When they did it with female human beings, the woman would give birth to female babies—at least they've always been female so far—without male sperm. So it's now been established absolutely that this can happen.

Two other things: (1) These female children born through parthenogenesis are absolutely identical to their mothers and (2) in all cases the female children have been sterile. It seems to me that there's a lot more going on around this subject than we probably ever thought. This is true of many subjects we *thought* we knew so much about.

Conception on a Different Dimension

After thinking about this idea of virgin birth for a long time, I came up with this question: When scientists induced parthenogenesis, is it possible that they might have created a baby that is based on a different principle? Is it possible that the female child isn't really sterile, but that she is no longer in a binary sequence, but the Fibonacci sequence? And is it possible that she can conceive *only* interdimensionally? They haven't thought about that because they've been watching to see if she can conceive *physically*. Interdimensionally means you don't even have to be on the same side of the planet—or even on the same planet, for that matter. You connect on another level of existence. This way of conceiving still has the sexual energy and the orgasm, but it does not require physically being together.

Here's another thing: When conception is created synthetically through parthenogenesis, when a sharp object is used to break the surface, it always ends up being a girl. I believe now that when mating is done interdimensionally, it will be a boy every time. Of course, just because Mary and Joseph had Jesus, a boy, and Krishna was a boy and so on is not enough proof to say it will always be a boy, but it looks like it. There has never been an exception that I am aware of.

Thoth's Genesis and Family Tree

My attention to immaculate conception began a long time ago. I was doing geometry one day and Thoth was watching me. I was trying to figure out something he was trying to explain to me. Of course, the last thing in the world I was thinking about was immaculate conception, especially parthenogenesis. He asked me if I would I like to hear the story about his mother. I said, "Yeah, sure"—you know, while I was figuring out the geometry, not really too interested in his story. Then he told me a very unusual story. I didn't know what to think about it. He simply told me the story and left. After he left I wondered, What was *that* about?

He said his mother's name is Sekutet. I had the opportunity to meet her once, only once. She's an exceptionally beautiful woman, and she's about 200,000 years old, in the same body. Thoth said that after the time of Adam and Eve, when humans were learning to mate physically and go through the binary sequence, his mother did it in a different way. She found a man and fell in love with him, but they learned to mate interdimensionally. They had a baby boy—not a girl, but a boy. And in the process of having this baby, very much like Ay and Tiya [see chapters 3, 4 and 5], they understood immortality and became immortal.

This happened a long, long time ago, near the beginning of our race. Thoth's mother and her husband were part of the newly created race that was developed to mine gold. I don't know if they came from the Adam and Eve lineage or from the part of the human lineage that was supposedly sterile. At any rate, they figured out how to mate interdimensionally almost at the very beginning of our evolution. They might actually have been the very first ones to use this way to give birth.

An Earth Lineage Travels into Space

When their baby grew up and became a man, his father, Sekutet's first husband, left Earth and went to the fourth-dimensional level of Venus, merged with their evolution and became a Hathor. This is referred to in Egyptian stories and myths. Over and over again their stories tell about how they would die and ascend to the level of Venusian consciousness.

After the father had left for Venus, Sekutet mated with her son interdimensionally and became pregnant again. She had a second baby boy, and when he grew up, her first son (the second son's father) went to join *his* father on Venus. After the first son arrived on Venus, his father went to Sirius. Later, when the second baby was grown, Sekutet mated with *him* interdimensionally and had still a third son. When her third son was mature, the second son (the third son's father) joined *his* brother/father (the first son) on Venus. After the second son got settled on Venus, the first son left for Sirius. And after the first son got settled in Sirius, then his father (the *original* father) went on to the Pleiades. But the Pleiades was just the beginning.

This began a living lineage that traveled deeper and deeper into space, each son following his father out farther and farther. It's an interesting story. Thoth said that this has continued all the way from shortly after the Adam and Eve period in history up to the time of Atlantis.

Thoth's father, Thome, was one of the three who acted as the corpus callosum connecting the two sides of the island of Udal in Atlantis [see page 96]. At one point Thome left Atlantis—he simply disappeared off the Earth and went to Venus, leaving Sekutet and Thoth here on Earth.

But then Thoth broke the lineage. He married a woman, Shesat, and according to Egyptian legend, they had a baby, whose name was Tat [see page 123ff]. But Thoth said, "That's not true. It's more complex than that." He said that before he met Shesat, he mated with his mother interdimensionally, and that's who conceived Tat—his mother. He and Shesat did have a baby, which was *not* in the records; it was conceived in Peru and was a baby girl. She was physically conceived. So he says that he has the Fibonacci sequence, in his children with his mother, and also the binary sequence, simultaneously. According to Thoth, that's never happened before.

After telling me about his mother, he said, "That's that," and left. I wondered what that was all about. It was weird. Why did he tell me that? Later on he came back and said, "You really need to know more about virgin birth," and he told me to study it. So I started reading everything I could find on the subject. The more I read, the more amazing it became.

If you want to take the subject further, go ahead. You may find that having a baby can be a doorway into immortality. If you really do love someone and that person really loves you—if the love between you is true love—then you may have another option available, in terms of ascension through sacred marriage and interdimensional conception. Through your union you re-create the living holy trinity on Earth.

The experience that Ay and Tiya had with sacred marriage and birth on Lemuria now becomes clear. Perhaps there really is more to life than we know.

In the preceding pages we have explored parts of the feminine pathway, the Left Eye of Horus Mystery School. Realize that your emotions and feelings need to be balanced and that you simply must overcome your fears before you can truly work with the lightbody's energy field, the Mer-Ka-Ba.

The Flower of Life Seen from the Feminine Side

We will now examine one more aspect of Egyptian philosophy from a purely feminine point of view, from the way the Left Eye of Horus Mystery School would see it. What follows can also be seen as proof that the Egyptians knew about the Flower of Life and *lived* it.

Fig. 10-23. The Flower of Life.

We're going to unfold the Flower of Life in a completely different way than we did before. We're going to look at it in a right-brain feminine way rather than a left-brain masculine way as we did earlier. It will not have a male logic as it did before, but a female logic.

Fig. 10-24. Genesis pattern within a circle (turned 30 degrees).

We will begin, as we did earlier, with the Flower of Life [Fig. 10-23]. There's a certain image inside the Flower of Life that we will bring out. If you remove the Genesis pattern and put a circle around it, you get this image [Fig. 10-24].

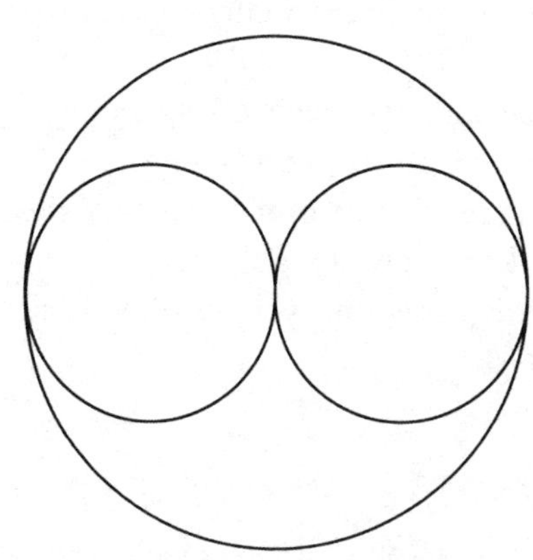

Fig. 10-25. Two circles circumscribed by a large circle.

Then after you take out the four circles on the top and bottom of the large circle, you get this image [Fig. 10-25]. As you can see, this image is derived from the Flower of Life.

Now, once we have this new image, we're going to use it over and over. We'll take the image of the two circles and make half-size circles inside the medium-size circles [Fig. 10-26]. We keep making half-size circles in each of the smallest circles, until we have Figure 10-27.

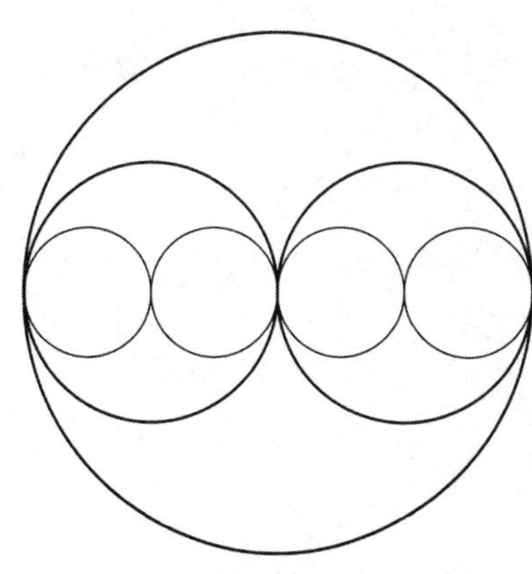

Fig. 10-26. Doubling the circles.

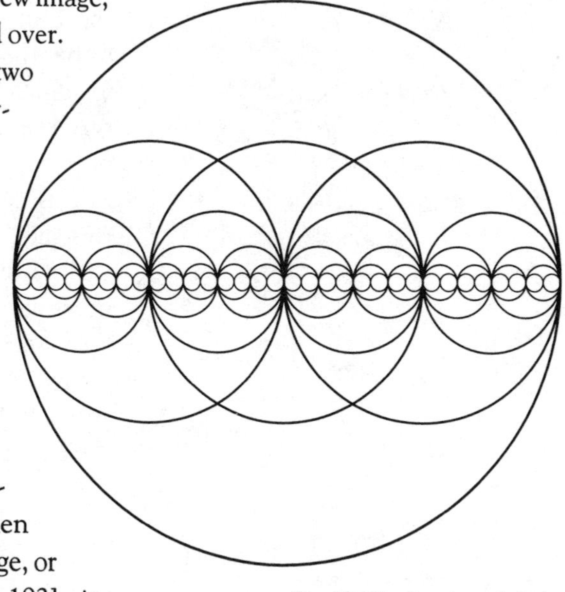

Fig. 10-27. A string of circles.

Remember the zona pellucida and the egg? Remember how the egg first went within itself to understand how life works, then when it got to the morula stage, or the apple shape [see page 192], it

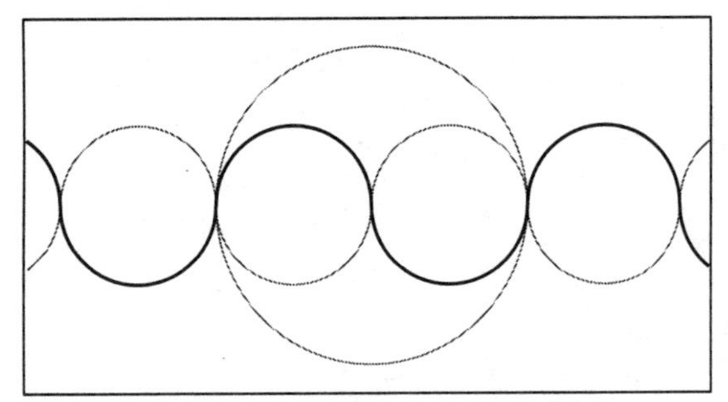

Fig. 10-28. Sine wave going beyond itself.

went out beyond itself? I would like to show you this same idea geometrically. This pattern you see in Figure 10-27 is in a binary sequence; you have 2 circles, then 4, 8, 16, 32 and so on. When the egg first went within, it did so geometrically. So geometrically, you can go *into* a pattern to discover how it can go *beyond* the pattern. You can go within a pattern to see how the sine wave works in order to go beyond the original pattern [Fig. 10-28]. The dark line here shows the sine wave of the pattern in Figure 10-25 continuing beyond the original pattern. Once this is understood, life can go beyond itself. Life simply needs to know how something works geometrically in order to use it in larger patterns. As above, so below. So with this understanding, we will look at the Flower of Life again, but in a different way.

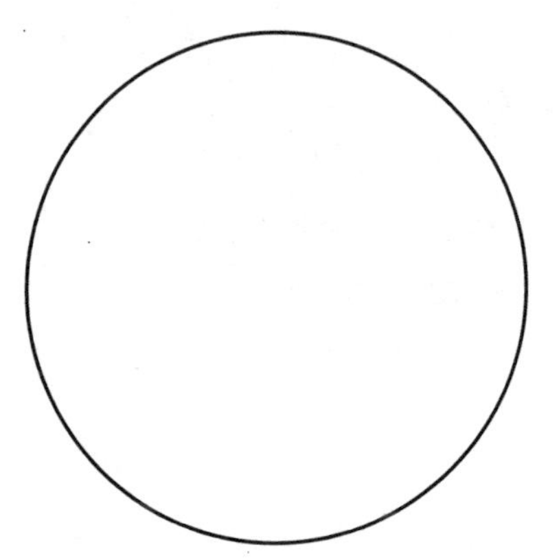

Fig. 10-29. A circle, the basic pattern.

The basic principle of the Flower of Life is a circle, or a sphere [Fig. 10-29]. And in every circle, no matter what its size, seven smaller circles can fit exactly inside it in this pattern [Fig. 10-30]. This is an eternal truth.

You see this in the Flower of Life, where there are seven primary circles hidden inside the larger circle. This relationship of 7 in 1 is also the basis of the Fruit of Life pattern. In the Flower of Life the Fruit is hidden in such a way that when you finish all the unfinished circles around the outside edge, one more vortex rotation *beyond* that leads to the Fruit of Life—*outside* the pattern [see Fig. 6-12].

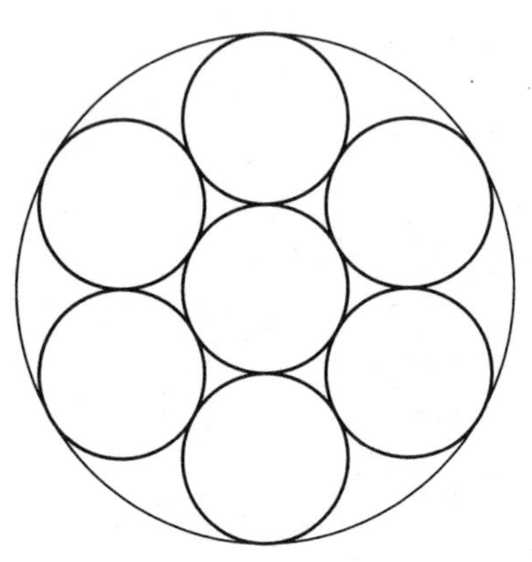

Fig. 10-30. Seven circles in one.

But there is a way the Fruit of Life can be obtained *within* the system. All you do is use the *radius* of the middle circle (or any of the seven) as the *diameter* of your new circles, starting the first new circle in the center of the original seven-circle pattern. Then you line them up, and when you've drawn twelve circles beyond and around the center one, you have the Fruit of Life *inside* the pattern [see Fig. 10-31].

You can see that you come directly to the Fruit of Life by going *within* rather than without as we did in earlier chapters. You can see the incredible harmony that moves in this geometry. Is this not the same with music? Seven notes are in the octave, and *within* the octave are the five additional notes of the chromatic scale.

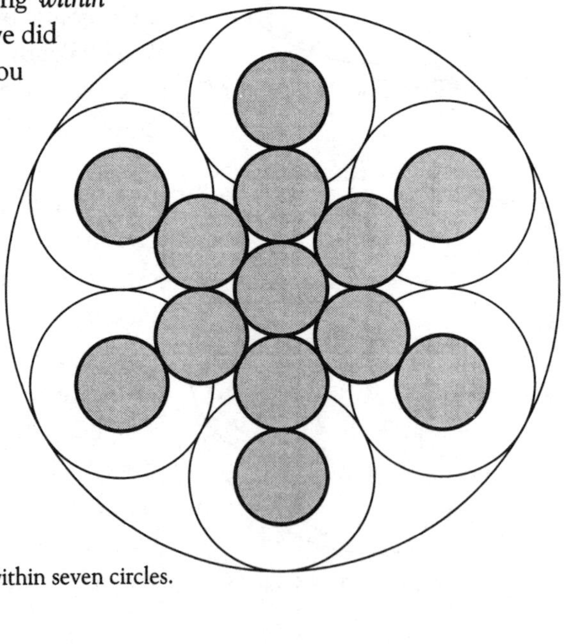

Fig. 10-31. Thirteen circles within seven circles.

I was next instructed to continue that process, so in Figure 10-32, I used the radius of the smaller circles as the diameter of an even smaller series of circles and expanded them out over the page.

You begin to see something that isn't certain yet, but it looks like the Fruit of Life is holographic. In other words, you see 13 circles connected to 13 circles connected to 13 circles connected to 13 circles and so on—little Fruits of Life all around, perfectly and harmonically arranged on the page.

Once again, if we draw a series of even smaller circles using the radius-to-diameter proportion, we get the grid of circles in Figure 10-33.

I deliberately did not extend the grid over the whole pattern so that you don't get lost in the image. You can see again that it keeps repeating, 13 circles connected to 13 circles and on and on. If you keep doing this, the grid will continue forever, yet inside, perfectly harmonic within each pattern and fully holographic, in what is called a geometric progression. You can go *inward* forever and you can go *outward* forever, because a circle around the whole drawing would simply be the central circle of a still larger grid.

This geometric progression is similar to the Golden Mean ratio—it has no beginning and no end. And when you have these no-beginning-and-no-end situations, you're looking at something very primal. It was this understanding that enabled us to do certain things in science, such as theorizing the creation of an infinite storage bank for a computer that would be considered impossible by conventional mathematical thinking.

Fig. 10-32. Going one more radius within, or reproducing at half size.

Fig. 10-33. Going inward one more radius.

Fig. 10-34a. Egyptian wheels on ceiling.

Now that we understand how this new grid works, let's see what those wheels represent that were found on the ceilings of Egyptian tombs that we showed you in chapter 2 [pages 42 and 43]. Here are two of those photos [Figs. 10-34a and b] and a simplified schematic [10-34c]. No one knows what they are. Perhaps what follows will give one answer. [See descriptive text later, on page 293.]

First, observe in Figure 10-35 the beautiful geometric harmony of this circular grid from Figure 10-32 over the Flower of Life. See how this flows with perfection. See how this proves its source—the Flower of Life!

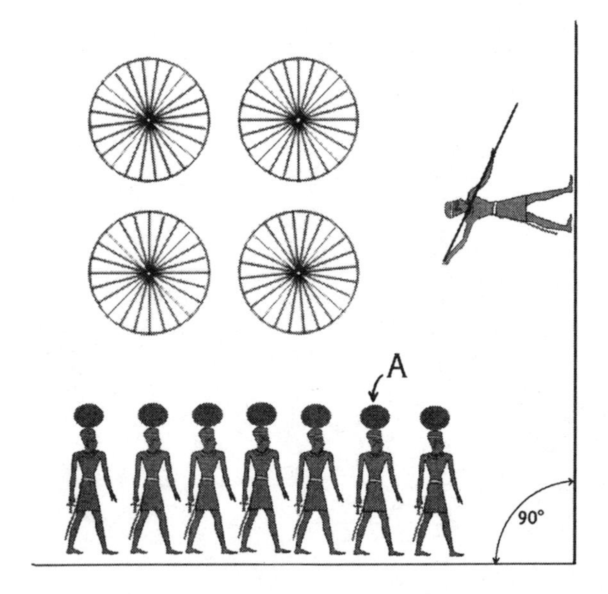

Fig. 10-34c. Simplified schematic of the wheels on the ceiling.

Fig. 10-34b. Detail of wheels on a different ceiling.

Now see how the star within the star of the Fruit of Life moves harmonically over this grid [Fig. 10-36]. In Figure 10-36b I have rotated the star within the star and the entire grid 30 degrees. You can still see the star tetrahedron inscribed in the sphere, but now you see it lying on its side. Figure 10-37 is a polar grid from chapter 8. See or sense how these two inner Fruit of Life patterns could be overlaid and that they would be harmonic.

As a side note, these two drawings, if superimposed, would be a partial top view of your personal energy field, which is about 55 feet across, about 27 feet from your center to the circumference. You contain all these geometries around you. When you look carefully at these various drawings, you'll see that they can all be overlaid, superimposed one over the other, over the other, over the other. As you study these drawings, you begin to see a single image emerging, all from the Flower of Life.

We have already seen how the image in Figure 10-38 is linked to the harmonies of music [see page 222]. And we have seen how the harmonies of music and the dimensional levels are interrelated, and that the differences in the cycles per second between musical notes and the wavelengths of successive dimensions or universes are proportionally exactly the same [see pages 45-47]. Since you know that this drawing is linked with

Fig. 10-35. The Flower of Life and the new grid.

Fig. 10-36. The star within the star of the Fruit of Life.

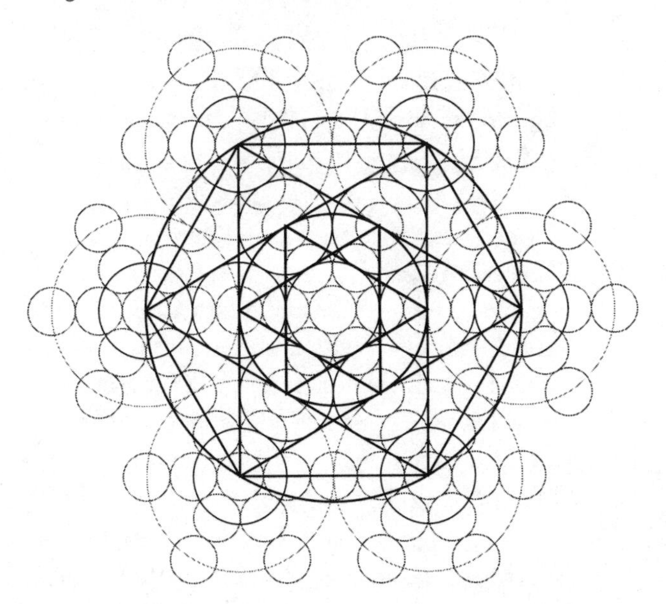

Fig. 10-36b. The star within the star of the Fruit of Life rotated 90 degrees.

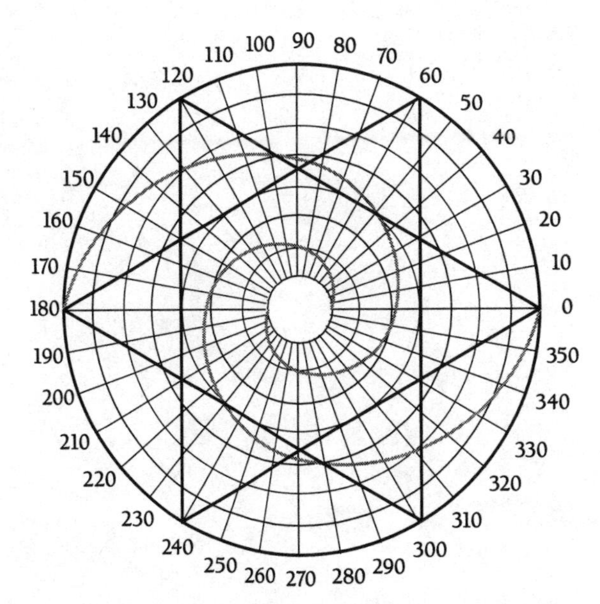

Fig. 10-37. The star tetrahedron inscribed in a circle and over a polar grid, from chapter 8, page 223.

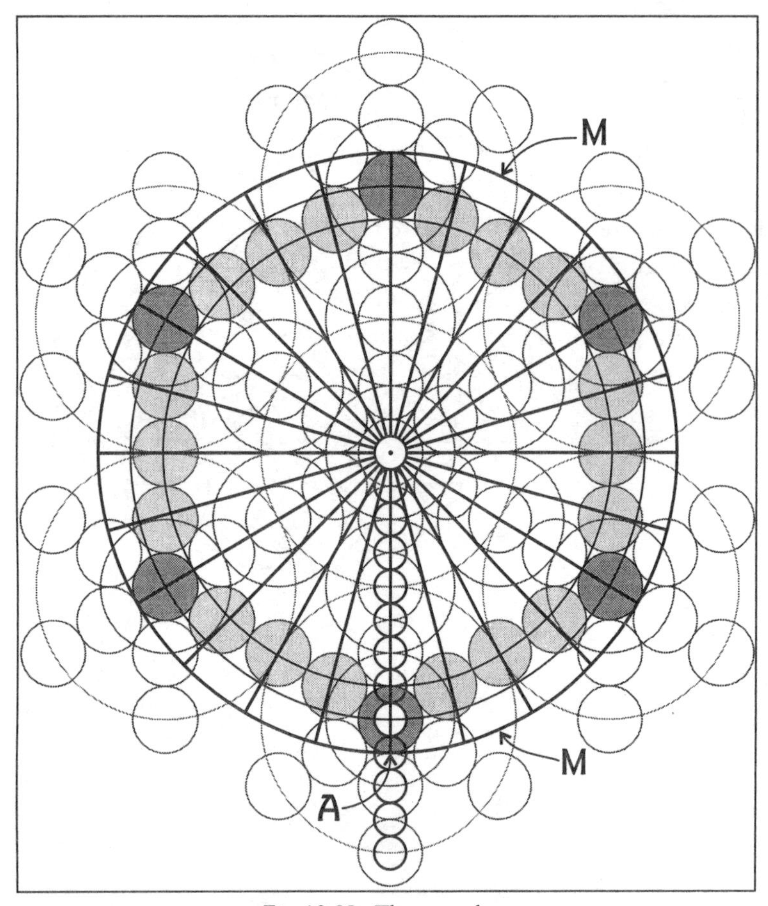

Fig. 10-38. The secret key.

the harmonies of music and sound, you can study this figure [10-38] to gain more understanding about the wheels on the ceilings of tombs in Egypt.

Notice first that there is a series of shaded circles in this grid that go around the center in a hexagonal pattern and that they are connected to each other. Exactly 24 of these little spheres are touching each other. If you scaled downward one more level to the next smaller-size circle, like the little one in the middle of the drawing, you would discover that there are exactly nine diameters of these smaller circles between the center and the edge of the outer circle at M, which contains the 24 connecting circles. The outermost of these nine circles is indicated by arrow A, and the count of nine includes the *radius* of both the central circle and the outer circle as one diameter. You can see these nine diameters; you don't need to measure them. Now notice the dark outer circle, shown by arrows M, that fits around all those 24 spheres perfectly, and the 24 radial lines that cross only 12 of the centers of those circles. The other 12 radial lines are at the circumference of the next larger size circles.

Wheels on the Ceiling

That circle M and the 24 radial lines produce an image that is identical to the wheels on this Egyptian ceiling [Fig. 10-39] shown again here.

Do you remember near the beginning when you saw a picture of those wheels on the ceiling? It was among the first photos I showed you [page 42], and I said that those were proof that the Egyptians understood the information that was in the Flower of Life, and that this wasn't just some funny little design on an Egyptian ceiling. Now I'm going to show you what I believe they are, at least in a right-brain way, so you'll be able to understand the way the ancients thought.

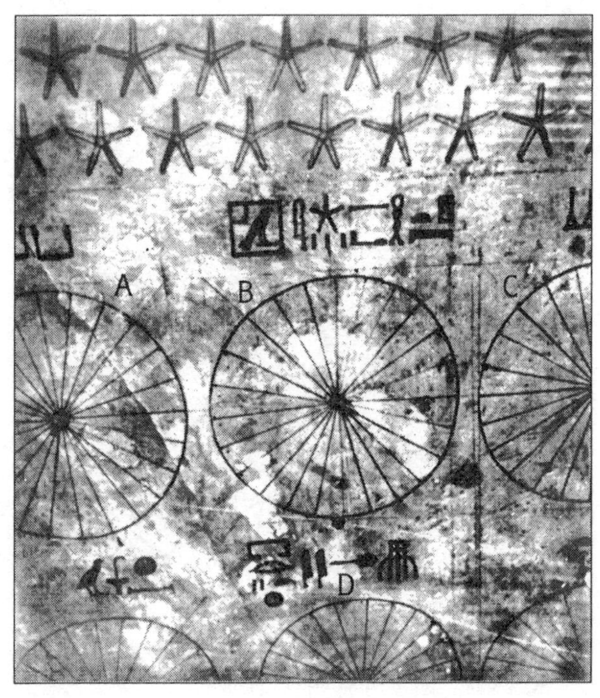

Fig. 10-39. The wheels A, B, C and D illustrate how the spokes do or do not line up with each other.

I've had every part of these wheels in Egypt carefully measured. If you measure the diameter of the little hub in the middle and line up the same-size circles going from the center to the edge of the wheel, there would be exactly nine diagrams, showing that the proportions between the little circle in the middle, the outer circle and the 24 spokes are identical to the previous two images [Figs. 10-37 and 38].

Arrow A [Fig. 10-34a, more clearly in 10-34c] points out the Egg of Metamorphosis over the heads of the figures, who are making a 90-degree turn and are showing the progression of resurrection, I believe, based on the above geometries. These wheels are keys. They exhibit the proportions that indicate and precisely locate the dimensional level where these ancient Egyptians went. They left a map on these ancient ceilings.

You'll notice that each wheel is rotated differently [Fig 10-39], so that the spokes in one are not always lined up with those of the next. The lines between wheels B and C look like they're precisely lined up, but between wheels A and B and wheels B and D the lines are off center. They're all slightly turned to a different angle. I feel sure they're indicating the dimensional level or world where they went.

But no matter how you look at it, whatever these wheels are, the fact that they painted them on the walls means that they understand the deeper geometry within the Flower of Life. It took tremendous knowledge to arrive at these designs; it could not have been an accident. So from my point of view, we *know* they knew about the Flower of Life. The Egyptians knew at the very least what we're talking about here, and more than likely they understood the Flower of Life on levels of life that we in modern times are just now beginning to remember and understand.

The Geometry of the Egyptian Wheels

Now, in order to complete the geometrical understanding of these wheels on the ceiling and other Egyptian hieroglyphs, I offer the following. There are two other Egyptian hieroglyphs that are equally important coming from these same drawings, and it is clear to me that they must be integrated if we wish to truly understand more about what the Egyptians were expressing.

In Figure 10-40 I revert back to an older drawing that shows the Fruit of Life pattern in a deeper progression. Notice that these six divisions separate the drawing into exactly six parts, each at precisely 60 degrees.

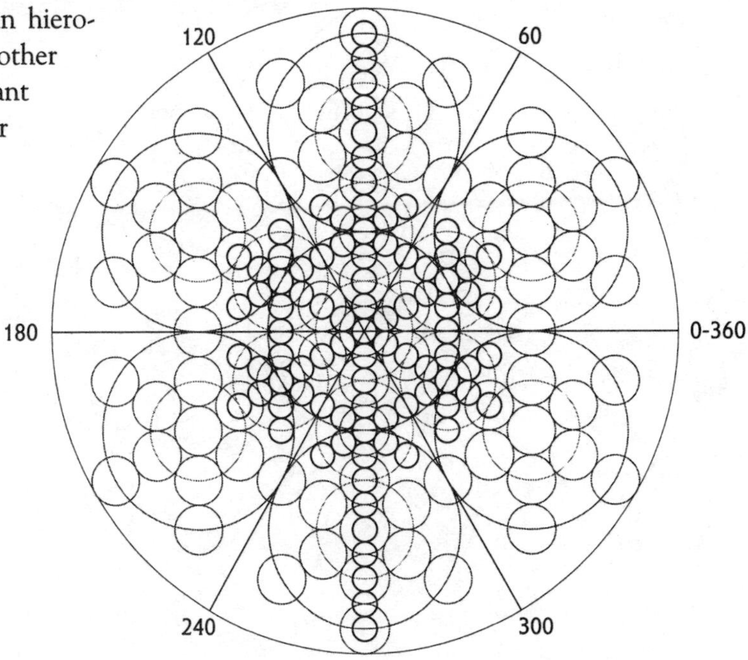

Fig. 10-40. Fruit of Life with 6 divisions.

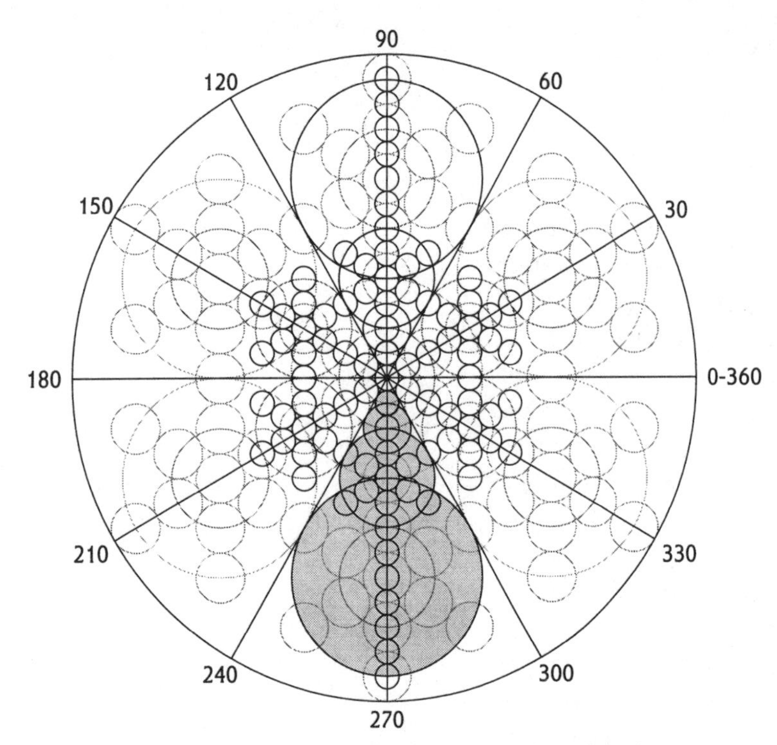

Fig. 10-41. The shaded circles show the 60-degree angle, and the lines running through the center of the Fruit of Life show the 30-degree angle.

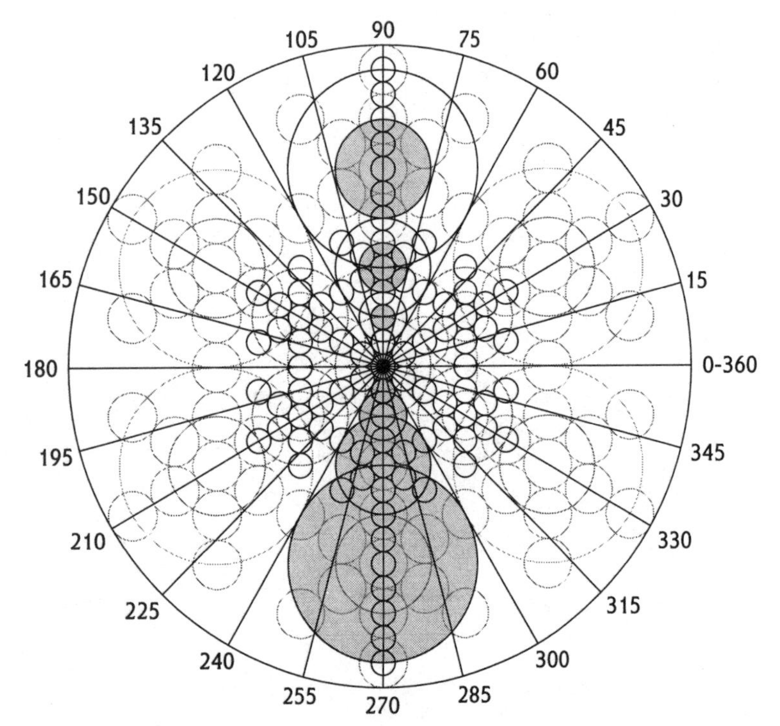

Fig. 10-42. The circles between 75 and 105 degrees at the top of the wheel also show the 30-degree angle.

In Figure 10-41 in the bottom and top 60-degree arc you can see the circles that exactly define this arc. If you then draw the lines down the middle of each arc defined by the center of each Fruit of Life pattern, you arrive at the next six secondary divisions, resulting in 30-degree divisions on the outer wheel. This divides the outer circle into 12 divisions, and is, of course, the wheel the ancient Egyptians used at the Temple of Dendera to define the astrological chart, divide the heavens and group the star patterns.

Continuing in Figure 10-42, the shaded circles in the upper 60-degree arc define the 15-degree arc on either side of the central line at 90 degrees, from 75 to 105 degrees. What is left over in this upper 60-degree arc is exactly two 15-degree arcs, dividing the outer wheel into exactly 24 divisions—the precise geometry found in the burial ceilings in Egypt.

Since these 24-division wheels were also found on the ceilings with five-pointed stars that represent the stars, it would only make sense that they were related to the astrological chart at Dendera, by which the Egyptians were plotting their way into the heavens. More proof of this idea can be seen directly from the astrological chart at Dendera [Fig. 10-43]. Notice that there are eight males and four females on the outside of the "wheel," supporting it. This represents the 12 divisions of the heavens. But also notice that they have 24 hands actually holding this wheel. Then notice that directly inside the wheel are 36 images. All three primary divisions of the wheel are in this image at Dendera: 12, 24 and 36.

Further, if you examine Figure 10-44, you will see something pretty amazing. At first this drawing will seem a little confusing, but it will unfold clearly. Look first at the 30-degree line and see the seven circles (starting with the number zero) moving from the central one out to number 6. The white circle number 1 was used to define the six divisions of 60 degrees. The white number 2 circle was used to define the 30-degree arc of the 24-division outer wheel. The third circle will break the outer wheel into 20-degree arcs and, when split in half, create 10-degree arcs, the same 10 degrees of the polar graph that is believed to come from Egypt. (If it didn't, it could have.) Look at the 150-degree line with its shaded number 3 circle. Finally, the two shaded circles on either side of that dark circle number 3 define the same 10-degree angle, splitting the entire 60-degree arc into six 10-degree divisions, which, when completed in all six divisions, results in the 36-division outer circle of the polar graph.

Notice the math. The first circle is a full 60 degrees. The second circle is 60 degrees times one-half = 30 degrees (the 24 outer circles). The third circle is 60 degrees times one-third = 20 degrees (the 36-division circle). If we were to continue, the next circle, the fourth, is 60 degrees times one-fourth = 15 degrees (48-division circle). The fifth circle is 60 degrees times one-fifth = 12 degrees (60-division circle). Finally, the sixth circle is 60 degrees times one-sixth = 10 degrees (72-division circle).

The last one would create the polar graph directly, and it must be noted that dividing the outer circle into 72 divisions creates the platform to move into pentagonal geometry, since the angle of the pentagon is 72 degrees. Now female geometry would begin to form.

This subject has hardly been touched, but it seems very interesting. The 12-division wheel defines the heavens; the 36-division wheel defines the Earth, and the 24-division wheel is between the Earth and the heavens.

Update: Days before printing this book, and anomaly was discovered as we were checking the math on the final diagram. At first I was going to completely rewrite this section, but then I decided that future researchers may need this example and understanding of how a mistake can lead to even greater discoveries. So I have left it as it is because the essence is correct, and simply present the evidence.

Fig. 10-43. Astrological chart at Dendera.

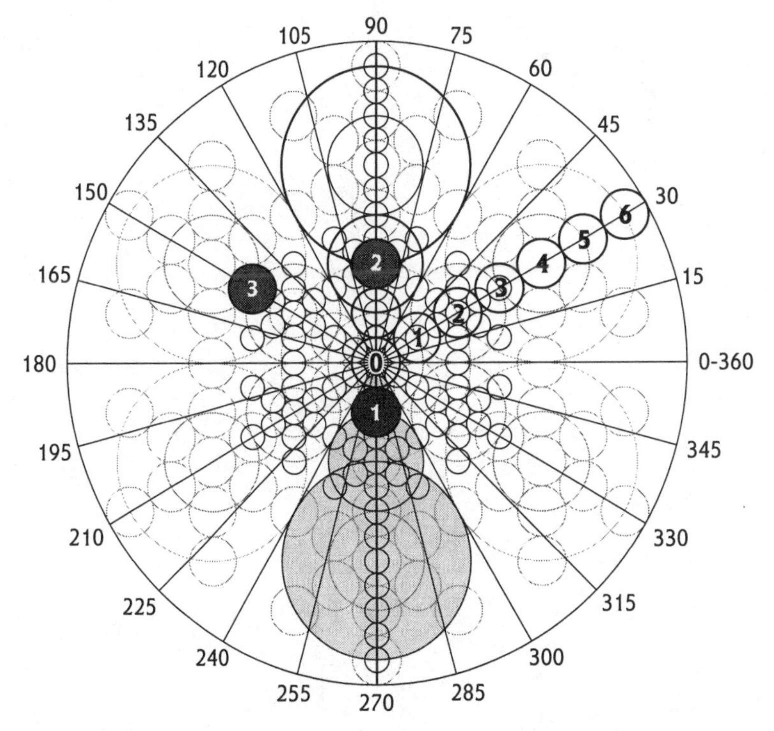

Fig. 10-44. The circles, 0 through 6, show the different angles of the different wheels.

First of all, sacred geometry is an exact science. There are no mistakes whatsoever. In all of sacred geometry I have noticed that whenever something "looks right," it probably is—but not always. However, whenever something is proven to exist in a geometric progression within a specific drawing, all related progressions within that first progression should also be true. I have never seen this *not* to be true.

So what is the problem?

In the progress of the first six divisions of the outer circle at 0, 60, 120, 180, 240 and 300 degrees in Fig. 10-40, they are absolutely perfect. The second set of six lines, creating the 12 divisions in Fig. 10-41, are also perfect. It is clear that the circular progression, as emphasized at 90 and 270 degrees, separates these lines at exactly 60 degrees and the central line into two exact 30-degree divisions. This is positive.

But when looking at Fig. 10-42, the internal circular progression *inside* the original progression does not apparently continue in further progressions. The math shows that the lines at 75 and 105 degrees do not perfectly fit the circle. Each line is off by about one-half of one degree—such a small amount you can barely see. So what does this mean?

When the wheels were measured, it was assumed that the divisions were equal, but perhaps this is not the case. If the ancient Egyptians were using these wheels to map space and the Earth, what is important? Is it more important that the divisions are equal or that they conform to the actual geometries? If they were using this pattern out of the Flower of Life, then the actual geometric progression would be important, since no matter how far the progression expanded into space, the map would be perfect.

This means that someone must go to Egypt and with extreme accuracy measure these wheels to know the truth. If 12 of the lines are perfect and 12 are off this tiny bit and they conform to these geometries, then a deeper understanding of ancient Egypt would become apparent. We could re-create the map.

There are other possibilities, but this is up to you to discover.

At the end of this book will be a short message to announce a new Internet Web service to the world that will enable us to find the truth not only of something like the above, but the truth of almost any subject.

My prayer is that you will become a spiritual researcher seeking the truth. For in the truth we will not only discover what wheels on ancient Egyptian ceilings mean, we will find our true selves. ✧

E L E V E N

Ancient Influences on Our Modern World

This is the Golden Mean rectangle [Fig. 11-1; see also chapter 7] derived from the pyramids, which can be recognized only when seen from the air. This Golden Mean spiral approaches the pyramid complex from over a mile away (at A) and passes over the center or apex of each of the three pyramids in the Giza complex. The Fibonacci spiral appears almost identical as it passes over the pyramids. As we saw in chapter 8, the Fibonacci sequence approximates the Golden Mean. What this means is that its source is in a slightly different place from that of the Golden Mean. They start out differently but soon become almost identical.

The Golden Mean spiral's connection with the Giza complex was discovered more or less recently, around 1985, whereas the source of the Fibonacci spiral was discovered about ten years earlier and given the name, the Solar Cross. No name has been given to the source of the Golden Mean spiral as far as I know.

This Golden Mean spiral at Giza is very interesting. The Egyptians put a stone pillar over the exact center or source of this spiral as well as one on either side—three pillars. I haven't physically seen this one yet. (I actually walked right by it the first time I was in Egypt but didn't know it was there.) According to the McCollum survey [*Giza Survey: 1984*], which was done in 1984, there are three pillars there. When John Anthony West went there, he said there were *four*, so I don't know—they're either growing or somebody was mistaken. Not only do these pillars mark the center of the vortex, but they also mark the diagonal line B very, very carefully; they wanted us to know about this line. Why? We will have to give some background information before we answer this question.

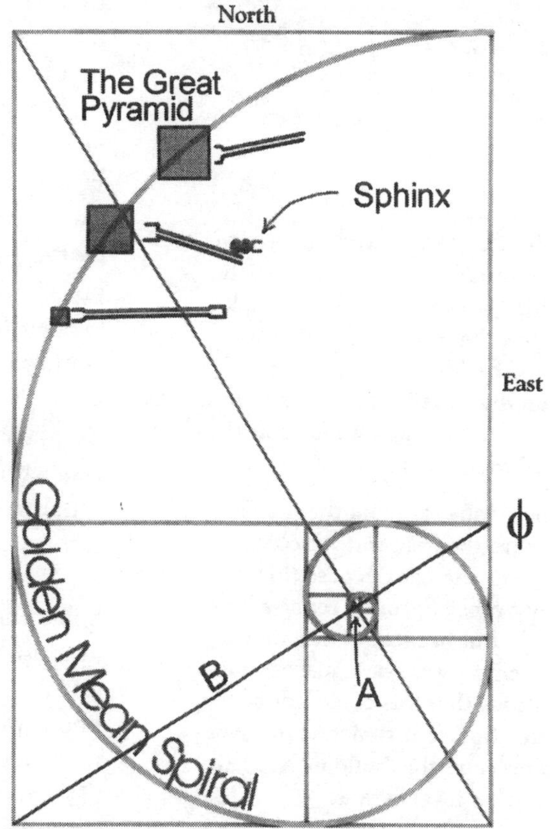

Fig. 11-1. The Golden Mean spiral. The phi symbol ϕ indicates one of the two places where the right vertical edge is bisected at a phi ratio of its length.

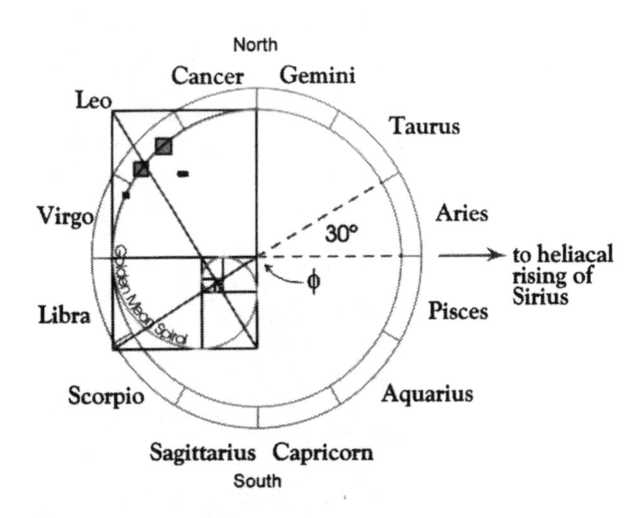

Fig. 11-2. Egyptian astrological wheel, Fig. 11-1 seen from farther away.

There's an enormous astrological wheel connected with the Great Pyramid complex that can be calculated only from the air [Fig. 11-2]. Making such astrological wheels that you can see only from the air is not unusual for the Egyptians if you follow the Druids, who came out of Egypt. The Druids went to Glastonbury, England, and created exactly the same kind of aerial view of the astrological wheel as in Egypt, except that it was more graphic. The one in England clearly shows the different signs on the ground, but it can be seen only from the air. Approximately five or six other Druid-made astrological wheels have been found in England that can be seen only from the air. So it seems to have been an Egyptian-Druid trait to create these wheels.

There is further proof located at the Dendera Temple in Egypt. High on a ceiling is a full astrological wheel similar to what we are used to. So we know the Egyptians knew about and used the astrological wheel. The only thing that was really different was the direction of movement of the heavens. The wheel was moving backward relative to modern observations.

The other bit of information shown on this drawing is that the angle between the ramp that comes off the Great Pyramid and the ramp that comes off the second pyramid is a precise 30 degrees [Fig. 11-3]. That's an important bit of information, which we will use in a minute.

From the McCollum survey we see that the ramp in Figure 11-3 that comes off the third pyramid points exactly to the other phi-ratio point on the long side of the Golden Mean rectangle that contains all these geometries. This is further proof that the Egyptians understood the geometric implications of the spirals moving out of these strange holes in the desert.

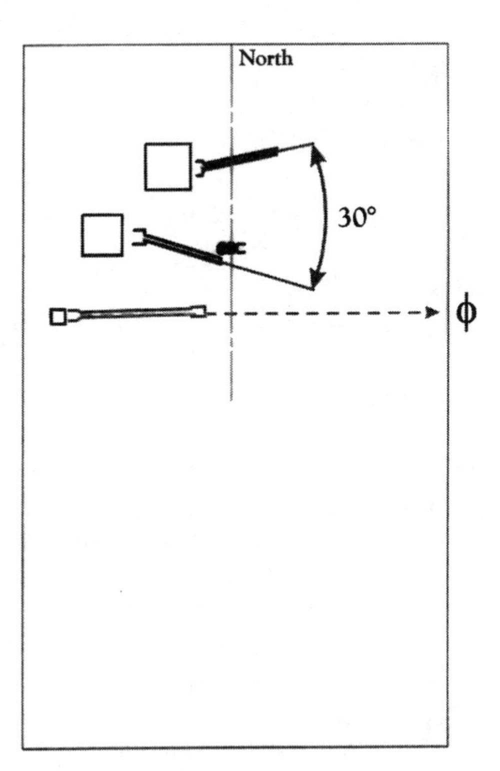

Fig. 11-3. The two ramps, showing the 30-degree angle.

The placement of the Sphinx appears to be random, just sitting there out in the middle of nowhere, who knows why and what for? But now you know about the Golden Mean rectangle around the Giza complex that can only be known from the air. If you bisect that rectan-

Update: About two years ago we discovered the great secret to the entire layout of the Giza complex. It was the building that was located beside the "hole" from which we first thought the spirals arose. Since then we have discovered much more.

I originally said that the building next to the hole was a Golden Mean rectangle because this is what other Egyptian reports have said. But because of certain research we were doing, it became obvious that this could not be true. So I sent someone to Egypt to measure this building and tell me what it really was.

It was found to be a square with four outer chambers around it. It was in the exact proportions as

gle vertically [Fig. 11-4]—put your compass on the right edge and draw a little arc in the middle, then do the same from the left edge (like the compass lines at A show)—and draw a line down the middle, that line passes exactly through, and parallel to, the plane of the vertical front of the flat headdress of the Sphinx. Simultaneously, if you extend the line of the southern base of the second pyramid, it skims the right shoulder of the Sphinx, marking a specific spot [Fig. 11-5].

Figure 11-6 shows the flat headdress of the Sphinx. And the center of the long edge of that Golden Mean rectangle passes exactly through the front edge of the headdress. To put it another way, *the headdress* marks the precise center of the long direction of the Golden Mean rectangle, proving that the Sphinx was not placed in the sand at random. And the line of the south face of the second pyramid skims right along the surface of the shoulder of the Sphinx.

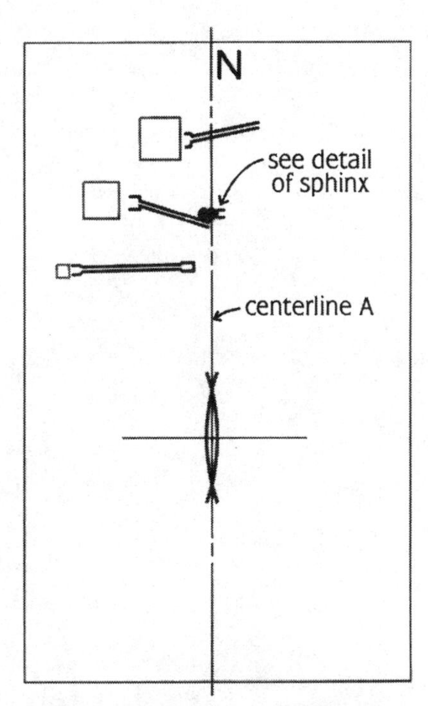

Fig. 11-4. The placement of the Sphinx. See the vertical bisecting line, created by finding the center of the Golden Mean rectangle (see curved lines made by a compass from each side). This line marks the vertical front of the Sphinx's headdress.

These two lines that mark this spot on the Sphinx are evidential, not perchance. For those of you who are involved in Edgar Cayce's work, you'll remember that about 60 years ago he said that someday we would find a room associated with the Sphinx that would lead to the records that were proof of superadvanced civilizations on Earth going back for millions of years, and that the opening to this room would be located in the right paw of the Sphinx. To be more precise, the pyramids' placement relative to the Sphinx is not random, since the Sphinx is older than the pyramids.

While we were in Egypt, we were told by Thoth that there would be 144 people—48 sets of three people each—who would come from the West to Egypt. And that these sets of three would each have something specific to do there. Eventually one particular set of these sets of three would walk up to the Sphinx and enter this special room containing what Edgar Cayce called the Hall of Records. Thoth said their voices would open the way to one of three hallways deep under the sand that would lead to the Hall of Records. This room Japanese scientists have already found; Thoth said there would be a clay pot in the corner with some hieroglyphics on it that would tell them which of the tunnels they were supposed to move through. Even the clay pot has been found by the Japanese instruments, along with a coil of rope.

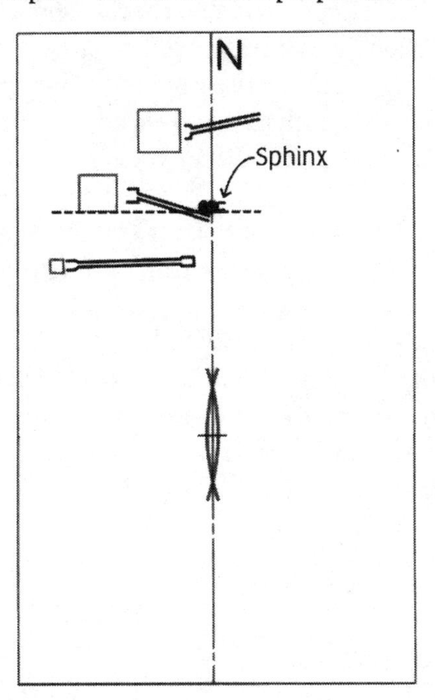

Fig. 11-5. The alignment of the Sphinx's right shoulder/paw and the second pyramid is shown by the horizontal dashed line within this Golden Mean rectangle.

the drawing around Leonardo's body.

In this building were four pillars. Two were at the exact beginning of two Fibonacci spirals. One passed exactly over the top of the three pyramids and was no doubt the source of the Fibonacci spiral that had been previously discovered. The other one spiraled out into the desert in the opposite direction. This design was a square lattice pattern, the same as that around Leonardo's body. From this grid everything in the Giza complex was defined. It was the key to everything in Giza and possibly every major sacred site in the world.

The other two pillars seemed to be placed in a completely arbitrary position, but they were not. These two pillars were the source

Fig. 11-6. Sphinx with flat headdress. Scaffolding shows that reconstruction/stabilization were taking place.

When I went there in 1985 with two other people, the Sphinx was sitting nice and flat and perfect, with no problems. We were instructed by Thoth to put a particular kind of sound down a tunnel that sat directly behind the Sphinx, about a quarter mile back. We were to make a specific sound for a certain length of time and then stop and leave, which we did.

I won't say that we were responsible for what happened, but when we went back there in 1990, the Sphinx was slanted toward its right shoulder. The Sphinx began to rotate, not a little bit, but a lot, and the right shoulder/paw kept breaking open. The Egyptians did everything they could to keep it patched up, as you can see by the scaffolding in Figure 11-6. The other thing is that the head of the Sphinx seems to be trying to fall off. Thoth said it *would* fall off someday, and when it does, it will expose a golden sphere in its neck that is some kind of time capsule. He didn't go into it very much. So those were two things the Egyptians were having a difficult time with—trying to keep the head on the Sphinx and trying to keep its right paw from breaking open.

Now, one final piece of information: Thoth said that under the Giza complex there was a city that would hold 10,000 people. He said this around 1985, and I talked about it publicly as early as 1987. The people who lived in this city would be people who had reached immortal status and had become part of what we call the ascended masters. They were what the ancient Egyptians called the Tat Brotherhood. About six years ago their numbers had reached just over 8000. This underground city is the place where the Tat Brotherhood lived in isolation while the rest of humanity continued to evolve. We mentioned this in chapter 4. Now I would like to give you an update on what is happening around this city in the past five years. It is important to know, but because it cannot be proven, please hold your judgment until the truth is finally revealed.

What I am about to say about the underground city in Egypt is highly controversial, and most Egyptian officials will not admit to any of it. They say it is all just somebody's imagination. History will tell. From what I know and have seen, they are not telling the truth. Egypt has a very good reason for you to not know about this city, at least not yet.

of a series of pentagonal geometric progressions that defined the position of the Great Pyramid itself and everything in the Giza complex, but used a different system than the one above. A double check, perhaps?

We showed the Egyptian government this information. They responded by removing this building and destroying all signs of its original placement! It is as though it never existed. The ancient Egyptian building that is the key to all of Egypt has now been destroyed. Only God knows why. I guess they did not want people to know where everything was. ✧

Update: Thoth came to me in about 1992 and said that he was going to have to leave the Earth and that his work with me was finished, at least for now. He said he was sorry, but the events on Earth had accelerated, and the ascended masters, the Tat Brotherhood and what many call the Great White Brotherhood (which are all the same) were about to venture into a new area of consciousness, an area no human being has ever entered before. He said that whatever happened would determine the outcome of human evolution forever. I have not seen him since. (See the update at the end of this section, because he has now returned.)

Thoth explained that in the summer of 1990, he and the rest of the ascended masters had decided that the consciousness of the Earth was about to reach a critical mass in January 1991 during the Egyptian window of January 10 through 19. He said that it would begin in August 1990, and by the following month the outcome would be determined. He said that the human population was still highly polarized, but that a special "moment" had arrived where great change could take place.

They saw that it was possible at this moment that we, the Earth, could become one in spirit and ascend to a higher level of consciousness exactly in the middle of the Egyptian window. Thoth made it clear that the ascended masters were not really sure what was going to happen. It depended on the hearts of the people of the Earth. The ascended masters had all decided to leave at once as a ball of living light, giving the Earth a tremendous boost into the new level of consciousness. Their leaving for a higher level of life was to be a decision for the good of all mankind.

However, when August 1990 came, Thoth said that the ascended masters were not sure if we were going to make the shift (at that time), and that there would not be another window of opportunity for some time. They held back on their plan to leave. Later in August, Iraq and her assistants were the only energy in the entire world to evade unity on an outer level. By September 1990 the world had declared war on Iraq. And on exactly January 15, 1991, the moment in the middle of the Egyptian window when the ascended masters were hoping that the world would come together, we came together as an entire planet, except for Iraq, to wage war instead of peace. We missed the opportunity for unity by only one nation. This unity, however, was not just nations, but primarily the people of the world.

Instead, we went to war on that day—January 15, 1991—and the Egyptian window of opportunity moved us deeper into the darkness instead of the light.

Thoth and the ascended masters responded by setting up another plan where only 32 masters at a time would leave the Earth and attempt to find the place in the universe to which humanity was supposed to eventually translate. Leaving in small groups would be timed to certain events in human experience to (again) give power to these events. Thoth and his wife Shesat were part of the first group to leave. On an almost daily or weekly basis, the masters traveled in small groups into higher dimensions and a new way of being, a way that someday the rest of humanity would follow. As they left the city under the Great Pyramid, slowly the city became deserted. By the end of 1995 only a small group of seven beings remained behind to protect the city.

As this city emptied, it then could be used for another purpose—to prove

to the modern world that there is more to life than we know and that there is great hope for humanity.

Now let's talk about rumors. There is very little proof of what I am about to say, so hold it only as a possibility until the world knows the real truth.

In November 1996 I was contacted by a source in Egypt who said that something had just been discovered that was beyond anything that had ever been found in Egypt. The person said that a stone stele (a flat stone rock with writing on it) came out of the ground between the paws of the Sphinx into the daylight. This stele spoke of the Hall of Records and a room under the Sphinx.

The Egyptian government immediately removed the stele so that no one would see what it said. Then they dug into the earth between the paws and opened the room under the Sphinx that the Japanese had found in 1989. There was the clay pot and the coil of rope. The person said that the government traveled down a tunnel coming off this room into a round room that had three more tunnels coming off it. In one of these tunnels that headed toward the Great Pyramid, the government found two things they had never seen before.

First they found a light field, a sheet of light that blocked entry past this point. When the government tried to pass anything through this light field, it could not penetrate it. Not even a bullet could pass through it.

In addition, if one of the government officials tried to physically approach this light field, at about 30 feet from the light he/she would get sick and throw up. If he tried to press forward, he would feel like he was going to die. No one, to my knowledge, was able to touch the field.

From aboveground, the government found something just past this light field that was also extremely unusual. They found an underground twelve-story building at that point—twelve stories deep in the Earth!

The combination of these two things—the light field and the twelve-story building—were more than the Egyptian government could handle. They asked for foreign help. The Egyptian government decided that a particular man (whom I will not name) was the person who could turn the light field off and enter the tunnel. He would do this with two other people. One of these people was a friend I knew very well, so I was able to follow closely what was happening. My friend brought in Paramount Studios, which would be allowed to film the opening of this unique tunnel. Paramount had filmed the opening of King Tut's tomb, so they had a very good relationship with Egypt.

They planned to enter, or at least attempt to enter, this tunnel on January 23, 1997. The government wanted several million dollars from Paramount, which they agreed on. However, the day before they were to enter, the Egyptians decided they wanted more money and asked for one and a half million dollars under the table, which outraged Paramount. Paramount said no, so everything was off. For about three months there was silence.

Then one day I heard that a different group of three people had entered the tunnel. I heard that they had entered and shut off the light field by using their voices and the holy names of God. The primary person in this group, who is famous and does not want his name mentioned, went to Australia and showed a video of the trip into the tunnel and the twelve-story building, which proved to be much more than just a building. The building went on and on for miles under the ground and was really the edge of a city. I had three good friends in Australia who watched this film.

Then entered another person, Larry Hunter, who has been an Egyptian archaeologist for over 20 years. Mr. Hunter contacted me and began to tell me a story almost identical to what I had been receiving through my sources in Egypt, except that it was more detailed. He said that the city is six and a half miles by eight miles on the surface and twelve stories deep, and that the city perimeters are outlined by special and unique Egyptian temples.

What follows next overlaps the work of Graham Hancock and Robert Bauval in their book *Message of the Sphinx*. Graham and Robert had guessed that the three pyramids of Giza were placed on the ground in the exact arrangement of the three stars of Orion's Belt. In fact, they believed that all the major stars of the Orion constellation should be found in the placement of temples in Egypt, but they were never able to completely prove this theory.

Mr. Hunter, however, has proven the truth of this, and I've seen the evidence. Using the knowledge of star navigation that he obtained when he was in the Navy, Mr. Hunter found a temple at every single location that corresponds to every major star in the Orion constellation. He used the GPS system to locate these spots on the Earth with a 50-foot accuracy, and physically went to each place where a temple should mark a star. Thus it was verified. In each place there *was* a temple—which was surprising—and each temple was made of a unique substance not found in any other temple in all of Egypt. This substance is also what was used to create the foundation stones of the three Giza pyramids, including the Great Pyramid. It is called *coin in stone*. It is limestone that looks like it has coins stirred into it. It is unique, found only in these temples that span an area on the surface of six and a half by eight miles.

To be clear, this is a theory that has not been accepted by the Egyptian government, but the underground city that Thoth said was there that would hold 10,000 people is, according to Mr. Hunter, marked by temples made of a unique substance, and the temples match the star pattern of the constellation of Orion.

From what I have seen, I believe this to be true, but the Egyptian officials say this is fantasy. I am keeping an open mind. Eventually the truth will be known. I do believe that if this *is* true, this archaeological find will have an uplifting effect on human consciousness when the underground city is revealed. Now let's return to the discourse on Egypt. ✧

The Heliacal Rising of Sirius

Here are the pyramids and the Golden Mean rectangle that surrounds the whole complex [Fig. 11-7]. Notice the two main lines that pass right through the center of the circle at phi (ϕ). If we completed that circle on the ground, it would have a diameter of about two and a half miles. The McCollum surveyors who discovered this relationship, along with almost everyone who has ever written about the Giza complex, chose east as the direction the pyramids and the Sphinx were facing. But we now know that this is not correct. People have always believed that the pyramids were lined up to magnetic north-south, but computers have now shown that the three pyramids were never aligned this way. They're off a tiny, tiny bit. People have said that the reason they were off this little bit is because of continental drift.

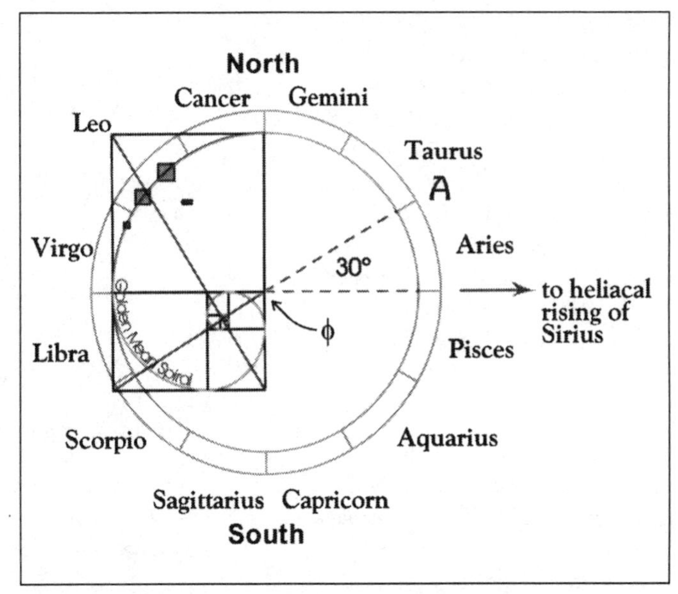

Fig. 11-7. Circular layout of the pyramid/Sphinx complex. Notice how the Golden Mean rectangle and spiral of the Giza complex touch the center of the astrological wheel at phi (ϕ).

But this "off a little bit" is not off at all—it's exactly correct. The three eastern-oriented pyramid faces are on a line that converges at a single point on the horizon—in other words, an arc. The point on the horizon happens to be the point of the heliacal rising of Sirius, which is not true east. This is the moment we talked about in chapter 1 (page 14), when on July 23 the star Sirius rises about one minute before sunrise, appearing as a bright red star. It is the moment when the Earth, our Sun and Sirius form a straight line.

Even more amazing is that the *eyeballs* of the Sphinx are looking at the same exact spot. This is what computers have shown. This makes sense because the ancient Egyptian religion and the Egyptian Sothic calendar were based on the heliacal rising of Sirius. Sirius was paramount to their very existence. So let's align this drawing to the heliacal rising of Sirius rather than to the east.

Because of the two ramps that were aimed exactly 30 degrees apart, let's divide the circle into 30-degree sections, which creates the twelve segments of the astrological chart (30 x 12 = 360 degrees). We already know that they totally understood astrology, because an entire astrological wheel was on the ceiling of the temple at Dendera [see Fig. 11-8], so it's completely logical to put those twelve segments in the circle. If you do, you have a very possible time wheel. The McCollum survey, for example, shows that when using this theory, the Great Pyramid sits in Leo and the time line of the point relative to 0 degrees Aries is at 10,800 B.C. (This is exactly the time when Edgar Cayce said it had been built.)

Fig. 11-8. A copy of the Egyptian astrological wheel from the ceiling of the temple at Dendera.

Update: In January 1999, the angels came and said that the ascended masters would begin to return to Earth during the Egyptian window, January 10 to 19, 1999. They told me they would bring with them knowledge of a new and completely different universe. The angels said that the Earth would soon begin to receive brand-new knowledge, knowledge that humankind had never even imagined before.

Then in November 1999, Thoth came to me for the first time in many years. He said he was back, and that at the right time we would work together again. It was interesting that a few days later, while at a lecture I was giving, a young man came up to me with a gift. He handed me an orange ibis feather, the ibis being a symbol of Thoth.

Shesat came in at the same time as her husband Thoth, and she began to communicate with me also. She stayed with me for two weeks. What she had to say was about my primary purpose for coming into this octave of dimensions. I am still learning about this lesson, so I will wait to talk about what she brought to me. ✧

Virgo and Leo, Aquarius and Pisces

Looking at the aerial view of the pyramids with a superimposed astrological wheel [Fig. 11-7], it places the three pyramids physically in Leo and Virgo on the wheel. This just happens to be where we are physically at this moment in our orbit in the precession of the equinoxes. More than that, the Sphinx was originally half lion and half human female, and it is believed that during the Fourth Dynasty the Sphinx's face was recarved into that of a man with a beard—which fell off. Now it has a kind of male face without a beard, but originally it was female, and combined Leo (the lion) and Virgo (the virgin)—further confirmation that this astrological drawing is accurate.

Further, McCollum's survey map shows that if you were to draw lines from the pyramids, the apexes, corners etc. across the circle of the wheel to the opposite side, it would throw a spectrum of accurate dates between Aquarius and Pisces, which is the time period we are in now—the Age of Pisces moving into the Age of Aquarius. So that's another consideration. But no one I know of has done enough research yet to be able to calculate this. With today's computers, we should be able to do this extremely accurately. Possibly one of you out there will do this work?

The Four Corners Implication

In the beginning of this chapter we asked why the ancient Egyptians had marked a certain line [see line B in Fig. 11-1] connected to the Golden Mean rectangle that encloses the Great Pyramid. Then we said we needed to give you more information first. Perhaps the following may be one answer.

There was an astrologer who had an amazing idea about this diagonal, which has to do with the stars and a specific area of the United States. Once the astrologer saw that there was an astrological chart in the sand around the Great Pyramid, she wanted to know about the diagonal line at A [see Fig. 11-7] that seemed to be so important to the ancient Egyptians. I can't quite explain what she did because I'm not an astrologer, but she took the astrological wheel and related it to the North Pole and aligned it somehow to Cairo. Then she looked to see where the other end of the line would point. It marked a specific spot on planet Earth. In her understanding, it was the Four Corners area of the United States, where Utah, Colorado, New Mexico and Arizona meet. To the Hopi and other native peoples, the Four Corners area is marked by four mountains, which create a much smaller area.

For years I sat on this information, waiting to see what would unfold, waiting to see if anything emerged that would somehow associate Egypt with the Four Corners. Then a few years ago a young man came to me and had an amazing story to tell. I listened because the story was saying that something Egyptian was connected to the Four Corners [see update next page].

The Philadelphia Experiment

Now we switch to a seemingly completely different and unrelated subject—but in fact it is related to everything in this book.

Most of you have at least heard of the Philadelphia Experiment. This experiment was performed by the Navy in 1943 near the end of World War II. An interesting fact is that in the beginning it was headed by Nicola Tesla, who died shortly before the actual experiment was completed. Tesla's part in this experiment, I feel, was paramount, but we will never know, since it has been so tightly hidden by the government. He was replaced by John von Neumann, who is usually known as the person who set up and oversaw this experiment.

The experiment tried to make a U.S. Navy ship invisible. This, of course, would give an incredible edge in warfare. In essence, the ship would be taken to another dimension and returned back to this one. It is my belief that Tesla had been communicating with the Grays and had learned the secret of interdimensional travel from them. It has been reported that Tesla was once asked where he got these ideas for this experiment, and he himself said that he got them from ETs. I'm sure that people in the '40s just thought he was kidding.

I realize that many people think that this information comes from the imagination of unstable people. But if you want to (and I have), you can get a copy of the original (then-top-secret) paperwork that the government still has. However, most of the paperwork has been blacked out for reasons of "national security." There is still enough that is visible to prove that the experiment did happen and to show much of its nature.

From what I have learned from this document and from many people studying it—and mostly from meditation with angels—is that the Philadelphia Experiment was energetically connected to other experiments through time, space and dimension. The first experiment was performed on Mars almost a million years ago when the Martians first came to Earth at the beginning of Atlantis. The next experiment was completed at the end of Atlantis about 13,000 years ago, which created the Bermuda Triangle and has caused major problems in many far-distant areas of deep space. That experiment, as I have said in the first book, was completely out of control, because in trying to create a synthetic Mer-Ka-Ba to control Atlantis, the Martians did not remember exactly how to do it.

This out-of-control synthetic Mer-Ka-Ba in the Bermuda Triangle, which is located near Bimini, has been causing real problems in deep outer space ever since. The primary reason the Grays first came to Earth was to solve this problem. They were the ones who were being affected most by this illegal experiment. Many of their planets were being destroyed. Later the Grays tried to use us to create a hybrid race to save themselves, but their experiments on us were completely unrelated to the original problem.

The Grays, trying to solve this problem of the out-of-control Mer-Ka-Ba near Bimini, assisted humans to do the first modern experiment to solve the

Update: What I am about to tell you is highly controversial. It may be true and possibly it is not. But it is worth it if some of you search out the truth.

A young man came to me and began to tell me this story. He said there is a mountain inside the Grand Canyon called the Temple of Isis. You might wonder why they called it that. In 1925 a great discovery was found in and around this mountain. It was written about in the *Arizona Gazette,* I believe, in 1925, and in a book published, as I recall, in 1926. He went to the still-existing newspaper and found the microfiche on file that shows what they found in this mountain. There are about six pages dedicated to the subject. I have seen it with my own eyes. [Perhaps readers can assist us to give exact references for both the article and the book, which had "Egypt" as part of its title and a picture of a flying saucer on its cover.]

The newspaper says that they found Egyptian mummies and Egyptian hieroglyphs on the walls "inside" the mountain called the Temple of Isis. I saw the photos where they were bringing out the mummies, and I saw the hieroglyphs. The newspaper said that the Smithsonian Institute was doing the fieldwork and quoted them as saying that this was the biggest find in North American history. A book was written about this about a year later, but I don't remember its name. Then there was silence for about 68 years, until 1994.

This young man said that he first found the 1926 book telling of this find, then researched the newspaper article of 1925. He told me the following story about hiking

into the Grand Canyon to find this place. It is important to know that this Temple of Isis mountain is located in the Grand Canyon in an area now closed off to the public, except that a permit can be obtained under certain conditions. Even then only a small group of people at a time are allowed into this area. There is no water there except for one or two springs that are far apart. Water has to be carried with you, which limits how long you can stay there. Also, it is so hot there that people have a difficult time staying alive unless they are trained.

He told me that he and a friend went into this area. They were both expert mountain climbers trained in survival. He says that as he and his teammate approached the mountain, they found an actual stone pyramid made by human hands not far from the mountain. It was large enough to be impressive to these two researchers. To reach the Isis Temple, they had to climb a rock face that went straight up about 800 feet. Since they were professional mountain climbers, this did not stop them, as they were prepared.

According to the original article in the *Arizona Gazette*, there were 32 large doorways entering the

problem at the Bermuda Triangle. It was performed in 1913, but it didn't work. In fact, I believe it made things worse and probably was the source of the First World War in 1914. Exactly forty years later (this time period is critical), the U.S. military performed the Philadelphia Experiment in 1943 during the Second World War. Again, in 1983 (40 years later) the Montauk experiment was performed, trying to solve the problems caused by the Philadelphia Experiment. A small experiment was finally completed in 1993 (a harmonic of the 40 cycle) to speed up the male component of the original problem caused by the Atlanteans.

All these experiments are connected. They are important to understand because they were all higher-dimensional experiments based on Mer-Ka-Ba science. The Philadelphia Experiment was based on the counterrotating fields of the star tetrahedron, very similar to what we are teaching here. The Montauk Experiment was based on the counterrotating fields of the octahedron, another possibility.

One day I gave a workshop on Long Island, New York, and while I was in the workshop I talked about the Philadelphia Experiment. Directly after that workshop I was scheduled to give another one on the next weekend, so I was hanging out for a few days at the home of the woman who sponsored the first workshop.

The next morning she said, "Have you seen the movie, *The Philadelphia Experiment?*" I didn't even know there was such a movie, so we watched the video. That night or the next morning, a man named Peter Carroll called me—he was then the coach for the New York Jets. He said that he had gotten my name from someone and had heard that I was talking about the Philadelphia Experiment. He wanted to know if I wanted to meet one of the survivors of this experiment.

I had already connected with one of the original engineers of the Philadelphia Experiment, and this engineer couldn't believe that I actually knew and understood what they had been doing. He was so excited about it that he had given us a few pieces of the original equipment and showed us exactly how it was done. It was all based on the star tetrahedron. So now someone was inviting me to meet a survivor.

I went to Peter's house, and there I met two people—Duncan Cameron, who was one of the people who allegedly survived the Philadelphia Experiment, and Preston Nichols, who has since written a book about this experience. I had a very enlightening moment there.

They had used Duncan and his human spine in 1943 to do this experiment, putting a synthetic Mer-Ka-Ba field around him. Later, when the experiment was tried again in 1983, it was called the Montauk Experiment, of which Preston claims to be one of the original engineers. When he said that, I said, "Okay, if you are who you say you are, then would you tell me exactly how you did it?" He described in detail how he did it. It was real stuff, I believe, based on his very high-level understanding of the geometry of the Mer-Ka-Ba. So I suspect that Preston is who he says he is.

Then Duncan came into the room. He had the strangest thing going on around him. He had two Mer-Ka-Ba fields rotating around him, and they were both out of control. They were wobbling and constantly changing positions relative to each other. They were rotating way too slowly, and they weren't phase-locked to make them work together.

When Duncan came into the room and entered *my* field, he stopped and couldn't get any closer. He seemed to be repelled almost like two magnets repelling each other. He tried to come closer, but he was so out of balance that he could not come into my field. He was forced backward. He finally ended up walking about 35 feet down the hallway until he felt comfortable, and we held our conversation from this distance. He was standing just a few feet outside my Mer-Ka-Ba field. We would sort of shout down the hall. I didn't have any problem getting closer to *him*, but when I did, he became very uncomfortable and asked me to move.

I am within my living Mer-Ka-Ba field all the time, and the first thing he wanted to know was, "What's that black ring around your field?" Approximately 55 feet in diameter, a spinning Mer-Ka-Ba has a thin black ring where the field rotates at nine-tenths the speed of light. (See again that photograph of the Sombrero galaxy from chapter 2 [Fig. 11-9]?)

Notice the black ring out where the galaxy is moving the fastest. When things start reaching the speed of light, you don't see the light. There's light there, but it starts turning black relative to where you are. What this told me is that Duncan could actually see my Mer-Ka-Ba, and that in itself is very rare.

The next observation I made was that Duncan had no emotional body. I asked him about that, and he said that the government gave him LSD and used his sexual energy to strip him of any emotions. I had never seen anyone in this state before. This, of course, was the problem he was having with his two Mer-Ka-Bas. He had two because he was linked to both the Philadelphia and the Montauk experiments. Neither of them were created with and by love, so they were completely out of balance.

Preston was sitting next to me, and I noticed that he was sweating and chewing his fingernails as if he were very afraid. I asked him about this, and

temple high above ground level. My friend said that they were still there, but looked like someone had attempted to destroy them. They picked one of the "doorways" that looked in the best condition and climbed up to it.

When they reached it, they found that the opening went into the mountain about 40 feet, where rubble blocked their way. However, above this doorway was a perfectly round cutout about six feet in diameter and several inches deep that had been created by human hands. Human beings had definitely been there to make this cutout. They found no hieroglyphics.

Their water was running out, and they made it back just in time. He said that staying another day might have been fatal, as the spring that should have given them more water was dry.

The other interesting part of this story is that another "mountain" in the Grand Canyon, on the same latitude and only a mile or so away, is being excavated by the U.S. government. This site is so important to the government that they have made it illegal to fly over the area under 10,000 feet! The entire mountain is surrounded by the military, which keeps everyone out of the area. What have they found?

Actually, the only reason I listened to this person about this possible Egyptian site was because of what we had learned about the diagonal line on the Giza Plateau that pointed to the "Four Corners area in the United States," indicating that something Egyptian and important seemed to be located there.

Why am I telling you this? Because I believe that Egypt will

Fig. 11-9. The Sombrero galaxy.

he said that yes, he was very concerned at this time. It seems that the Mer-Ka-Bas that created the Philadelphia and Montauk experiments were now linked, and because of some information they had, they were worried about these Mer-Ka-Bas returning to Earth and causing great harm. He was worried about his life and the lives of others.

After leaving, I talked with the angels. I could see exactly what was wrong with Duncan's Mer-Ka-Bas, and I thought it would be very easy to fix them. But the angels would not let me interfere. They said that in the year 2012, on December 12 a pretest on a new experiment would take place for twelve days that would solve all the problems and bring everything back into balance. They told me not to help.

eventually play a role in the unfolding of the consciousness of Earth, and I do not want what I know about this to be lost. ✧

However, Al Bielek, another survivor of the Philadelphia Experiment and Duncan's brother, called me a couple days later trying to get me to help Duncan. I could not help. They have to wait a few more years and all will be well.

I have brought up this subject because of the nature of these experiments. As I said, they are based on Mer-Ka-Ba science. At this point our government is using this information for purposes other than making invisible weapons of war. They have discovered that they can affect human emotions and control human minds. It is important for you to know, because you, in your Mer-Ka-Ba, can be immune to what they are doing by using the knowledge in this book.

There are many experiments that the governments of this world are doing on their populations, not to mention the problems with the Earth's environment. Knowing and using the power of the human lightbody, you can bring balance not only to yourself, but also to the whole world. It is this subject—learning to use your lightbody and how this can change everything—that I am bringing to your attention. You are more than you know. Great Spirit lives within you, and under the right circumstances, through you all things are possible. You can heal yourself and the world and assist in the ascension of Mother Earth into the next world if your love is great enough.

T W E L V E

The Mer-Ka-Ba, the Human Lightbody

The Egyptian Mystery School studied all the varied aspects of the human experience, more than we could possibly speak of here. But the one aspect that was central to the entire Egyptian training in the mysteries was the Mer-Ka-Ba. The Mer-Ka-Ba, the human lightbody, was everything! Without this knowledge and experience, the other worlds were impossible to reach, from their way of seeing.

"Mer-Ka-Ba" has the same meaning in several languages. In Zulu it is pronounced just like in English. The spiritual leader of the Zulus, Credo Mutwa, says his people arrived here from space on a Mer-Ka-Ba. In Hebrew it is *Mer-Ka-Vah*, and means both the throne of God and a chariot, a vehicle that carries the human body and spirit from one place to another.

In Egyptian, the word "Mer-Ka-Ba" is actually three words: *Mer* is a special kind of light, a counterrotating field of light; *Ka* means spirit (at least here on Earth it has the connotation of the human spirit); and *Ba* means "the interpretation of the Reality," which here on Earth usually means the human body. When you add these words together, my understanding of Mer-Ka-Ba is "a counterrotating field of light that will interact and translate the spirit and the body from one world into another," though it is really much, much more. It is the creation pattern itself through which all that exists has originated.

You know this. It's nothing really new to you. You just forgot for a moment in time. You have used the Mer-Ka-Ba a zillion times as your lives have unfolded throughout the creation of space/time/dimension. And you will remember again just as you need it.

This chapter will speak indirectly of the human lightbody, or the Mer-Ka-Ba. We will talk about the internal mechanics and energy flows of the lightbody, whereas in the next chapter we will give the understanding of the Mer-Ka-Ba meditation itself—a way to actually experience it, then remember. It will probably help you to know this internal structure first in order to work with your lightbody. If you don't feel it is necessary, then of course go on to the next chapter.

Let it be known that you can re-create or activate your lightbody without this knowledge. You can re-create it with love and faith alone, and for some people, that is the only way. I acknowledge this possibility, but my assignment here on Earth is to bring forth this pathway, using male knowledge, because some of you can understand only through the left brain. The female pathway is more intact within the Earth's biosphere, and it is the male that now needs the balance so desperately.

We will begin with the innermost points of energy called the chakras and slowly move outward to explain the entire human energy field. This is a lot of information; there is only so much I can do to simplify such a complicated subject.

Before we begin, there is one last image that must be seen, or you will never understand. No matter how much you try to know and understand the Mer-Ka-Ba through the sacred geometry, it will never be enough. There is the missing half that is experiential, and it can only be experienced while you are immersed in love. Love is more than just necessary; love is the very life of the Mer-Ka-Ba. Yes, the Mer-Ka-Ba is alive. It is nothing less than you, and you are alive. The Mer-Ka-Ba is not something separate from you; it *is* you. It is the energy lines that allow the life-force energy, the prana, the chi, to flow into you and from you back to God. It is your very connection to God. It is that which links you and God together as one. Love is half of the light that is swirling around you, knowledge is the other half. When love and knowledge become one, the Christ will be present, always.

If you think that within these pages you may find something useful to help you in one of the projects of your mind, you will never know the truth. It can only be experienced. If you are searching for the mechanics to have the Mer-Ka-Ba experience, I offer you the following.

The Geometries of the Human Chakra System

If the male pathway is your choice, then the human chakra system is imperative to know and understand when working with the subtle energies within and around the human body. These are often lumped together and called the human lightbody.

A *chakra* is an energy point within and sometimes outside the body that has a specific quality. When a person is focused in one particular chakra, their whole world is colored by the energy of that chakra. It is like a lens through which everything in existence is interpreted.

Although each chakra is different, both energetically and experientially, they all have certain aspects that are the same. There also is an underlying energy flowing through the chakra system and connecting them that is extremely helpful to comprehend.

The human chakra system is based on eight chakras along the spine. There is a more integral system of thirteen chakras, which we will examine later. Realize that there are many minor chakras we will not talk about at all, such as the ones in the hands and feet.

We are first going to focus on the flow of energy up the spine area, then branch off to many related subjects. In the next chapter we will see the sacred geometric fields of light that surround your body and are the basis of the living Mer-Ka-Ba.

We will explore the geometric source of the 8-chakra system, which is based on the structure of the Egg of Life, the same energy pattern as the original eight cells of the human body discussed in chapter 7. Note also that the original eight cells, the 8-chakra system and the eight internal electric circuits of the human body seen in Chinese medicine are all related to the cube or to the star tetrahedron, depending on one's point of view. The electric circuits have many conduits connecting to every cell in the body. In Chinese medicine these circuits are called meridians. A full study of the chakra system must include this knowledge, but not here, because it is so complex and not really necessary for our purpose. Here we will introduce only what is necessary to activate your Mer-Ka-Ba.

The Unfolded Egg of Life and the Musical Scale

Visualize the Egg of Life, the form with the eight spheres in the shape of a star tetrahedron [Fig. 12-1]. Now disconnect all the spheres and open it up into a chain [Fig. 12-2]. But it must be done in a specific sequence, keeping the half steps in place. What you have is the human 8-chakra system—the primary chakras running up and through the body. Human energy, from sexual to electrical, moves in the pattern you see here.

You have the same change-in-direction half steps between the third and fourth chakras and the seventh and eighth chakras. And there's still that special change between the fourth and fifth chakras, the heart and the sound chakras. These movements are also found in the harmonics of music. Seeing the structure of the musical scale will help you apply that structure to the human chakra system. Let's look at music to understand what was just said.

Fig. 12-1. The Egg of Life.

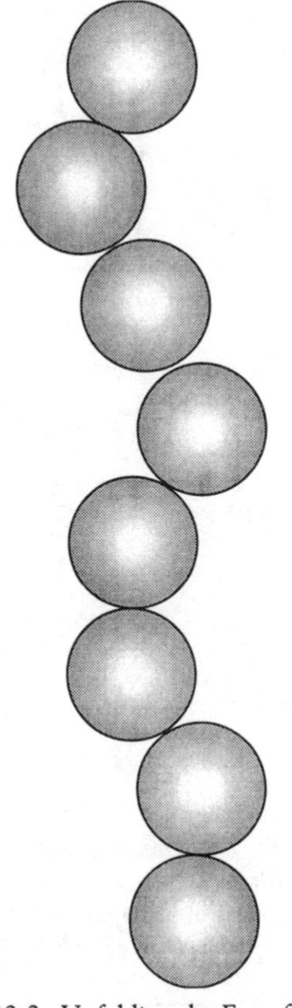

Fig. 12-2. Unfolding the Egg of Life.

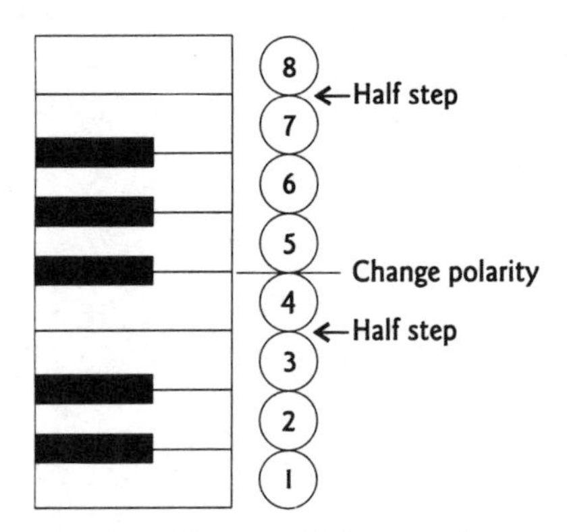

Fig. 12-3. The Egg of Life musically unfolded. On the left is an octave on a keyboard. The scale of C uses the white keys, making it easy to visualize the half steps (in relation to the black keys) and visually see the two tetrachords that make up a major scale. A major scale has half steps between 3 and 4 and between 7 and 8.

In the musical scale of any major key, there is a half step between the third and fourth notes and the seventh and eighth notes [Fig. 12-3]. These half steps are built into wind instruments such as the flute by the positioning of the holes. Likewise, there is a special place between the fourth and fifth notes that Gurdjieff talks about. It is the place where the polarity reverses, changing from female to male. Using the unfolded Egg of Life, we show how energy moves through music and through this shape, which is the same in the body chakras.

The energy of the Mer-Ka-Ba, the two tetrahedrons embedded in a human life form [Fig. 12-4], moves in the following way [Fig. 12-5]: 1 (*do*) goes to 2, 3 or 4, then to one of the other two vertexes, moving in a flat plane to do so. To reach the remaining vertex, it must now change direction—the half step.

Using the classical Western system of the octave as shown on the piano, the note *do* enters the star tetrahedron of the Egg of Life at the bottom point (vertex) of the female tetrahedron. The energy is male as it comes in from the previous octave, but it must change to female because it has just entered a new, "female" tetrahedron. The polarity reverses again when moving to the next tetrachord or tetrahedron [see Figs. 12-6 and 7]. The energy coming into a vertex has three planes (A, B or C) to move along [see Fig. 12-6]. To show the energy flow here we'll start in the middle/top. Once a plane has been chosen (C), it must move in that triangular plane, which gives it the next two notes, *re* and *mi*, at the other two points on that plane.

The movement takes place on one triangular plane and the distance between the notes is exactly the same. However, to reach the fourth and last note, *fa*, and complete this female tetrahedron, it must change to a new plane (half step), thus change its direction [see also Fig. 12-7].

Remember the movements of Genesis and the creation out of nothing [chapter 5, beginning page 147]? Spirit's projections in the Void—shadow forms—are the same concept. When spirit is in the Void, or nothing, the forms it creates are really nothing, too. The rules that spirit has chosen are

Fig. 12-4. The 3D tetrahedron within the Egg of Life.

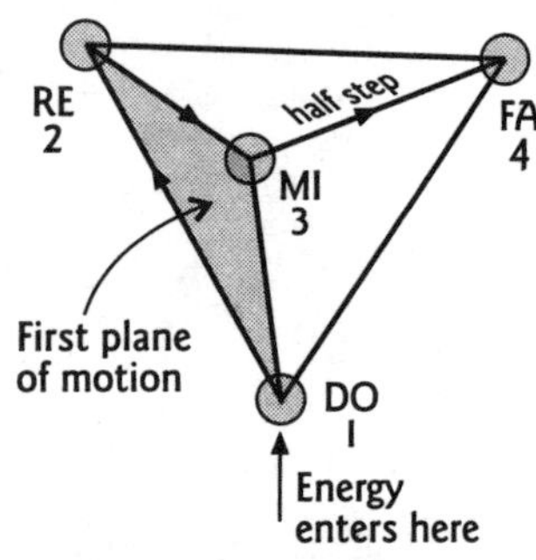

Fig. 12-5. The female tetrahedron. From the bottom point, *do*, a plane is chosen to reach *re* and *mi*; a change in direction (half step) is necessary to reach *fa* on the last vertex of the tetrahedron, completing the first tetrachord of the scale.

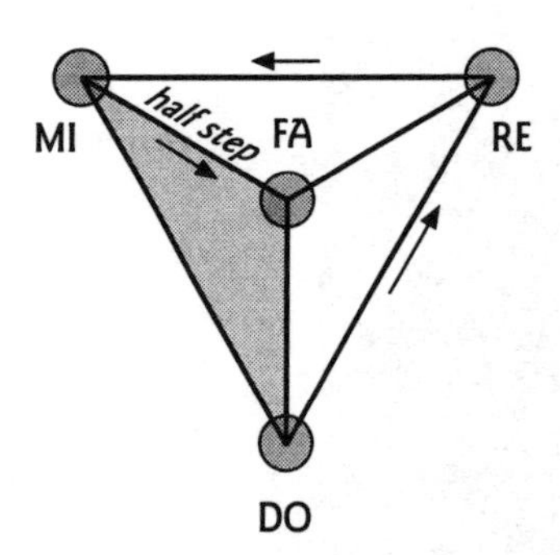

Fig. 12-6. The base of the tetrahedron is chosen for the plane of motion. The final vertex of the tetrahedron must then be *fa*, here seen at the "top" center.

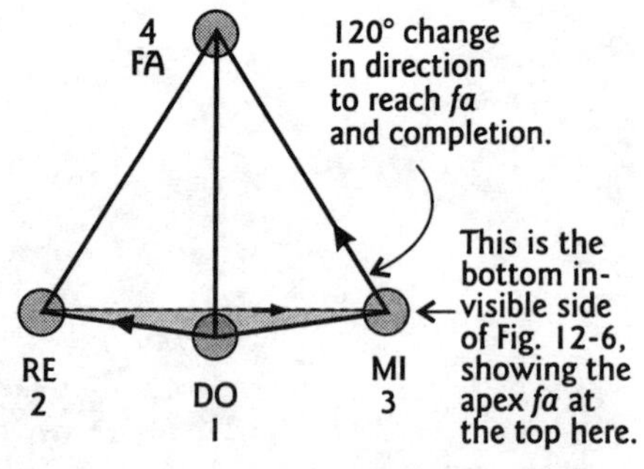

Fig. 12-7. The half step between the third and fourth notes. A 120-degree change in direction is necessary in order to move to another plane to reach *fa* at the last remaining vertex.

that everything can be seen as either 2D or 3D but must be in 2D first. Two-dimensional reality is primary, before the 3D world.

When spirit looks at the movement on one plane of the tetrahedron and a change of direction occurs, the shadow form of the 2D world (the distance traveled is seen as a shadow) appears about half the distance of the first two movements on the triangular plane. Geometrically, the shadow is slightly longer than half, and I believe this is the actual experience. It is labeled a half step. In truth, it is the same distance as the other three notes, but experientially for spirit, it seems like a half movement, which results in this world as a half step between *mi* and *fa*, because, as we said, the 2D world is the source. Now the first female tetrahedron is complete.

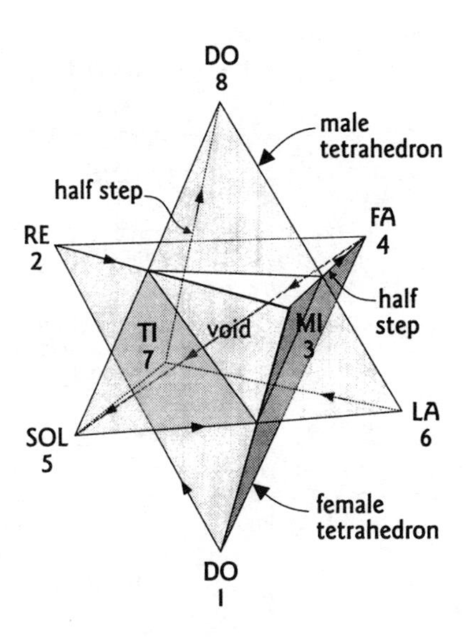

Fig. 12-8. Energy moving between tetrahedrons.

At this point the energy must change from the female to the male tetrahedron [see Fig. 12-8]. It does this by moving from *fa* directly through the center of the star tetrahedron (the interpenetrating male and female tetrahedrons), or the "void," to reach *sol*, the first note of the male tetrahedron. In so doing, it changes polarity from female to male.

The energy will move just as it did in the female tetrahedron, but the plane on which it must move is restricted to the horizontal plane at the bottom of the male tetrahedron (*sol, la, ti*). After choosing one of the three available vertexes for *sol* (5 on the left), it chooses *la* and *ti* to complete that plane.

The energy must now change direction again to complete itself, just as it did in the female tetrahedron. It makes this directional change [Fig. 12-9] to reach the last note, *do*, which becomes the first note of the next tetrahedron. Death becomes birth, transition from one form into another. Male becomes female and the procedure begins anew.

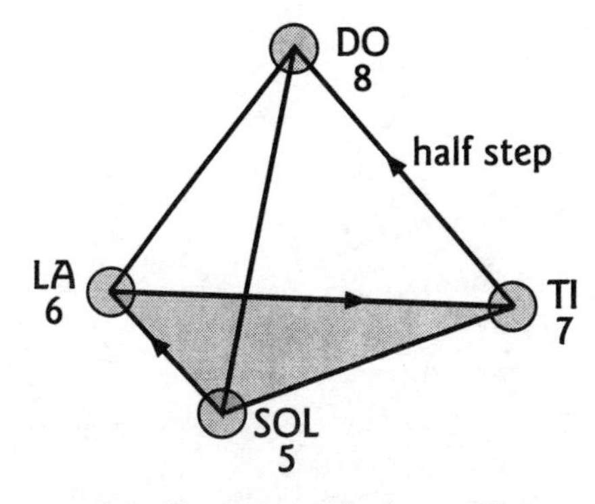

Fig. 12-9. The male tetrahedron, making its directional change to *do*, the first note/vertex of the next (female) tetrahedron.

Anew? Yes, because there is a complex of star tetrahedrons—at the very least a chain of star tetrahedrons—in all the systems we are discussing. Just as in music, there are octaves above and below this one, which theoretically continue forever. It is the same in music as it is for consciousness and even the dimensional levels we spoke of in chapter 2. As for the energy moving up the chakras, it is the same, too. There are chakra systems above *and* below the system you experience. This can be seen as the geometrical basis for immortality. Spirit just keeps moving up or down as it wishes, leaving one world (body) only to enter another.

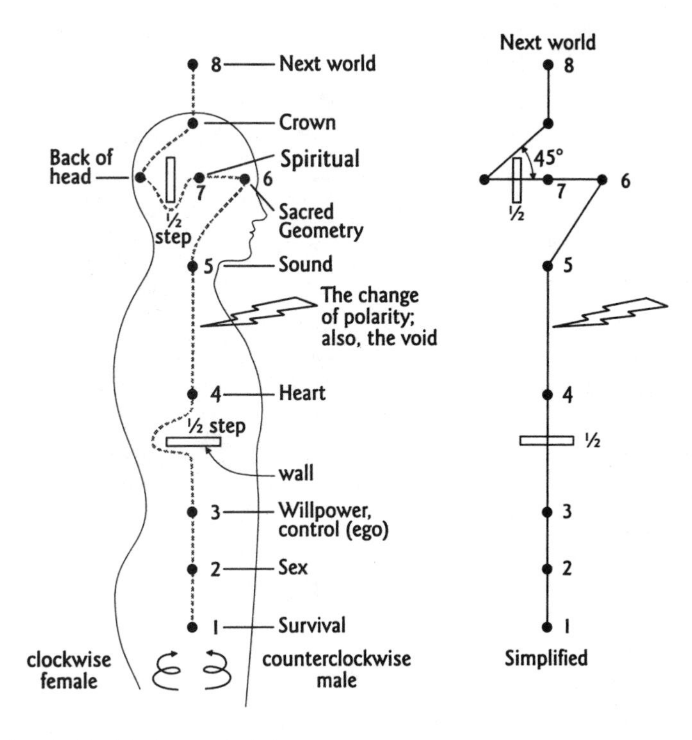

Fig. 12-10. The human 8-chakra system.

The Human Chakras and the Musical Scale

Let's look at the human chakras [Fig. 12-10] and see how they move in exactly the same way as the musical scale. (The chakra placement is not perfect on this drawing.)

Moving topographically on the surface of the body, notice the three lower chakra points. The first one is near the base of the spine, the second one is 7.23 centimeters higher, topographically, and the third one is 7.23 centimeters higher than that. This is an average for *all* humans, and it's the same as the average distance between our eyes, although you personally might be different. After the third chakra, there is a change in direction at the "wall" shown above it, which we'll call a half step.

This half step is crucial to human evolution, and it is revealed only when the spirit is ready and has mastered its position in this new world. To the spirit in the body, this half step is hidden, not apparent. The spirit simply cannot see it until the time is right.

Once this half step is found and passed, the energy flows to the heart, the throat, the pituitary gland and the pineal gland before it encounters another wall/half step that again stops the flow. This "wall" is located between the back of the head and the pituitary gland and is perpendicular to the plane of the first wall. Once the energy has moved past this second half step, it reaches the eighth and final chakra of this octave. This eighth chakra is, in Hindi, called the Godhead, for it is the goal of all life. It is located exactly one hand-length above your head.

The eighth chakra is just the beginning, or first note, of another set of chakras above the head. There is also another set of chakras below the ones in your body, and from which you have come.

There are two primary ways the energy can move up through the body, one male and the other female. First, the energy always moves in a spiral, and when it spirals counterclockwise relative to the body, it's male; when it spirals the other way, it's female, which is clockwise relative to the body. The human spirit's main focus starts at the bottom of the chakra system when you're born, then moves up during your life through the various stages.

Each chakra has a quality, which is noted on the above drawing. The first is survival, the second is sex, the third is willpower, the fourth is the heart or emotions, the fifth is sound, the sixth is the sacred geometry of creation, the seventh is spiritual and the eighth is the next world of existence.

When beings come into a brand-new reality where they've never been before—babies coming to Earth, for example—they have one thing on their mind and one thing only. They want to be able to survive and stay here; their whole focus is on being able to survive this new world, so they do everything they can to stay. As we mentioned, the first chakra becomes like a lens through which you interpret this new reality, and the interpretation requires your whole focus, just trying to stay in this new world.

The moment survival has been achieved, it becomes apparent to the spirit that one or two more chakras are available. (It's actually two, but spirit may see only one.) The rest of the chakras are not apparent because of the half-step wall. The half step hides the higher chakras from spirit, at least until spirit has learned to master the lower chakras and wisdom shows the way into the higher understanding.

Once survival has been achieved, you desire to make contact with the beings in that reality—this is instinctual. When you're a baby, that's usually interpreted as making contact with your mother, especially her breast in this reality, but in fact it is sexual in nature.

As you get older, the desire for contact becomes purely sexual; you want physical contact with the beings in this world. In higher worlds it takes on different connotations, but basically you locate and make contact with the life in that new world. So we call that chakra the sexual one. After you've survived and made contact with the beings, you now have the third chakra available, which has to do with wanting to learn how to manipulate and control the new reality, or what you might call willpower. You want to know how things work, what the laws are in this new world. How do you do it? You spend all your time trying to figure out physical things. Using your willpower, you begin to try to control the physical world. In higher worlds, physical is different from physical in the third dimension, but there is still a correspondence between the worlds.

Your efforts to understand the reality are interpreted in many ways as time goes on. When you're a baby there's a particularly interesting time, often called the terrible twos, where you want to know *everything* about the world around you and test to see what you can and cannot do. You pick up everything, break it, throw it in the air, look for something else—in short, do everything you're not supposed to do. This child will continue until he/she is satisfied in her understanding of the physical world.

When you're a baby, you don't know that there's a change in direction after the third chakra; there's something like a wall obscuring the next four chakras. The child is not aware of the many more chakra lessons to come. There's more to life, but the child is totally oblivious to it. On Earth, even when we become an adult, we may not know there are higher centers in the body. Much of the world is still living in the first three chakras. But that is changing fast, because Mother Earth is waking up.

The Wall with a Hidden Doorway

God put this wall or half step or change in direction there so that you won't know it until you've mastered all the lower centers to a certain degree. So when you're growing up, you're in only the three lower chakras. You may be in all of them at once or maybe mostly in one and partly in the others; or it could be a balanced blend or combination of all three.

This pattern is true of a person, a country, a planet, a galaxy or anything alive; at any level of existence, this same pattern of movement occurs. Let's take a country like the United States. We're a brand-new country in an old world; we're young relative to countries in Europe or elsewhere; we're just a baby. Until the 1950s, the vast majority of people in this country were in one of the three lower chakras—not everybody, of course, but most people. They were concerned with control, money, materialism, houses, cars, sex, food, especially with survival aspects, making sure they stored up enough money to feel secure. That was a really materialistic world. Then in the '60s changing consciousness began to rapidly alter what was thought to be normal. People began to meditate and enter the higher chakras.

If you go to an old country like India, Tibet and parts of China, places that have been around a long, long time and, as a country, have found their way through the wall with a hidden doorway to the next level, they moved up into the fourth, fifth, sixth and seventh chakras. And as they moved through these higher four centers, they eventually came to another block after the seventh chakra, stopping further progress.

The lower part of our body has three centers and the upper part has four. Once a country or a person goes beyond the first half step, they're never the same again. Once they *know* there's something more, they'll spend the rest of their life trying to figure out how to get back to the upper centers, even if they had just a fleeting experience of the higher worlds.

In terms of a person or a country, though, once it gets above the first half step, moving up into the heart, the sound currents, the geometries and the spiritual nature of things, what sometimes happens is that they lose their concern about the lower centers of consciousness. They don't really care about their physical side very much—whether their house is nice or anything like that. They're more concerned about the information and experiences they're learning about the nature of these higher centers. So sometimes when you look at these older countries, they seem to be physically almost devastated because their whole focus is toward trying to find out what this Reality is about on the higher levels. An example of this kind of country is India.

Once a country has actually reached and focused on the seventh chakra, which is very difficult, its only concern is what happens after death, the next level of life. This was the case in ancient Egypt.

The doorway or half step between these two chakra groups is in a place (direction) where, under normal conditions, you would never find it; you wouldn't even know it existed. You might have to go through quite a few lifetimes before you even learned of the existence of a doorway to these upper chakras—especially if you lead a simple, conventional life. But inevitably, especially in a country or person that's spiritually focused, the doorway will be found.

Ways to Find the Secret Doorway

I feel that in the beginning—in the *new* beginning, after the fall during the end times of Atlantis—humans first started experiencing this higher level of consciousness that had been lost. It was through near-death experiences, because death was something that everyone experienced. When someone dies, he goes through the first doorway and finds other worlds, other interpretations of Reality. They may experience another reality for only a short time, then something happens. Instead of totally dying, they come back into their body. But they still have that memory. People who go through this kind of experience are completely changed, and they're probably going to do everything they can to find out what happened to them. They'll really question this other aspect of life, which is related to the higher chakras.

Possibly the next group of humans who found their way through to a higher level were those who took psychedelics. Psychedelics have been used all over the world and throughout history by almost every religious culture I know of. Psychedelics are not drugs in the normal sense. They're very different from pleasure drugs like opium, heroin, crack and similar substances, which can actually do exactly the opposite of psychedelics. The pleasure drugs tend to enhance the lower centers and make you feel good, but they trap you in those lower centers. Gurdjieff felt that in terms of the spiritual path, cocaine was the worse drug of all. I'm not judging anybody about this, but that was his opinion of cocaine, because it causes a particular delusion and increases the sense of ego. It heads you in the opposite direction that spirituality normally takes.

But the psychedelics do something different, and they are not usually physically addicting like the pleasure drugs. The Incas used San Pedro cactus mixed with a little bit of the coca leaf. (Coca leaf is completely different from cocaine.) Some of the Native Americans (Indians) use a psychedelic called peyote, which is legal for them since it is part of their religion. All over the walls in Egypt, in about 200 locations, you'll find images of the *Amanita muscaria* mushroom, a big white mushroom with red dots. At least one book has been written solely about this subject [*The Sacred Mushroom* by Andrija Puharich].

In the United States in the 1960s, LSD took people through this doorway to the higher chakras—specifically, LSD-25. Over twenty million Americans took LSD-25 and were blasted through into the upper centers or chakras. Most of them were totally out of control, with no initiation. The ancient cultures made significant preparations before they used these kinds of psychedelics, but there was no preparation for most of these Americans in the '60s, and there were a lot of casualties. They were blasted through into the higher chakras. In most cases they landed in the heart; they had a major sense of expansion and of becoming love and all of creation.

However, they could have landed in the fifth chakra of the sound currents if they began their experience with music. There would have been nothing to stop them. Music automatically leads you into the fifth chakra, and many times that was the case. The fifth chakra is a totally different experience from the heart chakra, just as the sex chakra is extremely different from the survival chakra.

If the person experimenting went up far enough to reach the sixth chakra, he would have found the sacred geometries that created the universe. A person who went into this chakra would have had incredible geometrical experiences, where all of life would appear geometrical.

A few rare people may have found their way into the seventh chakra, which is spiritual. At this level there is really only one concern: how to find the way to become one with God, how to connect directly with God. It's the only interest a person in that center would have. Nothing else would matter.

But the problem with psychedelics is that the person is always thrown back down to the lower centers and the 3D reality when the drug wears off. They are changed forever by the experience, and usually they continue to seek a way to return to these higher worlds, and it is usually *not* through psychedelics.

The psychedelic era did one permanent thing for sure—it opened the doorway or the half step for the consciousness of the United States as a country. It gave people an experience that showed them the higher worlds really existed. Since then, millions of those people have been spending their lives trying to get back to those higher sacred places, and in so doing, they are changing the country and the world.

I think the next stage of evolution came along when people were trying to figure out how to get back to that higher state of consciousness without having to use drugs. We had our gurus and yogis, meditations and various spiritual practices, religious and spiritual experiences seeking the way. In the late '60s and '70s we were fixated with spiritual teachers. There are all kinds of meditations and spiritual paths that will lead you into a place calm enough for you to find the doorway and go through this wall. One way is not better than another; the concern is only about which one will work for you.

Eventually, after you've been dwelling in the fourth through seventh chakras and have mastered them, you'll come to another wall, which is at 90 degrees to the lower one. The angles you must negotiate to get through the top wall are different—and tricky. But if you can find your way through, you can actually transcend this third-dimensional world and go into next world, which all of life here on Earth will follow someday. You die here and you're born somewhere else. You leave this place and enter a new place. Spirit is eternal and always has been. We'll talk about this new place soon. It is not some*where* to go, it is really more a state of being.

In Egypt, after initiates had twenty-four years of training, they were given an appropriate psychedelic and put in the sarcophagus in the King's Chamber for three days and two nights (sometimes up to an extra day).

The primary experience they sought was to find this doorway and enter the higher worlds, then return to Earth to help others. This becomes apparent to almost everyone who reaches for these higher levels: There is only one thing to do when you return to Earth—serve all life, for it becomes very apparent through this experience that you *are* all life.

Eventually most seekers around the world search for a way different from a near-death experience or drugs. They search for a way that comes from nature, a way that is contained within themselves before they were even born. The search is always the same. No matter what religion or spiritual discipline, no matter what technique or form of meditation, no matter what words are used to describe their experiences, it is the doorway, either the first or the second one, that will always be the focus of their seeking.

Chakras on Our Star Tetrahedrons

Those eight chakras that run up through our bodies have duplicates in the space around our bodies [Fig. 12-11]. They are spheres of energy that vary in size, depending on the person's size. The radius of these spheres is the same length as a person's hand, measured from the tip of the longest finger to the first wrinkle on the wrist. (My sphere has about a 9-inch radius, or 18-inch diameter.)

They are actual spheres of energy that sit on the points of the star tetrahedral field that's around your body in space. They are, in fact, your chakras, "duplicated" in the space around your body. You can detect or feel the spheres when you enter the spherical area, but the actual chakra is like a pinpoint—it's very little and in the exact center—located at the apex of each point of your star tetrahedron.

When I had access to a molecular emissions scanner (MES), we were able to see these things. Days before I quit working in the field of technology, we measured our bodies and focused on the centers of our chakra points located at the tips of our star tetrahedrons. First we searched with the sensor head of the MES, but the machine didn't sense a thing. But when we went through the center point, the computer screen would light up. Once we found it, we had to lock in on it; then we could take a microwave "photograph," which looked like a chakra inside the body. We found out that each inner chakra has a living pulse associated with each external chakra and the system as a whole. I was preparing to figure out what this pulse was tied to when I left, so I don't know the answer. Of course, the first thing we would have checked was the heartbeat. But the body produces other rhythms, and at this time we do not know.

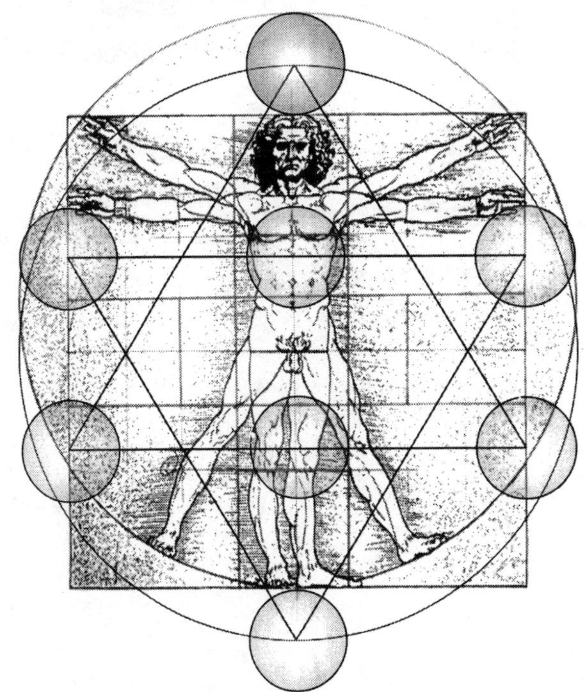

Fig. 12-11. Leonardo's canon with eight spheres.

The Egyptian 13-Chakra System

Now we will explore the expanded energies of the chromatic chakra system, the system with thirteen chakras. I would like to preface this section with the acknowledgment that this information is not necessary for most of you to know. It is very complex, and for some of you it will only make it harder to understand the energy flows within the body. Either skip this section or read it with an "information only" attitude if you feel you need to.

When a person uses the 13-chakra system instead of the 8, there is something that needs to be understood, or great confusion will occur. From what I have learned, you cannot use both systems at once. You must use one or the other, but not both simultaneously. It is a mystery, except to say that the very same thing happens in quantum physics: You can see the Reality as made up of either particles (atoms) or vibration (waveform), but if you try to superimpose both systems at once, neither will work.

For example the "void" step between the fourth and the fifth note of a scale happens between the heart and the throat chakras in the 8-chakra system. But in the 13-chakra system it happens between the two hearts, between the sixth and the seventh chakras. The reason is that spirit is using two entirely different views or systems of movement in the star tetrahedron. We will try to make it as simple as possible.

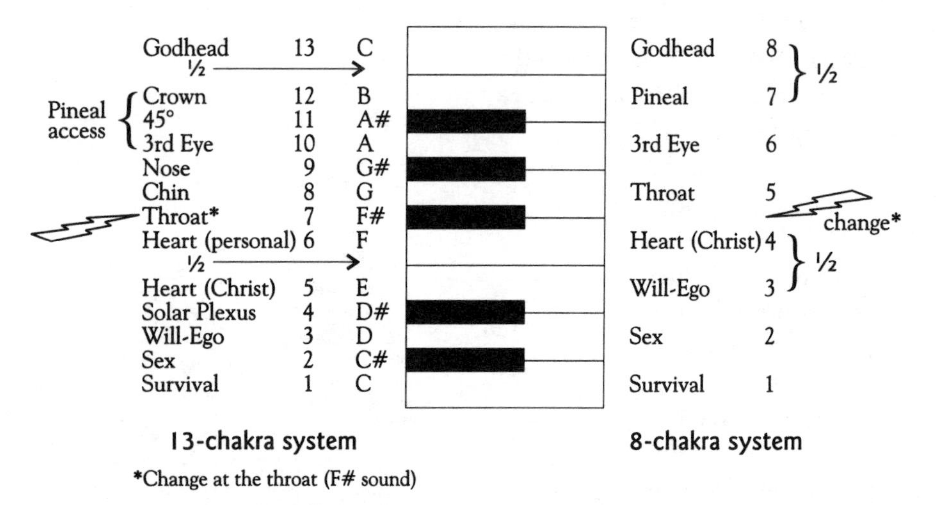

Fig. 12-12. The piano scale and the 13-chakra (chromatic) and 8-chakra (major scale) systems.

In the chromatic scale, best seen on piano keys, adding the five black keys to the eight white keys that make up the C major scale totals thirteen notes [Fig. 12-12]. In other words, when you add the pentatonic scale of the five black keys (C# D# F# G# A#) to the C major scale (the white keys C D E F G A B C), you get the chromatic scale. All other scales on the piano are similar, but they will use sharps or flats. Beginning with *do* (or C, since the C scale is easiest to see on a keyboard), we have the following chromatic scale:

C, C#, D, D#, **E, F,** F#, G, G#, A, A#, **B, C**

The half steps are between E and F and between B and C (bolded). Notice that there is no sharp (black) note in between these pairs. The special void between the fourth and fifth note of an octave is between F and G, where the second tetrachord begins [see the lightning bolt on the right in Fig. 12-12]. In the chromatic scale it is different, because the flow is based on a different view of the star tetrahedron. We will first look at how the chromatic scale is laid out, then talk about the flow.

The chromatic scale has twelve notes, and the thirteenth is the return, or the first note of the next scale. In every octave there are seven notes, and the eighth is the return. This means that the eighth chakra of the octave and the thirteenth chakra of the chromatic scale are the same note and have the same role.

Fitting these two harmonic systems together in the chakra system gives us the chromatic 13-chakra system, which is far more complete than the 8 system. Many questions that will arise are answered when using the expanded chromatic chakra system. For instance, it is only with this system that you will find the topographical (body surface) distance of 7.23 cm between chakras.

So some things are possible using the 13 system that are not possible in the 8 system and vice versa. Therefore, sometimes we will use the 8 system and sometimes the 13 system. We will always tell you which one we are using.

There are many other systems of harmonics and scales, all of which are used in various ways by nature to arrange the harmonic relationships around us. I say, however, that *all* harmonic systems of music are derived from a single sacred geometric form, but this is not necessary to know now for the work we are doing. This single sacred geometric form is related to the tetrahedron, but is too complex to bring up here.

One of the systems we talked about is the dimensional levels of creation (chapter 2, page 43). If you reread this section now, it will begin to make much more sense.

Discovering the True Chakra Locations

We were able to look into the body with the molecular emissions scanner, and we could see the microwaves coming from each chakra and locate them precisely. But we found that the images coming off these chakras were not always located where some of the books said they were. For one thing, many books I read said that the thirteenth chakra was anywhere from four to six finger-widths above the head—but there's nothing there! We searched and searched this area, because that's what the books said, but still there was nothing there. But when we went where the geometries were indicating, which is one hand-length above the top of the head, bingo, there it was! We could see the screen light up with activity.

Another obvious difference was the third chakra of the 8 system. According to most martial arts teachings and many Hindu philosophies, the third chakra is either one or two finger-widths below the navel. But there's nothing there, either—nothing! We searched and searched that area, but we found it in the most obvious place, also predicted by the geometries. When you look at the absolute geometrical center of the navel, you find the third chakra.

I suspect that somebody along the line told a white lie. They tried to make it secret because they knew that this chakra was a very important place, and I think they purposely distorted the information. Secrecy through distortion in the sciences and in religious and spiritual matters, especially in the last 2000 years, has been rampant.

A Body-Surface Chakra Map

The other thing the Egyptians say about the 13-chakra system is that the centers are found topographically—on the surface of your body—and evenly spaced. The actual chakras are not evenly spaced inside the breathing tube, but the *entry points* are evenly spaced over the surface of your body. And they're separated by exactly the distance between the centers of your eyes. The distance between your eyes is the same as the distance between the tip of your nose and the tip of your chin and several other pertinent places on your body. If you are overweight, this will not work, but you can try.

Make that distance your measuring unit, then lie down on a flat, hard surface, like a floor, and put one finger at your perineum. This locates the survival chakra, the first chakra. (The perineum is the piece of skin located between the anus and the vagina in females, and between the anus and the scrotum in males.) When you measure from there one length over the surface of your body, it will mark the second chakra, the sexual chakra, which is on or just past your pubic bone.

Measuring upward from the sexual chakra, you'll find that your thumb goes right inside your navel, locating the third chakra.

One measure beyond your navel, your thumb will go exactly inside the mouth of the solar plexus, the fourth chakra of the 13-chakra system.

When you come up one more measure, you'll come to the fifth chakra, the Christ chakra, the first heart chakra. It's located a little above the sternum bone.

When you take the next measure, it will exactly mark the sixth chakra, which is the second heart chakra. The first heart chakra, which is more primal, is universal unconditional love for all life. It is love for God, whereas the sixth chakra is love for *part* of life. If you fall in love with a person, you feel it in this upper center. Even if you fall in love with a planet, as long as it's only a portion of the Reality, no matter how big it is, you'll feel it in the upper heart.

Both heart chakras are on white keys in the chromatic scale. This is very interesting, because that happens to be exactly where the half step is located—between them on the 13-chakra system [see Fig. 12-12].

When you measure once again (remember, you have to be lying on a flat surface), you'll find that your thumb will hit the Adam's apple, if you're male. Of course, if you're female, you don't have one, so it's harder to tell. This is the seventh chakra of the chromatic scale.

When you take the next measure, it will touch your chin, which is chakra number eight. The chakra point on the chin is a really powerful one. It's seldom talked about, though Yogi Bhajan has talked about it in his discourses to his pupils. He considers it one of the most important chakras.

Measuring again, you'll reach the nose, which is the ninth chakra point. And when you take the next measure, you'll touch your third eye, the tenth chakra.

Measure once again, and it marks just above the top of your forehead to the eleventh chakra, a place we call the 45-degree chakra, which I'll tell you about below.

One more measure to the top of your head will touch the crown chakra, which is chakra number twelve. Then one hand-length above your head you will find your thirteenth chakra, the end of this system and the beginning of the next one.

The reason we call the eleventh chakra the 45-degree chakra has to do with how the tenth, eleventh and twelfth centers are connected to the pineal [Fig. 12-13]. Remember when I talked about the pineal gland as an eye? Well, it seems that when the pineal gland "looks" or projects energy to the pituitary gland, it produces the third-eye perception. There's another line of energy that projects from the pineal to where the eleventh chakra is located; this sits at a 45-degree angle (average) from the pituitary projection. I believe it is exactly 45 degrees, but I can't prove it. Then there's another projection, which goes straight up and out of the crown. All these last three chakras are focusing in on or projecting out from the pineal gland.

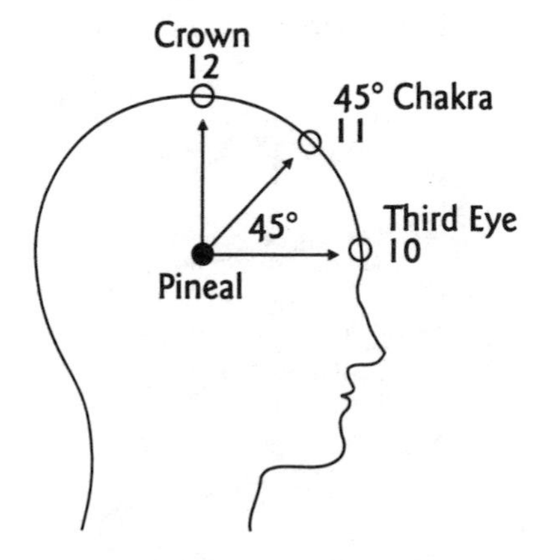

Fig. 12-13. Three chakras of the pineal gland.

Here is another contradiction between the two chakra systems. The 8 system sees the pineal as the chakra from which one moves into the next world. In the 13 system, this chakra has three access points and has ways of working with this energy that are different from the simple 8 system.

Another interesting note: In the 8 system, the first half step is found between the universal heart and the throat (sound). However, the first half step in the 13 system is located between the *universal* heart (the love for all life everywhere) and the *personal* heart (the love for someone or something). This is between the fifth and the sixth chakras in this system. This difference between the Christ consciousness and the personal love of human consciousness is one of the most important areas of understanding in spiritual work; and that happens to be exactly where the change in direction takes place. The next half step above, between the twelfth and thirteenth chakras, is also a crucial place, and this again is different from the 8 system. It's a crucial place, because that's when you move from one world or dimension to another. But both half steps (and the individual chakras themselves) provide the essential lessons of life.

A Different Movement on the Star Tetrahedron

It seems as though spirit decided that there was more than one way to move through the star tetrahedron. When we use the 8-chakra system, it is pretty simple, but in using the 13-chakra system, spirit becomes far more complex. I was going to offer a possible way that spirit could move through

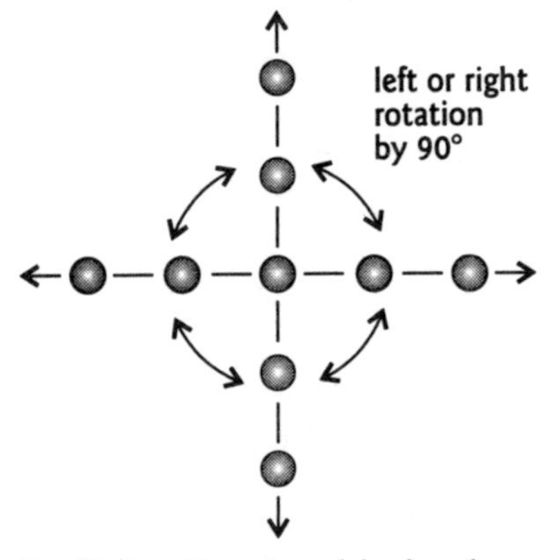

Fig. 12-14a. Top view of the five channels, seen as a horizontal line that rotates up the spinal column.

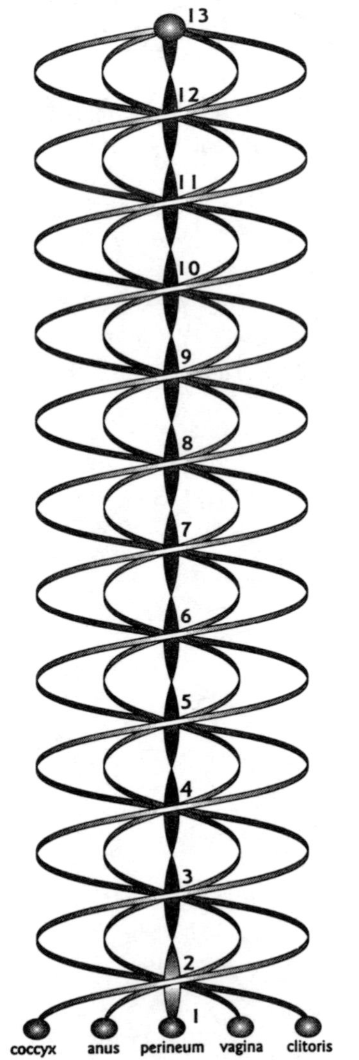

Fig. 12-14b. Rotation of the spiral of light up the chakras, a female seen from the side.

the star tetrahedron and still meet the requirements of the Reality perfectly, but after looking at it, I decided that it would probably cause more confusion than help. So if you really want to know, do it yourself. Try the top or bottom view of the tetrahedron first. Clue: One tetrahedron will give only the white keys and the other only the black keys (sharps or flats).

The Five Spiraling Light Channels

Both of the previous two chakra systems show a very simplified understanding of the full chakra system, which is really much more complex than what has been presented so far. Although we have been talking about one channel that connects all the chakras that the energy flows through, there are actually *five different channels* and four additional chakras associated with each major chakra. They are set out in a horizontal line, 90 degrees to the vertical [Fig. 12-14a], and they rotate in 90-degree increments as they rise up the central column [Fig. 12-14b].

Three of these channels are primary, the outside two and the central one, and the two others are secondary. This relates to the five different kinds of human consciousness that Thoth talked about in chapter 9. Remember, the first, third and fifth are unity consciousness and the second and fourth are disharmonic consciousnesses. It further relates to the five senses and the five Platonic solids, but in order to keep it simple, we will not elaborate further.

Before we can discuss these five channels, we must talk about light. By understanding the way light moves in deep space, it will be easier to understand the movement of prana up these chakras. All forms of energy have a single source, and that source is prana or chi or life-force energy. It is consciousness itself, awareness, spirit—spirit, which began its journey in the Void, creating imaginary circles and lines.

To study light is to study the movements of spirit through its sacred dance into nature. Spirit made it so. We have been studying the movements of spirit, but now we will become more specific in our discussion. We will study light first, then return later to this discussion of chakras.

Let There Be Light

This simple drawing in Figure 12-15 is the most important one I've ever done for my understanding of the Reality. Do you remember that when I talked about the first day of Genesis—which probably seems like a thousand years ago—we went from the Void to the top of the first sphere? And when we got to the top and formed the second sphere, we formed a vesica piscis? In the Bible, after the first motion of God upon "the face of the waters," He immediately said, "Let there be light." Remember that I said I would show you that the vesica piscis *is* light? Well, Figure 12-15 shows the energies of a vesica piscis. It's much more complex than this, but this is enough to show the relationship between it and light.

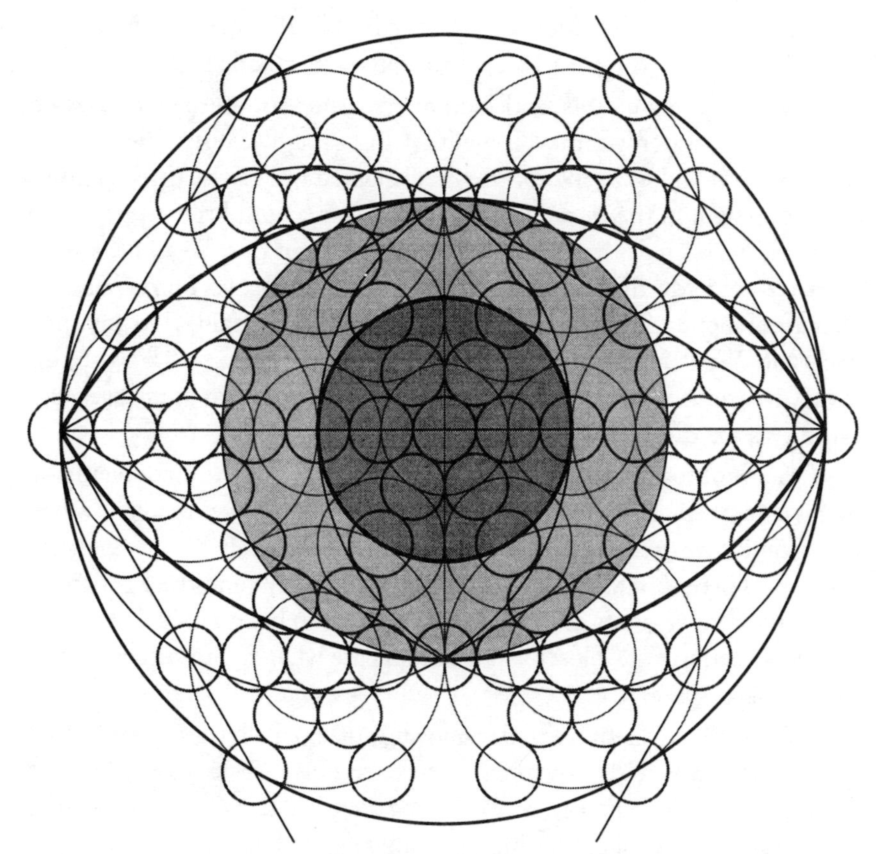

Fig. 12-15. "The Eye," a sacred geometry drawing.

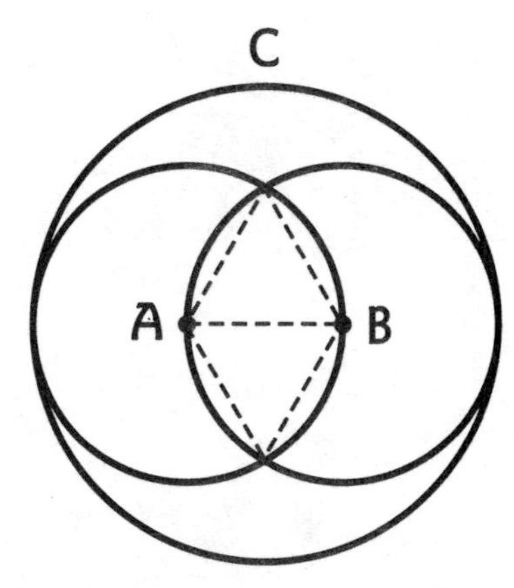

Fig. 12-16a. Vesica piscis created by two circles, here enclosed within a larger circle.

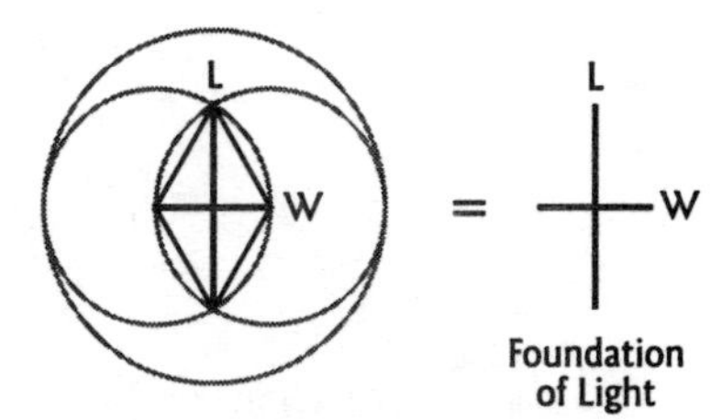

Fig. 12-16b. Same drawing with diamond and cross inside the vesica piscis.

In Figure 12-16a circles A and B pass through each other's centers, forming a vesica piscis, and both fit perfectly inside circle C. This vesica piscis is further delineated by the lines inside it, which form two equilateral triangles. The length (L) and width (W) of these two triangles together form a cross [see 12-16b]. This cross is the foundation of light.

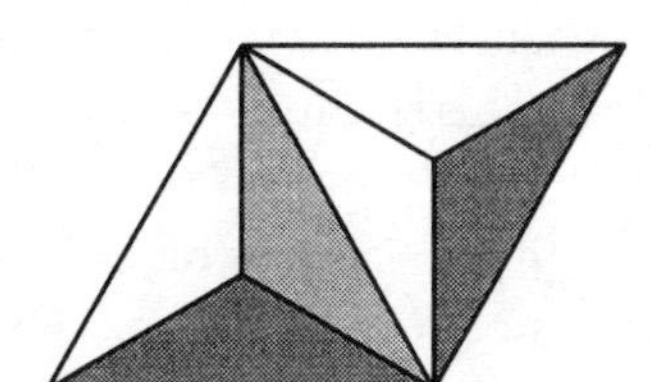

Fig. 12-17a. Top view of two 3D tetrahedrons with edges touching.

Notice now that these two triangles are really two edge-to-edge 3D tetrahedrons [Fig. 12-17a] (imagine two tetrahedrons sitting on a table with their edges touching, viewed from above), fully visible and contained perfectly inside the vesica piscis in Figure 12-17b. L is the length of a vesica piscis and W is the width. Every time the vesica piscis rotates by 90 degrees, a new one is created [see the smaller and larger crosses in the figure], and the length of the smaller one becomes the width of the larger. The drawing begins to form a shape that looks like an eye. This progression can continue forever, moving both toward and away from the center. This is a geometrical progression of relationships within the vesica

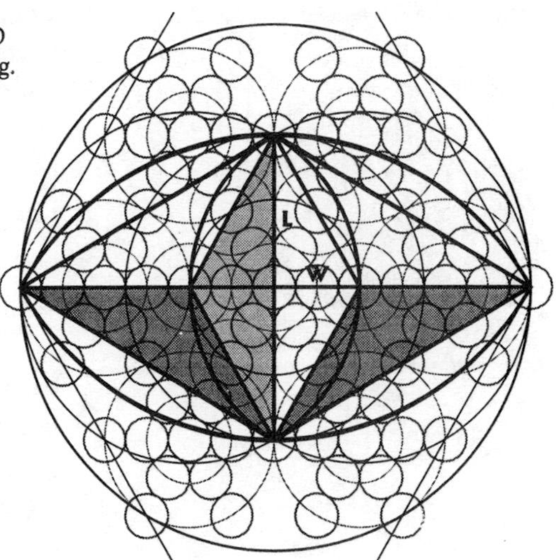

Fig. 12-17b. Two edge-to-edge 3D tetrahedrons.

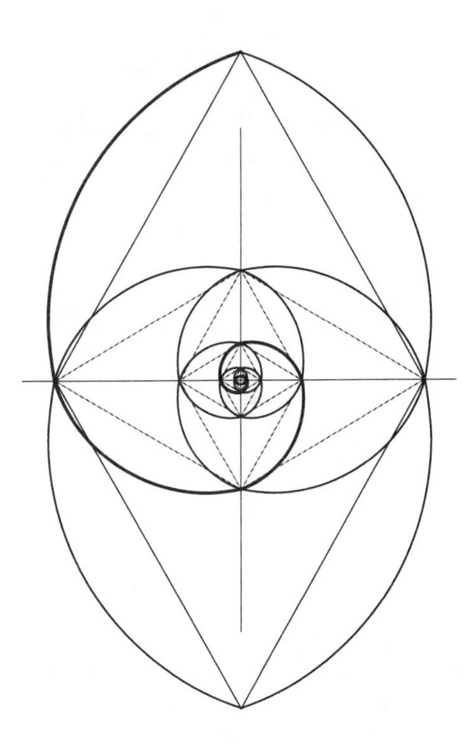

Fig. 12-18. Spirals of light.

piscis that identifies the blueprint of light based on the square root of 3. As you will see below in Figure 12-18, light moves in exactly this way.

When I was giving this workshop many years ago, there was a certain man present. I don't think I'll mention his name because I don't know whether he would want me to. He is considered one of the three greatest experts on light in the world. He is also one of the most brilliant people in the world. This guy's incredible. When he got out of college, he was 23 years old and Martin-Marietta signed him up and gave him a massive amount of money and a large team of scientists. They said, "Do anything you want. We don't care." That's how brilliant this person is. So with this money he studied light. One of the first things he did was study eyes, because eyes are the receivers of light.

If you want to study something in nature, you get to the components—in this case, the light wave and the instrument that receives the light wave, the organic eye—because one will reflect the other in its geometrical makeup. There should be a similarity between the eye and the light wave, and in their movements as well. If you're trying to build an instrument to receive something, the closer you can duplicate what you're receiving, the better you can receive it.

This gentleman discovered, after studying just about all types of eyes on the planet, that there are six categories, just like crystals. There are six different types of eyes on planet Earth, and each living thing within a type has geometric as well as physical similarities with every other living thing in that category.

I met this gentleman when he came to one of my first workshops, and when I flipped this picture on the screen [Fig. 12-18], he nearly fell out of his chair. He started to get a little angry, and he explained why. You see, after all his research—studying and typing eyes and study in related fields—this is the drawing *he* had come up with as the common thread between all eyes. This was how he had categorized them. At first he thought I must have stolen it from him. He knows now that I simply received it from Thoth. But as you know, this information doesn't and cannot belong to anybody. It belongs to all of us, and it's accessible to anybody who asks the right questions. It's embedded in every cell of every living thing.

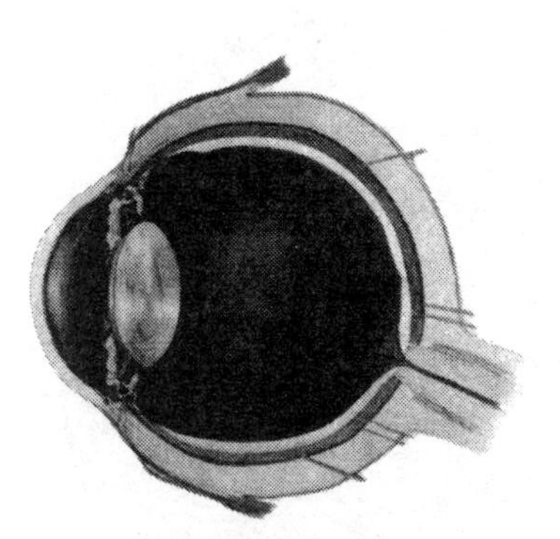

Fig. 12-19. The human eye.

If we look at someone's eyes, we see ovals, but the eye is actually round. It's a ball, a sphere, and there's a lens on one part of the surface [Fig. 12-19]. In Figure 12-15, you can see the round sphere, the oval shape of the vesica piscis and the smaller circle of the iris. You can almost *feel* the correctness of the geometries there with your right brain.

But that eye drawing is much, *much* more than just a drawing. It really shows the geometries behind the eyeball and the geometries of light itself, because they are one and the same. The geometries that create all eyes and the geometries of the entire electromagnetic spectrum, including light, are identical. When the spirit of God made the very first move in Genesis, it created a vesica piscis and immediately said, "Let there be light." It was not a coincidence that light came first.

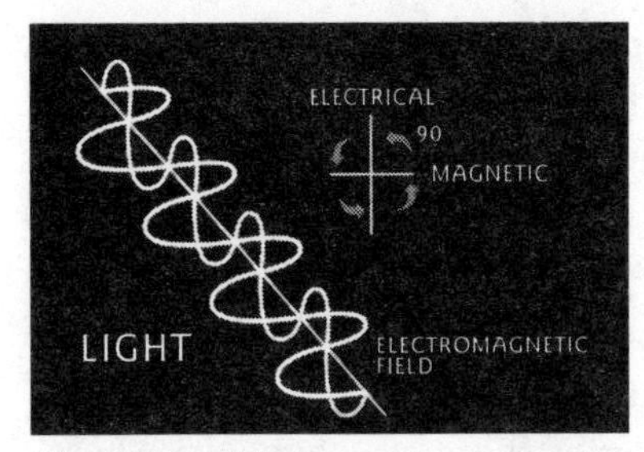

Fig. 12-20. A light wave's movement.

A light wave moves as shown in Figure 12-20. Here you can clearly see the relationship between the vesica piscis and light. An electrical component is moving in a sine wave on one axis at the same time a magnetic component is moving at 90 degrees to it, also in a sine-wave pattern. Simultaneously the entire pattern is rotating in 90-degree segments.

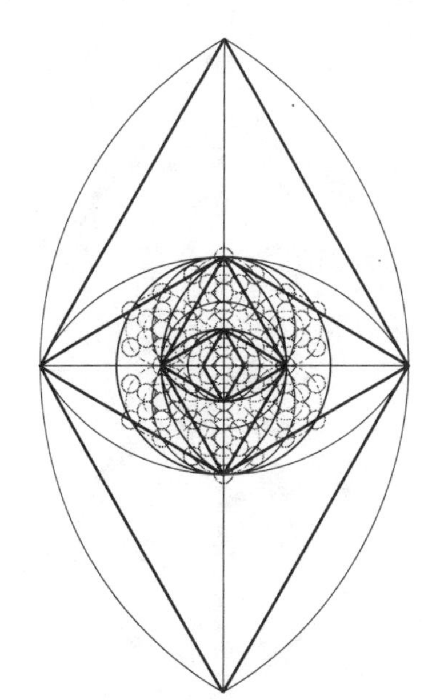
Fig. 12-21. The geometry of light.

If you look at Figure 12-21, you will see the geometry of light. The long axis, or length, of the vesica piscis is the electrical component and the short axis, or width, is the magnetic component, and they are in the square-root-of-3 ratio to each other. In chapter 2 [page 41] I mistakenly said that the length and width of a vesica piscis was in the Golden Mean proportion. Actually, they are related through one of the sacred numbers of the Egyptians, the square root of 3. However, when you look at the pattern created by two vesica pisces at 90 degrees from each other that are set to the Golden Mean and at the square-root-of-3 pattern, it becomes obvious that they are extremely similar. Perhaps nature is trying to duplicate the Golden Mean again, as it has done with the Fibonacci series.

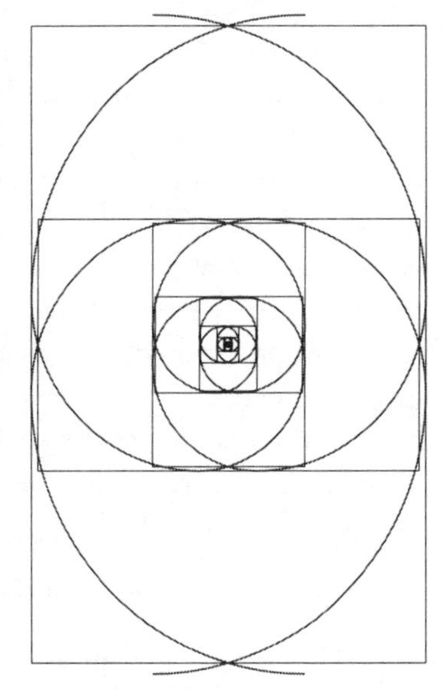
Fig. 12-22a. The geometry of light in Golden Mean spirals.

As light flows in 90-degree turns, it can be seen geometrically by examining how the vesica piscis turns 90 degrees as it moves in or out of the progression. If you can see this, then you will understand the geometry of light in Figure 12-18.

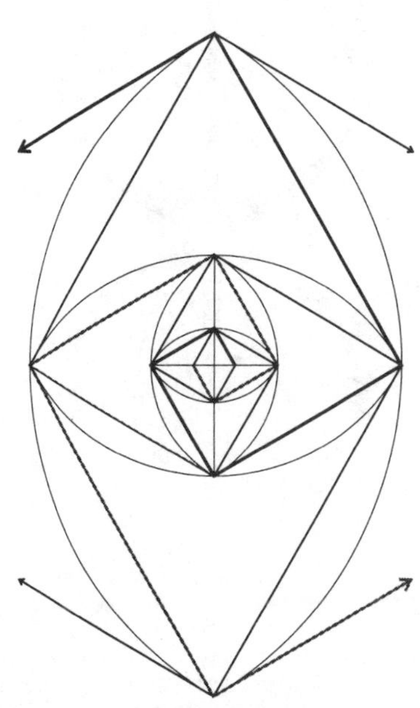
Fig. 12-22b. Four male square-root-of-three spirals coming out of a vesica piscis.

The Golden Mean spirals appear very close to the square-root-of-3 spirals of the vesica piscis, but notice that the rectangles in Figure 12-22a do not quite touch each other as they do in a true vesica piscis.

Interestingly, Figure 12-22b, a drawing of a true vesica piscis, is both the geometry of eyes and light. It is also the geometry of many other natural living things, such as the leaves in Figure 12-23. Leaves are designed by nature to receive light for photosynthesis. In these leaves you can see the same geometry that was in Figure 12-18, the spirals of light.

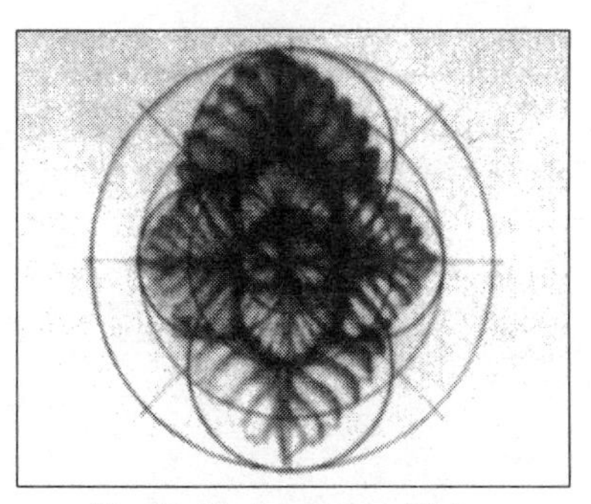
Fig. 12-23. Leaves and light.

Now we will see how the movement of energy up the chakras is similar to the movement of light. (I repeat that this information is for certain people who feel it essential, and that if you wish to skip or just scan this section if it feels too complicated, you can, because you really need only the information about the basic energy flows of the 8- or 13-chakra systems.)

Figure 12-24a is an image of light or energy, of how light spirals as it moves up the spine, just as it moves in deep space, except that in space it continually expands. Figure 12-24b shows how it looks from above.

Now let's see the energy flow. There are five channels where energy ascends the chakras. These five channels spiral up through the body in one of two ways, male or female. The male energy spirals counterclockwise and the female clockwise, as seen from the center of the body.

I'm going to have to be graphic to describe these five channels. There's no way to get around it. If you were beneath a person looking up at their subtle-energy channels (at the genital area), you'd see five channels of energy flowing up through the spine. There are very special connections and openings that appear on a horizontal line, 90 degrees to the vertical tube running through the chakra points. These openings are shown at the bottom of the diagram. That's at the base of a person's trunk at the perineum.

As we have said, the perineum is located between a woman's anus and vagina and a man's anus and scrotum. In that little bit of soft skin at the perineum, there's actually an internal opening, though it cannot be seen. In at least one body therapy, when pressure is placed on the perineum, the finger can actually move about two inches into a person's body. The perineum is the opening to the central tube in which the primary chakras are located. But there are four more openings and energy channels, two on each side [see Fig. 12-25].

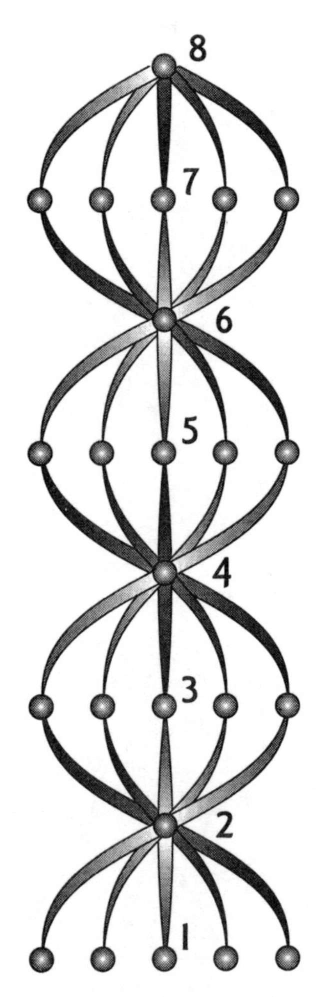

Fig. 12-24a. Spiral of light moving up the eight chakras.

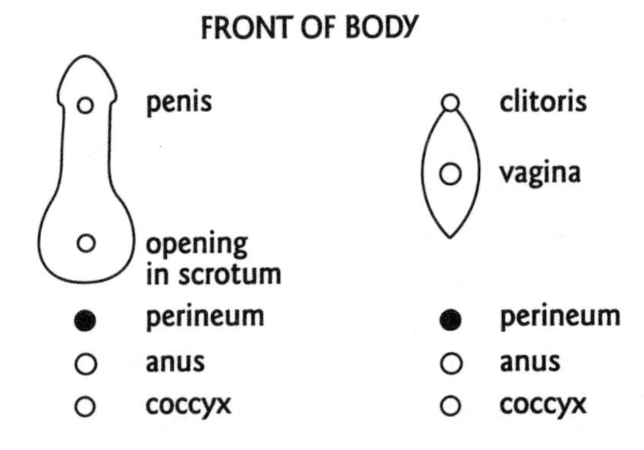

Fig. 12-25. The five openings to the five channels.

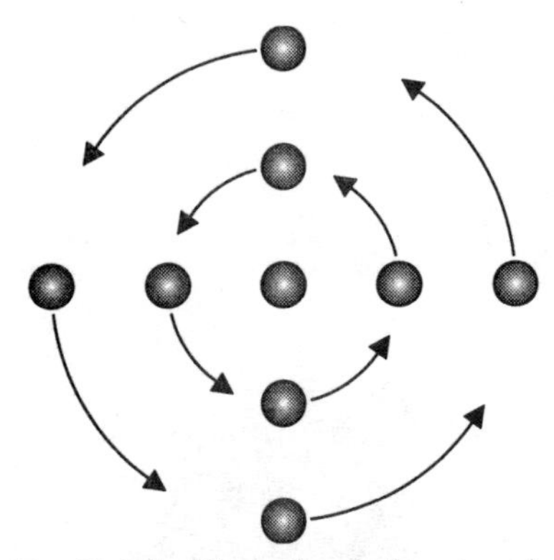

Fig. 12-24b. The male spiral as viewed from above. The female is reversed, or clockwise as seen from above.

Behind the perineum is another opening, the anus, which has an energy flow that spirals upward as shown in the diagram; and behind the anus is another energy flow. The flow originates below the triangular-shaped sacrum, at the tip of the coccyx. This point lines up horizontally with the anus and perineum. The swing is much wider from there (shown graphically in Fig. 12-24a) and it has a more powerful flow of energy than the anus. In front of the perineum is the vagina in females or the opening inside the scrotum in males, where the energy level is similar to that of the anus. In front of that is a more powerful energy flow that is similar in strength to the spine; this originates at the clitoris in females or the penis in males and swings wide, as shown in Figure 12-24a.

Looking at the five channels at the bottom of the trunk, notice that they are laid out in a straight line from front to back. Everything about them flows from back to front with the exception of the male testicles, which are side to side but placed close together. This exception makes sense when you see the fifth chakra in a few minutes. The opening to the vagina is a vesica piscis whose orientation is front to back. The opening to the penis is also a vesica piscis, also oriented front to back. The first-chakra flow itself is laid out front to back, with the single exception mentioned.

We reach the second chakra, rotating 90 degrees either clockwise (female) or counterclockwise (male). Life always tries to conform to these natural energies, and you can see that in many cases these directional energies conform to the physical body parts. Actually, the body parts conform to the directional flow of the internal chakras.

At the level of the second (sexual) chakra, the female fallopian tubes are located to the sides—at 90 degrees to the direction of the first chakra, which is front to back. Spiraling up one more time, we reach the third chakra and the navel. Think of the umbilical cord coming out in a front-to-back direction. As we spiral up to the fourth chakra, the solar plexus, it is shaped like a vesica piscis and is oriented from side to side, 90 degrees to the third chakra.

One more rotation brings us to just above the sternum, where we will see something different from anything below—except, perhaps, the first chakra. That difference can be seen when you look at the rotational pattern.

Figure 12-26a is an overhead view of a person who is facing the top of the page. When we begin this spiral up the spine, the first-chakra energy faces the front (the top of the page). To illustrate, let's say it rotates counterclockwise [shown by arrows at 26a and 26b]. When it comes to the second chakra (2), its rotation would face toward the left. At the third chakra (3), it would face the back (or bottom of the page). At the fourth chakra (4), the solar plexus, it would face to the right. And when it spirals upward to the sternum, the lower heart chakra (5), it has returned to its original direction, facing front again.

So the heart chakra is different because it knows the whole pattern; the energy has made one full circle of 360 degrees. This also happens with a sine-wave curve or a light wave [see 26c]; it has five places to complete itself. At the lower heart chakra, where the cycle completes itself, we find both front-to-back and side-to-side energies. It has made a cross in this very special place. The Egyptians felt that this was one of the most important centers in the body. It's the place of completeness, where we experience our love for God. At this center you see the breasts facing front-to-back in depth but side to side in placement; both directions are happening simultaneously, which we also saw at the testicles in the first chakra, which is the same point on the circle [1 and 5 in Figs. 12-26a or 12-26b].

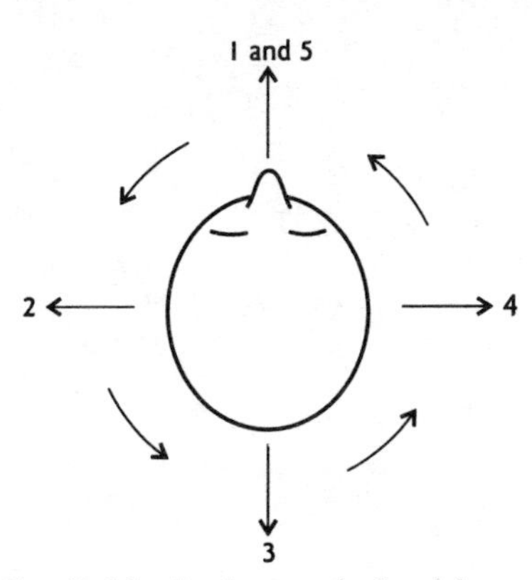

Fig. 12-26a. Looking at the head from above. One complete cycle goes up the spine in five movements, shown by the arrows facing each direction.

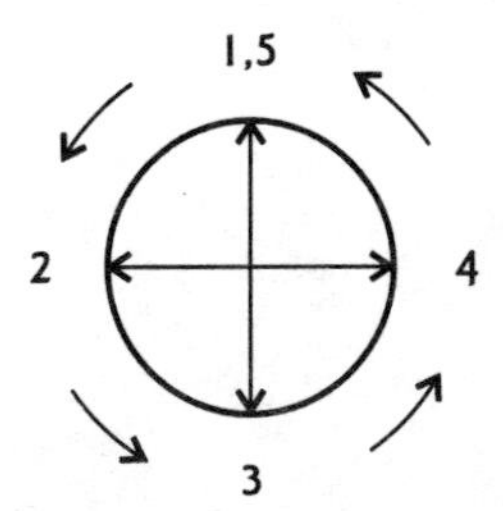

Fig. 12-26b. One complete cycle as a circle.

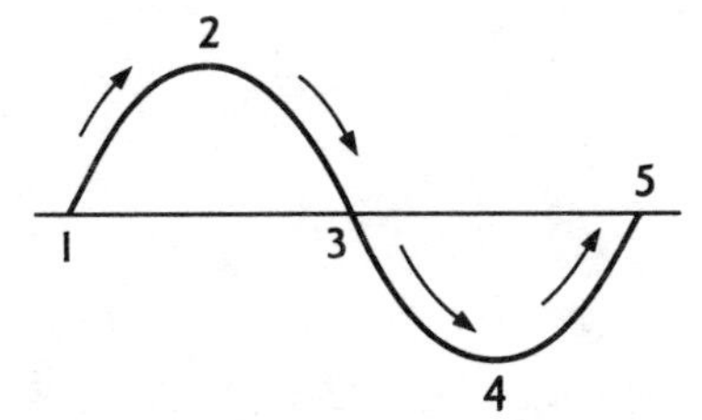

Fig. 12-26c. One complete cycle as a sine wave or light wave.

Egyptian Sexual Energy and the Orgasm

Here we will take a small sidestep to discuss an immense subject—the importance of sexual energy and the human organism. It was believed in ancient Egypt that the orgasm was the key to eternal life, and that it was intimately connected with the fifth chakra. First we will explain the connection to eternal life.

When humans today practice sexual energy and orgasm, little concern is given to what happens to this energy when it is released. Most people in the world are ignorant about what happens to their sexual energy after they have an orgasm. Usually the energy moves up the spine and out the top of the head directly into the eight or thirteenth chakra. In a few rare cases, the sexual energy is released down the spine into the hidden center below the feet, the point opposite the one above the head. In either case, the sexual energy, the concentrated life-force energy, is dissipated and lost. It is similar to discharging a battery into a ground wire. It is no longer in the battery; it is gone forever. This is what all the world's tantric systems I am aware of believe: that orgasm brings one a little closer to death because a person loses his or her life-force energy in the orgasm. But the Egyptians have found long ago that it does not have to be this way.

It is for this reason that the Hindu and Tibetan tantra systems ask the male to avoid ejaculating. Instead, they speak of these tiny invisible tubes where the sperm migrates up to the higher centers when a student learns to control the orgasm.

Both of these systems and the Chinese Taoist tantra system are all primarily concerned with the sexual energy flow, sometimes referred to as sexual currents. They are primarily concerned with what happens when the sexual energy is moved before the orgasm, but they all have entirely different views of this energy compared to the Egyptians.

The Egyptians believed that orgasm is healthy and necessary, but that the sexual energy currents must be controlled in a deeply esoteric procedure that is unlike any other system. They believed that if this energy is controlled, the human orgasm becomes a source of infinite pranic energy that is not lost. They believe that the entire Mer-Ka-Ba or lightbody benefits from this sexual release, that under the right conditions the orgasm will directly lead to eternal life—and that the ankh is the key.

What has the ankh to do with sexual energy? It is complicated to explain, but I will take the time. In order to see what took thousands of years for the Egyptians to grasp, we will begin with the fifth chakra. You can see from the section above that the fifth chakra is the first place where the rotating chakra system returns full circle. This is the first chakra that has the energies of both front-to-back and left-to-right. If you could see these energies from the top, they would look like this [Fig. 12-27a].

Fig. 12-27a. Top view of the upward-spiraling energies at the fifth chakra.

If you could see these energies from the front view of a human, they would look like this [Fig. 12-27b]

Notice that both of the above examples are Christian symbols. However, if you could see the same energies from the *side* of a human being, they would appear different than you would expect. There is another energy-flow "tube" there that the Egyptians discovered from their discourses with the Tat Brotherhood under the Great Pyramid. This information comes straight from ancient Atlantis. From the side, this is what a human being's energy field associated with the fifth chakra looks like [Fig. 12-27c].

Fig. 12-27b. Front view of these energies at the fifth chakra.

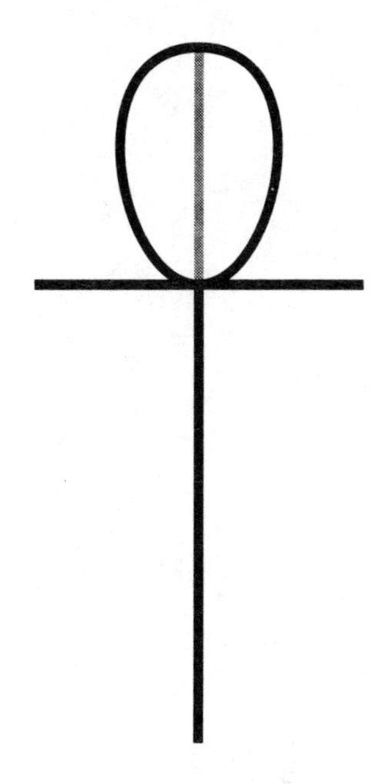

Fig. 12-27c. Side view at the fifth chakra—the Egyptian ankh.

I find it very interesting that the Christians must have understood this at one time, for on the robes of many Christian priests, at certain times of the year that are usually associated with resurrection, you will see the following symbol [Fig 12-27d]. This symbol shows all three views—the top, front and side at once. I believe the Christians omitted the complete loop of the ankh so that they would not show a connection with the old Egyptian religion. But it is obvious that they knew.

Now that you know that this "ankh" energy conduit is located in the human energy field, you will be able to understand the reasons for the Egyptians' sexual conduct.

Let me explain something about the ankh before I speak about its relationship to sexual energy. When I toured the museums in Egypt, I personally observed over 200 Egyptian rods. These rods were mostly made of wood, although other materials were sometimes used. They had a tuning fork on the bottom end, and the top end had four different types of devices that could be attached.

The 45-degree attachment that is used in the actual experience of resurrection is mentioned in chapter 5, but we didn't really discuss the ankh. This end piece is amazing. As the tuning fork at the bottom end vibrates, this energy is normally dissipated very quickly. But if you place an ankh at the top end, the energy seems to wrap around back into the rod, moving downward as it returns, thereby sustaining the energy.

I was in Holland a couple of years ago, and there some people had made many rods out of copper with a high-quality tuning fork at the bottom and a threaded end at the top, so that different end pieces could be screwed on. I experimented with this rod. Using it without a top piece, I struck the tuning fork and timed how long it would vibrate. Then I screwed on the ankh and struck the tuning fork again. With the ankh on top, the rod vibrated almost three times longer.

Fig. 12-27d. The Christian symbol that incorporates all three of the above views.

This is the key to why the Egyptians performed the particular sexual practices we are about to explain. They found that if they had an orgasm and let it go out the top or bottom of the spine, the sexual energy was lost. But if the sexual energy were guided by consciousness to move into the "ankh" conduit, it would come back into the spine and continue to resonate and vibrate. The life-force energy was not lost. In actual experience, it seems to increase the energy.

You can talk about it all day, but if you try it one time, you will understand. However, it is not easy to do in one test. For the first few times the sexual energy will often shoot past the point of the fifth chakra and continue on up and out of the body. So it takes practice. Once it is learned, I doubt seriously if you would ever have an orgasm any other way. It's too powerful and feels too good. Once your body remembers this experience, it is not likely to revert back to the old way.

The 64 Sexual/Personality Configurations

Once you have experienced what I am saying, you may change it slightly to fit your needs. I will begin by explaining the basic sexual practices of the ancient Egyptians as told to me by Thoth. It is hard to believe from a modern view how complex and intricate their system was.

First of all, they did not see just two sexual polarities, but 64 *entirely separate* sexual polarities. I am not going to go into great depth here, but I will lay out the simple pattern. This pattern was copied from the human DNA molecule and the 64 codons.

They see four basic sexual patterns: male, female, bisexual and neutral. These were further broken down into polarities. Male: Male-heterosexual and Male-homosexual. Female: Female-heterosexual and Female-homosexual. Bisexual: Male body and Female body. Neutral: Neutral-male body and Neutral-female body. This makes eight primary sexual patterns.

What I am about to say is, again, outside of normal human knowledge. The Egyptians did not see us in our body all alone. They perceived and identified eight completely separate personalities. All eight personalities are directly related to the original eight cells, which make the eight electrical circuits that lead to the eight primary chakras, which is the basis of the eight points of the tetrahedron around the body.

When a spirit comes to Earth for the first time, it arranges the tetrahedrons around the body in such a way as to be male or female. The personality that emerges is the first one. At the second lifetime, the spirit usually arranges the tetrahedrons in the gender opposite to the first lifetime. The spirit will continue to choose a different point of the tetrahedron to face forward until all eight points and all eight personalities have experienced life on Earth. After the first eight lifetimes, usually the spirit will choose a rhythm that keeps a sexual balance during its lifetimes on Earth. An example would be to choose three male lifetimes followed by three female lifetimes, then continue in that pattern. The rhythm could be almost anything the spirit chooses.

What happens in almost all cases is that spirit likes one of both the male and female personalities more than the others and uses it more often. The result is that one male and one female personality become dominant, like a grandfather and grandmother to the other six. Then there is a slightly younger one, equivalent to a middle-aged person. Next is a still younger one that would be about in the late twenties or early thirties. Finally, there is one that is seldom used and is like a teenager. It is the same for both sexes. These eight personalities together make up the entire personality complex of the spirit that first came to Earth.

The ancient Egyptians combined the eight primary sexual modes and the eight personalities to create the 64 sexual/personality configurations associated with Egyptian tantra. We are not able to work within this arena at this time. It is a fascinating subject, one that requires many years to master. The Egyptians took twelve years to pass through each of the sexual/personality configurations, resulting in a person who has great wisdom and understanding of life.

At the end of this training the student would have a "conference" with all eight personalities conscious at the same moment in order to bring the wisdom of the grandfather/grandmother to the younger personalities.

Instructions for the Orgasm

Here is exactly how to achieve the "ankhing" associated with the human orgasm. Whatever you do sexually before the orgasm is completely up to you. I am not here to judge you—and definitely the Egyptians would not, since they believe in knowing all 64 sexual modes before you enter the King's Chamber to ascend to the next level of consciousness. This is *their* idea, but it is important to know that it is not necessary. You can reach the next level of consciousness without knowing this information. However, from their point of view, the idea of ankhing is of paramount importance in achieving eternal life. You will have to decide for yourself if it is something you wish to practice.

1. The moment you feel the sexual energy about to rise up your spine, take a very deep breath, filling your lungs about 9/10 full, then hold your breath.

2. Allow the sexual energy of the orgasm to come up your spine, but at the moment it reaches the fifth chakra, with your willpower you must turn the flow of sexual energy 90 degrees out the back of the body. It will then automatically continue inside the ankh tube. It will slowly turn until it passes exactly through the eighth or thirteenth chakra one hand-length above the head at 90 degrees to the vertical. It will then continue to curve around until it returns to the fifth chakra, where it began. It will often slow down as it approaches its point of origin. If you can see the energy, it comes to a sharp point. When it approaches the fifth chakra from the front of the

body, there is sometimes a tremendous jolt as it connects with this chakra. All this takes place while you are holding your breath.

3. The instant the sexual energy reconnects with its source, take in the full breath. You had filled your lungs only 9/10 full, so now you fill them as completely as you can.

4. Now exhale very, very slowly. The sexual energy will continue on around the ankh channel as long as you are exhaling. When you reach the bottom of this breath, you will continue to breathe very deeply, but a change happens here.

5. At this point, continue to breathe a deep, full breath, but instantly see the sexual energy as prana coming from the two poles and meeting in your fifth chakra as before. Be aware of your entire Mer-Ka-Ba and feel this energy radiate into and throughout your entire lightbody. Let this energy also reach down into the deepest physical levels of your body structure, even past the cellular level. Feel every cell becoming rejuvenated by this life-force energy. Feel how this beautiful energy surrounds your very being and brings health to your body, mind and heart.

6. Continue to breathe deeply until you feel the relaxation begin to spread throughout your body; then relax your breath to your normal rate.

7. If possible, allow yourself to completely relax or even sleep for a while afterward.

If this is practiced for even one week, I believe you will more than understand. If it is continually practiced, it will begin to give health and strength to your mental, emotional and physical bodies. It will give great strength and power to your lightbody as well. If it does not feel right for some reason, then don't do it.

Beyond the Fifth Chakra

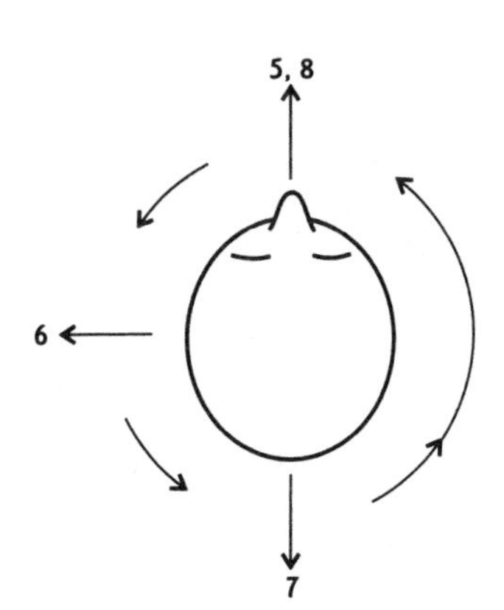

Fig. 12-28. The upward spiral from the fifth chakra.

Physiologically, you can't see the next chakras as clearly as the five below, but we will see the same phenomenon in the upper part of the body [see Fig. 12-28]. After the spiral exits the fifth chakra, it rotates to the left, to the sixth chakra, which is the personal heart chakra. The physical heart is off center on our left side and at 90 degrees to the fifth, Christ chakra.

Then the spiral rotates to the rear as it rises to the throat chakra. The Adam's apple of the male protrudes along this front-to-back plane.

But when it comes to the eighth chakra, the chin, the system seems to break down. It's clearly a front-to-back flow also, like the throat—no 90-degree change. Why? At this point the energy enters into a new configuration, perhaps because it is the eighth chakra, which usually completes the cycle in the 8-chakra system. A new, smaller chakra system emerges inside the head alone that defines the 13-chakra system, yet is separate from it.

What is going on? If you study Leonardo's canon [Fig. 12-29], you'll see that the head is drawn inside one of the 64 squares that is further broken up into a 4 x 4 grid of 16 squares. In this drawing you can barely see what I am talking about, but if you can find a good copy, you will see. A 16-square grid is a function of a 64-square grid in which the head is exactly the size of one of the 64 squares. So the head is 1/64th of the square around the entire body.

The chakra system goes all the way up through the body and through the head, but in the head there's a separate mini chakra system that runs from the tip of the chin to the top of the head. It seems to be an 8-chakra system, but I am not positive that the 13 system is not there also. Realize that this mini chakra system is in addition to and inside the 13-chakra system we have begun to study.

The chakra points are located at the tip of the chin, the mouth, the tip of the nose, the eyes and the third eye. The other three are inside the head and cannot be seen unless we study the internal parts of the brain.

Fig. 12-29. Leonardo's human canon.

Again you can see the rotational pattern in the shape of the body part. First, the tip of the chin extends outward, facing straight ahead, then the mouth, a vesica piscis, is 90 degrees, extending left and right. The nose faces front to back at 90 degrees to the mouth, then the eyes, also vesica pisces, extend to the sides at 90 degrees to the nose. Finally, the third eye is the place of completion, the fifth point, just like the Christ chakra. It is for this reason that both places, the Christ chakra and the third-eye chakra, are so important and unique. They both are the fifth and completing chakra within their respective systems.

This was the work I was involved with when Thoth left the Earth. I wish I had had more time with him on this subject, because it's not in any books. The Egyptians never wrote any of this down. None of the Right Eye of Horus information was written down anywhere except in the Hall of Records. It was all transmitted orally.

Through the Final Half Step

Figure 12-30 shows the head, the pineal gland and the thirteenth chakra. Eventually our consciousness is going to be located at the pineal gland, and we're going to want to get up to the thirteenth chakra. The most obvious way is to go straight up, but God made sure that that was *not* the way because it's the most obvious. He changed the angle so that you can't find it, so that you will stay in the pineal until you really master it. Just as on the 8-chakra-system drawing [Fig. 12-10]—where there's a block after the third chakra so you can't get into the upper chakras—there's another block toward the back of the head, where the half step is. Experientially, it is very difficult to figure it out. The Tibetans say that you can't go up to the thirteenth chakra unless you go to the back of the head first. You have to find the doorway, and once you do, you can step through it.

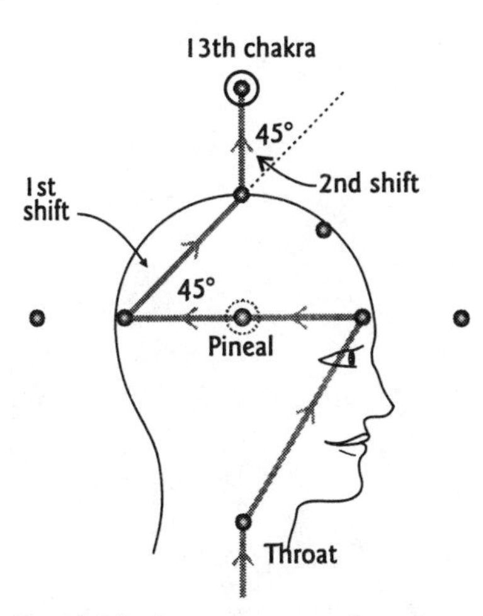

Fig. 12-30. Ascension in modern times.

There are actually five chakras in a straight line running from front to back, as shown. Three are inside the head, one is in space behind the head, and the other in space in front of the head. Most of us are familiar with only the pineal and the pituitary.

The Nefilim originally figured out how to get from the twelfth to the thirteenth chakra and change dimensional levels, but their secret was different from the way we're going to do it. The Nefilim went to the pineal gland first, then shot their consciousness forward to the pituitary gland and continued it out into space to the chakra that sits in front of the head. Once they entered that front chakra, they made a 90-degree turn and went straight up. That put them in another world. Because of this rapid-change technique they used, which is shaped like an L, the Nefilim became known as the L's or Els. It became their nickname. Later, when the Nefilim were becoming rare on Earth, they became known as the Elders, or the old ones.

I believe the Earth is going to do it another way—unless you *want* to go the way of the Nefilim. But I'm going along with the rest of the planet. The way I will describe now is how Thoth and Shesat left. The reason we're using this method of leaving is because it's the easiest way known. These were some of the instructions Thoth told me on his last day here.

We will find our way from the pineal to the point at the back of the head. We have to pass through the crown chakra to get out, so from that back point, we make a 45-degree turn to get to the crown. When we reach the crown, we make another 45-degree turn to move up to the thirteenth chakra. You may find the Mer-Ka-Ba becoming unstable because of the rapid 45-degree turn. Don't worry, it will stabilize.

Prior to the Fall in Atlantis, we made one 90-degree turn; but it's difficult that way—it's a real shock. It's easier to make two 45-degree turns. When you make that first 45-degree turn, you'll find that your Mer-Ka-Ba field will sort of wobble, and you may feel really strange. You've got to sit there and center until your Mer-Ka-Ba field restabilizes itself. You will make two shifts separated by about a minute to a minute and a half. When you feel it stabilize again, make another 45-degree turn to connect to the thirteenth chakra.

This is what many of the ascended masters have done during their ascension. They make the first shift, wait till everything settles down, and immediately make another shift. For just a moment you're in a kind of no-man's-land, and it's not very stable; you can't stay there. If you stayed there too long, I don't know what would happen. But you stay there for only a moment and then whooosh, you make the second shift, which puts you into the next dimensional level, in this case the fourth dimension.

I'm telling you this again so you will remember; you might find this useful at some point. There are lots of ways to directly experience other dimensions, but it requires a more mature soul to make that rapid 90-degree turn. Making these two 45-degree turns is like using training wheels. It's easier, and it's not as likely to throw you off balance.

The Energy Fields around the Body

Now we're going to look at the energy fields around the human body that are created by the movement of energy and consciousness *within* the chakras.

The first energy field that comes off the body is the prana or chi field, sometimes called the etheric field. Although it comes out of the whole body, it's seen primarily around your hands, your feet, your head and on your shoulders a little bit, too. Usually it's a soft, white-blue light. Immediately next to the skin is a black field, and just beyond it begins a light bluish light. This bluish light is the prana or the life-force energy of your body. If it's around your hands, it'll show up anywhere from a quarter inch to maybe 3 or 4 inches away. But around the rest of your body it usually extends less than an inch from the skin.

Even if you don't believe in it and have never seen it before, you can see it easily. I'm going to describe how to do it if you wish to try it. All you do is take a piece of black construction paper and get directly under an incandescent light with a dimmer switch. Hold your hand about an inch away from the paper and slowly turn down the dimmer switch until you can't see your hand. Wait 11 seconds. Your eyes will adjust, and when they do, you'll see your hand again. When your hand reappears, you should see the prana aura. You may have to do it a second time.

Then look at, say, the last section of your middle finger, with the black paper maybe an inch behind it. Lock your eyes on it and don't blink. Now wait. Within 10 or 15 seconds you'll begin to see this soft blue glowing light around your fingers.

Once you see the field, you can do different things. You can put the tips of two fingers on opposite hands together, whereupon the flames that shoot out the tips of the fingers will lock. Then move your fingers apart and you'll see the flames stretch out like bubble gum. When your fingers get about five inches or so away from each other, the flames will snap back. You can do this over and over. Most people can see this.

Then you can take a crystal—it doesn't have to be a fantastic one—and hold it against your wrist. Start doing yogic breathing deeply and rhythmically—really deep and really long—to bring in prana. You'll see the flames at the tips of your fingers begin to grow. Sometimes these flames can go out four to six inches. (You can actually see this.) Then you'll notice that it's connected to your breath. As you inhale, the field will slightly contract; as you exhale, it will expand. You can see with your own eyes how the breath and the prana field interrelate.

Kirlian photography is done by placing your hand or finger or a leaf on a charged plate, then exposing it electrically on a special film. You can see these fields in the photograph. Figure 12-31 is from the Human Dimensions Institute, and the pictures are from the finger of a well-known local healer. On the top, when the healer is sitting there doing nothing, you can see the whitish blue light coming off the tip of her finger and around the edges. The photo on the bottom shows what happens after she begins to

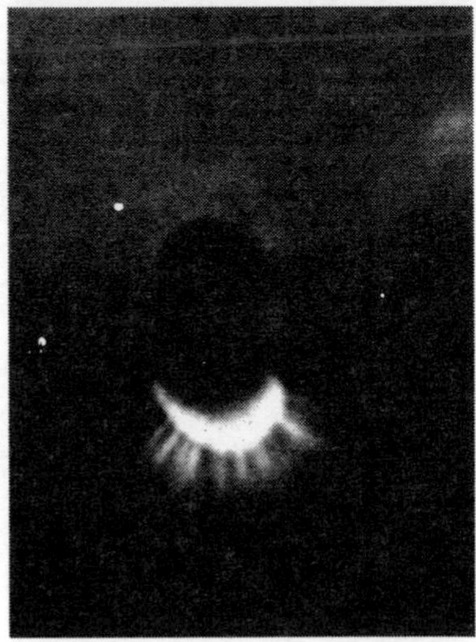

Fig. 12-31. Kirlian photos of fingertips, pointing downward.

breathe and focuses on healing. Whitish blue flames are coming out the tip of her finger. In this case, it's not just the breath that's doing this—it's also which chakra she's centered in, which I will talk about in the chapter on healing.

Beyond the prana field, as it radiates away from the body, is another field of energy that is not associated directly with your breath, but with your thoughts and emotions. Your thoughts emit electromagnetic fields from your brain. And your emotions also put out electromagnetic fields. You can see them, they're visible. However, most people have tuned them out, so we don't know they're there. Cameras have now been connected to computers that can photograph the aura, so it is no longer guesswork, but a scientific fact. Look into the work of Dr. Valorie Hunt to see how far science has opened up the secrets of the human aura.

Tuning out incoming information is an interesting subject. It's like living in a big city where all kinds of horns are going off, fire engines and police sirens, auto crashes, people screaming—everything imaginable. All this loud noise is going on all the time, and in the human experience, it is heard as a low drone, although it's really loud. There's a continual drone going on in every city, but if you live there all the time, you don't hear it. You tune it out. For most people it's just not there. Yet if someone comes from the woods or a little town into a big city, it seems deafening. But that's only because he or she is so sensitive to it. If that same person stayed in the city long enough, he would do the same thing, just tune it out. Then it's gone for him, too. We have done the same thing with human auras, for whatever reason. Perhaps because it has been too painful to see the truth of another person's thoughts and feelings, most of us have turned off our ability to see auras.

How to See Auras

If you wish to really see and know the aura, I suggest that you first read a couple of books on color therapy. This will give you the meaning of different colors, but as I have found, this meaning is within all of us, and we all understand color on a subconscious level. I have read 22 books on color therapy and found that they all say the same thing. There is hardly any difference between their definitions, so if you read two or three, I feel sure you will get the message. The book by Edgar Cayce [*Auras: An Essay on the Meanings of Colors*] is excellent, simple and to the point.

The military trains some of their special forces to see auras because they can then look at someone and know exactly what they're thinking and feeling—which obviously could be very advantageous to the military. They have a special training technique, which I'm going to give you.

Get some construction paper with many colors, then a big piece of white paper, maybe 2 feet by 3 feet. You'll see a phenomenon of vision that has nothing whatsoever to do with auras, but through this technique you can learn to see the real human aura.

Put the white paper on the floor under a lamp that has a dimmer switch.

In the middle put a piece of colored construction paper. Use red the first time. Now lock your eyes in the middle of the colored paper and don't blink. Wait for 30 seconds. Keeping your eyes locked on the colored paper, quickly pull it away and keep staring at the same place on the white paper. Within less than a second you'll see the *complementary* color of the color you stared at. If you used red, you'll see green. The afterimage will always be different from the original color, but always the same shape.

The afterimage will be glowing and transparent and appear to float above the surface. If you do this experiment with four or five different colors in a row, which would take just a few minutes, by the time you get done you'll have a certain sensitivity to being able to see this type of color image—glowing, transparent and floating in space. These colors are very much like auric fields, except that they are more ideal, because few people have auric colors that are quite so clean and clear.

For the next part of the training you need a partner; preferably both of you will wear white clothing. That's the easiest way to see the colors. Clothing certainly won't block an aura, but the color you wear could make the aura harder or easier to see. Have your partner stand against a white wall, then take the light with a dimmer switch, turn it up to its brightest and shine it on your partner. Now take one sheet of colored paper and put it an inch or so in front of your partner from the nose down, letting your partner hold it there. Get back and look at the color in the same way as before; lock your eyes on it, count to 30, then have your partner remove it. Now you'll see the complementary color floating in space in front of your partner. In this way you can get used to colors floating in space around a person and your mind can adjust to this idea.

After that you might put a colored paper behind the head or the shoulder, maybe a foot or two in front of your partner. Do that four or five times, until you get used to seeing colors floating around the body. Then remove the colored paper and continue watching your partner while you turn the dimmer switch down very, very slowly. You will come to a magical place where the person's body will start to get very dark—then bingo!—all the colors will pop out and you'll see the aura.

You'll see it *all*. You'll know that these are the *real* colors of the aura, not the complementary colors you were seeing earlier, because you'll see a variety of *changing* colors. Whatever that person is thinking and feeling at the time will be projected at that moment. Usually you'll find that the colors around the head and shoulders will primarily be what the person is thinking. The colors around the chest and the body, wrapping around the back, are going to be primarily your partner's feelings and emotions, though there can be a slight overlap sometimes.

In addition to the aura showing the person's thoughts and emotions, there's a third possibility. Sometimes a physical problem in the body shows up in the aura. If something inside your body is hurting, it'll often show up as a colored shape in your aura. The colors emitted from your thoughts will glow and change as your thoughts change, and the colors that are your emotions usually tend to float or move. But the ones associated with an illness will be fixed and generally have angles or a shape, and the shape won't change. As the body moves around, it will be fixed at a certain place. Sometimes you might not see an illness at all because the light of that illness is totally inside the body and there's nothing emerging outside. But usually something will stick out.

There's a physician at the Human Dimensions Institute who teaches courses about diagnosing human illnesses by reading human auras. He discovered a long time ago that once you know how to read auras, you can simply look at someone and see all their fixed auric patterns to know exactly what's wrong with that person. You don't need to go through MRIs or anything. Just look, and you know exactly. Most people can do this, and he teaches it. All people are capable of seeing auras, I believe, unless there is some real physical or emotional problem.

Here's how you can tell if these fields are real or not. In a class I would say to the person we are looking at, "Okay, think about your car." (People have all kinds of mixed feelings about their cars.) And immediately you'll see the auric colors change around their head where they're thinking. And then you can say, "Think about someone you don't like." You'll probably see a muddy red color, the color for anger, because we usually have anger associated with someone we don't like. That will come out around the head and shoulders, perhaps even all the way down around the body. Then you can say, "Think about someone you really love. Get into it. Find one person you really love and think about that person." You'll usually see pink colors coming out around the chest area and gold or white colors coming out around the top of the head. If you have the person think about spiritual matters and God, you'll usually get lots of golds and violets. These colors will change the moment a person changes his/her thoughts. That's how you know it's real.

Once you have this ability, you can turn it on and off at will. I leave it off all the time unless I'm asked to do it. But it's real easy. It's kind of like a stereogram; you can just look at the paper normally if you want, or you can focus softly and go into the other level, which is what you do when you see auras. You can either look at the surface of the body, or you can focus softly and look around the body. Looking at the space around the body is similar to looking at stereograms. You can do either one.

The Rest of the Human Lightbody

The human aura is contained in an egg-shaped field that encloses the body. Out from that are hundreds of geometric images that are very, very specific. They're electromagnetic in nature (at least in this dimension), and you can pick them up on a computer screen and see them if you have the instruments. They're very hard to see without instruments. You can sense them with the mind, you can feel them, but they're difficult to see because the energy is so subtle. Once you get the Mer-Ka-Ba field going, it's easier because the Mer-Ka-Ba has so much power.

In the next chapter we will investigate these geometric fields and make them clear. Once seen, they offer the possibility of ascension into worlds of light, which will result in immortality and the direct knowledge of God.

T H I R T E E N

The Mer-Ka-Ba Geometries and Meditation

To summarize the last chapter: First there is the energy flow through the chakras, and from the chakras the meridians reach each cell in the body. Then there is the prana field close to the body, generated by the chakra/meridian energy flow. Next there is the auric field that extends out a few feet off the surface, generated by the thoughts and feelings/emotions and surrounded by an egg-shaped energy field. Out past that we begin to see the geometric fields of light that make up the bulk of the human lightbody. The Mer-Ka-Ba is a potential of the geometric fields of light and is created through consciousness. It does not happen automatically except over a very long period of evolution, and at this moment in history less than 0.1 percent of humanity has a living Mer-Ka-Ba. I believe that will change dramatically over the next few years.

The human being is surrounded by numerous geometric fields of energy that are electromagnetic in nature within this dimension [Fig. 13-1]. The Mer-Ka-Ba extends into all possible dimensions, and in each dimension uses the laws of that dimension to manifest. In the figure above, you are seeing only one of hundreds of other possibilities that exist around the body. You are looking at the star-tetrahedral field that is the first geometric field off the surface of the body, sometimes referred to as the "opening" to the Mer-Ka-Ba. This field will be the one we will use (at least most of us) here on Earth at this time in history, but we are going to show you the more complete geometric lightbody, because for some of you this information will become very important. For the vast majority of you, this first star tetrahedral field is all that is necessary to know. Once you reach the next world, the fourth dimension of this planet, you will receive all the additional information you will need at that time.

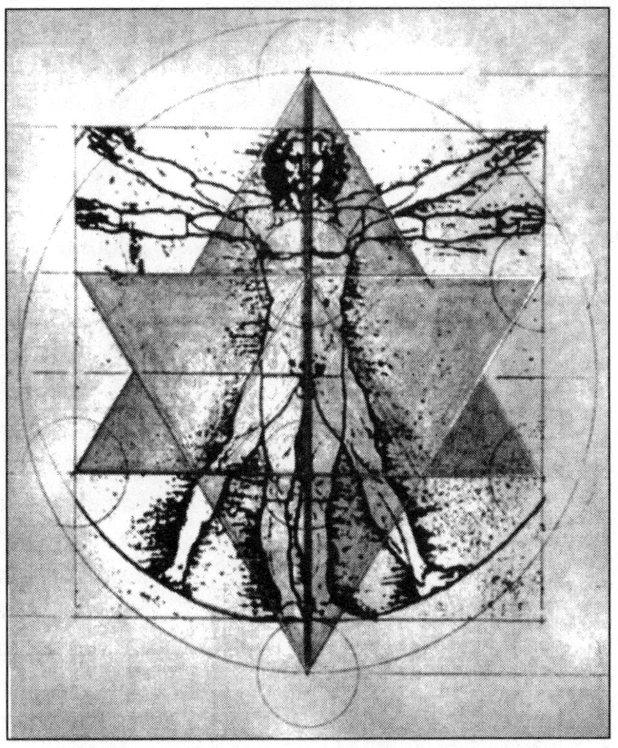

Fig. 13-1. The human star-tetrahedral geometry.

Why do I keep giving information that is only for a few? I am speaking to an audience that is on many levels of evolution. All of you are important to life. In fact, if even one spirit were to become nonexistent, the entire universe would cease to exist. In order to reach the whole audience, I must go beyond what most people need.

The Star Tetrahedron, Source of All Geometric Fields around the Body

If you were to follow these energy lines of this star-tetrahedral field to their source within the body, you would be looking at the tiny star-tetrahedral field of the original eight cells—the Egg of Life, located in the exact geometric center of the body. As you saw in chapter 7, the creation of life is geometric. Mitosis moves through sphere to tetrahedron to star tetrahedron to cube to sphere again, and finally to torus. This geometric beginning of life does not stop there. It continues out to a distance of about 55 feet around the body, creating an amazingly intricate array of interconnected and interrelated geometric energy bodies that will be used over time by life as it evolves.

Now that you understand the source of these geometric fields around the body, let's take a look at them. We will begin with the star tetrahedron. First we will repeat part of the information on pages 48 and 49 to save you from having to look it up. It is the beginning.

The work that is to follow is sacred and will result in your being changed forever. If it does not feel like the right path for you to follow at this time, then don't. Wait until you feel sure. Once you have entered upon this path, there is no turning back. You will know and will have experienced too much in the higher chakras. You can read this chapter, but that is not what I am talking about. It is the actual *experience* of the Mer-Ka-Ba that will change you and your life. It will alert your higher self that you are becoming aware, and your higher self, which is you on a higher level of consciousness, will begin to alter your life here on Earth and you will rapidly begin to grow spiritually.

You may find major changes in your life begin within days or weeks of beginning this practice. Friends and relationships that have been in your way spiritually will recede, and new friends and relationships will appear. Whatever has stopped you from growing spiritually will disappear and whatever you need will appear. It is a spiritual law, as you will soon see if you choose to enter this path within the higher chakras and the Mer-Ka-Ba. I say this to you so that you will know and not be surprised. Once life is aware of your awakening, it will assist you; then once you have begun to awaken, life will use you to further unfold it. Do you remember? This is, of course, not the first time you have entered this path. In truth, you do know. So let us begin.

This star tetrahedron with the human image within it [Fig. 13-2] is going to become one of the most important drawings for understanding and working with the Mer-Ka-Ba as taught here in this book. What you're looking at is two-dimensional, but think of it in three dimensions. In three dimensions it is two interlocked tetrahedrons that are perfectly contained within a cube. It would really help if you were to make or buy one of these forms so that you can get the image perfectly in your mind. [In the back of this volume is a template that can be copied, cut out and taped to form the star tetrahedron.]

One of the first things the angels did when they were teaching me was ask me to make a star tetrahedron out of cardboard. Somehow, holding this form in your hands really helps your understanding. In fact, it is almost essential, for a misunderstanding at this point could completely stop your further growth.

One simple way to construct a star tetrahedron is to first construct an octahedron with eight identical equilateral triangles. (You see, there is an octahedron inside the center of a star tetrahedron). Then make eight identical tetrahedrons that exactly fit over each face of the octahedron. Now glue the eight tetrahedrons onto each face, and you have a star tetrahedron. There are other ways [see the pattern in back of this book], but this way is easy. I highly recommend that you somehow obtain a star.

The next thing is to understand how your body fits into this star tetrahedron, or how the star is arranged around your body. By carefully studying this 3D star tetrahedron you have obtained or constructed and by studying Figure 13-1, your mind will begin to remember. Please do this first.

On Leonardo's drawing, the tetrahedron pointing upward to the Sun is male. The one pointing down toward the Earth is female. We're going to call the male one a *Sun* tetrahedron and the female one an *Earth* tetrahedron. There are only two symmetrical ways that a human being can look out of this star tetrahedral form with one point of the star above the head and one point below the feet and with the alignment of the human body looking toward the horizon.

For a male body looking out of his form, his Sun tetrahedron has a point on the bottom plane facing forward and the opposite flat face is behind him; his Earth tetrahedron has a point on its top plane facing backward and the opposite flat face is in front [see Fig. 13-2, left].

For a female body looking out of her form, her Sun tetrahedron has a flat face forward and a point facing the back; her Earth tetrahedron has a point facing forward and the opposite flat face is behind her [see Fig. 13-2, right]. Fur-

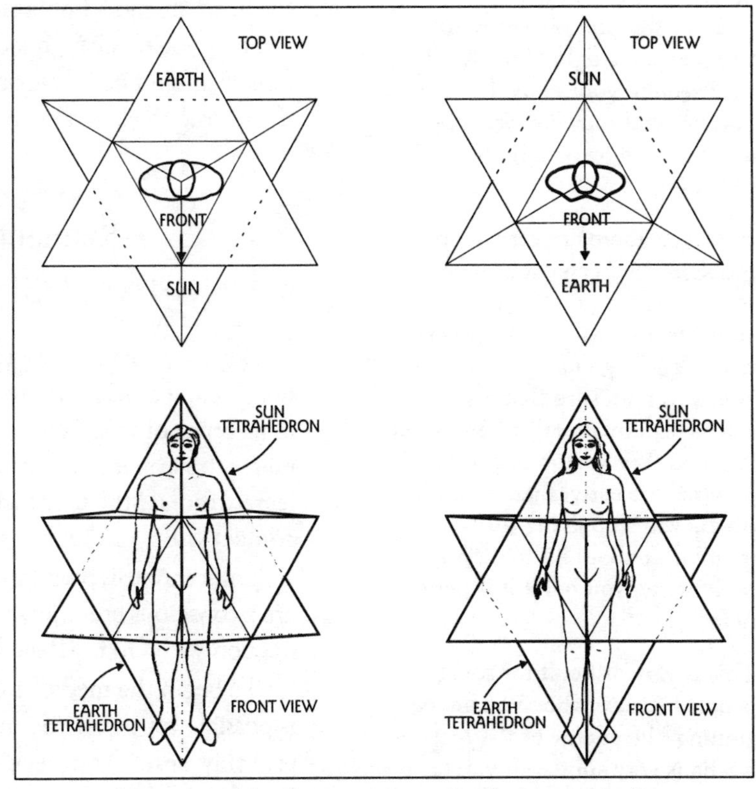

Fig. 13-2. The male and female orientation within the star tetrahedron.

Update 1: If you have been on Earth and did not recently come from somewhere else, your Mer-Ka-Ba has been dormant for 13,000 years. So it has been a very long time since your body has sensed this experience. This breathing practice will reestablish the living Mer-Ka-Ba around your body. The practice functions much like a spinning wheel that has to be spun every so often to keep it spinning. In a Mer-Ka-Ba, however, eventually the repeated spinning begins to take on a life of its own, and at one point in the practice the spinning will continue indefinitely. But it takes time. This state of the Mer-Ka-Ba is now being called a "permanent" Mer-Ka-Ba, which means a person is what is called a *conscious breather*. A conscious breather is someone with a permanent Mer-Ka-Ba who is consciously aware of the Mer-Ka-Ba breath. To be clear, the daily practice that follows is a method to construct a living Mer-Ka-Ba field around your body, but the practice will someday be stopped and replaced by conscious breathing.

However, there are very definite problems that can occur if you stop doing the practice before your Mer-Ka-Ba is really permanent. Your ego may say to you, "Oh yes, I am sure that *my* Mer-Ka-Ba is permanent" when in fact it is not. If you stop doing the practice too early, then your Mer-Ka-Ba will stop living (or spinning) after about 47 to 48 hours. So how can you tell if it is permanent?

This is very difficult for some people because when you are beginning, the energy of the Mer-Ka-Ba is very subtle. If you have been doing the Mer-Ka-Ba for

ther, there are actually three complete star tetrahedrons around the body, all the exact same size and superimposed over each other along the same axis. If you could see them, they would appear as only one, but there are really three. We will explain in breath fifteen.

Now we are going to give the actual ancient Mer-Ka-Ba meditation and special updated information to help you solve most of the problems that people have encountered in the past when attempting to activate their Mer-Ka-Ba using these or similar instructions. These instructions, which I have slightly edited here, were originally used by the Flower of Life facilitators and have been posted on Web sites around the world, but most people have not been able to do this work from these instructions because of problems that have been hidden until recently. Read these updates as referenced to avoid the earlier problems.

The problems that people have had in understanding these instructions have been identified over the last five years by direct experience in workshops, and they will be clearly noted in the updates format in the margin and in a special section. I believe this new way will work, but the best possible way is still to seek out a Flower of Life facilitator to teach you. These FOL facilitators are in over 33 countries and can be located on the Internet at www.floweroflife.org. Or you can call the Flower of Life office in Phoenix, Arizona, USA, direct at (602) 996-0900. They have been carefully trained not only to teach the Mer-Ka-Ba instructions, but also to teach the oral instructions of the heart that cannot be taught from a book. And the lessons of the heart are more important than the knowledge itself. It is, of course, up to you how you proceed, but once you begin to understand the Mer-Ka-Ba, the FOL facilitator could become indispensable. With this preface, we will begin the instructions. These instructions will be in four parts.

Spherical Breathing and the Remembrance of the Mer-Ka-Ba

Like the Sun, we must breathe, radiating out to all life. And from all life we will receive our manna.

Begin by creating a place in your home that is used only for this meditation. Make a space where no one will walk through or disturb you, such as in a corner of your bedroom. A small altar with a candle and a cushion or pillow to sit on may be helpful. Make this place holy. It is here that you will learn to create the living Mer-Ka-Ba around your body and make conscious contact with your higher self.

Enter into this meditation once each day until the time comes when you are a conscious breather, remembering with each breath your intimate connection with God. [Read Update 1.]

To begin the meditation, first sit down and relax. Any human position is possible for doing the meditation, but sitting lotus style or on a chair is probably best. You decide. Begin by letting the worries of the day go. Breathe rhythmically and shallowly in a relaxed manner. Be aware of your breath and feel your body relax. When you feel the tension begin to fade, place your attention on your Christ chakra, which is located just about one centimeter above your sternum, and begin to open your heart. Feel love. Feel love for God and all life everywhere. Continue to breathe rhythmically (the same length of time in and out), being aware of your breath, and feel the love moving through your spirit. When the feeling of love is in your beingness, you are ready to move toward the experience of the Mer-Ka-Ba. The degree you are able to love will be the degree to which you will be able to experience the living Mer-Ka-Ba.

An Overview of the Meditation

There are seventeen breaths to reach completion. The first six are for the balancing of the polarities within your eight electrical circuits and for the cleansing of these circuits. The next seven, which are quite different, are to reestablish the proper pranic flow through your chakra system and to re-create what is called *spherical breathing* within your body. The fourteenth breath is unique. It changes the balance of pranic energy in your body from third-dimensional to fourth-dimensional awareness. The last three breaths re-create the counterrotating fields of the living Mer-Ka-Ba within and around your body.

Part 1: The First Six Breaths

The following instructions are broken into four areas: mind, body, breath and heart.

FIRST BREATH: Inbreath

Heart: Open your heart and feel love for all life. If you cannot do this completely, you must at least open to this love as much as is possible for you. This is the most important instruction of all.

Mind: Become aware of the Sun (male) tetrahedron (the apex facing upward to the Sun, with a point facing to the front for males and for females a point facing to the back). See this Sun tetrahedron filled with brilliant white light surrounding your body. (The color of this brilliant white light is the color of lightning as you see it coming from a thundercloud. It is not only the color of lightning, it is the energy of lightning.) Visualize it the best you can. If you cannot visualize it, sense or feel it surrounding you. Feel the Sun tetrahedron filled with this energy. [Read Update 2.]

Body: At the same moment of inhalation, place your hands in a mudra where your thumb and first finger in both hands are touching. Lightly touch the tips of the two fingers, not allowing the sides of your fingers to touch each other or any other object. Keep your palms facing up. [Read Update 3.]

Breath: At this same moment, with your lungs empty, begin to breathe in a complete yogic breath. Breathe through your nostrils only, except at certain places, which will be described. Simply breathe from your stomach

more than one year *and* you find that you are aware of your Mer-Ka-Ba many times a day, then it is fairly certain that it is permanent. If you are in contact with your higher self and you are sure of it, then simply ask. However, one thing is also for certain: If you stop doing your practice and you find that you have not even thought of or remembered your Mer-Ka-Ba for several days, you must begin again. Once you are a conscious breather, you will remember your Mer-Ka-Ba every day. ✧

Update 2: You will need to have a small three-dimensional physical star tetrahedron to look at. Realize that each edge of this star tetrahedron is the width of your outstretched arms from the middle finger of one hand to the middle finger of the other hand (or your height, if you prefer). So the star around you is very big. You can draw a triangle on the floor or use strings to see with your mind the actual size of your tetrahedrons. This will help tremendously. In the Flower of Life classes they often use a full-size 3D star tetrahedron and get inside it. This really works.

When you visualize your tetrahedrons, do not see them outside yourself. Do not see a small star out in front of you with you inside it. This will disconnect you from the actual field and will not create the Mer-Ka-Ba. Your mind needs to connect with the real field, so see the tetrahedrons *around your body* with you inside.

Second, you have different options to connect your mind with your tetrahedrons. Some people can visualize them; their ability to visualize is amazing. Other peo-

ple cannot visualize them, but they can feel them. Both ways are equal. To see is left-brained and male, and to feel is right-brained and female. Either way works; it really does not matter. Some people use both ways at once, which is also okay. ✧

Update 3: A mudra is a hand position. Many spiritual practices use mudras. The Tibetans and the Hindus both use them in their practices. What this does is connect your body consciously with a specific electrical circuit within your body. As you change mudras, it will connect you with a different electrical circuit.

There are eight electrical circuits in the body, coming from the eight original cells. It is hard to explain here, but it is necessary to balance only six circuits to achieve balance in all eight. It is similar to the global positioning system (GPS) system that locates a specific spot on the surface of the Earth. This system is based on the tetrahedron. If three points of the tetrahedron are known, then the fourth can be located. In the same way, if three electrical circuits are balanced, it will balance the fourth. Therefore, if six points of the star tetrahedron are balanced, the last two, located above the head and below the feet, will automatically become balanced. That is why there are only six balancing (and cleansing) breaths for the eight electrical circuits. ✧

first, then your diaphragm and finally your chest. Do this in one movement, not three. The exhalation is completed either by holding the chest firm and relaxing the stomach, slowly releasing the air, or by holding the stomach firm and relaxing the chest. The most important point is that this breathing becomes rhythmic, meaning the same time duration in and out. Begin by using seven seconds in and seven seconds out, which is what the Tibetans use. As you become familiar with this meditation, find your own rhythm. The breaths can be as long as you are comfortable with, but should not be less than five seconds unless you have a physical problem and cannot do it that long. Then, of course, do the best you can.

The following instructions for a complete yogic breath are from *Science of Breath: A Complete Manual of the Oriental Breathing Philosophy of Physical, Mental, Psychic and Spiritual Development* by Yogi Ramacharaka [Yoga Publishers Society, 1904]. Perhaps this description from his book will be helpful:

> Breathing through the nostrils, inhale steadily, first filling the lower part of the lungs, which is accomplished by bringing into play the diaphragm, while descending exerts a gentle pressure on the abdominal organs, pushing forward the front walls of the abdomen. Then fill the middle part of the lungs, pushing out the lower ribs, breastbone and chest. Then fill the higher portion of the lungs, protruding the upper chest, thus lifting the chest, including the upper six or seven pairs of ribs.
>
> At first reading it may appear that this breath consists of three distinct movements. This, however, is not the correct idea. The inhalation is continuous, the entire chest cavity from the lowered diaphragm to the highest point of the chest in the region of the collarbone being expanded with a uniform movement. Avoid a jerky series of inhalations and strive to attain a steady, continuous action. Practice will soon overcome the tendency to divide the inhalation into three movements and will result in a uniform, continuous breath. You will be able to complete the inhalation in a few seconds after a little practice.
>
> Exhale quite slowly, holding the chest in a firm position and drawing the abdomen in a little and lifting it upward slowly as the air leaves the lungs. *[Author's Note: Some teachers reverse this part by holding the abdomen in a firm position and relaxing the chest. Most teachers use the first method. Either way is fine.]* When the air is entirely exhaled, relax the chest and abdomen. A little practice will render this part of the exercise easy, and the movement, once acquired, will be afterward performed almost automatically.

FIRST BREATH: Outbreath

Heart: Love.

Mind: Become aware of the Earth (female) tetrahedron (apex pointing to the Earth, with a point facing to the back for males, and for females a point facing to the front). See this tetrahedron also filled with brilliant white light.

Body: Keep the same mudra.

Breath: Do not hesitate at the top of the inhalation to begin the exhalation. Exhale quite slowly for approximately seven seconds, in the yogic manner. When the air is out of the lungs, without forcing, relax the chest and abdomen and hold the breath. When you feel pressure to breathe again after five seconds or so, then do the following:

Mind: Be aware of the flat equilateral triangle at the top of the Earth tetrahedron located in the horizontal plane that passes through your chest at approximately 3 inches below the Christ chakra, or approximately at the solar plexus [see Vitruvius' canon on the frontispiece before chapter 1]. In a flash, and with a pulselike energy, send that triangular plane down through the Earth tetrahedron. It gets smaller as it goes down because it conforms to the shape of the tetrahedron and pushes all the negative energy of the mudra or electrical circuit out the tip or apex of the tetrahedron. A light will shoot out of the apex toward the center of Earth. This light, if you can see it, will usually be a muddy or dark color. The mind exercise is performed simultaneously with the following body movements. [Read Update 4.]

Body: This following exercise can be achieved with your eyes either open or closed. Move your eyes slightly toward each other; in other words, slightly cross your eyes. Now bring them up to the top of their sockets (by looking upward). This motion of looking up should not be extreme. You may feel a tingling sensation between your eyes in the area of your third eye. Now look down to the lowest point you can, as fast as you can. You may feel an electrical sensation move down your spine. The mind and the body must coordinate the above mental exercise with the eye movements. The eyes look down from their uppermost position at the same time the mind sees the horizontal triangular plane of the Earth tetrahedron move down to the apex of the Earth tetrahedron. It will naturally return to its normal position.

This combined exercise will clean out the negative thoughts and feelings that have entered your electrical system in this particular circuit. Specifically, it will clean out the part of your electrical system associated with the particular mudra you are using. Immediately upon pulsing the energy down your spine, change mudras to the next one and begin the entire cycle over again for the second breath.

The next five breaths repeat the first, with the following mudra changes:

SECOND BREATH	Mudra:	Thumb and second [middle]finger together.
THIRD BREATH	Mudra:	Thumb and third finger together.
FOURTH BREATH	Mudra:	Thumb and little finger together.
FIFTH BREATH	Mudra:	Thumb and first finger together (same as first breath)
SIXTH BREATH	Mudra:	Thumb and second finger together (same as second breath)

Part one, the first six breaths (balancing the polarities and cleansing your electrical system), is now complete. You are now ready for part two.

Update 4: Do not worry about this negative energy entering Mother Earth. She is fully able to assimilate this energy with no problem. However, if you live in a two-story building or higher, it may be necessary to do one more thing in order to be responsible. When passing through a building into a lower floor, if this energy comes in contact with other people, it will contaminate them. In order not to cause harm, the following is necessary:

We have not explained psychic energy yet, so you must go on faith if you do not understand it. You must *see and know* that this negative energy you have emitted will not become attached to another person and will completely enter Mother Earth without causing harm. *By simply thinking this thought,* it will be so. ✧

Part 2: The Next Seven Breaths, Re-creating Spherical Breathing

Here an entirely new breathing pattern begins. You do not need to visualize the star tetrahedron at this time. You only need to see and work with the breathing tube that runs through the star, from the apex of the Sun (male) tetrahedron above your head to the apex of the Earth (female) tetrahedron below your feet. The tube extends from one hand-length above your head to one hand-length below your feet. The diameter of *your* tube will be the size of the circle formed by touching your own thumb and middle finger together. (Because all people are different, each person must be his/her own measuring stick.) The tube is like a fluorescent tube with a crystalline tip at each end that fits into the top and bottom apexes of the two tetrahedrons. Prana enters the tube through an infinitely small hole at the tip.

SEVENTH BREATH: Inbreath

Heart: Love. There is another refinement that can be used after you have first perfected this meditation. [Read Update 5.]

Mind: Visualize or sense the tube running through your body. The instant you begin the seventh inbreath, see the brilliant white light of prana moving up and down the tube simultaneously. This movement is almost instantaneous. The point where these two prana beams meet within your body is controlled by the mind; this is a vast science known throughout the universe. In this teaching, however, you will be shown only what is necessary to take you from the third- to the fourth-dimensional awareness and move with the Earth as she ascends.

In this case you will direct the two beams of prana inside the tube to meet at your navel—or more correctly, within your body at the navel level. The moment the two beams of prana meet, which is just as the inbreath begins, a grapefruit-sized sphere of white light/prana is formed at the meeting point centered within the tube exactly at this chakra. It all happens in an instant. As you continue to take the seventh inbreath, the sphere of prana begins to concentrate and grow slowly larger.

Body: For the next seven breaths, use the same mudra for both inbreath and outbreath: the thumb, first and second fingers touching together, palms up.

Breath: Deep, rhythmic yogic breathing, seven seconds in and seven seconds out, or whatever is best for you. There is no holding your breath from now on. The flow of prana from the two poles will not stop or change in any way when you switch from inbreath to outbreath. It will be a continuous flow that will not stop as long as you breathe in this manner—even after death, resurrection or ascension.

Update 5: The following refinement is optional. If it does not feel necessary, then don't do it, and continue to use only love. Use this refinement only after you are comfortable with this practice and are no longer concentrating on how to do it. It is as follows: Replace the feeling of love that is held for all seven breaths with the following seven feelings or qualities of mind, holding them during the entire breath.

Breath 7	**Love**
Breath 8	**Truth**
Breath 9	**Beauty**
Breath 10	**Trust**
Breath 11	**Harmony**
Breath 12	**Peace**
Breath 13	**Reverence for God**

This pattern is necessary for entering a stargate such as the one found in Orion in the middle of the Crab Nebula. Only a person (or spirit) who is living these qualities can enter such a stargate. This pattern has a subtle field that will help you in the future. If you do not understand now, you will later. ✧

SEVENTH BREATH: Outbreath

Mind: The prana sphere centered at the navel continues to grow. By the

time of the full exhalation, the prana sphere will be approximately eight or nine inches in diameter.
Breath: Do not force the air out of your lungs. When your lungs empty naturally, immediately begin the next breath.

EIGHTH BREATH: Inbreath

Heart: Love
Mind: The prana sphere continues to concentrate life-force energy and grow in size.

EIGHTH BREATH: Outbreath

Mind: The prana sphere continues to grow and will reach maximum size at the end of this breath. The maximum size is different for each person. If you put your longest finger at the edge of your navel, the line on your wrist that defines your hand will show you the radius of the maximum size of this sphere for you. This sphere of prana cannot grow larger; it will remain this size intact even when we expand another sphere beyond this one later.

NINTH BREATH: Inbreath

Mind: The sphere cannot grow larger, so the prana begins to concentrate within the sphere, causing it to grow brighter.
Breath: The sphere grows brighter and brighter as you inhale.

NINTH BREATH: Outbreath

Breath: As you exhale, the sphere continues to grow brighter and brighter.

TENTH BREATH: Inbreath

Mind: As you inhale the tenth breath, the sphere of light in your stomach area will reach maximum concentration. Approximately halfway into the tenth inbreath, at the moment of maximum possible concentration, the sphere will ignite and change color and quality. The electric blue-white color of prana will turn into the golden color of the Sun. The sphere will become a golden sun of brilliant light. As you complete the tenth inbreath, this new golden sphere of light will rapidly reach a new and higher concentration. At the moment you reach full inhalation, the golden sphere of light in your body is ready for a transformation.

TENTH BREATH: Outbreath

Mind: At the moment of exhalation, the small sphere of golden light, two hand-lengths in diameter, bulges to expand. In one second, combined with the breath described below, the sphere expands quickly to the size of Leonardo's sphere (the fingertips of your extended arms). Your body is now completely enclosed in a huge sphere of brilliant golden light. You have returned to the ancient form of spherical breathing. However, at this point the sphere is not stable. You must breathe three more times (breaths 11, 12 and 13) to stabilize the new golden sphere.

Breath: At the moment of exhalation, make a small hole with your lips and blow out your air with pressure. Notice how your stomach muscles contract and your throat seems to open. In the first moment of this breath, you will feel the sphere begin to bulge as you force the air through your lips. Then at the right moment (usually within a second or two), relax and let all the remaining air out through your lips. At that moment the sphere will immediately expand to the size of the Leonardo sphere. Notice that the original smaller sphere is also still there. There are two spheres, one within the other.

ELEVENTH, TWELFTH AND THIRTEENTH BREATHS: Inbreath and Outbreath

Mind: Relax and drop your visualization. Simply *feel* the flow of the prana flowing from the two poles, meeting at the navel and expanding outward to the large sphere.

Breath: Deep, rhythmic yogic breathing. At the end of the thirteenth breath you have stabilized the large sphere and are ready for the important fourteenth breath.

It is important to note here that the original small sphere is still inside the larger sphere. In fact, the small sphere is actually brighter and more concentrated than the larger one. It is from this inner sphere that prana is drawn for various purposes such as healing.

Part 3: The Fourteenth Breath

FOURTEENTH BREATH: Inbreath

Heart: Love.

Mind: At the beginning of the fourteenth inbreath, using your mind and your thoughts, move the point where the two beams of prana meet from your navel to about two or three finger widths above the bottom of the sternum, the fourth-dimensional chakra of Christ consciousness. The entire large sphere, along with the original small sphere, still contained within the large sphere, moves up to the new meeting point within the tube. Though this is very easy to do, it is an extremely powerful movement. Breathing from this new point within the tube will inevitably change your awareness from third- to fourth-dimensional consciousness, or from Earth consciousness to Christ consciousness. It will take awhile to have this effect on you, but as I have said, it is inevitable if you continue this practice.

Body: The following mudra will be used for the rest of the meditation. Males will place the left palm on top of the right palm, both faced upward, and females will place the right palm on top of the left palm. Let the thumbs lightly touch each other. It is a relaxing mudra. [Read Update 6.]

Update 6: Because there is a sexual change taking place on Earth at this time triggered by the new light from our Sun, many people have found that their sexual polarity has changed. Since this mudra is not really important except to relax the meditator, it is now suggested that you use whichever mudra feels right for you. And if it seems to change sometimes, then change with it. ✧

Breath: Deep, rhythmic yogic breathing. However, if you continue to breathe from your Christ center without moving on to the Mer-Ka-Ba (this is recommended until you have made contact with your higher self), then shift to a shallow, comfortable rhythmic breath. In other words, breathe rhythmically but in a comfortable manner where your attention is more on the flow of energy moving up and down the tube, meeting at the sternum and expanding to the large sphere. Just feel the flow. Use your feminine side to just be. At this point don't think; just breathe, feel and be. Feel your connection to all life through the Christ breath. Remember your intimate connection with God. [Read Update 7.]

Update 7: **For many years it was recommended that people breathe only from the spherical breath until they had made conscious contact with their higher self. Because the Earth has moved into a higher consciousness in the last few years, it is now recommended that you immediately continue to part four of the living Mer-Ka-Ba.** ✧

Part 4: The Last Three Breaths, Creating the Vehicle of Ascension

It used to be taught that you not attempt this fourth part until you had made contact with your higher self and your higher self has given you permission to proceed. We are now giving you permission to proceed, but continue to be open to communication with your higher self. This part is to be taken seriously. The energies that will come into and around your body and spirit have tremendous power.

FIFTEENTH BREATH: Inbreath

Heart: Unconditional love for all life.

Mind: Be aware of the whole star tetrahedron. Each is composed of one Sun (male) tetrahedron interlocked with one Earth (female) tetrahedron. These two, the Sun and Earth tetrahedrons together, form the whole star tetrahedron (the three-dimensional Star of David). Now, realize that *there are three separate star tetrahedrons superimposed over each other*—three complete sets of double (star) tetrahedrons that are exactly the same size and appear as one but are actually separate. Each star tetrahedron is exactly the same size, and each star tetrahedron has a polarity of its own, either male, female or neutral. Each star tetrahedron will turn or spin on the same axis.

The first star tetrahedron is neutral in nature. It is literally *the body itself*, and it is locked in place at the base of the spine. It never changes its orientation, except under certain rare conditions that have not been discussed. It is placed around the body according to the sex of the body.

The second star tetrahedron is male in nature and electrical. It is literally *the human mind*, and it can rotate counterclockwise relative to your body, looking outward. To put it another way, it rotates toward your left, beginning from a point in front of you.

The third star tetrahedron is female in nature and magnetic. It is literally *the human emotional body*, and it can rotate clockwise relative to your body, looking outward. Put another way, it rotates toward your right, beginning from a point in front of you. [Read Update 8.]

Update 8: **This is one of the biggest misunderstandings people have. Not being clear that there are really *three sets* of tetrahedrons around the body, they simply rotate the Sun tetrahedron counterclockwise and the Earth tetrahedron clockwise. This is a**

On the inhalation of the fifteenth breath, as you are inhaling, say to yourself in your mind the code words, "**equal speed.**" This will start the two rotatable star tetrahedrons spinning in opposite directions at equal speeds. Your mind knows exactly what your intentions are and will do as you say. This means there will be a complete rotation of the *mind* tetrahedrons for every complete rotation of the *emotional* tetrahedrons. If one set goes around 10 times, the other set will also go around 10 times, only in the opposite direction.

Body: Continue the mudra of the cupped hands from now on. [Read Update 9.]

Breath: Deep, rhythmic yogic breathing again, but only for the next three breaths. After that, return to shallow, rhythmic breathing. We will mention this again.

FIFTEENTH BREATH: Outbreath

Mind: The two sets of tetrahedrons take off spinning. In an instant they will be moving at exactly one-third the speed of light at their outermost tips. You will probably not be able to see this because of their tremendous speed, but you can feel it. What you have just done is to start the "motor" of the Mer-Ka-Ba. You will not go anywhere or have any exciting experience. It is just like starting the motor of a car but keeping the transmission in neutral. It is an essential step in creating the Mer-Ka-a.

Breath: Make a small hole with your lips just like you did for breath number ten. Blow out in the same manner, and as you do, feel the two sets of tetrahedrons take off spinning. [Read Update 10.]

SIXTEENTH BREATH: Inbreath

Mind: This is the most amazing breath. On the inbreath, as you are inhaling, say to yourself in your mind, "**34/21.**" This is the code for your mind to spin the two sets of tetrahedrons at a ratio of 34 to 21, meaning that the *mind* tetrahedrons will spin to the left 34 times while the *emotional* tetrahedrons will spin to the right 21 times. As the two sets speed up, the ratio will remain constant.

Breath: Deep, rhythmic yogic breathing. [Read Update 11.]

SIXTEENTH BREATH: Outbreath

Mind: As you let out the breath, the two sets of tetrahedrons take off in an instant from their setting at one-third the speed of light to two-thirds the speed of light. As they approach two-thirds light speed, a phenomenon occurs: A flat disk quickly extends from the original eight cells within the body (at the level of the base of the spine) to a distance of about 55 feet in diameter. And the sphere of energy centered around the two sets of tetrahedrons creates, with the disk, a shape that looks like a flying saucer around the body. This energy matrix is called the Mer-Ka-Ba. However, this field is not stable. If you see or sense the Mer-Ka-Ba around you at this point,

mistake that does not cause any real harm, but it stops further spiritual growth.

This type of Mer-Ka-Ba will take you into an overtone of the third dimension of this planet, which has been used by medicine men and women and shamans for thousands of years to gain power and to heal. It has been used even for warfare. But it leads nowhere, and it definitely will not allow you to ascend into the higher worlds that the Earth is taking us to. If you are doing this now, begin anew and start the practice as described here. ✧

Update 9: You can also use the mudra of the interlaced fingers: Interlace your fingers, thumbs lightly touching. ✧

Update 10: After you have created the Mer-Ka-Ba and have been doing it for about two weeks, you can do this blowing out more symbolically because your mind knows exactly what your intentions are and can achieve this step with or without this blowing out. (But if you like to do it, that is okay.) ✧

Update 11: This is why the numbers 34/21 are used: As you know from chapter 8, these are Fibonacci numbers. All counterrotating fields in nature, such as pine cones, sunflowers etc., that have different speeds, are Fibonacci numbers. (There may be exceptions, but I am not aware of them.) That explains it on one level, but why 34/21?

Without going into a long dissertation, each chakra has a different you will know it to be unstable. It will be slowly wobbling. Therefore, breath number seventeen is necessary to speed it up.

Breath: Same as breath number fifteen. Make a small hole with your lips and blow out with pressure. It is at this point that the speed increases. As you feel the speed increasing, let out all your breath with force. This action will cause the higher speed to be fully obtained and the Mer-Ka-Ba to be formed in a stable position.

speed ratio associated with it in this dimension. The chakra we have moved into with the fourteenth breath and are breathing from is the Christ chakra, and that *is* the speed ratio of that chakra. The chakra above this one is 55/34, and the one below it, the solar plexus, has a ratio of 21/13. It is not important for us to know this now, for when we reach the fourth dimension we will be given full knowledge about this subject. ✧

SEVENTEENTH BREATH: Inbreath

Heart: Remember, unconditional love for all of life must be felt throughout this meditation or no results will be realized.

Mind: As you breathe in, say to yourself the code "**nine-tenths the speed of light**." This tells your mind to increase the speed of the Mer-Ka-Ba to 9/10 the speed of light, which will stabilize the rotating field of energy. It will also do something else. The third-dimensional universe we live in is tuned to 9/10 the speed of light. Every electron in your body is rotating around every atom in your body at 9/10 the speed of light. This is the reason this particular speed is selected. It will enable you to understand and work with the Mer-Ka-Ba in this third dimension without having to have fourth- or higher-dimensional experiences. This is very important in the beginning. [Read Update 12.]

Breath: Deep, rhythmic yogic breathing.

Update 12: Many teachers in the world have decided to teach people to move faster than the speed of light with their Mer-Ka-Bas. This is their decision, but I feel it is extremely dangerous. Most of the higher selves of these people will not allow this to happen even if the person commands it to take place. If a person really did have the Mer-Ka-Ba moving faster than the speed of light, that person would not be visible in this world and would exist somewhere else in the universe. They would no longer live on 3D Earth.

There will come a time when this will become appropriate, and it is called the 18th breath. We will talk about this in a moment. ✧

SEVENTEENTH BREATH: Outbreath

Mind: The speed increases to 9/10 the speed of light and stabilizes the Mer-Ka-Ba.

Breath: Same as breaths fifteen and sixteen. Make a small hole in your lips and blow out with pressure. As you feel the speed take off, let all your breath out with force. You are now in your stable, third-dimensionally-tuned Mer-Ka-Ba. With the help of your higher self, you will understand what this really means.

After you are finished with the breathing exercise, technically you can immediately get up and return to your everyday life. If you do, try to remember your breathing and the flow through your body as long as you can until you can realize that life is an open-eyes meditation and everything is sacred.

However, it would be desirable to remain in the meditation for a while longer, perhaps fifteen minutes to an hour. While you are in this meditative state, your thoughts and emotions are amplified tremendously. This is a great time for positive affirmations. Talk to your higher self to discover the possibilities of this special meditative time. We will talk about this in detail in the chapter on psychic energy.

EIGHTEENTH BREATH:

This very special breath will not be taught here. You must receive it from your higher self. It is the breath that will take you through the speed of light into the fourth dimension (or higher, if higher self directs it). It is based on whole-number fractions, just as in music. You will disappear from this world and reappear in another one that will be your new home for a while. This is not the end, but the beginning of an ever-expanding consciousness returning you to the Source. I ask that you do not experiment with this breath. It can be very dangerous.

When the time is right, your higher self will cause you to remember how to do this breath. Do not be concerned about it; it will come when needed.

There are many people teaching how to do this 18th breath now, especially on the Internet. I can't tell you what to do, but please be careful. Many of these teachers are saying that they know how and that they can take you there and have you return to Earth. But just remember, if you *really* take this breath, you will no longer exist in this dimension. The idea that you can go to a higher dimension and return to Earth is highly unlikely. Not that it is impossible, simply highly unlikely. If you were to truly experience the higher worlds, you would not want to come back. So please be careful. As I said, when the time is right, you will remember what to do without any outside help whatsoever.

Additional Information, and Problems That People Sometimes Experience

All the problems or misunderstandings will be placed in this section for convenience. Some may be repeated from above and some will be new. We already mentioned the number-one problem associated with the creation of the human Mer-Ka-Ba with the spinning of the male and female (Sun and Earth) tetrahedrons in opposite directions instead of spinning the Sun and Earth *star tetrahedrons* (the set) in opposite directions. We are going to reprint this update here again since it is so important. Below are other related problems and additional information, but they use different terms to help your understanding.

1. Spinning the tetrahedrons, top and bottom only.

This is one of the biggest mistakes people make. They are not clear that there are really *three sets* of star tetrahedrons around the body, and they simply rotate the Sun tetrahedron counterclockwise and the Earth tetrahedron clockwise. This is a mistake that does not really cause any harm, but it stops further spiritual growth.

This type of Mer-Ka-Ba will take you into an overtone of the third dimension of this planet, used by medicine men and women and shamans for thousands of years to gain power and to heal. It has been used even for warfare. But it leads nowhere, and it will definitely not allow you to ascend into the higher worlds that the Earth is taking us to. If you are doing this now, begin anew and start the practice as described.

2. Experiencing the tetrahedrons as either too small or too big, or one bigger or smaller than the other.

Sometimes when people examine their tetrahedrons, they find that they are either too big or too small or that one is bigger or smaller than the other. These instructions also apply to a crooked or unaligned field. What does this mean?

Your tetrahedrons are an exact measure of the polarity balance within your body. The first and primary polarity within your body comes from your parents. The Sun tetrahedron is your father's energies as given to you at conception; the Earth tetrahedron is your mother's energies as given to you at conception. If you experience a trauma originating from your parents during your childhood, especially from conception to about three years of age, your tetrahedrons will mirror this trauma.

For instance, if your father spanked or hit you in such a way as to cause real fear, almost for sure your Sun tetrahedron will contract and become smaller than normal. If this happened only once, perhaps it will heal and return to normal if the father is truly loving. But if this hitting continues, the Sun tetrahedron will remain distorted and smaller than normal, which will affect the child's life as long as he/she lives unless a healing is received in some manner.

The tetrahedrons should be the same size, and each edge-length should be the length of your outstretched arms. But this is seldom the case. Almost every human being on Earth has had trauma during childhood and beyond. What can we do? This is where emotional healing or therapy becomes necessary.

In the ancient schools, such as in Egypt, the female or right-brained aspect of the mystery school (the Left Eye of Horus) always came first. The student began there, and after the emotional healing took place, then the left-brained aspect was taught (the Right Eye of Horus). Here in the United States and in other left-brained countries, we have introduced the left-brained studies first because these countries are having a difficult time understanding the female pathway. In many cases they have simply rejected this simple pathway. Therefore we have introduced this male pathway first just to get their attention. But now that we have your attention and you are beginning to study this pathway, I find it necessary to tell you that you must now, or at least at some point on this path, begin to study the female way.

Emotional healing is essential if you really wish to find enlightenment in this world. There is no way around it. Once you begin to find out about the higher worlds, you yourself will stop your growth past a certain point until this emotional healing has taken place. I am sorry, but that is the way it is.

The good news is that there has been a great success in refining techniques to assist the human to heal the emotional body in the last 70 years. From the time of Freud until now, an incredible understanding has come to humanity around the human emotions. Wilhelm Reich was the primary person, more than perhaps any other, who opened the door to this great understanding. It was Reich who realized that as children, not wanting to feel the pain of an emotional experience, we stored these painful emotions within our muscles, our nervous system and in the space around our bodies, our lightbody. We now know it is not just anywhere in our lightbody, but specifically in our tetrahedrons.

Since the time of Reich, Dr. Ida P. Rolf decided that if this emotional pain was stored in our muscles, then let's go in and get it. So Rolfing was born. Then many great souls came to this idea of Reich's, such as Fritz Perl and Sandy Goodman with the related ideas of Gestalt therapy and psychodrama. In more recent times, hypnotherapy was born, which opened even newer doors of understanding, including our past (and future) lives and their effect on our present lives. The existence of entities or dysfunctional spirits and energies such as found in witchcraft, voodoo and so on have become more understood with an easy method of release.

My suggestion is that you trust yourself and open to the possibility of someone coming into your life who can help you with your emotional imbalances (even if you are not aware of them). It almost always requires help from the outside. We usually cannot see our own problems, so this is one area of human experience where outside help is just about the only way.

Only when a person is in a relatively healthy emotional balance can he or she successfully function through the Mer-Ka-Ba.

3. When the disk that extends from the Mer-Ka-Ba is in the wrong location.

The 55-foot disk that extends from the body comes from the original eight cells, and this disk is in that exact location. It passes through the area of the perineum, near the base of the spine. It is fixed at that location, or should be.

Sometimes it is mistakenly seen emerging from other chakras or other locations in the body. It is very important to move this disk with your mind to the correct location, as this will change the nature of the whole chakra system. This is one mistake that will distort the entire Mer-Ka-Ba experience, yet is easily corrected. You simply "see" it returning to its proper place, then hold it there for a while to stabilize. Make sure each day, as you do the steps of the Mer-Ka-Ba, that this disk is in the proper place, and after about a week it will remain there.

4. A reversed-spin field.

Various mistaken understandings could cause a reversed-spin field for the Mer-Ka-Ba. In other words, instead of the *mind* tetrahedrons spinning to the left (from within the body) at the rate of 34 and the *emotional* tetrahedrons spinning to the right (from within the body) at the rate of 21, the speed ratio is reversed. By this we mean, the mind moves at 21 and the emotional at 34. No matter how you arrive at this state, it is very dangerous. A reversed field is antilife. If you do this long enough, it will almost surely result in sickness or even death.

The solution is simple—just correct it. But when you correct the field, it is like starting all over again to create a permanent field.

To be very clear, since this is extremely important, we will give these instructions again: From within the body looking out, and from a point in front of the body as the point of reference, the *mind* tetrahedron moves to the left 34 times while the *emotional* tetrahedron moves to the right 21 times.

5. Seeing yourself in a set of small star tetrahedrons in front of and outside of your body.

If you see yourself in a small star tetrahedron in the space in front of your body, this will not create the Mer-Ka-Ba. Your mind *must* connect with the *real* energy field of the star tetrahedrons. You must see yourself *inside the center* of the real field that exists around your body. You can see this field or you can sense or feel it. It does not matter, for either way will connect the mind to the lightbody.

Minor Problems and Misunderstandings

6. Perfect use of the mudras.

For the first two weeks, the exact use of the mudras is very important. However, once the mind and body know what you are attempting to do, then the mudras can be relaxed or even not used at all. The body needs to know that you are attempting to connect to a particular electrical system within it. Once the body knows which system it is, it can go there simply by your intention. It's kind of like riding a bicycle. At first your attention must be placed on keeping your balance. Once your body knows how to keep this balance, your attention is no longer necessary; it happens automatically.

7. Blowing outward—the tenth, fifteenth, sixteenth and seventeenth breaths.

This is similar to #6. The blowing out is very important in the first two weeks, but after that it can be done very lightly or not at all. Once the mind and body understand, they will perform this function purely from intention.

8. Colors.

For the first two weeks to perhaps a month, we ask that you use the color of lightning in the tetrahedrons and the breathing tube. Many of you may find or have found that color(s) have entered your Mer-Ka-Ba experience, and you are not sure if this is all right.

We are asking you to use the color of lightning because that is the truest nature and color of pure prana. But many people will find that they cannot help color from coming into their Mer-Ka-Ba. First the tetrahedrons will fill with color and finally the entire Mer-Ka-Ba. This is not wrong, but normal.

After about one month, we ask that you allow color to enter your Mer-Ka-Ba without using intention. In other words, simply allow whatever happens to happen. Feel what happens within your body when these colors begin to emerge. See within your mind if images begin to appear. What these colors and images are is communication from your higher self. It is the beginning of direct communication, and it connects with the rest of life.

9. The other senses.

To be clear, it is not only color or sight, but all the five human senses (eventually some senses that you may now not be aware of) that will begin to interact within your Mer-Ka-Ba. Do not be afraid, just relax and allow it to happen. It is completely healthy.

Beyond the colors and images, you may begin to hear sounds, voices or even music or harmonics. You may smell fragrances, feel touches or sensations from somewhere or someone and even experience tastes in your mouth. You may even begin to see in a new and unexpected way that does not seem to be coming from your eyes. You are awakening to life! Have fun, for this is a new world beginning to emerge, and you are a child.

10. Feelings and emotions.

Feelings and emotions play an enormous role in the experience of the Mer-Ka-Ba. It is the female emotional body that brings the Mer-Ka-Ba to life, not just the male knowledge of how to create it. To begin to understand what is being said, study the stargate breath pattern in update 5, page 350 and also Figures 18-1 and 18-2 on page 441, and live it within your Mer-Ka-Ba. Just so you know, there are many other stargate patterns, but every one I know of all have *love* and *truth* as part of their pattern. You know this information. As you live and feel how emotions and feelings engage within the Mer-Ka-Ba field, you will remember. Experiment.

11. Sexual energy.

Sexual energy is primary to the Mer-Ka-Ba on this level and within human consciousness. The full knowledge of Egyptian tantra is too complex to transmit at this time and is not necessary. The only aspect of Egyptian tantra that is necessary to understand is what is called *ankhing*, which is described in chapter 12 [page 333]. If you no longer use sexual energy, then do not be concerned with that section, and continue.

The Acceleration of Spirit in Matter

The following is a very important issue that must be discussed. Because of the nature of the subjects we have talked about in this book, many of you may experience emotional releases after experiencing the Mer-Ka-Ba. If you do, it is normal.

I know that we talked about this before, but I would like to say it again since it is so important. When you start the breathing, and the prana flow begins again after 13,000 years of not functioning, higher self may begin to take control of your life and purify it. By this I mean that persons, places and things in your life that were blocking spiritual development will often leave you. At first this seems like a loss or a negative. But when your new life comes into focus, you will see why certain things had to change. Do not be afraid during this transitional period. God and your higher self are watching over you.

The degree to which you experience this transition will depend on how clean and unattached your life is now. It's like when you take a medicine.

At first you may appear to be getting more unhealthy as the disease comes out of your body. How long the transition takes depends on how sick you were in the first place. Of course, once it is out, you feel and live a much healthier life.

An Overview of the Human Energy Field beyond the Mer-Ka-Ba

The following information is, again, needed only for certain people. You can read this section, but if it is not seen as something important or necessary, then simply skip it or read it for information only. A day may come when it will be important to you.

The energy field of the human being is far more complex than was taught through the Flower of Life workshop. As we have said before, the star tetrahedron is the opening to higher consciousness, but there is much more.

Every possible level of consciousness in the universe is within the human energy field now, but it is only a potential. There is only one Reality. There is a nearly infinite number of ways that these energy fields can interact to create different Mer-Ka-Bas, which interrupt the one Reality and make it seem different. Depending on the Mer-Ka-Ba, the whole universe will experientially be entirely different and even seem to have unique laws. Most of the conscious universe is working on all possible solutions to this "problem." One thing is for certain: All the possibilities are based on geometry and the knowledge of how to combine these geometries.

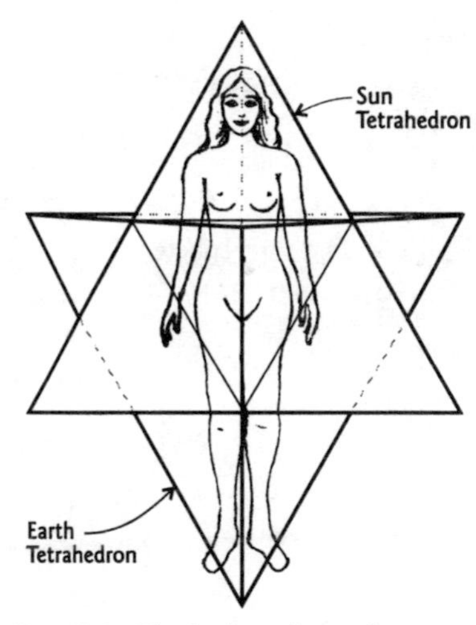

Fig. 13-3. The body and star, front view.

To assist humanity and the future of humanity, I will offer the following geometrical possibilities. I in no way claim that this information is complete, only that it is a possibility. We will begin with the star tetrahedron and give a pictorial view of the basic complete field beyond the Mer-Ka-Ba. We will present this in steps until we have reached the full field.

First there are the original eight cells, and from there the adult human body. Of course, the human body can be replaced with any kind of body and may vary depending on the environment and the needs of spirit, but the geometries will always be the same. In many cases there is no body, simply spirit. Then around the body or spirit there is the star-tetrahedral field, which always begins the geometry shown in Figure 13-3.

Next is the star-tetrahedral Mer-Ka-Ba field, which looks like this when it is alive [Fig. 13-4].

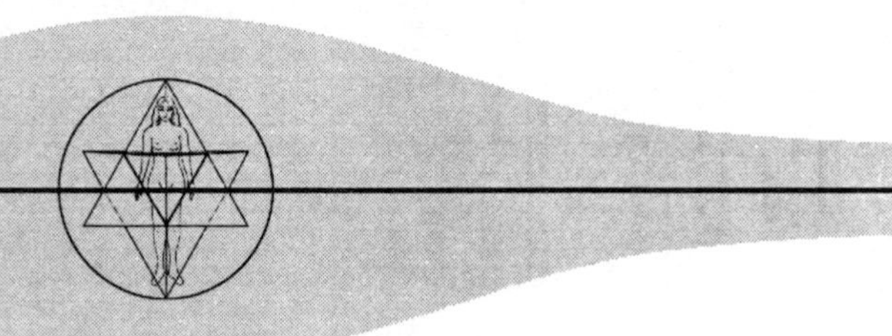
Fig. 13-4. Body, star and Mer-Ka-Ba.

Surrounding the Mer-Ka-Ba is a sphere of energy that is the exact diameter of the Mer-Ka-Ba disk. It looks like this [Fig. 13-5].

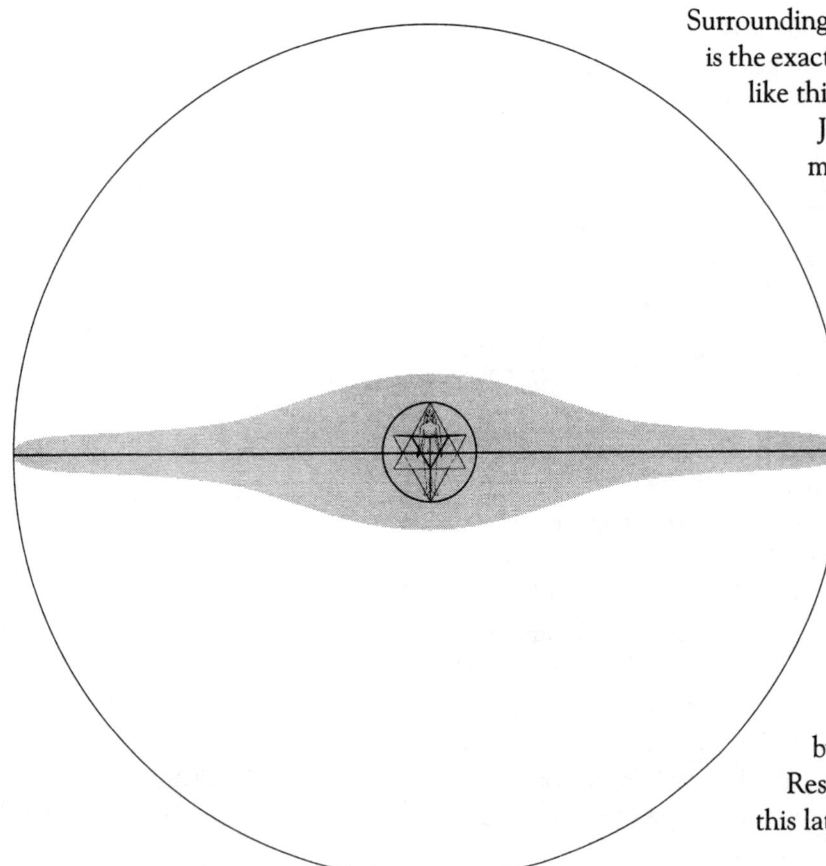

Fig. 13-5. The outer sphere.

Just inside this outer sphere is an electromagnetic field in the shape of an icosahedron. Immediately inside that is the dual of the icosahedron, the pentagonal dodecahedron. The icosahedron is actually created by a stellation of the dodecahedron, where one edge-length of the dodecahedron is used to determine the length of the stellation. All the edge-lengths of the stellated icosahedron are the same.

This energy field is the same as the Christ grid that now surrounds the Earth. This is important, since it gives us a direct possibility of consciously connecting with this Earth grid by connecting with our own outer grid. Resonance is the answer. We will talk about this later. This is what it looks like [Fig. 13-6].

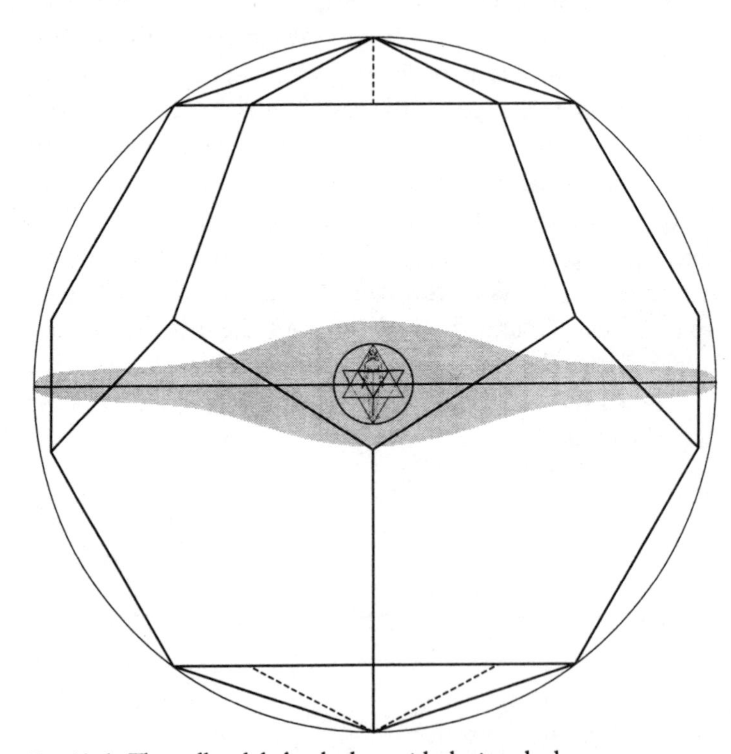

Fig. 13-6. The stellated dodecahedron with the icosahedron.

Next, the breathing tube that we were taught that ended at the tips of the star tetrahedron actually continues both up and down to connect with the stellated dodecahedron. It looks like this [Fig. 13-7].

In between the Alpha (the star tetrahedron) and the Omega (the stellated dodecahedron) are many other geometric energy fields, all symmetrically centered on this breathing tube. There are so many of them, including the internal lines of force, that if you could see the complete geometric field, you could hardly find a place to see through it. We will not draw all of them in now for two reasons: One, it would be impossible to distinguish between them here without making hundreds of special drawings. Two, it is not necessary for ascension in the immediate future. We will give one example and talk about that. This information will be the same for all the other geometric forms.

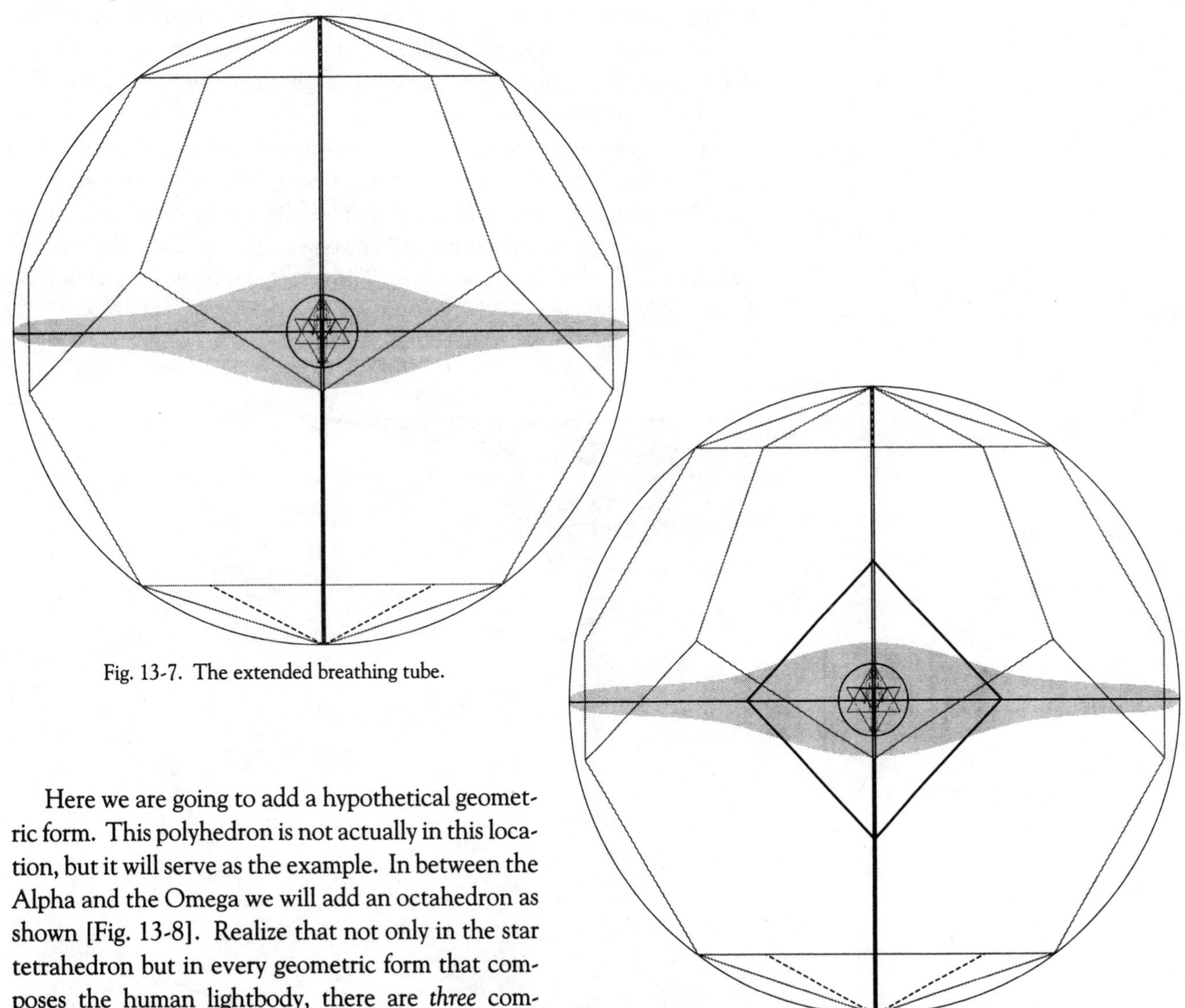

Fig. 13-7. The extended breathing tube.

Fig. 13-8. The hypothetical octahedron (visualize the fluorite octahedral crystal from Fig. 6-35b in the center).

Here we are going to add a hypothetical geometric form. This polyhedron is not actually in this location, but it will serve as the example. In between the Alpha and the Omega we will add an octahedron as shown [Fig. 13-8]. Realize that not only in the star tetrahedron but in every geometric form that composes the human lightbody, there are *three* completely different superimposed and identical polyhedral or geometric forms, although you see only one.

Remember that with the star tetrahedron there are three sets, one that is fixed, one that will rotate to the right and one that will rotate to the left. This is true with *every single geometric form around the body.*

We will say this again in the chapter on psychic energy: All psychic energy comes down to two parts, *attention* and *intention.* Where the mind places its attention and whatever intention the mind has, that is what will happen. Of course, one's belief systems control the possibilities.

Therefore, the breathing tube passes through many geometric energy fields with many extended possibilities. How do you select which one to use? You simply place your attention on a specific field (first you must know it is there) and with your intention open the field. The breathing tube will now work, but only from that place and through those geometries.

The breathing tube has a special geometric or crystalline cap that fits perfectly into the new energy field and allows the new prana to enter your breathing tube. Yes, prana has different qualities that come from different worlds and that change consciousness in addition to the Mer-Ka-Ba. Figure 13-9 shows three possibilities.

Finally, there is a toroidal field (a doughnut shape) that is centered on each Mer-Ka-Ba the spirit is using. Sometimes spirits will be running many Mer-Ka-Bas in the same moment, which usually results in "wheels within wheels." The geometric forms are so close together that the possible toruses look almost like onion skins. These toroidal fields extend beyond the actual Mer-Ka-Ba and enclose it. See Figure 13-10.

top view

Tetrahedral cap | Octahedral cap | Icosahedral cap

Fig. 13-9. Three possible breathing-tube caps. They will always have the same number of faces that the polyhedron has.

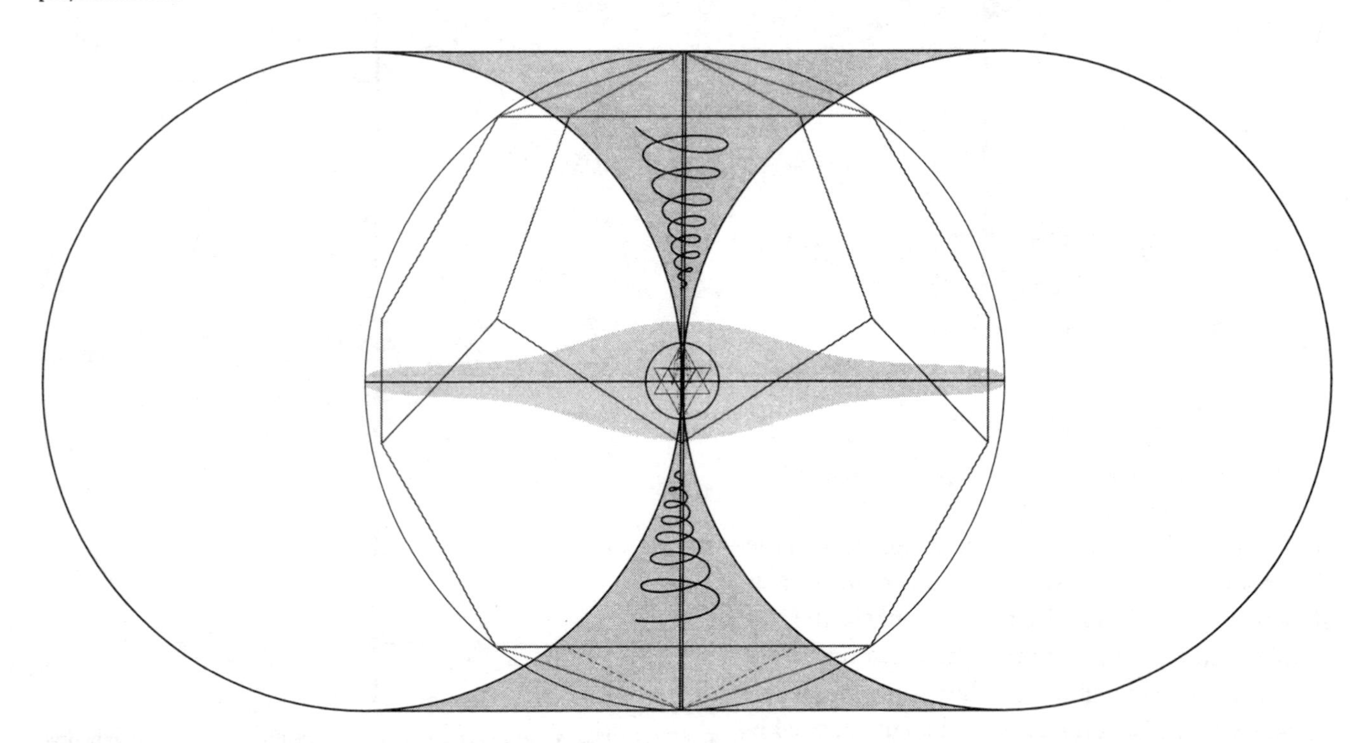

Fig. 13-10. The toroidal field of the inner star tetrahedron. (Visualize a doughnut cut in half.)

In this last drawing we will put everything together except the middle geometries between the Alpha and the Omega. This will at least give you a better image and understanding of the extended nature of your lightbody [Fig. 13-11].

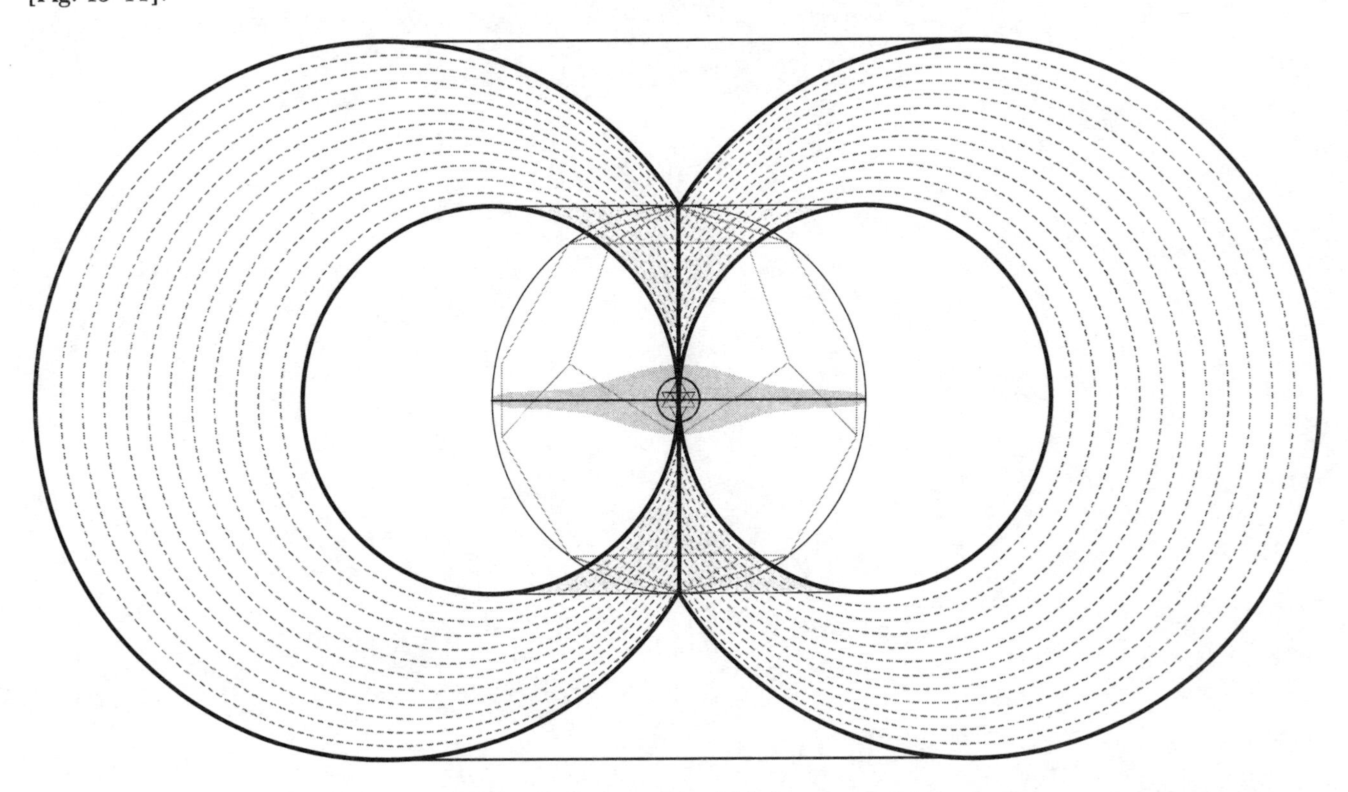

Fig. 13-11. The full lightbody surrounding all life forms—and all forms are alive.

The full lightbody surrounds all life forms—and all forms are living.

Although Figure 13-11 is an almost complete image of the energy field around the human being, the following image is what primarily manifests in the Reality as the Mer-Ka-Ba or human lightbody [Fig. 13-12].

This is an infrared photograph of the heat envelope of the Sombrero galaxy, slightly tilted. It looks like a flying saucer. It has a huge ring around the outer edge, which is dark because the outer edge is moving very, very fast. This heat envelope is in the exact proportions of the Mer-Ka-Ba around your body when it's activated through breathing and meditation. With the proper equipment, you can see it on a computer screen, since it has an electromagnetic aspect that is partially within the microwave range.

Fig. 13-12. The Sombrero galaxy.

It is now up to you. Having come this far, you hold the basic knowledge to activate your lightbody. If in your meditation and in your heart you know that this is the right thing to do, then begin. But perhaps you should wait until you have read the next chapter, for there is a great deal more than just turning on your Mer-Ka-Ba. This achievement is only the beginning.

F O U R T E E N

The Mer-Ka-Ba and the Siddhis

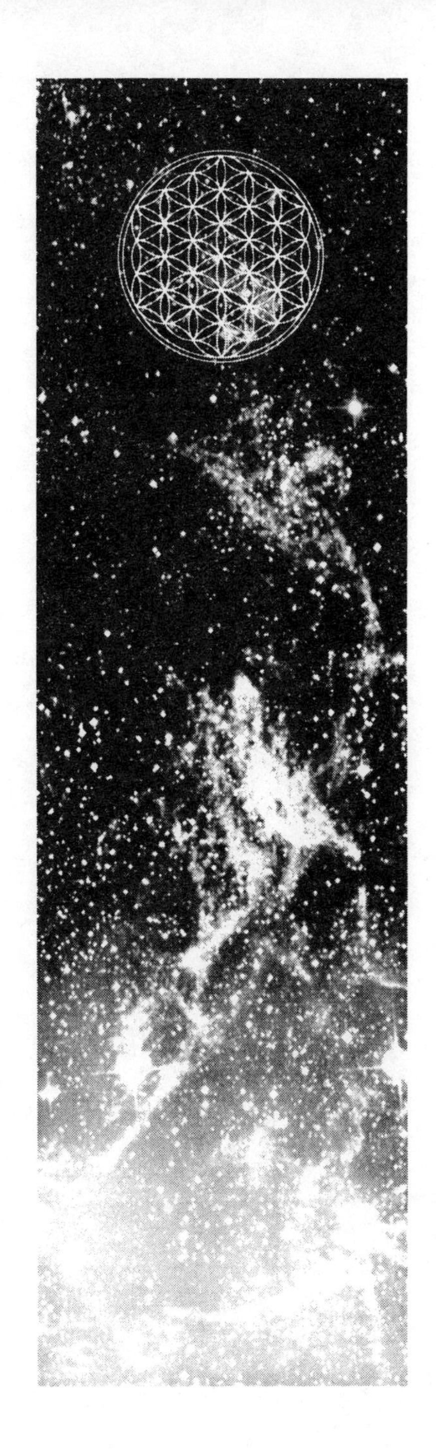

In the last two chapters we have defined the energy flow and field of the human lightbody. We have also given instructions for activating the human Mer-Ka-Ba. When this information was first given in the Flower of Life workshop, it was assumed that the students would find their way to their higher self, and their higher self would instruct them on the content of this chapter (and of course much more). This did happen with some students, but only a small percentage. The majority never really understood what the Mer-Ka-Ba was or how to use it—in other words, how to meditate inside it.

For this reason, the subsequent Earth/Sky workshop was created to assist students in further understanding and living the meaning and purpose of the Mer-Ka-Ba. In this chapter we will give you the basics to help you begin, but it is still essential that you consciously connect with your higher self at some point to really unfold your purpose in life.

In the Flower of Life we taught only how to activate the Mer-Ka-Ba, and many students thought that was all there was to it. They thought that *was* the meditation, but they simply did not understand. The Mer-Ka-Ba is the pattern that all things visible and invisible were created through. There are no exceptions. Thus the Mer-Ka-Ba has infinite possibilities.

Further Uses for the Mer-Ka-Ba

It is generally believed that the Mer-Ka-Ba is the vehicle for ascension, and yes, that is true. But it is much more. It is *everything* more. The Mer-Ka-Ba can be anything whatsoever, depending on what the consciousness within the Mer-Ka-Ba decides. The only limitation it has depends on the memory, imagination and limits (belief patterns) held in consciousness. In its purest form, this tetrahedral Mer-Ka-Ba's only limitation is that it cannot take the spirit through the Great Void or past the "Great Wall" into the next octave of dimensions. This act requires a person to give up individuality and merge with at least one other spirit to form a special kind of Mer-Ka-Ba, which is definitely not necessary to know at this time.

If a human ego decides that it is going to use the Mer-Ka-Ba in a negative way, to cause harm or control others or profit personally or do anything that is not in integrity and not based on the purest images of love, then that ego will learn a hard lesson. Many have tried, including Lucifer. God knew this would happen and arranged the universe in such a way that this cannot happen, for the Mer-Ka-Ba needs love to be alive. As soon as the Mer-Ka-Ba is misused, it begins to die. Very quickly, the higher self enters and that person is "arrested" or stopped, and they must wait to continue the upward climb in consciousness until the lesson of love is learned. Do not underestimate what I have just said or you will simply waste your time.

In chapter 17 we will talk about what happened when Lucifer found that he could not manipulate the Mer-Ka-Ba.

The Mer-Ka-Ba is very much like a computer. If a person simply activates his or her Mer-Ka-Ba and does nothing else, then this is like buying a new high-tech computer with superadvanced potential without loading any software. The computer just sits on the desk humming away, but nothing is accomplished. It is not until the software is loaded that the purpose of the computer can be accessed. And the software you choose will determine the nature of the possible uses of the computer.

It is not a perfect analogy, but it is close. It is true that just by activating your Mer-Ka-Ba, it alerts your higher self and the awakening process begins. But eventually *you* must consciously connect with your higher self to download the higher meaning and purpose in order to fulfill your purpose on Earth. This chapter's purpose is to help you in that process.

Meditation

We usually think that meditation is when we close our eyes and go within, which ultimately leads us to self-realization. This is a way, but meditation can also happen when your eyes are open. With a wider perspective, we can see that all of life is meditation. Life is a school of remembrance.

If you connect with your higher self, its instructions will lead into meaningful meditation and self-realization. This is the ideal way. However, if you do not connect, then you can use the traditional forms of meditation techniques such as Kriya Yoga, Vapasana meditation, Tibetan, Taoist etc. You can use these forms of meditation and practice the Mer-Ka-Ba at the same time without problems as long as the teacher you are learning from does not mind. If your teacher says that you cannot use another method such as the Mer-Ka-Ba, then you must either follow their instructions or find another teacher if you wish to continue with the Mer-Ka-Ba.

Now, while one is learning meditation, whatever the method, a particular level of consciousness will emerge. It is inevitable. It has to do with the relationship between the inner and the outer worlds. One begins to realize that all is light, and the miraculous phase begins. The siddhis begin to manifest. It is this stage of development that we are going to discuss here, because it is the stage that, when mastered, is closely followed by an understanding of the meaning and purpose of life. It is also a stage that the whole world is now beginning to enter. We must understand, and we will.

Siddhis, or Psychic Powers

What is a siddhi? This is a Hindu term that means "power"—more accurately, it means psychic power. The siddhis are considered by many Hindu teachers to be an aspect of consciousness we must pass through, but they are usually considered dangerous. Why? Because it is very easy to get spiritually lost in this area of consciousness when the ego has not been transcended by the time this area is reached. The ego can become so charged by the siddhi experience that it forgets it is God that it is returning to; it may even think that it (the ego) *is* God. Still, it cannot be overlooked or avoided. This level of consciousness must be mastered.

So when I talk about the siddhis, please remember that I speak about them so that you can master them, not use them for personal gain or to enhance the ego.

When the angels first taught me how to do the Mer-Ka-Ba in 1971, I began to have some strange experiences that I could not explain. Very often when I was around electrical equipment (especially when the Mer-Ka-Ba disk popped out on the sixteenth breath), I would blow up or burn out electrical equipment close by. This experience went on for almost fifteen years. I thought it was just a side effect and there was nothing I could do about it. It also became very expensive over time. I lost many TVs, radios and other electrical equipment.

One day in about 1986 I was working with Thoth in my meditations. I happened to be visiting Hawaii. I sat down in a circle with a few friends to meditate with them, and I was sitting next to a wall that had a light switch directly above my head. At the very instant that I popped out the disk on the sixteenth breath, the light switch blew up in the wall behind me and started a fire. We had to quickly dig a hole in the wall and squirt it with a fire extinguisher.

I felt embarrassed. It had plagued me for many years, so after the fire was out, I went into the other room and brought Thoth into my meditation. I felt that perhaps he could explain what I was doing wrong. I asked him what I could do. He simply said, "Don't do it. Tell your Mer-Ka-Ba that it will no longer affect electrical fields." My first thought was, "Is it really that simple?"

So right then and there I "told" my Mer-Ka-Ba not to affect electrical fields anymore, and that was the end of my electrical problems and the beginning of my understanding of the siddhis associated with the Mer-Ka-Ba.

The siddhis are no more than commands to do something, and *if done right,* that thing will happen. If the commands are given to your Mer-Ka-Ba, your Mer-Ka-Ba will continue forever to fulfill that command until you stop, change or alter that command with your intention. I realize this is simple to say but more difficult to truly understand. I will do my best to explain.

Programming Crystals

Computers are made of crystals, and both computers and crystals have traits similar to the Mer-Ka-Ba. The programming of crystals is extremely similar to what could be called the programming of the Mer-Ka-Ba. Many books have been written about programming crystals. Katrina Raphaell has at least three books on crystals and how to program them. There are many other authors.

As I have said before in this work, everything in psychic energy is based on two things: attention and intention. I have also said that crystals are living beings. They can receive and send frequencies and even complicated waveforms anywhere within the electromagnetic field (EMF), and this includes our human thoughts, emotions and feelings. Remember the first radio, a crystal set? It was nothing but a wire touching a natural quartz crystal in a certain place. The crystal would pick up the signal, and we could hear sound through the radio speaker.

Marcel Vogel was a great scientist working for Bell Labs. He held over a hundred important patents, including the invention of the floppy disk. This was a man who knew crystals and computers from a deep scientific understanding. At one point in his life, just before he died, he referred to the number of programs that a natural crystal could hold at one time. He said that the crystal could hold only as many programs as there were faces on the end of the crystal. At the time, I thought this was incredible, and I sought to prove or disprove this statement.

I contacted a scientist I knew, Bob Dratch, and we did a simple experiment to see if this was true. We placed a quartz crystal on a lab bench with the sensor head of his molecular emission scanner (MES) aimed at the crystal to pick up the microwave emissions and send them through special homemade software into the computer to be analyzed.

Bob watched the screen as I programmed the crystal with my thoughts. Our thoughts are long EM waves that transmit into space and can be received by scientific equipment, so why not put them into a crystal to be received just like a radio signal?

Of course, Bob did not know what I was thinking, so seemingly he would have to rely on my telling him when I did it. But this was not the case. The instant I programmed the crystal with a thought (the idea of love), Bob noticed an immediate change in the sine-wave signature on the screen in the shorter wavelengths. It was not long before Bob could tell me instantly when I had programmed the crystal and when I erased one of the programs. (You erase a program or remove it simply by telling the crystal to do so.)

I could not fool him. I would put three programs in and take out two, and Bob could see the three added blips on the sine-wave signature, then he would see two blips being removed. He could track me perfectly. We were also able to confirm Mr. Vogel's statement that a crystal could hold only as many programs as there were faces on the tip of the crystal. As soon as I exceeded the number of faces on this crystal, the blips would no longer show up on the sine-wave signature. The crystal simply could not or would not accept them. I was amazed.

From this experiment I believe we can see that crystals hold thoughts (and emotions and feelings), and that they can send them back out. Your Mer-Ka-Ba is no different. In fact, it is even crystalline in nature in that it uses the same geometries that crystals use to structure their atoms. Whatever thoughts, emotions or feelings you emit, with your *attention* on the Mer-Ka-Ba and your *intention* to place them into the Mer-Ka-Ba, they will be received by your Mer-Ka-Ba, which will continue to send them out forever until you stop them. And no one, not even Lucifer, can stop or alter your Mer-Ka-Ba programs except you. Unless, of course, you have a program that says they can.

One difference between crystals and the Mer-Ka-Ba is that the Mer-Ka-Ba *has no limit* on how many programs it can hold. It seems like this is true, anyway. I have put vast patterns of programs in my Mer-Ka-Ba and it works perfectly. If there is a limit, I know for sure it is not a low number such as six or eight as is found in crystals.

Mer-Ka-Ba Programs

The programming of the Mer-Ka-Ba and all psychic energy is very interesting. It happens to us every day, but few people see it for what it is. I would like to tell you a couple of stories before I begin this section. I feel they will help explain the nature of this subject. However, I will begin with a definition.

Ways to Manifest Wine

Let's say you wanted a particular kind of French wine or some specific thing like that. It's your favorite wine, and you think, "I really wish I had this particular bottle of wine here." You see it in your head, your mouth is watering and your desire is strong. You want it but you don't know where to get some.

Well, you could create the wine on a 3D level. You could grow the grapes, wait several years for them to fruit, pick them and press them, then wait ten years or so to age the wine before you have your favorite bottle of wine. It might be a little trouble and a little slow, but if that's what you accept as your reality, then you can do that.

Or you could run down to the store and buy a bottle of the wine you desire.

Or you could just sit there thinking about the wine, and somebody walks into the room with a bottle of it and says, "I've got an extra one of these. Do you want one?" and sets it on your table.

If that happened just once, you'd say, "Boy, that was a fantastic coincidence!" But if every time you think of something the coincidence happens, after a while you're bound to start thinking, "Hey, this is weird. Whenever I think of something, I want something or I need something, it just happens."

Eventually the coincidences will lead you to the realization that there is definitely a connection between what you're thinking and feeling and these "coincidences." Many of you on the path know exactly what I am talking about, for it is the beginning of the spiritual path.

This then leads you to the next step of the siddhis, when you begin to explore exactly how you make these things happen and how you can make them happen on purpose instead of seemingly accidentally. And that leads to performing acts like Jesus did when he converted water into wine. In this instance you're taking one element and changing it into another. Thus you prove to yourself and to others that what you believe about this Reality is real. You've established it and made it real. This is the area that is dangerous, however, because usually the ego has not yet been transcended.

Then you may go another step beyond that, which would be to actually make the wine from nothing—not just converting the elements, but creating it directly from the Void. At this stage your higher self and you have merged.

A step beyond that is not even having the desire for the wine in the first place—to not have a need or want at all, knowing that all things are whole, complete and perfect as they are. You are now outside of polarity. The pathway home becomes clear.

The Gas Can

When I was living out in the woods in Canada, I began to first realize this idea of coincidence. The angels had already appeared to my wife and me and we were being guided by their words. They had told us not to worry about money while we were in this beginning stage with them. They said that they would give us everything we needed. They said that there was a "natural law" that God had made with man. Mankind could either rely on God to give them substance, or mankind could rely on themselves. If they relied on God, everything needed would always be "within reach," but if they relied on themselves, He would not help them as they requested.

My wife was getting very upset with me because we needed a gas can for our car. She had run out of gas several times, and we were over 20 miles from the nearest gas station. She had just run out again the day before and had to walk several miles, so she was very upset at me for not buying her this gas can. She was going on and on and on about it, making a big deal out of this little gas can. I kept saying, "You've got to trust in God." She said, "God? I need a gas can!" And I said, "You know the angels said we aren't to work at this time, and they'll supply everything for us. Yes, we are really low on money, but please have faith." Actually, they did supply us with everything; we already had absolutely everything we would ever need—except a gas can.

We took a walk down to the lake where we were living, and all the way down to the lake she was going on and on and on, "We have to go back to the city. We have to quit this living by faith. This is too hard. We need money." We sat down on a rock and looked out onto this beautiful lake surrounded by majestic mountains that God had given us, and she continued to complain to me, to the angels and to God.

I kind of glanced over to the side as she was talking, and there, about 20 feet away, was a gas can just sitting there between two rocks. Somebody had evidently pulled a boat up there and left it. But it wasn't just any old gas can. It must have been the most incredible gas can on the planet! I didn't even know they made such things. It was a beautiful red can made of thick, solid brass trimmed with a heavy, solid brass handle. This gas can must have cost $100 or more!

So I said, "Just a minute," and went over and picked it up, came back and set it down next to her, saying, "How about this one?" It kept her quiet for about two weeks.

The Stack of Money

This little house out in the woods we were living in was located in one of the most beautiful places on Earth. It had been given to us by the Catholic church to stay in as long as we wanted to for free. We had nothing . . . but we had everything—even a gas can. But at one point, as we mentioned, we were starting to run out of money. Because the angels asked us not to work during the time we were out in the woods and only continue with our meditation, our supply of money kept dwindling.

And as the money got lower and lower, I could see my wife getting more and more nervous. Finally we were down to $16 and no way in sight for us to get more. As the money supply shrank, you could see her patience shrink with it. Her fear grew. That was it, she was ready to leave me. We had to make a payment of about $125 on our car the next day or we would lose it. We didn't have it, and that was that. She complained all day and all that evening. Finally we went to bed. She rolled over as far on her side of the bed as possible and drifted off to sleep.

About midnight there was a knock on the door. Now, we were out in the middle of a deep forest. There was a four-mile walk just to get to the house from the closest road, and our nearest neighbor was two miles away. So we were surprised by this rare nighttime visitor.

I rolled out of bed, threw on a robe and opened the door. Standing there was an old friend I hadn't seen for about two years with a big smile on his face. He came in and said, "Oh man, I've been looking for you everywhere. You are really isolated. Are you trying to hide from someone or something?" I said, "Well, no. I just like nature. Come on in. What are you doing here in the middle of the night?"

Well, I'd loaned him a bunch of money a long time ago. I basically just gave it to him and had actually forgotten about it. He said, "I felt really compelled to come here and pay you this money! I couldn't think of anything else." And he put a huge stack of twenty-dollar bills on the table, amounting to $3500. To my wife and me, living as simply as we were, this might as well have been a million dollars!

The Second Stack

My wife was dumbfounded. That shut her up for about six months or so. Not a word.

As this money began to dwindle, her faith became weaker. This time we were down to about $12 to our name and her faith began to be shaken again. She went on and on and on; she was going to leave me and the family and return to the States. Hours went by, the Sun went down and she continued to complain. Then we went to bed after a long stressful day arguing about money and about having faith in God. Then again in the middle of the night came another knock on the door.

This time it was another friend, one who went *way* back, all the way back to Berkeley to my beginning days in college. I couldn't believe it! I don't know how he found me. He came in, and the same thing happened, only it wasn't quite as much this time. It was only $1800. But he said, "Here's this money you gave me once when I was in need. I hope it helps you."

My wife went through the same exact changes. First she was very happy and didn't complain for a few months, but as that money began to run out, she lost all faith. She just could not believe that the angels—who were appearing to her as well as me—could really supply us with "everything we needed" as they said they would, even though they had demonstrated it for almost two years.

When this money ran out, she forced the issue and returned to Berkeley to get a job. It was the beginning of the end of her spiritual life. Soon she could no longer see the angels anymore. Then she had to rely on herself to live. She got a job, and for her, life returned to its normal state before the angels appeared to us. Life became solid and the magic faded from her life.

The angels have never left my side. To this day I leave my substance up to them and give my life energy to God. I have faith and trust in the unseen. As my faith became stronger with each stack of money, my wife's became weaker. It is like the story of the glass that is either half full or half empty depending on how you see it. Remember this story, for we will all be tested when it comes to the siddhis and the natural laws of God.

During this time my wife and I experienced firsthand many, many miracles. We saw these miracles almost every week, sometimes every day, for about two years. Most of them were way beyond just someone giving us money. They were truly impossible happenings that anyone would call a miracle. Yet it was a great lesson for me to watch how a miracle could cause one person to become deeper in love with God and another to move deeper into fear.

There is a great spiritual danger with the siddhis in more ways than one. It is not just that the ego may become enhanced and attempt to use the siddhis for personal power and gain, but also that the ego may enter fear and stop meditating. Either way, it stops further spiritual growth until the time is right. No one is truly lost, only delayed.

Four Ways to Program the Mer-Ka-Ba

Now that we have introduced you to the siddhis and the possible pitfalls, let's see exactly how the Mer-Ka-Ba can be programmed.

First of all, there are four ways the Mer-Ka-Ba can be programmed. These four ways correspond to the four primary sexual pathways, which are male, female, both and neither. Each of these four sexual pathways also have a polarity, so under "male" there is "male-male" (heterosexual male) and "male-female" (homosexual male). Under "female" there is "female-female" (heterosexual female) and "female-male" (lesbian female). "Both" is bisexual, and under that category is "bisexual male" and "bisexual female." Finally there is "neither," which also has the polarity "asexual male" and "asexual female." These eight polarity breakdowns have further polarity breakdowns that are unnecessary to unfold at this time.

The four ways to program the Mer-Ka-Ba follow this same sexual classification: male, female, both and neither.

Male Programming

In the Shiva religion there are 113 ways to meditate. They believe that there are exactly 113 ways and no more. They feel that no matter what way you meditate or what you call it, even if you invent a new form, your way will fit into one of these 113 ways.

The first 112 ways are male, and the last (or first) way is female. The male ways are pathways that can be written down or verbally described to another person. Exact descriptions are possible and logic is the rule. You are told that if you do this, this and this, then a particular result can be expected.

But the single female way has no rules. It is never done the same way twice (it could be, but that would not be known beforehand). The female pathway has no logic in the normal male way of thinking about things. The pathway moves according to feelings and intuition. It is like water in its movements, following the path of least resistance.

Thus male programming in the Mer-Ka-Ba is very specific and logical. One example is the following:

When I began the Tri-Phased Mer-Ka-Ba workshop in between the Flower of Life and the Earth/Sky workshops, I experienced a particular problem. The Tri-Phased Mer-Ka-Ba was a huge Mer-Ka-Ba field with a distance across the disc of 1.6 million miles. It required two or more people to create it. The energy release at the time the disk popped out was enormous. It was picked up on military computers, and they sent four black helicopters to investigate this new phenomenon. They would not leave, and they interfered with my teaching program.

The angels told me that I would do nine of these workshops, then never again. This Tri-Phased workshop became one of the most misunderstood and misused information ever. About thirty international teachers and untold Internet sites, without asking permission, began to use this information, but no one knew what its true purpose was. They thought it was for the evolution of people, but it was not. It was only for the awakening of the spirit of Mother Earth and for the activation of the Earth's Mer-Ka-Ba. This has now been accomplished, along with the misuse of this information by many teachers and the spiritual misguidance of many of their students.

At any rate, groups of three or four black helicopters continued through each of the first six workshops. Within fifteen minutes after the group entered the Tri-Phased Mer-Ka-Ba, the black helicopters would arrive, and they would stay for about one or two hours, using their instruments to run tests on us.

In the sixth workshop the FBI sent a man, who fully identified himself, and three other FBI agents who did not, and it was through their interaction with the group that I decided to use the siddhis of the Mer-Ka-Ba to protect the group from further harassment. The angels gave me permission to do this.

All I did was set up a surrogate Mer-Ka-Ba. I will explain this idea completely toward the end of this chapter, but briefly, a surrogate Mer-Ka-Ba is a field created by a person separate from the person's own Mer-Ka-Ba. This Mer-Ka-Ba can remain in a fixed area, such as your house or land. It can have completely separate programming from your personal Mer-Ka-Ba, though it remains alive through your life-force energy.

This surrogate Mer-Ka-Ba I created was placed in a spot on the land where the Tri-Phased workshop was taking place. It was big enough to surround the entire area so that when the group entered into the Tri-Phase, my special "male" programming would protect them from the black helicopters. The male programming I used was simple: It simply stated that the internal area within the Mer-Ka-Ba and the external effects of the Mer-Ka-Ba would be "invisible and undetectable" by anyone, and it was.

When the group created their Tri-Phased Mer-Ka-Ba, for the first time in seven workshops, no black helicopters appeared. They could no longer see us. It was that simple. And as you might have noticed, it was the same method that stopped the electrical disturbances.

However, we made a human mistake, and this shows the problems of male programming. This same group, on the last day of the workshop, decided that they wanted to go to Sedona, about 50 miles away, to do the last part of the workshop. In traveling to this spot, we were outside the surrogate Mer-Ka-Ba with the "invisible and undetectable" programming, and we all forgot about it. We were miles out in the forest with no one around, but about fifteen minutes after this group popped out their Tri-Phased Mer-Ka-Ba, six black helicopters arrived and would not leave. They just continued to swarm around us like flies for almost an hour.

In the last two Tri-Phased workshops, we used the "invisible and undetectable" programming and stayed inside this Mer-Ka-Ba. Not one helicopter of any color appeared to harass us. This is the nature of the male programming—the need to be specific.

I am not here to tell you what to do or what to program into your Mer-Ka-Ba. I am here only to tell you how. The rest is up to you and your higher self. But when we talk about healing yourself and others or about healing the world's environment, for example, this information will begin to make more sense.

Female Programming

As we just said, female programming has no logic. Any man in a relationship with most women knows exactly what I am saying. (Just kidding.)

Female programming is formless, and an example would be difficult even to explain. But I will try. Thinking of psychic protection, one may come up with many male programming ideas on how to do that. For example, to reflect psychic energy back to its source or into the Earth or convert it from negative to positive. There are many, many male ways to do this. But a female would do something like program her Mer-Ka-Ba to choose whatever possibility that is appropriate without being specific. In other words, *all possibilities*. Therefore, she has no idea how the Mer-Ka-Ba is going to respond to a psychic attack, but it will, and it will always be successful.

Another way is to put your fate into the hands of God. It is very similar, except that it accepts the possibility that might mean the psychic attack appears to be working. God has a greater wisdom when it comes to these matters. Remember, even the idea of psychic attack falls within the area of polarity. It is thinking of an us and a them.

Both Programming

This is pretty simple to explain. It is a spirit in either a male or a female body that uses both ways at the same time. It will run a female program for whatever it is doing, and at the same time it will run specific male programs to accomplish a particular purpose.

Neither Programming

The idea of "neither" programming is paradoxical. A neither person (extremely rare on Earth but major in the cosmos) does not program at all. They are persons who are outside polarity and do not respond to it. Even the Taoist idea that "nakedness is the greatest defense" would never cross their minds. They see life and the Reality in a completely different perspective that would be almost unimaginable to us.

Since almost no "neither" persons exist on Earth, there is little point in discussing this type of person. Besides, if you are one of those persons, you don't need to do this work. You are already living the Way.

The Surrogate Mer-Ka-Ba

As we said, a surrogate Mer-Ka-Ba is a living Mer-Ka-Ba field separate from the Mer-Ka-Ba that is around the person who creates it. It is a Mer-Ka-Ba field that can remain in a fixed area, such as your house or land. It can have completely separate programming from your personal Mer-Ka-Ba, though it remains alive solely through your life-force energy.

It is simple to create:

1. Pick a spot where the "breathing tube" will be.
2. Decide where the outer limits of the Mer-Ka-Ba will be—in other words, where the radius of the disk will end. For example, the edge of your property. The size of this surrogate Mer-Ka-Ba can be very big. (We are still experimenting with this. At the moment I have one 228 miles in diameter that is helping with the environment in the area where I live. It took me several years to learn how to use one of this size.)
3. Do not be concerned with the sex of the Mer-Ka-Ba or which way the tetrahedrons are facing. It will work anyway.
4. The size of the tetrahedrons will automatically adjust to the size you set for the disk, so you do not have to think about that, either.
5. As you do your personal meditation with your Mer-Ka-Ba, "see" the same thing happening to your new surrogate Mer-Ka-Ba. Each step of the meditation 1 through 17 you "see" it happening to your surrogate while you see it happening to your personal one.
6. You must remember your surrogate Mer-Ka-Ba every day, just as you must remember your personal Mer-Ka-Ba. This means that every day as you do your Mer-Ka-Ba meditation, you see the same thing happening with your surrogate, step by step, breath by breath. When the disk pops out for your personal Mer-Ka-Ba, then the surrogate's disk pops out, too.
7. You can have more than one surrogate, but it becomes complex, since you must remember them to give them life energy.
8. Program your new surrogate to whatever you set immediately after completion. Once programmed, it will stay until you remove it.

One last thought. *If* you have a permanent Mer-Ka-Ba, then you will find that you can create a surrogate Mer-Ka-Ba instantly with a single breath. And it requires less attention to stay alive.

Conclusion

We have discussed the subject of the siddhis and some of the pitfalls of higher meditation with the Mer-Ka-Ba. However, we have not discussed the real purpose of meditating within the Mer-Ka-Ba. We will say again that it is through the conscious connection with your higher self that you will realize who you really are—self-realization. This primary realization is the beginning of all meditation that leads to fulfilling your purpose for existing. We will discuss this in another chapter.

FIFTEEN

Love and Healing

Love *Is* Creation

Love is the source of all of creation. It is the consciousness that actually forms the created universes, dimensions and worlds that we live within. As we look into the other worlds with our dualistic minds, we always see everything in threes, as we have said before. We see time as the past, present and future. We see space as the x, y and z axes. And we see size in the microcosm, the everyday world and the macrocosm. We will call this the trinity of the Reality.

Everything in this trinity of the Reality, from atomic particles to the grand galaxies, is held together by forces that we have given different names, seeing these forces as separate and unrelated. The atoms are held together by atomic forces that seemingly are different from the forces of gravity that hold planets to suns and suns to other suns, but are they really different? Perhaps the only real difference is the dimensional level they manifest in.

Love is a particular vibration of consciousness that, when it is between humans, holds people to people in all our relationships. Without love, marriage is just a shell and will usually break apart. Sometimes a marriage will stay together only to save the children, but is it not still love that holds the marriage together, love for the children? We may have other reasons to continue a relationship without love, but it is never the same as true love. Love is the bond that is stronger than any other. People will die for love.

I believe that everything in the universe is a mirror of consciousness. From what I have seen, all energy is consciousness no matter what the name of it is, whether it is called electricity, magnetism, electromagnetic fields, heat, kinetics, atomic forces, gravity and so on. And from this belief we can see that according to $e = mc^2$, energy is related to matter—and to the speed of light squared, a number. Therefore, matter is also consciousness, only crystallized. From this view of the world, everything is consciousness. And consciousness is the light that reflects off the matter of the outer world and creates the entire outer world, breath by breath. The inner world of consciousness—the dreams, visions, feelings, emotions, sexual energy, kundalini, and even our interpretations of the outer reality—are all the source of matter and how this matter is arranged, $e = mc^2$. And love is the binding agent within this equation. Love is the exact vibration that matter responds to. We have a great power to create. We have forgotten, but now is the time to remember.

This is why the living Mer-Ka-Ba needs love to become alive. Without love the Mer-Ka-Ba is lifeless and will soon die. The female aspect must be present in love to balance the male, or life will not be.

It is love that can change water into wine. It is love that can bring a person back from the dead. It is love that can heal yourself and others. It is love and love alone that will heal this world. So to speak of healing without speaking of love is not speaking with truth. In medicine only certain things are possible. But with love all things are possible. With love, the incurable disease is nothing but light, and the atoms of the body can be re-formed into perfect health. The absence of love is the source of all disease, for it is love that binds matter into order out of chaos, and without love, chaos will always ensue.

Healing takes place only when love is present.

In the late '80s we did research to see if all healers might have something in common. We looked at many healers, most of whom used different forms or techniques. Just about every technique of healing known was present. Hands-on healers, psychic surgeons, Reiki masters, prana healers, medicine men and women, shamans, practitioners of witchcraft, psychic healers and so on were all present. We studied the energies coming off their bodies and found that they all had an almost identical sine-wave signature, the same pattern of three high waves and one low wave that continuously repeated—and that the source of this pattern was located in the universal heart chakra.

This was very interesting from a geometric point of view, because the length of the breathing tube above and below the heart chakra was exactly one part male to three parts female. This was the one aspect that was the same in each of these healers, at least while they were healing. They were centered in the Christ chakra just above the sternum at the moment they were healing—the primary chakra of universal unconditional love!

From this research and other experiences I have had, I now believe that whatever healing technique(s) a person uses is of little importance. The technique simply gives the healer a structure for the mind of that person to focus on, but the *real* healing comes from the love that healer is giving to the person being healed. The healer's love for that person heals, not their knowledge. So speaking of healing without speaking of love will always evade the truth.

Healing people, healing villages or healing the entire planet is all the same. The only difference is simply the greater degree of love.

The mind has the knowledge to manipulate matter, but love has the power to not only manipulate matter, but to effortlessly create matter from nothing. No matter what the problem is that needs to be healed, love can always find a way. *True love has no limits.*

What is the veil that keeps us from seeing and living this great truth? It is the belief patterns we hold that limit us. What we believe to be true is always our limitation. If our doctors tell us that a certain disease is incurable and we believe them, we cannot heal ourselves. We are frozen in that belief. We must then live out that belief even if it means living in great pain and discomfort for the rest of our lives. Only a miracle, something much greater than ourselves, can overcome a frozen belief. So it is our minds that can arrest a healing. When our minds are in control and not our hearts, we will almost always suffer.

Let me tell you a true story about one woman's triumph over her mind and her belief patterns. Her name is Doris Davidson.

Doris contracted polio and was restricted to a wheelchair for about twelve years before I met her. Her doctor had told her that she would never walk again, and she had resigned herself to this "fact." She lived alone with her son, who sacrificed his life to take care of her.

One day she began to read Katrina Raphaell's books on healing through crystals. She became excited by Katrina's words, which spoke of how any and all diseases are curable. Through Katrina's words she began to have hope again for the first time in many years. She called Katrina to ask her for advice, but for whatever reason, Katrina asked her to call me.

When Doris called me and asked for help, I told her that I would have to ask permission before I could help her, and that I would call her back. (We will talk about the importance of asking permission later in this chapter.) I spoke to the angels, and all the channels opened up for this healing to begin. They told me not to do any of the healing work that I usually do, but to work *only* on her belief patterns. They said that as soon as she *really* believed it was possible to be healed, she would do it herself.

So I called her back and all we did was talk. Once a week for many months we would talk, always leading the conversation to allow her to believe that she could heal herself. For all these months nothing happened.

Then one day she called me, and it was obvious by her voice and commitment that she had changed. She told me how she had made certain decisions. First, she had decided that she was never going to sit in her wheelchair again. So she sold it and had her doctor rig her up with special braces that confined her hips and legs. Her legs had deteriorated from sitting for so many years and were very weak. Along with this, she needed a four-legged walker to keep her from falling over. Many months went by with these restrictions.

Then one day she felt that her legs were getting strong enough and she switched to regular crutches. This began to work, and Doris became even more certain that she could heal herself.

Her legs became so strong that the hip braces were no longer necessary, and she switched to braces that held only her knee joints in place. She was walking so well and feeling so confident that she asked her son to leave home so that he could have a life. She was now able to take care of herself without any outside help.

Then the big day came. Doris was able to walk without the crutches using only the braces. She became so excited, I could hardly talk to her on the phone. A few days later she went to the California Department of Motor Vehicles and managed to get a drivers license. Immediately after that she sold her house and bought a brand new RV and drove to Taos, New Mexico, where I was living, and attended one of my Flower of Life workshops. She walked into the workshop without help and with a smile so big that she looked like she was going to lift off the ground. She was a changed woman.

Nine months later I was walking down the street in Taos, and I saw Doris come running up to me. It was the first time I had seen or talked to her since the workshop. She had gone to work for Katrina and had disappeared for a while. She whirled around in a circle to show me that all her braces were gone. She looked at me and said, "Drunvalo, I am completely healed, 100 percent. I am so happy. I love you." And she danced away. I watched her as she skipped down the street with not even a trace that she'd ever had polio or had ever spent twelve years in a wheelchair.

Every year for about five or six years she would send me a Christmas card out of gratitude. But I hadn't done anything; she had healed herself. She understood the problem, and *believed* from the depth of her heart that it was really possible to heal herself—and of course she did.

Remember the lady who simply touched the garment of Jesus to heal herself, to whom Jesus said, "Daughter, be of good comfort; thy faith hath made thee whole."

What you *believe* to be true is always your limitation. If you do not believe in limitations, you are free.

"Heal Thyself"

First of all, there's healing yourself and healing others. You always begin with yourself. If you cannot heal yourself, how can you truly heal others? So let's begin with your own energy field, your Mer-Ka-Ba.

As far as the breathing and the Mer-Ka-Ba meditation is concerned, I believe that if you do the breathing daily and get the prana moving through your body, you will eventually find health. However, "eventually" can be shortened considerably with the understanding that the Mer-Ka-Ba is alive and responds only to the conscious intentions of the spirit within the field.

Because of the perfectly balanced male and female prana one receives by breathing within the Mer-Ka-Ba, some diseases are going to go away just from the breath. You should feel a tremendous change quickly in some health problems, but not all. There are other problems that can be healed only with a deeper understanding of the nature of what disease is.

This story will emphasize the nature of disease. In about 1972 I was living in the forest in Canada with my wife and children. My wife and I had been studying hypnotism. We had learned that we could leave our bodies and fly from room to room in our house. We even set up tests to see if our perceptions were real.

One of the tests was simple. When my wife was in a trance state, I left the room and went into another room, changing the room in a certain way that only I knew. When I came back I had her fly into the other room and tell me what she saw. She described it perfectly. It was then that I began to understand that life on Earth was different from what I believed.

We did many tests, some of which became more complex. One was when she would fly (astral-project or remote-view) down to a bookstore and pick out a book that neither of us had read. Then she would pick a certain page in the book and read it to me. I would write it down, including the page number. Then the next day we would check this book to see what was on that page. It was always perfect. As time when on, we became more and more confident of the nature of what the Reality was and how consciousness fit into the big picture.

Then one day I was drying a cast-iron pan on the stove. I had forgotten it for about fifteen minutes and it was practically orange-red. My wife walked into the room and without thinking, picked up the pan. I tried to speak, but it happened so fast I couldn't. She picked the pan up with her left hand and moved about three feet before her body responded with pain. She dropped the pan and began to scream and went into instantaneous shock.

Immediately, without thinking, I ran over to her and looked at her hand. She had really burned it badly, and I didn't know what to do but put it in cold running water. I did that for a few minutes, but then something else took over within me. I looked at her and told her that I was going to put her under. She agreed. The first thing I did was tell her that all her pain was going away. Immediately the pain stopped. Her eyes were closed now and she was relaxed. I decided to go one step further.

I watched her palm as I held her burned hand. I told her, under hypnosis, that her hand was going to go back to absolute normal on the count of three. The moment I said the word "three"—about two or three seconds later—the hand returned to normal. I saw this with my own eyes, and it changed my life. I knew in that moment that everything society and my parents had ever told me about the Reality was not true. The body was light, and it responded to consciousness. It responded to whatever the person truly believed.

After that day we performed many experiments that proved beyond any doubt that the Reality is light, meaning like light, not solid, held in place by consciousness. It was the first important lesson in healing in my life. It took me many more years to understand that what had happened with my wife's hand could be applied to all healing situations in this Reality. A diseased organ, for example, that is almost destroyed can be returned to health simply through consciousness alone.

I had a friend named Diana Gazes who did a TV show in New York for a while, called "Gazes into the Future." She used to film all kinds of spectacular healings to put on her show. She stopped her show after many years, but one of the last shows she was going to put on (though it never made it) was one about an incredible healing with an eleven-year-old boy. She had been taping on video this boy's progress over about a year, and it was almost done when her show was canceled.

When this boy was very young, he used to collect salamanders. You know, you can pull off a salamander's leg or tail, and it'll just grow another one. Well, the parents hadn't told him that that applied only to salamanders and not people. Because they hadn't told him, he didn't know. He believed that all living things did that, including people. When he was about ten years old he lost his leg above the knee. So what did he do? He just grew another leg.

It's all on Diana's video. In the last part of the video he was growing his toes. It took about a year or so for him to do it. What's possible? It all depends on your belief systems, what you believe is possible and the limitations you put on yourself.

Once you have healed yourself and know the nature of what I am talking about, spirit may ask you to heal others. If you are asked to be a healer, then there is more to understand.

Healing Others

You don't have the right to heal anybody you want, even if you *could* go around and touch everybody and they'd be absolutely healed. It's illegal. This is a school we live in, and everybody's experience is their own experience, and they need it. You can't heal someone just because you want to or they need or deserve it. *You have to get permission first.*

Why get permission? We cannot see very well from this position within the third dimension. We do not know what our actions are really going to do in the bigger picture. We may think that we are doing this person great good by healing him when in fact we are harming him. We all live in a cosmic school of remembering. An illness may be just what that person came to Earth for. Through this illness this person may learn compassion, and by healing him you take away that possibility. Keep your ego out of the way, and healing will come naturally.

This is how I proceed. First I ask permission from my own higher self, asking whether this is in divine order. (I will talk about what the higher self is in chapters 16-18.) If I get a yes, then I must verbally ask the person (if possible) if he wants me to heal him. If I get a yes, then I must now bring in *his* higher self and ask it if this healing is in divine order. Sometimes I will get permission and sometimes not. If I do not get permission, then I simply say I am sorry that I cannot help them, and allow nature to move the way it will. If I get a yes, then this is what I do.

To be clear, when I say, "This is what I do," I do not mean that this is necessarily what *you* should do. I am using myself as a guideline to help you understand, but I am in no way saying this is dogma.

The person's higher self knows exactly what is wrong down to the most minute detail, so continuing to talk to the person's higher self after you have permission will give you great knowledge about this illness. I have found that the person's higher self, if I ask, will even tell me exactly what to do to heal this person. Sometimes it is a traditional pathway, but sometimes it will not make sense to the mind at all. The higher self may tell you to paint a red star (for example) on your forehead while you are working with this person. Your mind will not understand, but the person will see the red star and suddenly it triggers something inside, and an immediate healing takes place. Use the person's higher self, for it knows everything.

The following ideas may be different from what you have learned about healing. Just keep an open mind. First of all, I realize that people have many concepts about what disease is, but as I have said above, to me the body is simply light and can be changed easily once the mind can accept the healing. Coming from that place, I see the whole body as just energy, including the disease. To me it does not matter what the story is around the disease—what the person thinks caused this disease. To me, both the body and the disease are just energy.

I have found that it is easiest to heal if the old negative, "diseased" energy is removed before one attempts to put positive energy into the body. I have found that energy, negative or positive, responds to human intention very well. Let's say a person has cataracts on both eyes and can't see at all. Medical doctors would say there is nothing that can be done except to have cataract surgery.

From my view, it is only energy. I would reach down to the eyes with my fingers, and with my intention, I would get hold of the energy with my fingers and pull this old diseased energy out of their body. Different healers around the world have many different ideas about what to do with this diseased energy once it is out of the body. Obviously, you can't just leave it sitting around for it to become connected to someone else.

The prana healers of the Philippines visualize a bowl of violet light that burns and consumes the diseased energy. Everyone has different instructions. The angels told me to just send it toward the center of the Earth and that Mother Earth would take it and convert it into useful positive energy. It has worked perfectly for me.

Everyone has different ideas about how to generate the healing prana or positive energy to put back into the body. Chi Gung masters pull the energy from nature. The Philippine pranic healers pull it from the Sun. You have a special advantage, since you are learning the Mer-Ka-Ba, and you will be able to pull unlimited pure prana from the fourth dimension for this purpose. As you were shown in chapter 13, there is a sphere of prana two hand-lengths in diameter that surrounds the heart chakra, where the two pranic flows meet. On the tenth breath this sphere expands to enclose the human body, but the original smaller sphere is still there. It is from this source that one can get this prana for healing.

So from this sphere around your heart chakra, you simply visualize *with intention* that this energy move from around your heart into the person who needs healing. It is unlimited, so as fast as you use it, it is replaced. You can see this energy moving down your arms into your hands and then into the person to wherever the person needs it. And it does not actually matter where this person is located in the world. You can send your energy to him with your intention, and it will be received.

Once you have removed the diseased energy and replaced it with pranic energy, the last step is to see the person becoming healed in your own mind—and also (extremely important) see them healthy about three months in the future. You *know* it will be so.

This form of healing is very simple, but it works. Remember, it is really love that allows the healing to come to pass.

Now, there is a slightly new subject that I will address here. Most healings that do not take place no matter what the healer does, are because there is something within the person that is stopping the healing. We are talking about something other than belief patterns. This is something that many healers wish to avoid, but it is *absolutely necessary to address* if the person has this problem.

This brings up the subject of entities and dysfunctional thought forms that are not part of a person, yet live within that person. These entities act as parasites. They are not the person, but that person has, by his thoughts, emotions/feelings or actions, attracted these entities. By their presence these entities can keep a healing from taking place as well as directly cause major diseases.

What is an entity? It is a living being who has come from another dimension but somehow entered this world. In the world from which they came, they are useful and necessary to the universe as a whole. But here they are a problem.

There is another kind of entity that is simply a human spirit who, out of fear, has not left the third dimension and has chosen to reside within another person. And there are other possibilities, such as ET spirits who may or may not be from this dimension but are in the wrong place at the wrong time.

The understanding is similar to the cellular levels within your body. Each cell in your body is unique and lives in a particular body part. It has a job to perform for the body as a whole. They appear different; brain cells look different from heart cells, which are different from liver cells and so on. As long as the cells are in the right place, there is no problem. But if we were to cut your stomach open, blood cells would pour into your stomach. They should not be there, so a healing would be necessary to remove these blood cells and stop this influx of alien cells.

What is a dysfunctional thought form? It is the thought of a human or other being that has arrived within a person, usually by intention. A spell, a curse, directed hatred and so on can all come to life within a person. Once within someone, it will usually take on a form, which might have almost any shape, and a life-force energy. It will appear to be alive. It is removed in the same way that spirits are.

All these possibilities have a detrimental effect on human health, with the exception of the "good" entity. Yes, rarely there is a spirit of a highly evolved nature who is good for the person. When one is discovered, I usually do nothing to remove it. At the right time it will leave on its own.

Hypnotherapists deal with these issues all the time. It is usually the first thing they do. And I agree with them. After you get permission from a person's higher self, the first thing you do is check to see if he has any of these entities or dysfunctional thought forms. I have found that about half the people I have seen have them. The source of these entities is often from the time period when the Mer-Ka-Ba was misused on Atlantis and the dimensions were ripped open, about 13,000 years ago. And very often these entities have remained with a particular soul for all this time.

Ask your higher self if you are to become involved with this part of healing. If not, then forget it, but be prepared that sometimes there will be nothing you can do as long as an entity lives within the one to be healed.

I will explain what I do to remove them, but please remember that it is not the technique, but love that is so important. And my path is definitely not the only way or technique to assist in healing. If you are just beginning, some of what I say may not make sense. I will do my best.

In the past, the Catholic Church and others have used exorcism to evict the entity out of the person's body. This was usually done with very little understanding on a spiritual level and mostly by brute psychic force. The priest just wanted to remove the entity and didn't care what happened to it. Little did he know that this spirit is simply going to move into someone else's body as soon as possible, which is usually the first person the entity sees. The entity *must* live within someone's body. It is not capable of living long outside some form.

So what good is this form of exorcism? The disease, the entity, still stays alive within humanity. It is in a world that is not its own. It is afraid and very unhappy. These entities are similar to little children, but in order to protect themselves in this alien world, they have learned to take on frightful appearances and noises to keep humans away. If they are approached in love, honesty and integrity and you can convince them that you really are going to send them back home, they will not resist but will usually even help. So my suggestion is that you treat these entities like children, no matter what they do.

Now let's see what they might do. If you understand the Reality, that it is just light and that it conforms to your intentions, then you know that you can remember and create the intentions that will heal all things. Do not be afraid of these entities or dysfunctional thought forms. They can do nothing to you as long as you connect to them only through love. In this particular state of consciousness, you are immune. If you connect to them through fear, sexual energy, drug-related experiences or any experience that brings them into your internal world, they can possess you.

With love, I begin by asking the person's higher self if there are any entities or dysfunctional energies within that person. If it says yes, I immediately put up a mind field in the shape of an octahedron (two back-to-back pyramids) that surrounds the person and usually myself, too. This is done for two reasons: It will not allow the spirit to escape and move into someone else's body, and it provides a dimensional window at the tip of the octahedron to move the spirit back into its home world.

Then I personally invoke Archangel Michael to assist me. He loves to do this work because it brings the universe just a little bit closer into order. He stands behind me and watches over my shoulders. We work together as one. He will work with you if you just ask.

Then I place my hand over the person's navel and ask the entity to come forth to me. I then go into telepathic communication with the spirit(s). I have found it is not necessary to have the entity talk out of the person's mouth. (This just makes matters more complex and can produce fear in the person.) Once I am in telepathic communication with the spirit, I send it love so it knows that I am not there just to "get it," but that I am interested in its well-being, too.

Every spirit in existence was created by God for a reason and serves a sacred purpose in the overall scheme of life. Nothing has ever been done at random. I tell the entity that my purpose is to return it to the world from which it came. And I mean it. Once the spirit is convinced that I will really do this, it is easy.

Then I feel and internally see this spirit. These entities have many shapes and forms, which will seem very strange to a novice. Often they are shaped like a snake or insect, but they can appear in almost any form. At the right time I begin to pull this spirit out of the body. Once the spirit is out about three feet, I hand it over to Michael, and he brings the spirit up to the apex of the octahedron and sends it through the dimensions back to its home. Michael knows exactly what to do.

This becomes a win-win situation for both the person and the spirit. The spirit returns home, which to it is like going to heaven. There it can fulfill its sacred purpose in life and be happy. And the person being healed is inside his own body all alone, sometimes for the first time in thousands of years, and he is able to function in a new and healthy way. Many diseases will often simply go away all by themselves, since it was the spirit that was causing the problem in the first place.

A little side note: The reason I put my hand over the navel is because I have found that that is the easiest place from which to remove spirits. They usually enter a body from a specific chakra at the base of the skull, at what is called the occiput. Usually a person has entities because he has used heavy drugs or alcohol and become vulnerable to them or because entities may have found an opening from the person's use of sexual energy or because the person has entered extreme fear and become helpless. There are other ways, but these are the three major reasons I have found.

Once one spirit leaves and demonstrates that going home is real, almost always, if there are other spirits, the others will line up and help you, without a fight, so that they too can go home.

I know this is a strange subject, but it is real. I have observed the results in thousands of people and seen how this has helped them become whole and healthy again

I'll give a couple of examples. Last year in Mexico a young man I didn't know came up to me after a workshop, saying that he needed help. He said that for about a year, he had not been able to control himself in many ways. He felt like a spirit was inside him, and asked me if this was true.

After getting permission, I talked to his higher self, who said that there was only one spirit inside him and to proceed in my normal way. The spirit came forth and began to speak in English, but with a thick Italian accent. I giggled inside, since I had never heard a spirit that had an Italian accent before. We talked for about fifteen minutes. Finally he told me he would leave, and in a few more minutes it was over.

The young man felt much better, and we began to talk. I asked him how he thought he had opened up to this spirit. He said he didn't know that for sure, but he did know where it happened. I asked where. He said, "Italy." Inside I said, "Of course." This spirit was human and was simply afraid to leave until now.

Another example was from Europe. A woman and her husband came to my workshop. They had been married for years and loved each other very much, but as they began to get older, she began to sexually fantasize about this "imaginary" man. It was not because the sex between her and her husband was not good. The fantasies simply began.

As time went on, this imaginary man began to take more and more of her sexual energy until one day she could not have an orgasm *except* with this imaginary man. So she stopped making love with her husband, and from her point of view, she couldn't help it. This imaginary man made her have sex at least two or three times a day, whenever *he* wanted, not her. She had no control.

This could have been an emotional or mental problem, but in this case it wasn't. This was a real "imaginary" man from another dimension. She had opened the doorway through drugs. She had stopped taking the drugs, which she had done only twice, but it was too late. The man was inside her.

After getting permission, I talked with her higher self for a long time. The spirit inside her was a highly intelligent being. There was no fooling this one. When I contacted him, he already knew what I was going to do. He held a deep conversation with me for about twenty minutes and then wanted to see Archangel Michael. So I invited him to stick his head out of this woman's stomach and look for himself. When he saw Michael, I knew by the expression on his face that he was impressed. He immediately popped back into her body, looked at me and said that he needed more time to think about it. He told me to contact him the next day.

The next day, the lady told me that she had talked with him almost all night. He said he loved her and didn't really want to go, but he had decided that it would be best for both of them. And then, of course, they had sex again.

That evening I held my hand over her stomach and contacted him again, as he had asked. He simply said, "Good evening. I want to tell you that I like you very much, and I want to thank you for assisting in this manner." Then he said that he was ready to go. I lifted him out and Michael held onto his shoulder and took him into the world from which he came. No resistance whatsoever.

When I told the woman it was over, she was amazed. She said she hadn't felt anything. Then she looked at me and said, "He wanted me to tell you that he likes you."

That evening she and her husband made love together for the first time in a long time. The next morning they were so happy that they decided to have a second honeymoon. Life was to begin again.

Details: Make sure you get *all the debris* out of the body. Many of these entities will lay eggs or leave behind some kind of debris. Ask where it is, or feel it and pull it out and let it go back with them. If you leave this debris, the person could get sick from it or even keep the diseases caused by the spirit.

One last statement. Personally, if I get sick or something begins to go wrong, which is seldom, I wait a little bit before I heal the situation. Why? Because I want to know why I caused this unbalanced experience in my life. I examine my life. I want to know what I thought, felt, said or did or how I lived that created this disease so that I can correct it so that it does not come up in some other form. I wait for the wisdom.

A Final Message and a Story

I'm sure you've heard this one: "There are no limitations in this world except the ones you place on yourself."

Diana Gazes, from the above story, left her TV show and went to Hawaii to learn about herself. She took a leave of absence from the whole film world. She could look at spoons and bend them with her thoughts, and she taught people, mainly in corporations, how to work with psychic energies. She's a very psychic person, and she wanted to explore this part of herself more. Anyway, she was in Hawaii and we decided to do this psychic experiment she wanted to do. The details of the experiment are not important, but we were going to do it for ten days, and each day after it was done, I would call her and we would verify our results.

I did it the first day and called her, then I did it the second day and called her. On the third day I decided, "I think I'll *not* do the experiment today and see what'll happen." After the experiment was supposed to be completed, I called her up, but there was no answer. Something had happened. She wasn't there. I didn't know what to do, so I asked the angels, "Well, what do I do with this?" They said, "Here's her phone number. Call her up."

So this phone number came out of the blue and I called it, wondering what was going to happen. To my sort-of surprise (the angels are never wrong), Diana picked up the phone. I said, "Hi Diana," and she said, "Who's this?"

"It's me, Drunvalo."

"Drunvalo?"

I said, "Yeah, how're you doing? You sound funny."

She said, "Drunvalo? How . . . ?" She was quiet for a moment, and then she said, "How can this be? Drunvalo, I was just walking by this phone booth, and the phone rang. How did you do this?"

Soooo, just have faith in yourself, trust yourself. God is within you, definitely. You can heal anything. You can bring your body *and* your world into perfect balance with love. Life flows and becomes easy, not diseasy.

S I X T E E N

The Three Levels of the Self

We think of ourselves as living on Earth in this human body, but have you ever considered that you may exist on another level, or even levels, of life at the same time you are here? This is the belief of many of the Earth's indigenous peoples, such as the Maya and the kahunas of Hawaii. They see us as multidimensional beings literally living other lives in other worlds, which is the truth, from everything I know.

Under normal conditions we humans are consciously connected to these other parts of ourselves, but because of the Fall during the time of Atlantis, we are separated from our higher selves. When we do connect and it becomes a reality, we live life in a manner that would seem impossible to us now. We can see the past and future clearly and are able to make decisions based on higher knowledge, which affects our spiritual growth in positive ways. This we have lost due to our actions long ago.

These higher levels of ourselves that exist in other dimensions are called our higher self or higher selves if we consider it from the bigger picture—though to think of our higher self as a single being is right and wrong at the same time. There is only One Being in the universe, yet there are many levels that exist within this One Being. Remember the way we spoke of the levels of consciousness in chapter 9?

Your higher self is connected to even higher selves. So there are higher selves connected to higher selves connected to higher selves. Each higher self is on a different level of consciousness that is still larger and more encompassing, until finally the ultimate level is reached before transcending this waveform universe of dimensions altogether. Each person has the *capability* of existing within every possible level of consciousness at the same moment, but this is rare.

So it is similar to a lineage or a family tree that grows upward until finally it connects with God and all life. But we were separated from our multidimensional self at one point when we, as the human race, fell to this present third-dimensional consciousness. There was a division that took place. We fell so far down in consciousness that the other aspects of ourselves could no longer communicate. Although we are not, for the most part, aware of our higher selves, they have always been aware of us.

As time has progressed since the "Fall," communication has been sporadic and rare. Our higher selves have mostly waited for us to awake. They have been waiting for the right moment in time. It's been kind of a one-way separation—they are aware of us, but we are not aware of them.

If the kahunas of Hawaii are correct, our higher selves have placed us on hold and are out there playing and communicating with each other, preparing for the day when we will wake up to the rest of life. Most of us have not truly connected with our higher selves for almost 13,000 years, except for short periods of grace and light.

This reconnection with your higher self is not channeling or anything of that nature. It is just a reconnecting of your own essence and spirit to itself. Perhaps, more accurately, it is a remembering—a re-membering, bringing the various members of spirit back together. Some people call it the soul. For me, I see only spirit. I see Great Spirit, and all spirits that come from that source are just a portion of Great Spirit. In this view we are all related to Great Spirit, or God. Some of the connotations of the word "soul" imply that souls are different from each other and are somehow unrelated. To me, all souls or spirits are from the same source. If you want to see God as our Father/Mother, then we are all brothers and sisters in the entire universe.

What I have found—and it has been found by almost all native tribes in the world—is that we have this higher aspect within us. If we can make the connection with conscious communication, we then get clear guidance from within us about how to move moment by moment in life. The movements become filled with grace and power, with little or no effort. This guidance comes from only you, and it cares about you in the same way you care about yourself. And it's a guidance that you could never figure out or understand from this third-dimensional level.

A side note: Superimposed over the levels of life and the higher selves is what many people call the Spiritual Hierarchy. The Spiritual Hierarchy is composed of beings who have been given responsibility for organizing and running the government of the universe. The Spiritual Hierarchy is interwoven with our higher selves and is not directly related to us. Just because you connect with your higher self does not mean that you have connected with the Spiritual Hierarchy. I bring this subject up only as a reference, to answer the question before it is asked.

Following is the example that the angels originally gave me when I was trying to understand how the higher self could see so clearly. Suppose you were rowing down a river in a canoe. Let's say you're in a jungle and it's the blue skies and green water of the Amazon. There's foliage all over. You're having a good time, just row, row, rowing your boat down the stream of life. And when you look behind you, you can see only a little way. The trees are so high on each side of the river that you can't see outward or beyond the bend.

Your memory of the river goes back only a little, and that's all you can see. As you pass the bend into the next area of the river, you kind of forget the past. You can remember a little bit, but the farther you go down the river, the more unclear it gets in your memory. You can look ahead and see the next bend, so you can see ahead into the future up to the next bend in the river, but after that you don't have any idea what's coming up. You've never been on this river before.

Your higher self is like a huge eagle flying high over your head. Your higher self is in another dimension and perceives time spherically. It sees the past, the present and the future all occurring simultaneously. It can see way back along the river, way, way, way back, much farther than you can, and it has a good memory. It can see far into the future, too. It has limitations, but they're expanded. It's a fantastic view compared to yours on the river, so it can see things as they're about to happen. It can also see relationships in the reality that you, from this human place, just simply can't see because of your position. Let's say you're following the instructions of your higher self, and your higher self, a great bird, comes down to you and says, "Hey, take your canoe over to the side of the stream here and get out now."

If I didn't follow my inner guidance very well, I might say, "Oh, I don't want to do that. It's beautiful, you know. No, let's wait awhile, and then I will leave." But if I were following the guidance of my higher self, I would simply do it and ask few questions. Then the higher self might say, "Carry your boat through the jungle." So you carry your canoe over logs and tree roots and red-ant hills, and you're thinking, "Oh man, these higher selves!"

If you have been following your inner guidance, you know what I mean. You're going through all these changes, moving this heavy canoe through the jungle, wondering why the higher self has asked you to do this seemingly crazy act. You might go for half a mile through this dense jungle before you reach the river again and can look back up the river. From there you see that around that last bend was a 500-foot waterfall crashing onto massive rocks. Had you continued as your ego had wanted, you would have been killed. But because you changed your path and went another way, you continue to live on Earth. You avoided a disaster by following an invisible inner guidance that has an ancient wisdom.

I used to give a technique for reconnecting with higher self. I now realize that this technique works only under certain conditions. It worked for me, but I didn't realize that it actually didn't work for me in the way I originally thought it did. Why doesn't it work for someone else? I tried to understand, but at first I couldn't.

I had tried for many years, but I just could not understand it. I finally just asked my higher self. (I usually wait until I can't figure it out any other way.) I asked the angels, "Please, just tell me. Show me what it is." A whole series of events happened after that, one after another, each leading to a better understanding.

The first thing that happened right after I asked for help was at a workshop I was giving in the state of Washington in Olympia. A man there was in his sixties, a native Hawaiian. When I saw him, I could not understand why he was at this workshop, because I could see that he didn't need to be there.

I waited awhile before I approached him, and I finally said, "What are you doing here?" He said, "I don't know."

"Oh, okay. Neither one of us knows why you're here." So I went back to teaching and waited a long time.

A couple of days later I was talking with him and said, "What do you do?" He said that he was a kahuna from Hawaii.

"What do you teach?"

He said, "I teach only one thing, and that's how to connect with higher self."

"Oh . . ." So when it came time for me to talk about the higher self at the workshop, I said, "Just a minute." I sat down in the audience after asking the kahuna from Hawaii to talk about the higher self. He talked for an hour and a half to two hours about connecting to higher self from a Huna point of view. It was perfect for me.

This talk changed my understanding. From the way I had understood it through my experience, there was me and there was higher self, because that's what my life seemed to tell me. But the kahuna made it clear that we are divided into *three* parts—the higher self, the middle self and the lower self. I should have known, since everything is broken up into thirds.

Since that time with the kahuna, I have had many experiences that have made the following clear. If we are the middle self in our duality consciousness, then what are the other two selves, the higher and lower selves? We will slowly explain who and what they are, but it is most important to understand that one cannot reach or connect with the higher self until one has first reached and connected with the lower self. Spirit must first move downward before it can reach to the heavens. This teaching has been verified in so many ways in my life. So we will begin by explaining what the lower self is.

The Lower Self—Mother Earth

In the most straightforward terms, the lower self is your unconscious mind. But contrary to the popular thought that the unconscious mind is connected only with yourself and your personal unconscious thoughts, this unconscious mind of the lower self is connected with all other human beings on Earth (Jung's collective unconscious), and it intimately knows every individual person's unconscious mind also. Further, it knows the unconscious minds of not only every human alive, but also everyone who has ever lived on Earth in the past as well as everyone who will live on Earth in the future. Yes, your subconscious mind knows the past and the future in detail, at least relative to the Earth. In addition to that, your lower self knows everything associated with *all life* on this planet, not just human—in other words, the entire living biosphere. It is a perfect record. And this lower self is alive and comes across as a single being communicating with you. *It is Mother Earth herself! She* is your lower self.

To be clear, the lower self is the Earth and all life on, in and above her. I am not sure at this time if the Moon is included with the lower self. It probably is, but I am not certain.

According to the Hawaiian kahunas, and really to most other indigenous peoples of the world, Mother Earth is a young child about two to six years old, depending on who you talk to. She is always a child, because she *is* a child.

To connect with your lower self, it is believed by indigenous peoples worldwide that you must begin by loving her and playing with her. Adult sophistication and all its technological thinking and trappings will not work to connect with the Mother. She is usually not interested. You could meditate for hours every day, you could spend all your time doing nothing but trying to connect with the Mother, but usually it is a waste of time. The harder you try, the less likely that anything will happen. Why? Because she will connect only with the innocent child within you. And of course most of us have lost our childhood innocence. We have lost the pathway to know and consciously connect with the Mother. Your inner child must be remembered and lived if you wish to proceed. Even Jesus said it: "Except ye become as little children, ye shall not enter into the kingdom of heaven."

Let's look at ourselves, our adult side that thinks it knows so much. You may have a master's or doctor's degree from one of the great universities of the world; you may be considered an expert in your field; you may even be famous and very highly respected. But if you wish to know Mother Earth, you must put all that aside and completely forget it. She is not impressed. Mother Earth loves children, and if your childlike nature and your innocence are allowed to emerge from the muck of your adulthood, then something real can begin in your spiritual life.

When the kahunas want to find fish, for example, they ask Mother Earth for substance. And she will answer them. The answer might very well come from within the reality itself. The clouds might turn into a human hand and point to the place where the fish are. The kahunas get in their boat and when they reach the spot that the Mother told them about, there the fish are. This is a way of living with nature that civilized mankind has completely lost, although a few indigenous tribes and Earth keepers still live that way.

Now let's look at you. You are at work or school, say, and you decide to go home. You reach in your pocket for your keys. Immediately your thoughts are in the future. You are already thinking about your car and going home. Once you get to your car and start it up, you are thinking in the future again. You are thinking about the drive home or your lover or perhaps even your cat or dog, but you are more than likely not thinking about what is right before your eyes. You are still in the future or the past. But *only from the present* can we truly experience anything. The present is usually too painful for most people to participate in.

Did you really look at the beauty all around you? Did you see the sunset? Did you see the billowing white clouds in the sky? Did you smell the air, or did you decide not to because it was filled with pollution? Did you see the incredible beauty of the colors of nature? Did you feel love for Mother Earth? Did any of your senses function except what was necessary to drive home? This is the problem. Our adult lives are deadened, and we are only living a shadow of what is humanly possible.

Have you ever noticed children when they are experiencing nature? They become lost in sensing the great beauty all around them, so much so that they sometimes are seemingly in another world. Do you remember?

If you wish to connect with your lower self, with Mother Earth, you must find your inner child and become a child again. Play with the Mother, have fun, really enjoy life. It means living a life that is joyous. It does not mean play-acting like a child and making silly sounds and faces—unless, of course, that is what is really coming from your heart. It means living your life in the way you really want to, not in the way that someone else feels you should. It means caring about people and about animals and other life, because you can feel the connection, not because it will profit you somehow.

I didn't understand what had happened to me at the time the angels appeared. All I knew was that I had given up on living life according to the rules that seemed to have no meaning. I had begun to live a life that I really loved. I had moved to the mountains of Canada, where I had always wanted to live. I moved deep into the forest because I had always wanted to do that. I wanted to see if I could live on nothing, and I became very close to nature. I had no fear. As I watched the sunrise, every day was like a new birth into life for me. Each day was special. I played music most of the day, which was my dream. I had to work hard for about three hours a day, but the rest of the time was mine. I loved life, and I still do. The seeds that were sown in those early years are still growing in my life today.

It was then, at the peak of this Canadian experience, when the angels appeared to me and my wife. It was the beginning of a lifelong love of life. It was a silent key to higher consciousness, but at the time I didn't understand. As I have found, in order to begin a true spiritual life, one begins in nature as a child. Once a true connection with your lower self has happened—and only then, according to the kahunas—you may connect with the higher self. It will be Mother Earth who decides if you are ready, and when she feels you are, she will introduce you to this grand part of yourself that we call the higher self. No amount of force or determination, no amount of begging or crying or feeling sorry for yourself, will bring this to you. Only love, innocence and a great deal of patience will allow you to find your way. You have to forget about trying. You even have to forget that you are connecting to Mother Earth. You simply must live life from your heart and not your mind. Your mind will function, but under the control of the heart.

The Higher Self—All That Is

Okay, if the Earth is the lower self, then what is the higher self? It is simple. The higher self is everything else in existence. All the planets, the stars/suns, the galaxies, the other dimensions—everything is your higher self. It is you. This is why there are higher selves to the higher selves as you expand into the infinite. The experience of the higher self is very different from the experience of Mother Earth.

Consider this for what it may be: Mother Earth will often play with you and tell you that *she* is your higher self, using the words that she knows will get your attention. She may come to you in your meditation and tell you she is your higher self and that you must listen to her. She may instruct you to do all kinds of earthly things, like run all over the world doing projects for her. But she is just playing, and you are taking her seriously, not realizing that it is just a game.

If you ask her to tell the truth, whether she is really your higher self, she will never lie. She will laugh and tell you the truth. At this point you are supposed to laugh also and begin to play with her. But most adults will simply get mad and think they are being used. Then the connection is lost. This is why the kahunas always ask, when they connect with the higher self, if it is really the higher self. The Mother is a funny girl, but she is wonderful to know when your heart is pure. And what escapes most meditators' understanding is that *Mother Earth is you.*

The higher self knows everything that has ever been known by any life form anywhere, and everything is alive. And it knows everything that will ever happen in the future, just like Mother Earth, except that it is for all the rest of creation.

Once you are connected consciously to the lower and higher self, life becomes a completely different experience from anything you have known before. Life works through you, and your words and actions have great power because they are not from your little limited middle self. They are from *all life*, from all of creation. Nothing is outside you, everything is within you. And the truth of who you really are will begin to unfold.

From My Old Writings—Living as a Child

I had been living in the forest for about a year. I had no plan and nowhere to go. I was just being. I was just simply playing, just like I played when I was a kid. I would go outside and look at tall pine trees and feel and see their great spirits. I could talk to them, and they would talk back to me. I would find animals and walk up to them with no fear. I became so in tune with my surroundings that I could walk right up to deer only three feet away and look them in the eyes, and they wouldn't even think of running. They would just look back with their open and innocent eyes. I could feel them connect with me in my heart. All the animals knew that my home was theirs and that it was safe.

As time passed, life became very simple, and I was really enjoying each

moment. I felt like I could spend eternity here amongst the life that seemed to cuddle me in its arms. It was at that moment, when I least expected anything spiritual to happen, that the angels appeared, these two beautiful angels, one green and one purple. I really didn't know what was going on. I started following their direction because I could feel their immense love for me. And once the angels appeared, all these things started happening in my life. The coincidences began . . .

First they were just little ones, then incredible ones. Then more incredible, and then ridiculously incredible. And then it went beyond ridiculously incredible—it went into flat-out, plain, total miracle. I began to see things that were absolutely impossible according to my logical mind. I just watched these impossible happenings all around me and I would think, "Oh boy, this is really fun! I like this a lot!"

In that entire time I never really understood what was happening to me. I never understood when the angels came and told me that the green angel was the spirit of the Earth and the purple angel was the spirit of the Sun. I didn't get it. I didn't know what that meant. When they told me, "We are you," I understood even less.

Mother Earth is connected to all of us in the whole world; our subconscious mind *is* the subconscious mind of the planet. When I would start thinking about the nature religions such as the Druids and the Shintos and how they were connecting with the Earth, the Moon and the Sun, it began to make sense. It all started falling into place. I began to understand.

You see, we've lost this truth so much that we've severed our bond with the Earth. We don't have it anymore. We're sophisticated now. We're adults, we're civilized. Did anybody see the Peter Pan movie? You know, the one with Robin Williams called *Hook?* That movie is exactly what we're talking about, exactly. If you haven't seen it, do so, and if you have, look at it again with new eyes. It might surprise you.

There was always a third angel in the background, a huge presence of a gold angel. It was always silent and was simply a witness whenever the two angels and I would communicate. Almost a year went by and never a word from the gold angel. One day the two angels came to my wife and me and said that the gold angel wanted to speak to us. They said he would speak on a specific day, which was about a week in the future.

My wife and I were so excited. We fasted and prepared for this wondrous event. We could only imagine what the gold angel would say. On the appointed day we went into meditation, and there he was, front and center. The two other angels were in the background. We had very high expectations. We thought he was going to lead us in some new way. Then he spoke the words, "It is only light." He looked at us for about a minute in silence and then disappeared. We had no idea what this message meant. We thought it was too simple. We wanted more.

The green angel, the Earth, was our lower self, and the purple angel, the

Sun, was our higher self. Over the years we began to understand that the gold angel was the next level of our higher self. In about 1991 I was teaching a class, sitting in a medicine wheel on a hill on Orcas Island in the San Juans. I called in the angels during our opening circle.

The green and purple angel came in and looked straight into my eyes. Then the gold angel came in directly behind them. The gold angel then passed right through the other two and turned around, facing the same direction I was, toward the center of the circle. He then slowly moved back into the space of my body and merged with my being. The sensation was electrical, and I went, "*Wwwooowww.*" I felt an immediate change in my spirit, a huge surge of energy. I knew something really big had just happened, but I had no idea what it was.

I slowly began to understand. That was my first physically direct connection with my higher self. And the work with the purple angel, though it was also my higher self, seemed distant. This was somehow very different and straightforward. I began to notice that as I saw the angels from then on, they would not tell me in detail what to do, which I had become used to. After that they would tell me to find the answer within myself. They would say that I was older now and must find my own way. If I made a mistake, they would wait as long as possible before they instructed me to make a change.

From 1970 until about 1991, approximately 21 years, I was working with my lower self, although I didn't know what I was working with. You can know almost *anything* from the lower self because you have the entire knowledge of the planet. All the practices with dowsing rods, pendulums and psychotronic instruments I am convinced is just your lower self.

What I've found is that the connection with your lower self becomes a spiritual growth process during which you start slowly, then grow faster and faster. You can almost watch yourself becoming something new.

A question was once asked at one of my workshops, "Is there a particular sensation or emotion you get when you connect with your higher self?" I replied, "I always feel like I'm in the presence of God. Other than that, I don't know. It isn't God as religions define God, but it's such a higher aspect of us that it feels like it."

How Life Works When You're Connected with the Higher Self

Here's another story from the past. Directly after the angels entered my life, they led me to a school called the Alpha and Omega Order of Melchizedek. In a meditation with the angels, they gave me an address, 111-444 Fourth Avenue, Vancouver, Canada, and a man's name, David Livingstone. They instructed me to go to that address and talk to this man. I finally found the place, which was in an old industrial section of the city where there were warehouses and the like. The address itself was in an alley attached to an old rusty door with a freshly painted, colorful sign just above the door that read: *Alpha and Omega, Order of Melchizedek.* David Livingstone was a real person, and I met him under very unusual conditions. He allowed me to learn in this school, where about 400 people were studying meditation. I learned many valuable lessons there, of which the following is but one. If you understand the meaning of this story, you will know the importance of the higher self in your spiritual growth.

There was a young man who lived in Japan, and he was communicating with his higher self through a form of automatic writing. This in itself is not unusual, but the language was not from this planet. It was composed of all these weird symbols and shapes with lines and dots placed seemingly at random. He acknowledged that this language was not human, yet he could both read it and speak it. But he knew no one to speak it with.

All instructions from his higher self came to him in this language, and he guided his life by them. He did whatever his higher self suggested, for the truth of this being had been shown to him. He believed it completely.

One day in 1972 his higher self told him to get in an airplane and fly to Vancouver, British Columbia, on a certain day at a certain time, then stand on a certain street corner and wait there. That's all the higher self said to do; he didn't know what was to happen after that. Because he believed it completely and always did whatever it said, like a child would with its parents (as long as it was morally right, of course), he bought the ticket, flew to Vancouver and found the street corner and waited. He had total faith.

On that day I was studying at the school, and David was in the same room. He looked down at his watch and said, "Oh yeah, he's going to be there soon." He told another man, "Go to this location," handing him a piece of paper, "to the southeast corner. There will be a Japanese man waiting there." He told the student the man's name and asked him to bring the Japanese man back to the school.

So the student went to this corner, walked up to the young Japanese man, calling him by name. All he said was, "Come with me, please," and led him back to the school. The Japanese man spoke English, but not very well. He was taken to this little room that was only about 10 feet square, where he was asked to wait. David told me that he wanted me to watch what was about to happen, so he brought me into that same room and said to me, "Okay, you stand there," pointing to a corner of the room.

After a while, David entered the room and addressed the Japanese man by his name. They had never met each other in their lives. David asked him a few simple everyday questions, such as what city are you from in Japan and the like. When he finished his small talk with him, David told him, "Wait here. I'll be back in a few minutes." He asked me to stay with him, then he left. We just looked at each other.

A little while later a tall, beautiful woman quietly entered the room. I didn't know who she was. There were a lot of people in this organization, and I didn't know them all. She set up an easel up in front of the two of us, and over it was draped a piece of dark purple velvet that hid whatever was underneath. The easel was probably about four feet square.

Then four young men silently walked in the door. Two stood on one side of the easel and two stood on the other. There was another long wait, with the six of us just standing there. Finally David came in. The Japanese man looked genuinely curious, showing no fear or confusion, but he asked, "Okay, what's this all about? What's going to happen here?" David didn't answer him, but just looked at him and lifted the piece of purple velvet off the easel. The Japanese man's eyes widened. Written all over the board was this young man's secret language—which, as far as he knew, no one in the world knew but himself.

Now, the Japanese man had not shown this language to anyone since his arrival in Canada. David hadn't seen the language, yet there it was, all over the easel. I don't know what it said, but the guy's eyes got about as big as pies, and all he could say was, "Ooohhh." Then, as if to increase the shock of seeing his secret language written by someone else, the four men standing on either side of the easel began speaking to him in that language. When the first man spoke, the Japanese man looked as though he had gone into shock. He collapsed emotionally and began to cry and sob uncontrollably. The four men began to assure him that everything was all right—in his secret language, of course.

I'll bet there was a little piece of him that thought he might be nuts, you know, after these words had come from nowhere in a language that no one knew. Suddenly here was an incredible confirmation of the truth of his inner meditations. They were all from a particular planet somewhere, and they all knew exactly where. All of them went crazy with joy, particularly this Japanese man. He was so happy he could barely stand it. It was the beginning of an amazing adventure of life for him. I can't tell you what happened after that because they asked me not to.

Anything is possible, absolutely *anything*. But you have to believe in yourself, you have to trust yourself and open up this innocent childlike quality within yourself. And if you do, it's a process that will reconnect all of you back into this wholeness, from which this kind of direct connection to God is very obtainable, I feel. It's an in-between step, I would say, in what is in the transcendental meditation aspect of things.

Communicating with Everything Everywhere

Eventually, when you're completely connected to the lower and higher selves, it becomes clear that everything is alive. Once that realization becomes your life, then everything becomes communication and everything has meaning. The higher and the lower selves can communicate with you in all kinds of ways, not just in a vision as angels or as a voice that speaks in secret tongues in your head. Once connected, the entire Reality becomes alive and fully conscious, and everything is communicating at all times.

Your inner world is alive and directly connected to the outer world. The outer world can speak to your inner world. The shape of trees, the color of a car at the right moment, even the license plates on the car, can communicate to you. The movement of the wind, the flight of bird in a certain direction—everything. Everything becomes alive and communicates. This world is much more than we were taught by our parents. The truth is, they didn't know, though long ago their ancestors did.

I remember years ago when I asked the lower self for a sign to show me that what I was about to do was in divine order. If a sign did not appear that I could understand, I was not going to perform this particular ceremony I was contemplating. This was in the very beginning days when the angels first appeared and after I had made my first trip back to California.

I was driving up I-5 in California heading back toward Canada at that moment. Only seconds later I saw something I could hardly believe, so I stopped the car and backed up to see if my eyes were telling me the truth. I got out of the car and walked over to an old barbed wire fence and peered into a large, flat grassy field. And there they were: At least two hundred large black ravens were all standing facing each other in what appeared to be an absolutely perfect circle. It looked like someone had drawn a ring on the ground and asked them all to stand on it and face the center. It had the most amazing effect on my faith. Mother Earth sure knows how to get to your heart!

Now, you "know" those things don't happen—but they do, at least when you can see that Mother Earth lives. She has the greatest sense of humor!

Foretelling the Future

One last story. When I first met the angels, I was somewhat preoccupied about knowing the future. I would use the I Ching and the tarot cards to try to understand what was coming. I practically wore out my I Ching. In the beginning the angels knew my desire to know the future. Whenever I would ask for future information, they would seldom cooperate. Then in a single day it all changed.

The angels came to me and said that from now on they were going to tell me everything that was going to happen the following day. They said that because the time difference between when they told me and the time it happened was so quick, I would be able to see the truth about the future. And they actually did it.

They gave me a synopsis of the following day, then at their discretion, certain moments or events in great detail. They would tell me every phone call, who it would be, the basic nature of what would be said and the exact minute it would occur. They would list every piece of mail I would receive and, in certain cases, exactly what was said in the letter. They would also tell me the name of each person who would come to my door and what they wanted. They also would tell me exactly when I would leave my house and when I would return and the primary events in between. During this time we always knew where we were going the next day, so that many times we would prepare, because it would always happen.

On the first day I waited minute by minute for each event to happen. And *everything* happened exactly as they said. I was so happy, because I finally knew for sure that the future could really be known. My confidence in the angels increased even more, for now I saw them as having real powers, from my ego point of view. I remember after a while how I would pick up the phone and say, "Hi, John. I knew you would call." Of course, in the days before Caller ID, this was impressive—at least my ego thought so. I was so happy with myself.

One day I asked the angels about my papers to immigrate to Canada. I wanted to know if the government was going to allow me to stay. Instead of telling me, they gave my wife a vision. She described the vision as it was happening, and I carefully wrote it down. She saw us driving home in a silver car heading into the countryside. She opened the glove compartment and reached inside to get the mail. She leafed through about six letters and found the one from the Canadian government. She opened it and read it to me. I wrote down every word.

When she came out of this vision, we examined what was said, but nothing made any sense. First of all, we did not have a silver car, and second, our mail was dropped through our front door. Why would it be in our car? The letter would say that I had been approved and would give me all my scores in detail. We talked about this letter for a while, but when it hadn't happened within a month or so, we soon forgot about it because it seemed to be a mistake. It worried me, because the angels had never made a mistake.

A few months later we moved from our house in Burnaby to a farmhouse out in the countryside. We had bought a new silver car, and one day I was driving home from the post office, where we had to go to pick up our mail. I had thrown it into the glove compartment and was heading home with my wife, who was in the passenger's seat. By this time we had both completely forgotten the vision the angels had given us some months before. As she reached into the glove compartment, she shrieked, remembering the vision. She leafed through the mail, and the sixth letter was from the government. We opened it and later compared it with the vision we had written down. It was the same, word for word, even down to the scores that no one could have made up.

Meanwhile the angels' daily forecast of the following day continued. I remember how it put me through so many changes. In the beginning I thought it was the greatest thing that had ever happened to me. Then as time went on, I began to take it for granted as part of my life. As time continued, I became bored with it. I remember how I began to not want to take down the notes when the angels would give me the details of the future. You know what it is like? It is like seeing a movie for the second or third time. You know what is going to happen, and it lacks the surprise and impact. Life became boring.

Finally I couldn't take it anymore, and during my meditation with the angels I asked them to please stop telling me what was going to happen in the future. I might outwardly look now like I am pushing for the future; I might fight tooth and nail for a cause because I believe in doing my best in life. But inside, I am still. I know it will all be fine. From this experience I now believe that everything that happens in life is whole, complete and perfect. I know the wisdom of not knowing.

The Lessons of the Seven Angels

When the angels first arrived in my world, I listened to their every word. I followed them because I could feel their love and because they showed me their deep understanding of the Reality. As I told you, eventually the green and purple angels were replaced by the gold angel. When this happened, there was a change in how I related to all of them. They quit instructing me in my everyday and spiritual affairs and began to see if I could find my own way.

Slowly over time, my work with the gold angel became one of learning how to know the answer from within myself without asking the angels. When I found this knowingness, I also found that I attained it through certainty. It was a knowingness that did not require asking for an answer. It came from within, and it came from within the heart, not the mind. There was a certainty without a doubt, like knowing your own name, and it was this certainty that allowed knowingness to emerge from the heart. Along with this knowingness I found there was a loss of wanting to know.

It was clear they wanted me to become more independent. Is this not similar to how parents treat their children? In the beginning parents take almost complete control over their children's lives. But as the children get older, they begin to teach them to do things for themselves. Weaning a child from its parents is necessary if the child is to become an adult. I think it is the same here on this level of life, too.

What surprised me completely was that one day another angel entered my world. This angel was pure white and had the quality of uncomplicated form or simplicity about it. The gold angel receded into the background with the other two angels, but remained visible, and for about a year the white angel taught me. What it taught me I am not sure. It was about letting go, not feeling attached to anything, living perfection and knowing that all is well. Even though my life was now becoming increasingly complicated from the teaching I was giving around the world, everything seemed to slow down. I understood what was inside, but I found it difficult to put into words.

Then in the midst of this fuzzy experience, the white angel joined the other three, and a fifth angel appeared. This angel had no color or form. It was what I call the clear angel. It is an angel of completion. It brought to me lessons of bringing all things together. It was an angel of my higher self that I have never talked about before. I am still working with this angel, and someday I may talk about it.

This angel pointed out to me how the angels related to music, and how this angel and the other four were connected to the notes of the pentatonic scale—five angels and five notes of the pentatonic scale. The clear angel suggested to me that someday two more angels would come, and that they would complete the knowledge of the octave—seven notes and seven angels. I waited.

About a year ago, at the beginning of 1999, two new angels appeared together to me while I was about to give an Earth/Sky workshop. It was none other than archangels Michael and Lucifer. They were holding hands. Since that time new lessons about duality have been filling my days on Earth, lessons I will talk about in the next chapter.

After working awhile with your lower and higher selves, there is a transformation that takes place inside you. I don't know when that stops, if ever. I keep finding myself changing all the time, yet I am beginning to see that the patterns are repeating, and I am simply that I am.

People look at me and say, "You can't do that. That will never work." But it works. Why? It is not me doing it. As the gold angel said, "It's just light." Everything, all the stuff we think we need, is only light.

There's no problem with creating it. There's plenty of energy, there's so much of everything. You know, there are tons of places to go, infinite space and dimensions. Everything is in abundance. There's no reason for these limitations, but we place them on ourselves because of our fears.

If you have a hard time believing that you could play all the time, well, that's your limitation. Doesn't playing mean doing something you really enjoy doing? I always like to try to create my life in such a way that I am giving to someone, because if I create giving to someone, it automatically comes back so that I can keep on giving. This makes me happy. It will come back, whatever it is that you do. It could be anything. It doesn't really matter as long as it brings joy. Keep your little child happy.

Testing the Reality of Your Connection with Your Higher Self

This test will not work for all of you who read this, at least not at this moment, but it will at some time in your future. If you have not connected to your lower self, with Mother Earth, then do that first. If you are now connected to your lower self, then this might really work for you. If you are already connected to your higher self, then it could be an interesting and useful proof. But if you are just beginning, then just hold this idea for the future.

Once you feel that you are connected to your lower self and you feel and know that you have permission to connect with your higher self, this is a simple test you can do to prove your connection to yourself. This proof helps build confidence and leads to a stronger spiritual understanding. Not everyone needs this proof, but some of you may. So if after reading this test, if it does not seem necessary, then go on to the next chapter.

Begin by asking your lower self, Mother Earth, if this test is okay for you to do. If she says yes, then have fun.

Once you feel that you are ready to make this connection with higher self, then get a pencil, paper and a clipboard and write down a statement that you've got to put in your own words. Basically you're going to ask your higher self for a test to prove to yourself that this connection is real. Again, you may not need this test to prove their existence to yourself, and if you don't, then don't do it. You want the higher self to prove to you that it *is* the higher self and at the same time (which is important), you want this test to be spiritually healthy for your evolution.

If you get a green light to go ahead, then begin by making sure that the room is set so that you will not be disturbed by anyone or anything such as a telephone or visitors. Then write down on your paper exactly what you are going to say to your higher self. You are asking for a test, so something like "What can I do, a physical act, in this reality that will prove to me that I've really made this connection with you? It will prove to me in my heart and mind that I've made this connection, and it will be for the greatest good of my spiritual growth at the same time."

Put it in your own words and write it down exactly the way you want to say it to your higher self. Then put the paper and the pencil down in front of you. Next, enter into meditation with your lower self, Mother Earth, and go into the point where you're breathing through the fourteenth breath and have prana moving through you. Then remain in the meditation for at least 30 minutes or more, until you've reached a state where you're very, very still inside.

Just sit with Mother Earth with no expectations. At the right moment, ask your higher self to come forth. The kahunas say you must ask, or the higher self will probably not come. When you feel or sense its presence, speak to your higher self in your own words, coming from your heart, the request that you made on paper. Then you simply listen and wait. Feel the flow of the prana moving through your body. Feel the connection you have with the Mother, and listen for the Father to respond.

The kahunas say it won't always happen the first time. And sometimes the lower self doesn't feel you're ready yet, so she blocks your pathway. But you must ask anyway, and then wait for the higher self to enter into your awareness. When it does, the experience could be anything, just about anything at all that your imagination could think of. In my case these two angels appeared in the room. But that does not set a standard. Anything can happen.

I'm very visual, but you might not be. It does not matter. It doesn't mean that one way is better than another. You might simply have a voice appear in your head and say, "I'm the higher self. What do you want?" Who knows, it might sound like your voice or it might not. Maybe colors start appearing to you and you know what they mean. There's somehow a great meaning in *whatever* occurs. It could just be a feeling or sensation, but if it is really your higher self, this test will prove it or not.

It could be that geometric images start appearing and you know what they mean. Or it could be that you're sitting there and your hand just reaches down, picks up a pencil and starts writing, and you wonder what the heck it's writing. You usually don't know; it could be anything. And it doesn't matter, because you and your higher self already have a way that you worked out a long time ago, one you've probably used before. You can use whatever method you want. It will become apparent to you when it happens.

So a transmission is made to you, whatever it is. The act you're supposed to do, whatever that is, is transmitted to you. You go, "Aha, I'm supposed to do *this!*" The most important thing now is to say to your higher self, "Thank you. Goodbye," then put all ten fingertips on the ground, like roots [see Fig. 16-1].

Put them down on the ground like this, in front of you or on the floor; or wherever you're sitting, reach down and feel the Earth. That will ground you and pull you out of your meditation very quickly. If you've ever done this before, you know that. You could be sitting in a meditation for two hours and be way out there, then put your fingers on or in the Earth's soil, and you will come out of the meditation and back into your body very quickly.

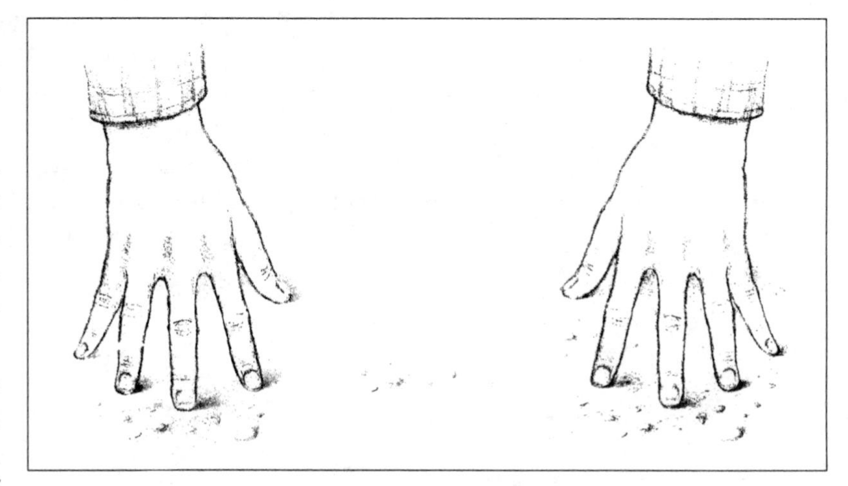
Fig. 16-1. A quick way to ground oneself after a meditation.

Why quickly? We want you to come out as fast as you can so that your mind does not interfere with the transmission. Don't think about what your higher self said, just get out of the meditation, pick up the clipboard and now write what you were just told. Don't think about it. That's very important. Just write it down, get it on paper, get it all the way down to the last word. Put the period on the last sentence. Once you've got it written down, you can relax.

It is so easy for the mind to interfere in this state because when the ego, the middle self, gets a transmission from the higher self or even from the lower self, it will very often change it before you even get out of the meditation. That's one of the biggest problems in interdimensional communication. If the middle self, the ego, thinks about what is said and says, "No, I don't want to bring that transmission back," it may change the words. It takes training.

So get it on paper, then pick it up and read it. You can look at it and think about it, whatever you want.

I have to say this, though the odds of this occurring are almost zero: If for any reason you are told to do something that is morally wrong, you absolutely did *not* contact your higher self, for sure, guaranteed. Your higher self will never tell you to do something that is wrong or harmful. If you understand what the higher self is, it is self-evident. If you received a message supposedly from your higher self that is morally wrong, then burn the paper and forget it. Forget about the higher self and go back to playing some more with your lower self. Definitely wait awhile before you try it again. But this distortion almost certainly will not happen.

However, if you get it on paper and it says to do something inconvenient or something you don't really want to do or that you think is silly—anything your ego doesn't really like or thinks is stupid to do—that does not matter. If you're going to follow this path, then the next thing you must do is *do it*, whatever it is. Then wait and see what happens.

In the act of doing it, look to see what happens in the Reality, which you are not in control of. The Reality itself will react to that act and should show you and prove to you, beyond any doubt in your mind, that you have reached your higher self. It might not prove a thing in anybody else's mind, but it will be very specific with you.

We have just entered a world where everything is light, meaning conscious, alive and a function of your thoughts and feelings. If it feels too strange or if you feel fear, wait. Everything is in the timing. If you have just connected with your lower and/or higher self, life is going to become beautiful, interesting and a lot of fun.

S E V E N T E E N

Duality Transcended

Judging

What I am about to say is a view of what we call evil that is different from what most of the religions of the world believe. I am in no way attempting to protect Lucifer or sanction his acts. I am simply giving a new/old perspective on what is behind what Lucifer is doing in the universe that, once understood, allows the possibility of transcending good and evil and entering pure oneness with God. The possibility of ending duality is impossible as long as we remain in the consciousness of good and evil. We have to transcend it and enter a different consciousness, but we cannot do that if we continue to judge.

As long as we continue to judge the events in our lives, we give power to them as either good or bad, which determines the course of our lives. To end it and then transcend it, we must step outside this polarity. We must change, and this change has to come in some way from our not judging this world. For it is in judging that we decide that something is good or bad. That is the basis of good and evil, or duality consciousness. The key seems to be viewing all the worlds in our universe and all events within them as whole, complete and perfect, knowing that the cosmic DNA, the cosmic plan, is proceeding exactly as directed by the Creator.

The Lucifer Experiment: Duality

The words "the Lucifer rebellion" carry a stigma that has haunted mankind for at least since the Bible has been on Earth. Many of us humans, especially Christians, believe that Lucifer is the cause of all evil and darkness that has ever transpired on this planet. We call what Lucifer did a rebellion, projecting an image that Lucifer is somehow going against the universal cosmic plan. But unity consciousness sees Lucifer's work in a slightly different light. His work is not known as a rebellion, but as the Lucifer experiment.

Why would it be called an experiment? Because that is exactly what it is, a test to see if certain parameters of life will work. *Life is an experiment!*

The instructions from God at the beginning of the Lucifer experiment were for humans to live free will. But what does free will mean? Does it not mean *all possibilities,* both good and evil? Does it not mean that we would be allowed to do *anything* we wanted, with the idea, from a biblical point of view, that we would learn discrimination for the good?

Life was given the ability to do anything it wanted, all possibilities; it was given free will. Therefore, how could free will exist unless consciousness created the format for this way of being? And who creates consciousness? The one and only God. Lucifer did not create free will, but it was through his actions and decisions that free will became a reality. It was God who created Lucifer so that free will would exist. Before the Lucifer experiment, there was no free will except during the three other attempts. All life moved according to the will of God, according to the cosmic DNA. There were no deviations, and free will was only a potential that life could someday try.

At one point, because free will was possible, we realized that there was a particular way we could experience this reality that had not been tried before. So we tried it. We actually tried three versions of it, and each time it failed. They were absolute disasters. The latest experiment and fourth attempt, with Lucifer heading it, used a different approach to create free will. This time God chose an area of consciousness that was just above human existence: This experiment began with the angels. So it was the angels who brought this new freewill consciousness to mankind to be lived here in these dense worlds, and life everywhere watched to see how it would fare.

With great respect between two brothers, the battle between good and evil began. It was a battle to the death, yet neither could die. It was a battle that had to be, for it was the will of God. For the overall sake of the universe, Michael supported the side of the light and the good and Lucifer backed the side of darkness and evil. A new possibility was about to be lived. And we humans thought it was a great idea, this idea of free will.

The Bright and Shining One

It becomes clear in the study of sacred geometry that nothing was created without intention and reason. It wasn't just a mistake; in fact, there *are* no mistakes. And when God created Lucifer, as you can read in the Bible, he was the most magnificent angel God had ever created. He was the most intelligent, the most beautiful, the most amazing of all angels. So he had no peer; he was the top-of-the-line model of the angelic worlds. God gave him the name Lucifer, meaning "the bright and shining one." God gave him this name, so do you think God made a mistake?

If you think back to our own human nature, we always tend to look to our heroes as that which we want to become. We look up to those people who have gone before us, who have blazed the trail in the direction we feel we want to go, and we model much of our behavior after our heroes. Because of the understanding of "As above, so below," it is the same for Lucifer. He wanted to be like his heroes, but he didn't have anyone higher than himself in his realm. He didn't have any heroes.

He was the greatest archangel in creation. There was no one greater than he. Rather, the only hero he had was God, who was the only being beyond him, from where he could see. So Lucifer did something very natural—and I feel sure that God was aware that this would take place when he created him. He wanted to be as good as God—to actually *be* God—from a *creation* level. There's nothing wrong with merging with God, but that isn't exactly what he wanted to do. He wanted to be *just like* God. In fact, he wanted to be even better than God. Lucifer wanted to surpass his hero.

Lucifer was so intelligent that he knew how the universe was created. He knew the images, the patterns and the codes that had created the universe. But in order to be greater than God, he decided that he would have to separate from God. As long as he was part of God, he could not go beyond Him. So, evidently with God's blessing (since He created him), Lucifer started on a great experiment to see what could be learned by creating in a different way from how God/Spirit had made the original creation. He severed the love bonds between himself and God and created a Mer-Ka-Ba field that was not based on love, because once he severed the love between himself and God, he could no longer make a living Mer-Ka-Ba.

Archangel Lucifer and many other angels started on this great experiment to see what could be learned in this new way. As we said, similar experiments had actually been tried three times before by other beings, but those experiments had ended in massive destruction and pain for everyone involved. Many planets had been completely destroyed, including one in our own solar system—Mars. But Lucifer was retrying this old experiment with a new method.

So he severed the love bonds between himself and God (at least it outwardly appears this way) and created a Mer-Ka-Ba field that was not based on love. What he did was make an interdimensional time-space machine that we call a spaceship. This flying object—sometimes seen as a flying saucer but also many other shapes—was more than just a vehicle as we think of it, much more. It could not only move throughout the spectrum of this multidimensional Reality, but it could *create* realities that seemed to be just as real as the original creation. It is similar to what we are now calling virtual reality, only this was a virtual reality that could not be distinguished from the real thing.

So Lucifer made this synthetic Mer-Ka-Ba to create a reality separate from God so that he could ascend to the heights and be just as good as God, at least in his own mind. He couldn't *be* God, but he could be *like* God, his hero.

In order to convince other angels that this experiment was necessary, he chose a different pathway out of the Great Void to create his synthetic reality that was unique unto itself. To explain this in detail, we will move to the Garden of Eden.

In the Garden of Eden there were two trees: the tree of life, which led to eternal life, and the tree of the knowledge of good and evil. In the Genesis pattern of creation as seen in the Flower of Life, the pathway the little spirit took, coming up to the top of the original sphere of creation, was associated with the first tree, the Tree of Life [see chapter 5, page 151]. The spirit came from a single point in the center of the first sphere and began to rotate in a vortex, creating the images that created the reality that leads to eternal life. The Tree of Life and the Flower of Life are of the same creation.

But there is another way that spirit can exit the Great Void, and it is associated with the tree of the knowledge of good and evil. It is actually the same geometry, except that it has a different view of the geometry. In other words, there's another path to follow in sacred geometry to exit the Great Void and create a reality that appears the same but is geometrically and *experientially* different. Lucifer knew this, and he chose that pathway to create a new kind of reality he could control. At least controlling this new reality was part of his original intention. Archangel Michael's original intention was to simply create free will. Their inner agendas were different.

Creating a Dualistic Reality

Lucifer convinced a third of the angels in heaven to go with him to support him in this new reality. He convinced them because his particular pathway out of the Great Void resulted in a unique viewpoint that had not yet been lived or explored. From their angelic viewpoint of reality, it was a possibility of life and someone needed to live it.

Important to at least the angels who followed Lucifer, this new pathway also contained a system of knowledge that was able to give an experience that had never been fully lived before in the original Reality of God. This experience centered around two pieces of geometric knowledge—rather simple pieces too, it would seem. These two geometric forms were primal knowledge about the Egg of Life and the source of all living forms.

The first sphere they were seeking fits in the center of the Egg of Life and touches all eight spheres [see A in Fig. 9-36a]. The second sphere fits perfectly inside any of the six holes in the center of each face of the Egg of Life (just visualize the eight spheres of the Egg of Life inside a cube, which has six faces). This knowledge had always been known, but from within the original Reality it was not possible to actually live and experience it. Remember, all sacred geometry has an experiential aspect. For your information, see Figure 17-1. The diamond view—a square turned 45 degrees—shows the Luciferian geometry of these two spheres.

Lucifer told the angelic worlds that we needed to do this experiment because the universe had missing information, and the only way to get the information was to live it. So he chose this particular view of geometry in which to start his new, separate reality creation. Through this new geometry he interpreted his creation in a new way. This gave the experience of being *inside* a life form *separate* from the rest of reality. Many believe it was

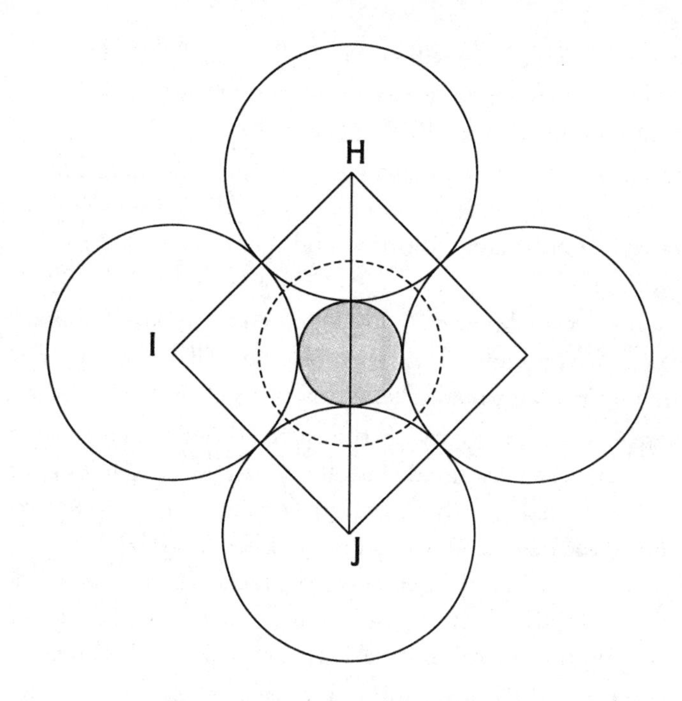

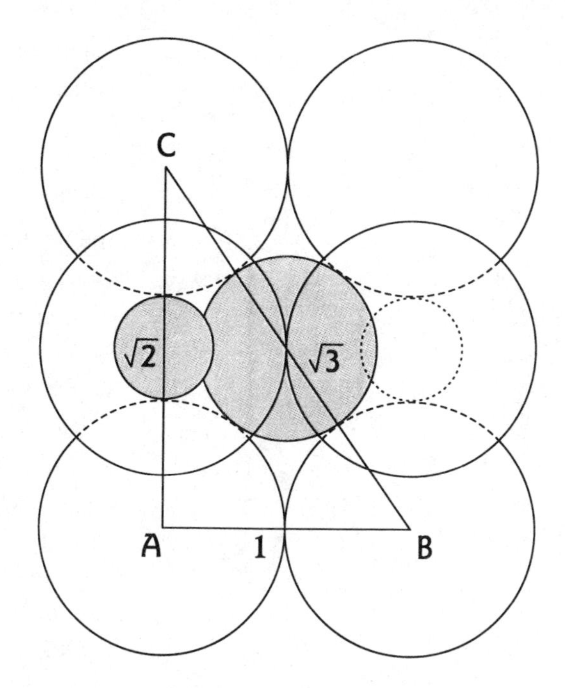

Egg of Life, diamond view
Large sphere diameter = 1
HI = 1
IJ = 1
$HJ^2 = HI^2 + IJ^2$
$\therefore HJ = \sqrt{2}$

Egg of Life, turned on edge 90°
AB = IJ = HI = 1
$AC = HJ = \sqrt{2}$
$BC^2 = AC^2 + AB^2$
$BC^2 = 2 + 1$
$\therefore BC = \sqrt{3}$

Fig. 17-1. Quest for the experience of two primal spheres. On the left: The sphere that touches only 4 is related to matter (the square root of 2). On the right: The sphere that touches all 8 is related to light (the square root of 3).

great and, most important, that it was new. There was hardly ever anything new in creation.

The way of Lucifer was the diamond view of the Egg of Life, the same dimensional view that humanity happens to be living at this moment in history. Yes, we did follow Lucifer.

Remember the ninth chapter, "Spirit and Sacred Geometry," where we were at the second level of consciousness? Remember how the Earth is now living the three levels of consciousness (out of five possible levels) and how we had to rotate the second level of consciousness 45 degrees to the diamond view to get it to point to the next level, Christ consciousness [see Fig. 9-4, page 228]?

Lucifer chose the square view, then turned it 45 degrees to the diamond view, the view in Figure 17-1. It was this view of the Egg of Life he wanted to obtain, because this view was the one that was needed to experience both the inner and outer spheres that would fit into those openings we spoke of above. The seemingly innocent need for this information from this view (remember, on an experiential level) was a huge deal to the angels whose purpose was to create free will and live all possibilities. This was a possibility that might work. And it was a possibility that had never been lived before, or at least never been lived successfully.

So these are the details of how Lucifer did it. Again, I am merely reporting this information so that you can transcend the dualistic view of life into the next higher level, Christ consciousness, and "get thee behind me," Lucifer, as Jesus would say.

The trick to this new reality was that spirit can separate itself; it can be in two or more places at one time. It is very much like cell division, or mitosis, except without form. It is what makes mitosis possible in the first place.

So the new reality was created with the same sacred geometry as the Flower of Life, except that spirit divided itself into two and began to rotate out of the Great Void in a double helix pattern *from two completely different centers*. *This* created the new reality. In addition, Lucifer used the diamond view of the Egg of Life, turning it 90 degrees to the rectangular view in order to focus the new, untried consciousness through it. It became the lens through which we interpreted the new reality. This was revolutionary.

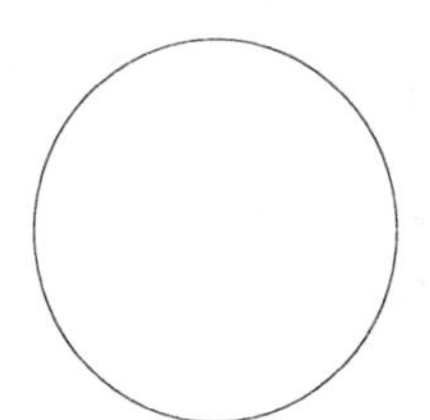

First creation

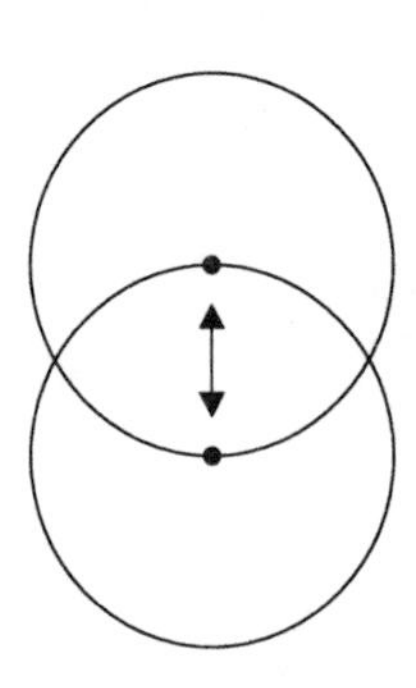

Day one

Fig. 17-2. First day of Lucifer's creation. Spirit resides in both centers at once.

In creating the original Reality, on the first day of creation at the first motion of the spirit of God, spirit moved itself to the top of the first sphere [see chapter 5, Fig. 5-32]. Then we started the rotating pattern, which began creation. But there's another way to enter creation, where spirit would leave part of itself at the very first center. In other words, at the very first instant of the motion away from center, which is the very first moment that creation begins, spirit would divide itself in two and leave part of itself in the center and move the other part of itself to the top of the first sphere. Then it would create the next sphere at the top of the first sphere, the same way as in the other creations [Fig. 17-2].

But from then on, the *next* motion, on the second day of Genesis, spirit begins a *double* rotation motion, where the center half of spirit rotates over one way and the top half of spirit rotates over the other way and forms the two spheres, which make this pattern [Fig. 17-3].

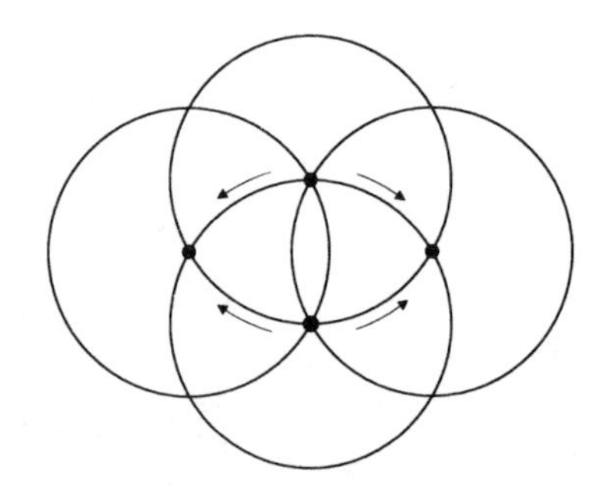

Fig. 17-3. Second day of Lucifer's creation.

From there it divides itself again, to create this pattern [Fig. 17-4].

It then begins a pattern of dividing and coming together. But it is primarily division, separating from one's self. It expands into this pattern [Fig. 17-5], then continues outward.

This can keep going on and on and on . . . and eventually you end up with exactly the same grid as the Flower of Life—the same laws, the same apparent reality, the same planets and suns and trees and bodies. Everything's the same except for one *huge* difference. The Flower of Life pattern has a *single* geometric center—one eye, and a being who enters creation this way is connected directly to all life and to God. But Lucifer's pattern has not a *single* geometric center, but *two* specific centers—two eyes. No matter how big the grid is, when you come back to its center, you'll find two centers or eyes. And it has been separated from God. There is no love. These angels of Lucifer have almost forgotten what love is. Remember what Jesus said, "If thine eye be single, thy whole body shall be full of light"? [See Fig. 17-6.]

But again, who is in control here? *God is.* And God created this situation. It wasn't Lucifer who created this situation—it was God, one step before Lucifer. God created Lucifer and knew what Lucifer was going to do. So there must be a reason for creating this separate reality.

Fig. 17-4. Third day of Lucifer's creation.

Earth Humans as the Focus of the Experiment

Lucifer began this new reality shortly before we humans came into existence as a race—a little over 200,000 years ago. And we have become the key players. There must be a reason why all these things have happened. I think that the purpose behind this Luciferian experiment, which has been going on for these millions and millions of years, is now coming to fruition on Earth, and that Earth has been chosen as the place to give life new birth. This is what it looks like.

Whatever the ultimate purpose for creating this new reality is I do not know, but it has become clear throughout the cosmos that the Earth has become the focus of this intense drama. And it appears as though the fruition of this experiment is about to unfold before our eyes. You and I are the players who take this new reality and transform it in the direction of the ultimate purpose. We are to go beyond anything archangels Lucifer and Michael had imagined. We are to be the children of the third way, a new reality born from the first two.

Fig. 17-5. Fourth day in Lucifer's creation.

We here on Earth are all part of this Luciferian experiment. All of us have chosen this path. Every one of us on this planet has chosen this way, whether you like it or not, whether you want to be identified with it or not. You chose this, because you're here. And our physical mother, the Nefilim, are also part of the Lucifer experiment, and so is our physical father, the Sirians, though the Sirians have almost totally extracted themselves. The race from Sirius B, the dolphins, were also part of the Lucifer experiment. If you remember, the dolphins came down in a *spaceship* to the Dogons. They were also involved in technology. They had little hard-shelled vehicles for a long time too, but they gave it up about 200 years ago and now they're making an incredible transformation back to unity.

I don't know if reverting back to a no-technology world as found in the original Reality is actually the answer. I'm not certain. I think that we here on Earth are going to discover the answer. The answer is on this planet, whatever it is, and the people on this planet have become the grand catalyst of the ex-

Fig. 17-6. As the days continue, the two eyes of Lucifer become clear. There is no "single" geometrical center, or "eye."

periment—the experiment upon which all life is now breathlessly focused to see what happens. Why? Because what happens here on Earth is going to affect everyone everywhere. And I believe that this answer is coming through our hearts.

Using the Intellect without Love

This is how Lucifer convinced all these angels that we really needed to experience this new way. What happened to these angels? They severed their love connection with God, with all life, and functioned on one side of their brain, not on both—they functioned only with intelligence, not love. This has created races of beings that were incredibly intelligent but had no experience of love or compassion—like the Grays and the Martians, for example. In the past this always resulted in their fighting each other, sending life into chaos.

This is where Mars comes in. Mars was one of those races (not of the Lucifer experiment, but the one before that) that was terminating almost a million years ago. At that time life was destroying itself everywhere. Mars destroyed itself. It was constantly warring, constantly fighting, because there was no love or compassion. Then at one point they just blew their atmosphere away and destroyed everything. But right before they did, there were certain people who knew that destruction was inevitable, and some of them were the Martians who came to Earth and settled in Atlantis, causing all the Mer-Ka-Ba troubles here on Earth.

This is the focus. The result of this Lucifer experiment was that the Lucifer beings created physical ships and focused on technology, creating an entire technologically based system and a separate reality from the original Reality, whereas the beings who did *not* separate from God had absolutely no technology whatsoever. They were led by Archangel Michael. Then the war of opposites began. Archangel Michael, the angel of light, and Archangel Lucifer, the angel of darkness, began the cosmic war of duality that created our good-and-evil, dualistic consciousness.

Archangel Michael and the angels of light have living Mer-Ka-Ba fields that can do anything that Luciferian technology can do, and even more. And Archangel Lucifer and his angels of darkness have their technological Mer-Ka-Bas and their synthetic reality. So we have two totally different approaches to life. Look at archangels Michael or Gabriel or Raphael—they don't have technology and spaceships. They live in lightbodies, and their reality, the original Reality, is based on light. It is what could be called light technology based on love. Then there's this other way, Lucifer's way, where you have all this material stuff to be concerned with. We have our houses and cars and all the things we feel we need. The whole web we're in is Luciferian technology. You can look out at the world and see the difference between nature, the original Reality, and what mankind has done with its separate reality created by the knowledge of Lucifer.

Of course, you can take this to the extreme—anybody, any life form whatsoever, no matter where they are, if they're flying around in technological crafts, they are part of the Lucifer experiment, flat out, I don't care who they are. But there's an entire spectrum of engagement with this experiment. There are some beings who are so far into it, who are so addicted to it, that they're helpless in a certain way. They cannot live without it. There's a spectrum of addiction to it all the way to and including people like us. We're addicted to it also, but we still have one foot in the original Reality, too.

It would be very difficult for us to take off all our clothes, which are now technological because they are made with machines, and walk into the woods again with nothing but our bodies. We're definitely addicted to our technologies. On the other hand, we do have love. We have a tiny spark of love; we haven't completely severed our love from life. Thus we're some of the beings in the universe who have somehow not completely severed our connection with God. We have technology, but we still sense and know what love is. It's weak, not powerful; it's not a blazing, blinding light. But we still have it. We have both aspects. We have the original Reality potential still within us.

The Third, Integrated Way

An important understanding is that we Earthlings are finding the universal answer in a totally unique way that's never been seen before. This whole thing between the original Reality and the Luciferian reality seems to be leading to a third way that is some kind of combination of the first two.

If you cross your eyes when you look at the two-eyes drawing [Fig. 17-6], you may see the third way when you see *three* eyes. Then the middle path becomes a combination of both. You're actually seeing both of them superimposed over each other. View this figure as a stereogram, and you'll see that it creates a third, unique pattern. This new third way is the hope of all life everywhere. The universe has been at "war" for 200,000 years—the battle between the dark and the light with no apparent solution. Now it appears this struggle is going to culminate in a new birth, a third reality.

The Sirian Experiment

Within the Luciferian experiment there was a second experiment that is changing everything here on Earth and is expected to change everything everywhere. Perhaps this second experiment will ultimately create a reality where both ways can be integrated. It does seem to the ascended masters that this is what God is doing. This next experiment was created and directed by the Sirians, who fathered our human race.

The story that follows is outrageous. Believe it only after you have found within yourself that it is true.

My Three Days in Space

More than 25 years ago, around 1972, not too long after the angels first appeared to me, one day I was sitting with my family and another couple who were living with us at the time. The two angels came in and told me that they wanted me to go into a room by myself and enter a meditation that would not be disturbed. (This was long before Thoth appeared on the scene.) I asked my family to leave me alone for a while, went to a separate room, sat down and went into the Mer-Ka-Ba meditation.

The next thing I knew, the angels had me lift out of my body, and we headed into outer space. That was the first time I saw the formation of the golden human grid around the Earth. I literally passed through it. I remember closely examining many geometrical parts being formed within this living space. Then the angels said, "We want to take you into deeper space." They communicated that I should not be worried or concerned about going so far away from Earth.

The angels and I together literally started moving away from the planet. I watched Earth recede, and the angels were right with me. We moved past the Moon—I will never forget watching as we quickly moved first toward it, then slowly past it. We silently moved out deeper and deeper into space, and I could see the Moon becoming much smaller. Then we flew outside a membrane that surrounds and contains both the Earth and the Moon. This spherical membrane is about 440,000 miles away from the Earth, though our scientists are not aware of it yet. On the other side of that energetic membrane sat motionless a huge vehicle that was about 50 miles long. It could not be detected from Earth because of the technology they were using. It was cigar-shaped, black and seamless. On one end was a huge opening covered with a clear material, and as I approached it, I was pulled toward the opening, where bright light streamed from the inside.

I felt sucked right into the opening and through the glass, or whatever it was, into a room where there were many people. They were very tall compared to me, and there were both males and females. Immediately as I asked the question, *Who are these people?*, within myself came the answer: "We are Sirians." They showed me instantly how they, the Sirians, are actually two humanoid races, one very dark and one very light, and they became brothers a long time ago. This was the white race I now found myself being curious about. There were about 350 members on this vehicle, and they wore white clothing with little gold insignias on their left arms. I sat down with three of them, two females and a male, who talked to me telepathically for a long time. Then they guided me through their entire ship. I ended up spending three days on this vehicle while my body sat at home in my room. They seemed to want to teach me as much as possible about how their ship was run and how they lived.

Everything in the inside of this ship was white, no other color. The rooms were seamless and had forms that came out of the floors and walls and ceilings—mostly the floors and walls—that looked like art forms, shapes like beautiful futuristic sculptures. It felt like you were in an art gallery everywhere you went. And these shapes *were* their technology. They had no moving parts in the ship, nothing except shapes. They had reduced their entire technology to shape, form and proportion, and all they had to do was connect with the shapes with their minds and hearts and they could do anything.

Those of you who have been to Peru have probably noticed that in the middle of the old Incan temples there would often be a large beautiful rock with many angles and shapes and sacred proportions cut and formed on its surface. Well, those rocks are not just rocks—those "rocks" were and still are ancient Incan libraries. They contain the entire records of their civilization. If you know how to connect with them, you can read every second of what happened during the entire Inca period. But the Sirians on this ship had taken it way beyond just record-keeping, so that anything you could think of could be done by this unbelievably simple and beautiful technology, even space travel. We on Earth today are just beginning to understand this technology. We call it psychotronics. It is a technology that requires human (or other than human) contact for the technology to work.

When I came back into my body, the angels began to tell me why they had taken me there. They weren't using words but were telepathically projecting images to me to explain what was happening to me. I expressed to them, "Wow, that was incredible! Their technology is amazing!" I went on and on, saying how great it was. They watched me for a bit, then said, "No, you don't understand. That's not the understanding we want you to have." I said, "What do you mean?"

Technology Reconsidered

My angels told me this: "Suppose your body gets cold in this room, and you decide that you're going to go out and make something to heat the room. So you invent a heater, a really good heater, and some kind of energy source, whatever you need to heat the room. Then you put the heater in the room, it heats up the room and you get warm. From the angels' point of view, if you did that, you just became spiritually weaker. Why? Because you were forgetting your connection to God. You could have heated the room or your body by your own inner essence, but instead you gave your power away to an object.

The angels projected to me that as civilizations make more and more advanced technology, if that is the choice they have made, they are separating further and further from the source of life and are becoming weaker and weaker because they have become addicted to the technology. They *need* it to survive. The angels were saying that the beings in that ship were spiritually very weak. In other words, I was not to look at them as a superadvanced race, but as people who needed spiritual help.

The bottom line of this experience was that the angels wanted me to give up technology and concentrate on pure consciousness as the way to remember God. I heard all that. I really thought I understood the lesson they were giving me. Then as time went on I completely forgot it. It's such a human thing to do!

Anyway, I knew I'd been in their ship for about three of our days, but when I got back in my body, my mind immediately said to myself, "I've been out for about two hours," because that was my middle-self mind rationalizing what had just happened. (That's what we do, rationalize unusual experiences.) So I stood up and walked into the other room where my family and friends were.

When my wife first saw me, she looked at me, pale-faced and fearful. Everybody came up to look at me with worried expressions. I asked, "What's wrong with you guys?" My wife answered and said, "Well, you've been sitting in that room for three days without moving. We couldn't get your attention, and we were just about to call the hospital for help." Then my mind realized that I really *had* been in space for three days. Even though I knew in my heart that it was true, I had to look at a newspaper to make sure. And sure enough, it was true.

The History of the Sirian Experiment

After this experience with the angels and the Sirian spaceship, I thought the reason the angels wanted me to know about this black cigar-shaped craft was to become aware of their technology and its technological relationship to Lucifer. I didn't know then that there was another reason, one that would have equally great importance.

On April 10, 1972, my spirit walked into the body of Bernard Perona, the person who was in this body before I entered. It is clear why I chose that particular time when I look at the timing of events in my past. For something would happen later that year that would forever change the course of history for this planet. It would actually change the course of history for all life everywhere, it now appears.

What I am about to say must be understood as higher-dimensional knowledge and history. The story you are about to read, from a normal human perspective, will seem absolutely outrageous and impossible, probably as impossible as the idea of going to the Moon would have been to people in 1899. From a cosmic perspective, it is business as usual, except that what has come out of this experiment is truly unique and of paramount importance to the entire creation. I know that by telling this story I will be pushing my credibility, whatever I have, to the max. But the angels have insisted that this story be told.

The reason that this Sirian experiment was undertaken in the first place goes back to Atlantis. In chapter 4, I wrote that because of the misuse of Mer-Ka-Ba knowledge by the Martians [page 98ff], the dimensional worlds of the Earth were cut open, causing us to fall in consciousness. And because of this misuse of energy, the human race fell deep into this dense third-dimensional world. As we said before, the Galactic Command, a body of 48 members, approved the rebuilding of the Christ consciousness grid around the Earth, using the system of sacred temples and special sites to re-create this grid geomantically so that humanity could regain its rightful place in the universe. It was a plan that had been used before by countless other planets in a similar position, and it had almost always worked. But when it hadn't, the consciousness of that particular race was lost.

It was calculated by those who know these things that we would be back into Christ consciousness before a particular cosmic event would occur in August 1972. This cosmic event was to be huge relative to this solar system, and if we were not back into Christ consciousness by that time, we would be destroyed, including planet Earth.

Thoth and the ascended masters of this human race, in conjunction with the Great White Brotherhood and the Spiritual Hierarchy of this galaxy, planned everything down to the last detail. This experiment by galactic consciousness was to be completed before August 1972 no matter what.

What was this cosmic event? In August 1972 our Sun was going to expand into a helium sun, a natural event. You see, it was then a hydrogen sun. All the light that comes to Earth and creates all life on this planet comes from the fusion of two hydrogen atoms to make helium. But as this helium builds up over billions of years, a new reaction begins, with three helium atoms coming together in a fusion reaction to form carbon. It was known that this reaction would take place in August 1972, which would mean that if humanity was not in the right state of consciousness at that moment, we would be burned to a crisp. If we were in the right state, namely Christ consciousness, we would be able to protect ourselves and life would go on. We absolutely *had* to be complete with the consciousness change before this date.

In the middle of the 1700s, after almost 13,000 years of this experiment to re-create the Christ-consciousness grid, it became clear to our physical father, the Sirians, that we were not going to make it. What was so sad was that we were not going to make it by only a few years. The Sirians and the Nefilim, our father and mother, both wanted to help, but our father was much further advanced in knowledge and understanding and was more prepared to actually do something. So the Sirians took the initiative to find a way to save humanity. The problem was, there was no solution known in the whole galaxy.

The Sirians loved us so much—we were their little child, and they did not want to lose us. So about 250 years ago they began to search the akashic records of the galaxy to see what other races had thought of concerning this problem. There was no known answer that worked. But because their love was so strong, they continued to search even though there was almost zero chance. Then one day as they were searching a distant galaxy, they found a single being who had proposed a possible solution to this human problem. It had never been tried or tested, it had only been conceived. But the idea was brilliant and could really work.

The Sirians went to the Galactic Command and asked permission to perform this unusual experiment on Earth humanity in order to save us. The Sirian council presented all the knowledge they had learned. You see, the problem was that our Sun was going to physically expand past the Earth and engulf the Earth in its flames in August 1972. This expansion would be only a pulse, returning to almost normal after a few years. But as far as humanity was concerned, five minutes would destroy us.

In order to make this experiment work, the Sirians first had to protect the Earth and humanity from the Sun's heat, but in order not to completely destroy our evolutionary DNA, we could not know they were doing it. It was much like the Star Trek mission statement of not interfering with a planet's indigenous cultures. But there really *is* a powerful reason for not interfering: This kind of ET interference would alter the human DNA forever, and the original human instructions would be lost. If we knew what they were doing, we would not be human anymore! As you may have surmised, this information is only for a few, not for mass consciousness.

The Sirians had to accelerate our evolutionary path so we could catch up with the cycle of the new reality and finish the 13,000-year experiment and return to Christ consciousness. Then we had to relive what we had missed because of the expansion of the Sun in order to put us back in sync with the new Luciferian reality. This was a very complex situation to manipulate.

The Galactic Command asked the Sirians if they expected anyone to survive if they *didn't* do the experiment. If the Sirians had said yes, even if it were only one man and one woman, they would not have been allowed the experiment. But since every last human was expected to be destroyed, then there was nothing to lose, so they agreed to it. Besides, this experiment had never *ever* been done before, not since the beginning of life. They too wanted to know if it would work.

The Sirians returned and locked into position just outside the membrane the huge, black cigar-shaped ship. They built this ship exclusively for this experiment. They then went to the Earth in the fourth dimension and placed objects at the remote corners of the star tetrahedral field of the Earth's lightbody and locked them in place. These were out in space over a thousand miles from the surface, one object at each of the eight points.

Then a special laser beam, unlike anything we know, transmitting unbelievable amounts of data, was fourth-dimensionally beamed down to the north or south pole of the Earth to one of the remote objects, which then sent a beam that was either red, blue or green to each of three of the other seven objects. The beam was relayed until it reached all eight remote objects. From the remote object opposite the one that received the initial beam, it penetrated the Earth to its center and from there outward to the surface into each human being on the planet. The animals and the rest of life on Earth were also inside this energy field, although they were not manipulated. It entered into the original eight cells at the center of each human, and from there outward to each human's star tetrahedral field. This last step created a unique holographic field around each human being, giving the Sirians a means to alter human consciousness. They could both protect and change consciousness without the humans' knowing about it.

This created a holographic field around the Earth that re-created the outer reality of space. It placed us in a holographic replica of the universe, twice removed from the original Reality. This same field was used to protect the Earth from the deadly expansion of the Sun. The Earth would be engulfed with fire, but we would not know it.

At the same time, they could gain control of human thoughts and feelings and project images into our immediate surroundings. This would give them the ability to influence the evolutionary patterns of every person on Earth. The overall system would allow complete protection while this change was taking place without the humans knowing it, and allow the complete alteration of our DNA if and when it became necessary.

The plan was to take away our free will for a short time in order to make rapid changes in our DNA, then slowly restore our free will to the point where *we* would begin to control the patterns—all this to lead humanity as fast as possible into Christ consciousness. Would a complicated, untried plan such as this work? No one knew. But the universe was about to find out.

August 7, 1972, and the Successful Aftermath

The big day came—August 7, 1972. The peak of the event actually occurred over a period of about seven days, but the seventh of August was its greatest expansion. What really happened on that day we humans will not know until we reach Christ consciousness, and no one on Earth would believe me if I put it into words. The real event was almost completely hidden from us through holographic means, but what did happen or what we were allowed to see was still the most powerful emission of energy from the Sun on record. The solar wind reached around 2,500,000 miles per hour for three days and continued at record output for 30 days. It was a truly spectacular cosmic event.

The experiment was incredibly successful. It did work, and we, the innocent humans, were still alive. We made it through the most crucial minutes without any problems. What the Sirians did was keep the programs running that would look to humans like there was little change, then continue the events in the exact way they would have unfolded without the holographic field. They didn't want to change anything until they knew that the system worked perfectly. After about three months they began their real work, rapidly changing consciousness.

For two years, from about June or July 1972 (just prior to the Sun's expansion) until about the end of 1974, we had no free will. All events were programmed, and our reactions to the events were also programmed to force rapid spiritual growth. This worked amazingly well. The Sirians were filled with glee. It looked like we were really going to make it.

The Return of Free Will and Unexpected Positive Consequences

Finally, as progress became apparent, the Sirians began to allow freewill choices. However, if we did not respond with the right choice, the Sirians would continue to give us a similar set of reality choices over and over again until we learned the spiritual lesson. The outer circumstances would change, but the same spiritual lessons would be applied. At one point we became adept and the Sirians allowed us to take back our free will completely.

All this was timed to another event, which was the completion of the Christ grid around the world that the Great White Brotherhood was focusing on. It was completed in 1989, which then made it possible for humans to actually ascend into the next dimensional world. Without this grid there could not be ascension to any level. There were a few minor adjustments in the immediate years that followed, but the grid was functional.

Since the early 1990s humankind has been in a most-remarkable position in the universe, and we don't even know it.

Within the first three years of this Sirian experiment, it became apparent that something very unusual was beginning to happen, something that no one anywhere had ever seen or expected. As this strange phenomenon began, people from all parts of the galaxy became very interested in us. Before this time we were just another speck in the worlds of light. As the experiment continued, even other galaxies began to watch us. And on dimensional levels, all of life shifted its attention to our humble little planet. We became a superstar in the universe—and everyone knew but us!

What was causing the attention was the speed with which we were evolving. From where we are, inside the holographic experiment, we can't tell how fast we are evolving, but from outside the system it is clear. We are evolving so fast that no life form ever known anywhere has ever even come close to achieving what we are doing naturally. And it is increasing exponentially, just as it is inside the experiment if we are observant. What this all means is not really clear to the Spiritual Hierarchy. It's hard to tell what any experiment is going to do when there is no history, no precedent.

The story we told about Thoth and Shesat leaving with 32 members to move into the higher-dimensional worlds and go past the Great Void [chapter 11, page 301] will begin to make sense now. The ascended masters were attempting to find out what this all meant. They began to follow and enter the dimensional windows that had been opened by our expanded consciousness. It now is clear that they lead all the way past the Great Void into the next dimensional octave. This is all so absolutely astounding, by normal galactic understanding of the universe, that few are willing to speak out about where this is all leading to. What is clear is that this is new.

Further, upon close examination, this tiny seed of information that came from a single life form in a distant galaxy (who had an idea that triggered the Sirian experiment) was contained within the original Reality. God put it there, not Lucifer. Of course, God knew what would happen, and only He knows where this will lead.

The reason for telling you this information so that you know the hidden reality behind the events of the day is simple: You are now, or about to become, one of the new ascended masters who will inherit the Earth. You, and those who work with you, will soon be responsible for awakening the rest of humanity. The primary information necessary to open your minds and hearts to the original Reality is within you. Within you is a wisdom older than time. May all that you do be a blessing for all life everywhere. God will always be with you.

May you transcend the good-and-evil, dualistic consciousness and open to the oneness of the One God and the original Reality. From this ancient perspective, the birth of something brand new will surely emerge into the light of this new day.

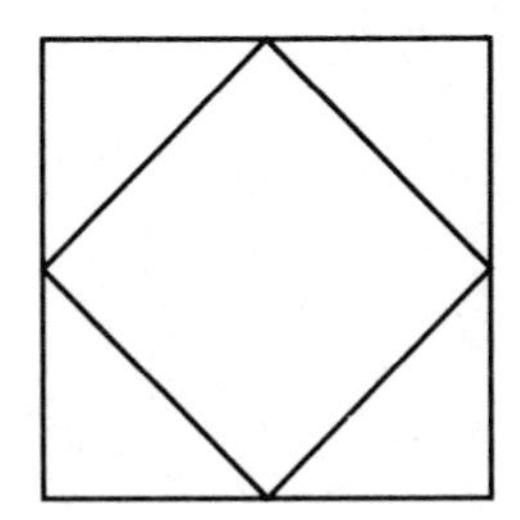

E I G H T E E N

The Dimensional Shift

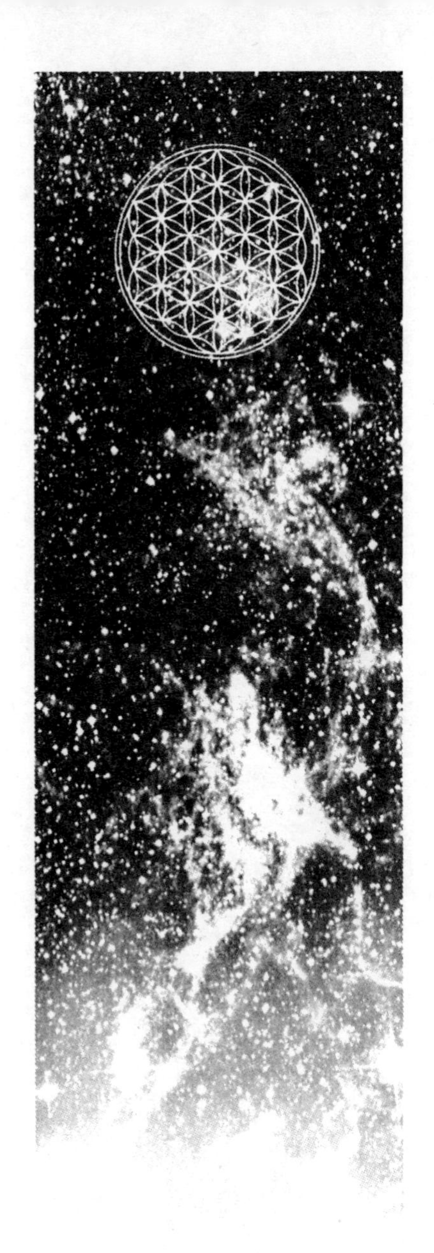

The Great Change

Most of the prophets and the indigenous peoples of the world see a "great change" coming to Earth and to mankind. We see this change, ultimately and specifically, as a planetary dimensional shift into a new level of existence associated with a change of consciousness into Christ or unity consciousness. In the final chapter we will look closely at the great change itself and what may be understood from it. In this chapter we will peer into the nature of the dimensional shift associated with this change to find wisdom that can now be lived here on Earth to bring balance to these changes. Understanding the nature of the dimensional shift is a way to speed one's spiritual growth and utilize to the greatest potential the time we have left on this beautiful planet.

A dimensional shift is when a planet or any cosmic body moves from one dimensional level into another. In our case it will be from the third to the fourth dimension. The whole planet and everyone on it will experience this translation from one dimension to another. The Native Americans believe that we are about to move from the fourth world into the fifth world, a change preceded by a day they call the Day of Purification. The difference in the numbers is because they see the Void as a world and begin counting from that point. So the third dimension of the Melchizedeks and the fourth world of the Native Americans are the same.

If you choose, you can understand the nature of this transformation into the next dimensional level, or next world. Even though it's probably going to be a very quick transformation, we can see the nature of it and understand what the changes are that we must enter. It also lifts the veil from the events of this world and explains why they are happening, which allows clarity of mind and heart about this transformation as we pass through it.

An Overview of a Dimensional Shift

On planets in this galaxy, normally the geomagnetic fields first begin to weaken and then become erratic, the civilization on the planet begins to break down and finally the last phase is entered. The final phase lasts usually no more than two years but nearly always at least three months. In this phase the civilization begins to dissolve, and it becomes extremely dangerous just to be alive. All the systems that keep civilization in place disintegrate and chaos rules. This is the period that most religions, such as the Mormon religion, have prepared for. It is the period when we are still on Earth in the third dimension before we actually make the transition into the fourth dimension.

Then there is a period of five or six hours before the dimensional shift begins. This is a very strange time, when the fourth dimension begins to leak into the third dimension. It really helps to know this is coming.

When the shift actually begins, there will be no doubt. There are specific changes of color and form that are outside of most human consciousness. From this point forward, we have left the Earth's third dimension. Usually the axis of the planet will shift at this time, but we will not know it because we will literally be in a new space-time dimension. There are always other possibilities for how this might happen, but this is the normal course.

Passing through the Void, we will enter into the Earth's fourth dimension. Life will be altered dramatically. Ascension, resurrection and final death will all take place before this phase. Birth into the new world will have begun.

The following scenario details the way a dimensional shift generally happens in the universe, but Earth is an exceptional case. I will first talk about a normal transition as though that is what will happen, but our own transition could and almost certainly will lead to something more anomalous. The course of history may turn into something very different from what I am about to tell you. It depends on the love we have for each other as a planetary race of beings. At the end of this discussion I will present another theory. It is too early to know for sure that it is happening, but it seems to be.

The First Signs

The first sign of a planetary dimensional shift is a sharp weakening of the geomagnetic field, which science knows has been dropping on Earth for the last 2000 years, since Jesus appeared. In the last 500 years, the Earth's geomagnetic field has been dropping more dramatically. As we approach the dimensional shift, the geomagnetic field will begin to go crazy, which has already happened. The world's airports have had to alter the magnetic error corrections for north for their airport maps in order to use automatic instruments. The last thirty years has seen very peculiar magnetic field changes. The birds are not migrating to their usual locations. Birds use magnetic lines to navigate their migratory routes home, and these lines have changed dramatically. I believe this is what is causing the whales and dolphins to beach themselves, because they too use these lines to migrate. Many magnetic lines that have always followed the coast have now moved inland. As the cetaceans follow them, they run into land and are beached. Eventually the geomagnetic field will probably collapse and fall to zero. It has happened many times in Earth's history.

If this happens, several scenarios might take place. The field could reverse itself and the poles would switch. Or it might return to the same polar configuration after it reaches zero, but with a completely different axis. There are various ways it could move, but it doesn't really matter to you and your ascension. You will not be here on this level of Earth's dimensions, so you won't have a direct experience of this change.

There are other more subtle energy changes, such as the Schumann frequency (the basic resonant frequency of planet Earth), which will change before the dimensional shift occurs, but the geomagnetic change is the biggest. I am not going to speak about the Schumann frequency, since the United States government has gone to great lengths to deny that this change is occurring. If you really want to know the truth, check with Germany and Russia, because both nations have information on this subject that utterly conflicts with our government's position. You can also study Gregg Braden's work. His work is more enlightened and honest.

The importance of the geomagnetic field lies in the effect it has on the human mind when and if it moves to zero *and* stays there for more than about two weeks. According to the Russians, in the early days when they put people into space and they were mostly out of the Earth's geomagnetic field for more than two weeks, their cosmonauts literally went crazy. This is exactly what happened after the Fall when Atlantis sank—people lost their memories and went nuts. It seems that Earth magnetism holds our memories intact, much like a cassette tape, and this is tied to our emotional bodies. So the Russians invented a small appliance to be worn on a belt that cosmonauts wear to maintain a normal geomagnetic field around the body when in space. I'm sure that NASA has done the same thing.

It may seem strange that geomagnetics would affect our emotions, but just think what happens during a full moon. The full moon makes only slight changes in the geomagnetics, but the effect is obvious. In any major city in the world, check out the police records on the day before, the day of, and the day after the full moon. There are more murders, rapes and general crime on those three days than at any other time. However, when the geomagnetic field moves to zero, it becomes a much greater problem. Even the fluctuations of the world stock market are based on human emotions, so you can see how major fluctuations in the Earth's geomagnetic fields that last for longer than two weeks can cause havoc in the world.

The Phase before the Shift

This is the period that usually lasts from three months to two years. It is triggered mostly by the geomagnetics driving people crazy. This is what causes the collapse of the social systems of the world. The stock market crashes, the governments become nonfunctional and martial law is invoked but doesn't work because the military is having the same problem. This is followed by the lack of food and other supplies and no help. On top of this, most people become paranoid and reach for their guns. Nowhere is safe on the Earth's surface.

However, because of the tremendous help that our spiritual ET brothers have given us and because of the dramatic changes in consciousness that we have accomplished ourselves, there is an excellent chance that we will not go through this dangerous period, and if we do, it will be very quick. In fact, I would not be surprised if we had *no warning at all,* except the five to six hours that we speak of below.

If we were to prepare for this phase on a *physical* level, we would put food and supplies in a hole in the ground to last at least two years. However, if we entered this underground fort when the shift began, we would not come out. Why? Because the dimensional shift will take us into a new dimension of the Earth's consciousness, a place where the third dimension, our normal world, will not exist. Once the shift begins, the third-dimensional world will pass away, so it is unfeasible to put food and supplies in a hole and expect to emerge after everything is over and resume life as usual.

A large portion of our population have recently done this in anticipation of a Y2K problem. There is nothing wrong about doing it, but it must be understood that it cannot save you. No *physical* preparation will help you in the higher dimensional levels. Success there depends on your spiritual awareness and mostly on your character. Yes, character. I will explain soon.

Five to Six Hours before the Shift

This phase is a weird one, from a human point of view. The Native Americans in the tribe I was first born to when I arrived on Earth, the Taos Pueblo, are told to enter the pueblo, pull the curtains, not look outside, and pray. To look outside would only cause fear, which is the last thing you need.

A strange phenomenon begins at this stage. The two dimensions begin to overlap. You may be sitting in your room when suddenly something appears out of nowhere that will not be explainable to your mind. It will be a fourth-dimensional object that will not fit into your understanding of reality. You will see colors that you have never seen before in your life. These colors will be exceedingly bright, and they'll seem to have their own light source. The color will seem to be emitted rather than reflected. And they have a shape your mind will not be able to explain. These objects will be the strangest things you have ever seen. It is okay; it's a natural phenomenon.

My strong suggestion to you is, *don't touch* one of these objects. If you do, it will instantly pull you into the fourth dimension at an accelerated rate. It would be easiest and best if you avoid moving that fast. If it is unavoidable, then it is the will of God.

Synthetic Objects and Lucifer-Reality Thought Forms

The other phenomenon that almost certainly will occur has to do with the nature of the reality that Lucifer created and that we live within. The original Reality is created in such a way that everything is in divine order with everything else. But in Lucifer's reality, technology has made synthetic materials. These materials, which are not found in nature, will not be able to pass into the fourth dimension. They will return into the elements they were created from. It is possible to send a synthetic material into the next dimension, but it requires a special energy field to keep it intact.

Further, these synthetic materials have a spectrum of stability. Some of them, like glass, are not far removed from nature. Glass is just melted sand. But other materials are far removed, thus far more unstable, such as our modern plastics. This means that some synthetic objects, depending on their stability, will melt or disintegrate quicker than others during this five- to six-hour period. Your car is made of plastics and other highly unstable materials, so it will definitely be unserviceable. Even your house is probably made of many unstable materials and will, for the most part, break down and partly disintegrate. Most modern homes will be unsafe during this phase.

Knowing that this time would come and what would happen when it did, the Taos Pueblo long ago made it illegal to use modern building materials inside the pueblo. The Taos people do make summer homes of synthetic materials away from the pueblo, but they know that when the Day of Purification comes, they are to head for their ancient homes on the pueblo. Sometimes they put windows in their pueblo buildings, but because the openings didn't have glass before, if they lose a window, it won't be a big loss. Other than that, their pueblo is made only of mud, straw, sand, stones and trees. They will not experience this problem.

Therefore, it would be best to be in nature when this happens, but if you cannot be, then it is the will of God. I would not worry about this. I am only informing you so that you will understand as the shift begins.

I will explain this a little further. Synthetic objects are really just thoughts created by and through the Luciferian experiment. They don't exist in the original Reality. It might be hard to understand that they're only thoughts. "Thought forms" would be a better term. They come from what the Hindus call the mental plane, from a higher-level dimension, and slowly filter down through the dimensions until they get here in the third dimension.

In human terms, a person thinks of something, imagines it, then figures how to do it. People create it in one way or another and manifest the object on the Earth. It can be an individual or a group of people, it doesn't matter. The person (or persons) who creates it does not hold the object here on the Earth plane even if they created it. It's held in place by our third-dimensional human grid around the planet. That's the consciousness grid of all the people on this level. It's an agreed reality held in place by the grid, so if someone dies who created an object, the object remains. But if the grid that holds these objects were to break down, the object would turn into the materials it came from, leaving no trace. And this grid will break down before or during the shift.

Obviously, the people who are already going crazy because of the collapse of the geomagnetic field will become much worse when they see the Luciferian reality collapsing, when objects begin to disappear or disintegrate. The good side is that it lasts for less than six hours.

According to Edgar Cayce and other psychics, there have been many extremely advanced civilizations here on Earth before, but there is little or no trace of them. This is because of what we have just described. Their synthetic materials did not make it through the last dimensional shift 13,000 years ago or through other prior shifts. God cleans up the original Reality environment every time there is a dimensional shift.

If an advanced ET culture comes here and wants to make a structure (like a pyramid, for example) last for tens of thousands of years, they don't make it out of a sophisticated metal like stainless steel. They use natural materials from the planet that are very hard and durable. This way they know that the pyramid will last through all these natural dimensional changes that every planet experiences. It's not a Stone Age limitation, it's just an intelligent thing to do, that's all.

Furthermore, these advanced ET cultures are also very careful not to leave any trace of themselves. They either take their bodies with them or vaporize them in order not to break the galactic law of noninterference.

Planetary Shifts

Every person who has ever lived on Earth has already experienced the shift. They had to in order to get here on Earth. It's just a cosmic fact. Unless we came from close by, wherever we came from before we came to Earth, we had to have passed through the Void to get here, so we had to change dimensions. On the day you were born on Earth as a baby, you experienced a dimensional shift. You moved from one world into another. It's only because of our poor human memory that we don't remember.

By not remembering the experience of being born or of the other dimensions, we have placed enormous limitations on ourselves. For one, we can't overcome the reality of great distance. The distances in our reality are so great that we can't cross them. We can't even leave our solar system, for in this present state of awareness we are prisoners in our own home.

Is it not true? Traveling great distances by spaceship in the conventional way of perceiving time and space is not possible. Scientific minds have come to that conclusion already. But of course it is a disheartening suggestion that we can never leave our own solar system. Reaching the nearest star (Alpha Centauri, about four light-years away) would take about 115 million years using current space technology. Humans do not live that long, and besides, that is only the closest star. To reach deep into space would simply be impossible. We would have to change our understanding of time and space to be successful.

As we have said, our problem is that we know about only time and space; the reality of dimension has been mostly lost. Because all things are perfect, we are remembering *now*, just when we need to. We first remember in our dreams, then in our movies. Movies like *Star Trek, Contact, Sphere* and many others all explore ideas about dimension. *We will remember*, for God is with us.

So let's do it. I'll tell you exactly what *normally* happens in a dimensional shift. I will give this description from my direct experience, but what really comes to pass may be slightly different, for the universe is always experimenting. Some of you would probably prefer that I tell this in story form, but I feel that a straight shot may be more appropriate.

The Experience of an Actual Planetary Shift

Remember that what I am about to say is what a galactic textbook would reveal. It is just the normal scenario. There can be many different details because life is flexible, but by knowing the norm, you can imagine the differences.

As we enter this new millennium, the ascended masters feel that there will be very little violence approaching this shift, for we have come a long way on the path. We have done a great job in helping to birth the new human consciousness! So I am going to say it now—relax, don't worry. Enjoy this transition. As you witness the perfection of life, you can be that little baby you may have wanted to revert back to. Know that you are going to be taken care of and that pure love is guiding the events. This energy wave is so much bigger than you that you might as well surrender to life and just be.

We have probably altered the possibility of the two years to three months of chaos. It is now believed that the period before the shift will probably be very short and with almost no disruption. They expect little or no warning except for the five- or six-hour shift. More than likely you will wake up one morning, and before sunset find yourself a baby in a brand-new world.

Six Hours before the Shift

Let's begin six hours before the shift. You wake up on a clear, cool morning feeling great. As you stand up, you realize that you are feeling very light and a little strange. You decide to take a bath. As you're watching the water, you sense something behind you. You turn and see a large, brightly glowing object of strange colors floating about three feet off the floor next to the wall. As you try to figure out what this is, a smaller one appears out of nowhere a few feet away. They begin to float around the room.

You jump up and run into the bedroom, only to see the whole room filled with these strange, unimaginable things. You might think you are having a mental breakdown or that maybe a brain tumor is affecting your perception, but neither is the case. Suddenly the floor begins to break apart and the whole house begins to distort. You run outside into nature, where everything seems normal except that there are many of these strange things everywhere.

You decide to sit down and not move. You remember your Mer-Ka-Ba and begin to breathe with awareness. You relax into the prana flow that moves through your body. The great spinning Mer-Ka-Ba has enclosed you in its warmth and safety. You become centered and wait, because what's about to happen is God's grace. There really is nowhere to go. It's the greatest ride you can imagine. It is ancient, yet it is brand new. It is beautiful and you feel fantastic. You feel more alive than you ever did when you were in the normal Earth reality. Each breath seems to be exciting.

You look across the meadow, where a red, glowing fog begins to slide into the space all around you. Soon you are surrounded by this red fog, which seems to have its own source of light. It's a fog, but it doesn't actually look like any fog you have ever seen before. It seems to be everywhere now. You are even breathing it.

An odd feeling comes over your body. It isn't really bad, just unusual. You notice that the red fog is slowly changing to orange. You no sooner see it is orange than it turns yellow. The yellow quickly changes into green, then blue, then purple, then violet, then ultraviolet. Then a powerful flash of pure white light explodes into your consciousness. You are not only surrounded by this white light, but it seems that you *are* this light. For you, there is nothing else in existence.

This last feeling seems to continue for a long time. Slowly, very slowly, the white light changes into clear light and the place where you are sitting becomes visible again. Only it looks like everything is metallic and made of pure gold—the trees, the clouds, the animals, the houses, other people—except your body, which may or may not appear like gold.

Almost imperceptibly, the gold, metallic reality becomes transparent. Slowly everything begins to look like golden glass. You'll be able to see right through walls; you can even see people walking behind them.

The Void—Three Days of Blackness

Finally, the gold, metal reality begins to dim and fade away. The bright gold becomes dull and keeps losing its light until your entire world is dark and black. A blackness engulfs you, and your old world is gone forever. You can't see anything now, not even your body. You realize that you are stable, but at the same time you seem to be floating. Your familiar world is gone. Do not feel fear here. There is nothing to be afraid of. It is completely natural. You have entered the Void between the third and the fourth dimensions, the Void that all things came from and must always pass back into. You have entered the doorway between the worlds. There's no sound and no light. It's total sensory deprivation in every imaginable way.

There is nothing to do but wait and feel gratitude for your connection with God. You will probably dream at this point. It is okay. If you don't dream, it will seem like a long, long time is passing. In truth, it will be only about three days.

To be concise, this period may last from two and a quarter days (the shortest ever known) to about four days (the longest ever experienced). Normally it is between three and three and a half days. These days are Earth days, of course, and this time is experiential, not real, because time as we know it does not exist. You have now reached the "end of time" that the Maya and other religions and spiritual people have spoken of.

The New Birth

The next experience is rather shocking. After floating in nothing and blackness for three days or so, on one level of your being it may seem like a thousand years has gone by. Then, totally unexpected and in an instant, your entire world will explode with a brilliant white light. It will be blinding. It will be the brightest light you have ever known, and it will take a long time before your eyes can adjust and handle the intensity of this new light.

More than likely the experience will seem brand new, and what you have just become is a baby in a new reality. You're a little baby. Just like when you were born here on Earth, you came from a very dark place into a very light place; you were somewhat blinded and didn't know what the heck was going on. The experience is similar in many ways. Congratulations! You were just born into a brilliant new world!

When you start adjusting to this intensity of light, which might take awhile, you'll begin to see colors you've never seen before and never knew existed. Everything, the whole configuration, the whole experience of the reality, will be bizarre and unknown to you except for the short time with the floating objects right before the shift.

In truth, it is more of a second birth. On Earth when you are born, you begin small and continue to grow until you are an adult. We usually think of human adulthood as the end of growth. What may sound strange until you see it is that a human adult body in the next world is a baby. Exactly as happens here, you begin to grow and get taller until you reach adulthood in this new world. Adulthood in this new fourth-dimensional world is surprisingly taller than here. An adult male is about 14 to 16 feet tall, and an adult female is about 10 to 12 feet.

Your body will seem solid, just as on Earth, but compared to third-dimensional Earth, it isn't. In fact, if you were to go back to Earth, no one could see you. You still have an atomic structure, but the atoms will have mostly converted into energy. You have become a great deal of energy and very little matter. You can walk right through a solid wall on Earth, but here you are solid. This new birth will be your last life in structure as you know it. In the fifth dimension, which will be coming soon after the fourth, there are no life forms. It is a formless state of consciousness. You will have no body, but will be everywhere at once.

Time is extremely different in the fourth dimension. A few minutes on Earth is several hours in 4D, so in what will seem like about two years, you will reach adulthood. But simply growing up is not what life is all about, just as here on Earth. There are levels of knowledge and existence that would be hard to imagine from where you will be when you first enter the fourth dimension, just as a baby here on Earth could not comprehend astrophysics.

Your Thoughts and Survival

Here you are, a baby in a new world. Yet in this new world you are far from helpless. You are a powerful spirit that can control the entire reality with your thoughts. Whatever you think, happens instantly! Yet at first you normally don't recognize this connection. Most people don't put the two together for several days, and those few days are crucial. They *could* keep you from surviving in this new world if you don't understand.

Here you are, only a few minutes old, and the first big test in life begins. When the fourth-dimensional window is opened, anyone can go through, but generally not everyone can stay.

What we have found is that there are three types of people at this stage. First, there are people who pass over who are ready. They have prepared themselves in this life by the life they lived. Then there are people who aren't ready, who are filled with so much fear that they cannot allow themselves to leave this third dimension past the Void, and they immediately return to Earth. Finally, there's a third group that passes over but isn't really quite ready for this experience.

They were ready enough to transition into the fourth dimension, but they weren't really prepared to stay there. Jesus spoke of these people when he said at the end of a parable that "many are called, but few are chosen."

There was another parable about a wheat farmer whose servants reported that many weeds were growing in his wheat fields and asked what to do. The farmer told them to let the weeds grow with the wheat, and when it was harvest time, to gather them both up and then to separate the chaff from the wheat. A farmer would normally attempt to get rid of the weeds before they got big, but that's not what he said to do. What Jesus was referring to is these two different kinds of people—the ones who are ready and the ones who aren't.

When people are not quite ready, it means they are bringing all their fears and hatred with them. When they find themselves in this very bizarre world, all their fears and anger arise. Because they don't know that whatever they think will take shape around them, their fears begin to manifest.

Because they don't understand what is happening, in the beginning most people reproduce familiar images of their old world, things they can recognize. They do this to make sense of what is happening. They are not doing this consciously, but from their survival instinct. They start creating the old images and emotional patterns. But this new world is so bizarre that all their fears come up. They say, "Holy cow, what's going on? This is crazy, insane!" They see people who had died long ago. They might begin to see scenes from their past, even their childhood. Nothing makes sense. The mind searches for some way to create order.

They think they're hallucinating, and this brings up more fear. Thinking in their Earthly way, they might feel that someone is doing this to them, so they need to protect themselves. The ego thinks it needs a gun. Manifestation follows thought, and when they look down, there's a rifle with a scope, just what they wanted. They pick up the gun and think, "I need ammunition." They look to their left and there are huge boxes of it. They load up and begin looking for bad guys who they think are trying to kill them. So who instantly appears? The bad guys, fully armed.

Now their worst fears start manifesting, whatever they are, so they start shooting. Everywhere they turn, other people are trying to kill them. Finally their biggest fear manifests, and they are fatally shot.

A scenario of some sort will happen that will remove them from this higher world back to the world from which they came. This is what Jesus meant when he said, "For all they that take the sword shall perish with the sword." But Jesus also said, "Blessed are the meek, for they shall inherit the earth," which means that if you're sitting in this new world thinking simple thoughts of love, harmony and peace, trusting in God and yourself, then that is exactly what will manifest in your world. You will manifest a harmonious, beautiful world. If you are "meek," you allow yourself to remain in this higher world by your thoughts, feelings and actions. You survive.

That's just the beginning, of course. So you are born into a new world and you survive. From this point on there are various possibilities. One that will invariably occur is that after a while you'll start to explore this reality, and at one point you will realize that whatever you think, happens.

At this point people often look down at their bodies and say, "Wow," and, with their thoughts, perfect their bodies and physically become what they always wanted to be. They will heal everything, grow back arms and legs. Why not? It's like a toy to a child. Because ego often still functions a little bit at this stage, you might make yourself really beautiful or handsome or taller. But you will soon get bored with perfecting your body. You will begin to explore the rest of your new reality.

One thing will almost certainly happen. You'll suddenly notice large moving lights around the area you are in. They're called mother and father. Yes, you will have parents in the fourth dimension. It is, however, the last time, for in the next higher world you will not.

In the area of the fourth dimension where you arrive, the family problems we have experienced here on Earth don't exist. Your mother and father there will love you in ways you probably have only dreamed of on Earth. They will completely love and take care of you. They will not allow anything to happen to you in a bad way once you have survived. You have absolutely nothing to worry about. It is a time of tremendous joy if you simply surrender and allow this love to guide you. You may realize that you've just won the big game of life.

All the pain and suffering you have experienced in life is over, and another beautiful and sacred level of life is emerging. Now the purpose and meaning of life begins to return consciously. You begin to experience another ancient, yet new way of being, and it's yours. It has always been yours, but you gave it up. So now you are returning to the state of awareness where God is apparent in all of life. He is apparent with every breath that enters your shining body of light.

How to Prepare: The Secret of Everyday Life

You ask, what can we do here on Earth that will prepare us for this experience of the higher worlds?

It's definitely not collecting food and making a hole in the ground or anything else like that. Not that this is wrong action, only that physical preparation has its limits. In heaven, in the higher worlds, you are what you create. It is true here too, but most of us don't know it. From the fourth dimension on, it becomes obvious.

Since we are what we create, then it becomes important and necessary that our emissions are in harmony with all life everywhere. We come to understand that everything we think, feel and do creates the world we must live in. Therefore, ordinary life here on Earth can be seen as a school, a place where each moment of life gives us lessons that can be directly translated into the next world. No wonder Egypt and most of the ancient civilizations regarded death with such reverence. Death, no matter how it comes, is the doorway of darkness into the Void that leads into the brilliant light of the higher worlds of life. If mastered, it leads directly into a conscious connection with all life everywhere—eternal life!

So what about these Earthly lessons? The truth is that the Source of all life is in the eyes of every person created. So even here on Earth, great intelligence and wisdom and love are present in every moment inside each person. Once this is seen, then it becomes clear that your thoughts, feelings and actions are the key. You know exactly what to do. In simple words, it's perfecting your character. The shining diamonds in your character become the survival tools of ascension.

Buddha, Mother Mary, Lao-tsu, Mohammed, Jesus, Abraham, Krishna, Babaji, Sister Teresa and about 8000 other great masters of the eternal light—these are your schoolteachers and the heroes of life. By their examples they show you how to build your character. All of them feel that loving your neighbor is the primary key. It brings order into the world you create. It gives you eternal life. Do you see?

In the Melchizedek transition, as you pass through what are called stargates and go from one area of existence to another, the only way you can get through is by thinking, feeling and being very specific emotional and mental patterns. These patterns generally come in sets of five or six [see chapter 13, update 5]. The pattern I used to enter this dimension was *love, truth and beauty, trust, harmony and peace.* There are many others. They are like codes or keys that allow you to pass the guardians. If the guardians sense that you are ready for the world they guard, they will let you through. If they do not, they will chase you back to the world from which you came. It's just their job—and you set it up that way.

If you can just sit there and keep chanting those patterns of love, truth and beauty, trust, harmony and peace, you don't have to worry about a thing. That's the female pattern [see Fig. 18-1]. There are other patterns. There's a male pattern [see Fig. 18-2], which is *compassion, humility and wisdom, unity, love and truth.* All stargate patterns have love and truth.

Wherever there is compassion and humility, there is wisdom; that's the male component. And wherever there is love and truth, there is unity; that's the female component. On the first stargate pattern, which is arranged differently, wherever there is love and truth, there is beauty, which is the male component. And wherever there is trust and harmony, there is peace, the female component.

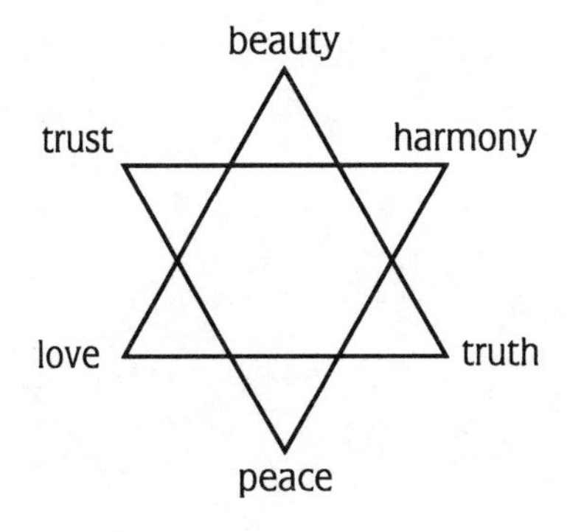

Fig. 18-1. The female stargate pattern.

So these mental/emotional states or stargate patterns become the most important possessions you could have when you enter the higher worlds. They'll become even more essential each time you pass higher. Where does this process lead?

When you reach the fourth dimension and see and understand your situation and begin to demonstrate your ability to control events, a funny thing begins to happen. Remember the painting on the Egyptian ceiling called the egg of metamorphosis [see chapter 10, Fig. 10-34a], the one with the red-orange oval over the heads of the Egyptians as they were making the 90-degree turn into the next world? Like them, you will begin to go through a metamorphosis. Like the butterfly, your body will rapidly change into something similar but uniquely different.

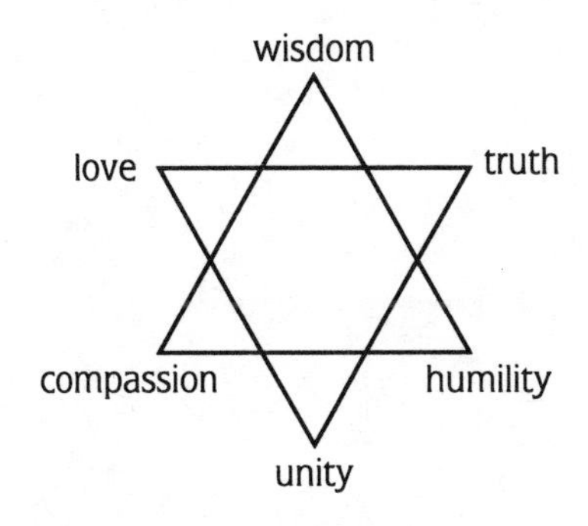

Fig. 18-2. The male stargate pattern.

"Pharaoh" means "that which you will become." The first king given the name pharaoh was Akhenaten, with his lovely wife Nefertiti. If you want to know what you will become, there they are to see. The race they came from, the Sirians, are our father, and we carry the genes they have given us. At the right moment we will change into their race. It is a race designed for the fourth dimension. When it happens, you will say to yourself, "Of course, I remember." The changes taking place in your body will feel so natural that you won't even think about it.

Life in the next world will seem normal and ordinary once growth begins. You will have entered one of the three highest overtones of the fourth dimension—the tenth, eleventh or twelfth overtones. In one or more of these three worlds you will gain the knowledge and wisdom to move into the fifth dimension, the beginning of a return trip straight back to God, ever changing as the truth unfolds.

The eyes of the universe are upon us, the great souls of the universe are following us closely. We are the children of God who offer the possibility of new life to life. In deepest gratitude, I thank you for being alive.

This Unique Transition

We have told you what normally happens when a planet transitions into the fourth dimension. Now we will propose a new theory of what may be happening here in the beginning of the 21st century of the third millennium on Earth. Occasionally a planet may enter into an anomaly in order to make the transition easier. It transits into the next dimension, but it re-creates the old dimension in such a way as to complete the old karma and make a smoother transition into the next world. It is rare on a planetary basis, but possible. It usually requires a very high level of consciousness to initiate it, though, and this is almost always lacking.

Edgar Cayce said that the axis of the Earth would change in the "winter of 1998," but it did not. Other predictions suggested that by August 11, 1999, we would have entered a higher dimension or destroyed ourselves, and it seems that we have not done that, either. Could it be that we already transitioned into the fourth dimension and don't know it? It is possible.

This is a subject so vast that I can hardly contain it. Perhaps the best way is to discuss where this higher level of consciousness could be coming from that would be making this kind of change. It just may be that the new children of Earth, the leading edge of consciousness, are here just for this reason. Vast numbers of our children today are high spiritual beings who have come to Earth to help us with this transition into a new world.

These new children have the ability to initiate the transition of this world into a new world through extraordinary means. We may be witnessing this miracle at this very moment in history. With their high level of universal understanding, they could re-create this world in the next world in such a way as to not lose a single soul—which is their desire, I believe. We would have to change Jesus' saying into "Many are called, and *all* are chosen." I believe he would be overjoyed. It has been the dream of the universe to transition every last soul, but it has never been possible before.

How could children save a planet in such an extraordinary way? A child's pure innocence and love in the higher worlds is the source of harmonic creation itself. If these children are real, and they appear to be, then anything whatsoever is possible now. God may have just blessed us with His perfect grace.

N I N E T E E N

The New Children

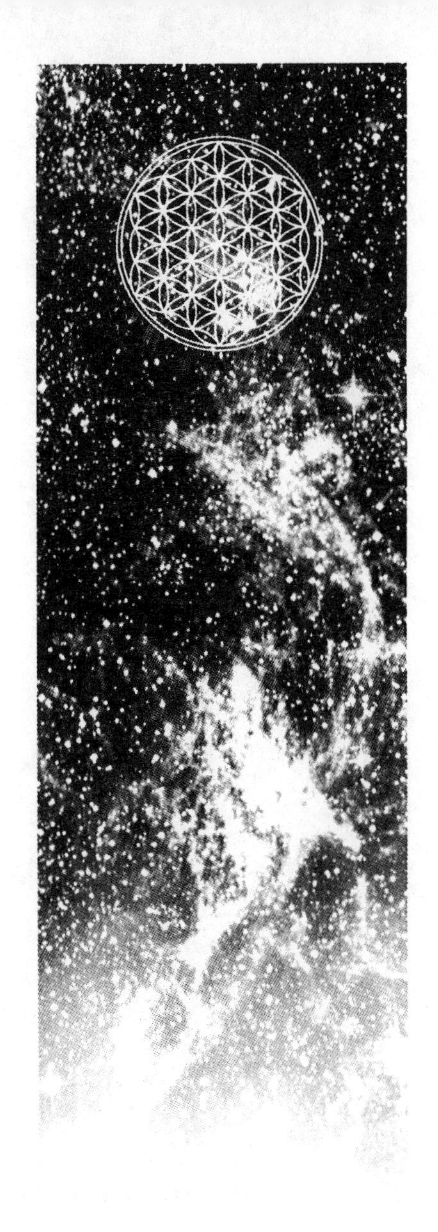

We humans are so funny. Exciting, earth-shaking miracles could be happening all around us, and we would rationalize them away so that our old world continues to be comfortable and unchanged. No one wants to rock the boat. Actually, most of us would just like to keep sleeping and hiding from the awesome changes that are everywhere in our daily lives. In the last hundred years the Earth has changed so much that no one, and I mean *no one*, would have believed the present if you had described it in 1899.

Y2K, the "year 2000." How did we get here to this supertechnological world so quickly? It's exponential, that's why.

The Current Growth of Knowledge

In the fall of 1999 I talked with Edgar Mitchell while we were in the Yucatan. We were both speaking at a Mayan conference during the time the shaman and Mayan priest Hunbatz Men performed the ceremonies for the "New Light of the Sun." This was a beautiful and important series of ceremonies, which had not been allowed for hundreds of years, that ushered in the beginning of a new light from the Sun and, as a result, a new Earth.

Dr. Mitchell said that NASA was in the middle of the greatest renaissance in the history of science, surpassing even the understandings of relativity and quantum physics. These theories had never quite fit together, and there were anomalies. Einstein had searched for the unified field theory that would bring all forces together in a single mathematical formula. Since Einstein's time, the scientific world has been searching for this theoretical holy grail.

Now, according to Dr. Mitchell, NASA has found the answer. He said that NASA has learned as many facts about our physical environment in the last five years (as of September 1999) as civilization has learned in the last 6000 years. Further, he said that they have learned as much in the last six months as in the previous five years! It is definitely exponential. Only a mere one hundred years ago the idea of going to the Moon, as Dr. Mitchell has so eloquently demonstrated, would have been considered absolutely impossible.

NASA has found the unified field theory. They feel that a great understanding has been born. In a nutshell, they have discovered that the Reality is holographic, that just as in a hologram, where you can take a small piece of the picture from anywhere on the image and retrieve the whole image, any physical piece of this Reality contains the image of the whole universe. Distant star patterns can be found in a piece of your fingernail.

Even more interesting is that the inverse is also true. That piece of fingernail can be located not only where we find it, but also anywhere in space. The Reality is not what we thought it was. The Eastern Indians called our reality maya, which means "illusion." They were right. It *is* a hologram. It is only light!

Thought follows attention. Attention follows intention.

Computers are changing everything—this special love affair between the two living atoms, carbon and silicon. The Earth has *two* eyes and can see in a new way. She can now see much better and farther. If only we can learn to live in peace, if only we can learn not to destroy our environment, I believe, I *really believe,* that Great Spirit will give us another chance with this Earth. In fact, perhaps it has already happened, this second chance.

The indigenous peoples of North, South and Central America performed the ceremony that brings together the condor and the eagle, acknowledging that the next 13 years are the last cycle of this Earth. Many teachers of the Mayan calendar have said that the last cycle ends on either December 22 or December 24, 2012. But the elder brothers, the Kogi, and the Maya themselves say no, that the last 13-year cycle begins on February 19, 2000, and ends on February 18/19, 2013.

What is so important is that the elder brothers believe that we, the younger brothers, are changing to remember the ways of Great Spirit. Joy sings in the jungle and old hearts are moved. We are learning quickly. We are waking up from a 500-year-old dream that was closer to a nightmare. The eyes of a child are blinking open.

And why would not the great change happen now? Were you not warned over and over long ago? Almost every prophet who has ever lived (speaking about the end of time) has placed it at this exact moment that you are reading this book. This period, different from the last 13-year cycle above, is from February 26, 1998 (an eclipse of the Sun) to February 18/19, 2013, and this is the time of the Great Change. Notice that this end-time date is different from the traditional date of December 24, 2012.

Edgar Cayce ("the sleeping prophet"), Nostradamus, the Holy Bible, Mother Mary, Yogananda and many others of the civilized world predicted that this time we live in is the time of the great change. Some saw this time as one of great destruction and pain, with huge Earth changes and a world altered beyond recognition; others saw a time of rapid spiritual growth, a time of ascension into a new world. Some saw both.

The indigenous peoples of the world—the Maori of New Zealand, the Zulus of Africa, the kahunas of Hawaii, the Eskimos of Alaska, the Maya of Mexico and Guatemala, the Kogi of Colombia, the Native Americans of North America, the Shintos of Japan and many others—all feel and predict that a great change is about to happen or, in some cases, is now happening.

Why would so many great people over such a long period of time point their finger at this particular moment in history? So I say again, why would not the great change happen now? And *is* it happening now?

In 1899 there were 30 million species of life on this planet. It took Mother Earth billions of years to reach this teeming variety of life forms from the one-celled amoebas to the magnificent humans and dolphins. It took mankind and his misuse of energy and his unconscious actions to reduce the number of life forms to less than half in a mere hundred years. Over 15 million species are now gone forever. How can we go so far up in consciousness and stoop so low at the same time?

If we can control our greed, if we can live from our hearts, we may make it. It is clear to me that Mother Earth has found a way to save us, the uncaring humans. Assuming this is true, do you know where this new hope is coming from? Not our great scientists or our greatest minds; it is coming from our innocent children. They are leading the way, just as the Holy Bible said would happen.

Human Mutations, Historical and Recent

The renaissance taking place in NASA is mirrored by what is happening inside our bodies. Deep in our DNA we are becoming new and very different. What appear to be genetic changes in our human DNA are showing up all over the world. What many scientists would call mutation has already occurred and, like it or not, the birthing of at least *three* new human races appears to be occurring at this very moment on the Earth—three very different kinds of races, filling the needs of a new humanity. The great change is definitely happening inside us, and hardly anyone knows. It is quiet, but it is getting louder with the first breath of each newborn baby.

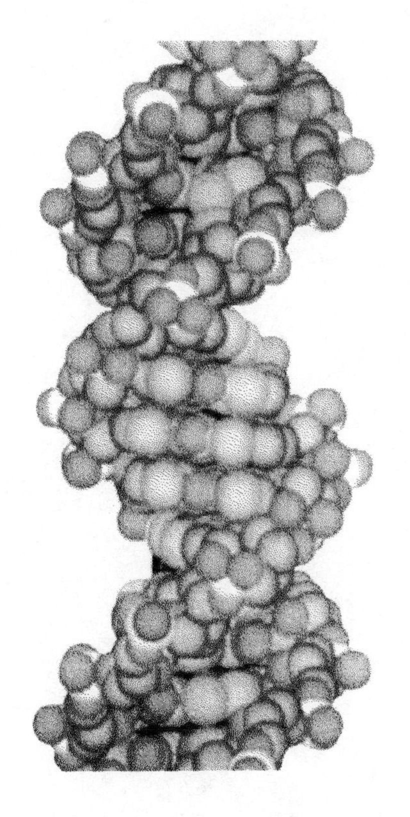

DNA Changes in Blood Types

DNA changes are rare, but they do happen. One of the most documented cases is associated with human blood. Mankind had only one blood type from the dawn of humanity until relatively recently. No matter what the outer skin appearance was—black, yellow, red, white, brown—the blood was the same. Everybody had type O blood flowing through their veins and everybody killed animals for their food. It was universal until a mere 15,000 years ago, the time when the great comet struck the Earth off the coast of Atlantis.

What happened? Most of the world, other than Atlantis, quit moving from place to place to hunt and eat animals; we became farmers. Our diets changed. We began to eat vegetables and grains in combinations that had never entered the human body before. The body responded to these dietary changes by mutating the human DNA and making a new, unheard-of blood type, type A. Besides this new blood, there were other DNA changes that affected the stomach acids and enzymes and other body functions to assimilate these new foods. Some scientists suggest that climate changes may also have had an effect on this mutation.

As time went on, twice more the human blood changed, each time in response to changes in diet and possible climate changes. Types B and AB were born. At the moment there are four types, but will this continue? Toward the end of the 20th century, foods from all over the world became available to almost anyone anywhere on Earth. Humanity for the first time began to eat all the foods of the world. You can go into almost any major market in the civilized world and get anything you want from anywhere—papayas from Mexico, avocados from California, olives from Greece, vodka from Russia and on and on. You can go into almost any American city and eat Chinese food or Mexican, Italian, Japanese, American, German and so on. Will a new blood type emerge to accommodate this unprecedented shuffle of foods?

As you can see, DNA changes do take place with seemingly innocuous changes in diet and climate. The changes happening on Earth today are astounding by anyone's standards. They are so huge that one would expect a human genetic response, and beyond doubt, humanity has responded.

A new change has taken place in human genetics that has such far-reaching implications to the future of mankind that I simply must discuss it. Most of the people who have made these DNA changes are children. There are three distinct categories, each with very different, exciting new powers. There might be more than three, but to date this is all we can see. I believe these children are leading us into a new future unlike what has been experienced in the last few million years. In addition, as I suggested before, these children may have altered the fourth-dimensional shift to complete the karma of the third dimension in such a way as to allow *all* humans to make this translation into the fourth dimension. Yet with or without this dimensional shift, the new human genetic change will alter us forever.

It was from China in 1974 that the first newly mutated child was noticed by the world. It was a young boy who was able to "see" with his ears. Yes, he could see with his ears in the same way you can see with your eyes—actually, even better. Do you think it is impossible? If you do, then you are in for a life-shaking surprise.

Perhaps I am getting ahead of myself. Let's start here in the United States with a completely different race of new children. These children are called the Indigo children.

The Indigo Children

The Indigo children, as they are now called by science, were first traced back to the year 1984. This was the year when suddenly a child appeared with very different human traits, and since that time this new type of human being has spread rapidly. As of 1999, science has suggested that approximately 80 to 90 percent of all the children born in the United States are Indigo children. I believe it probably will rise to nearly 100 percent in the future. You and I are obviously being phased out. These children are being born not only in the U.S., but also in many other areas of the world that seem to be connected with the wide use of computers.

Lee Carroll and Jan Tober have written a book called *The Indigo Children: The New Kids Have Arrived.* It is a book of compiled scientific studies, letters and notes written by medical doctors, psychologists and scientists who have been studying these new children since they were first discovered. It is the first book in the world, I believe, to discuss these new children. I have been aware of these children for the last ten years or more, and I have been discussing them with hundreds of people and children's groups that have also noticed the change. Yet no one officially recognized them until this book appeared. So I thank Lee and Jan for this timely edition. Please read this book if you wish to know more of the details.

Now, how are these children different? Science has not yet figured out exactly what the specific DNA change is that has taken place in this new race, but it is obvious that one has happened. First of all, these children have a different liver than ours, which means there *has* to be a DNA change. This liver change is, naturally, a response to the new foods we are eating. The new liver is designed to eat, of all things, *junk food!*

Sound funny? Why? We would all become increasing unhealthy or even die if we continue to eat these kinds of foods on a long-term basis. What happens to cockroaches when you feed them poison? At first they get sick and die, *but then they mutate*, change their DNA and end up loving our poisons. We have to keep changing our poisons because they keep adapting to them. Do you think that human beings are any different? We continue to feed our kids poisonous junk food, so they have to adapt to survive.

But this liver change is nothing compared to the other revisions in human nature and genetics. First of all, these Indigo children are brilliant. They have an IQ that averages around 130, and I do mean average, as many of these kids are way up in the genius range of 160 or higher. A 130 IQ is not a genius, but it used to be that only one person in 10,000 had it. Now it is becoming normal. The intelligence of the human race has just jumped into a new range.

Doctors and psychologists studying these children have found that the computer seems to be an extension of these kids' brains. They are far more able to function within the parameters of computer software than anyone ever before. Where this will lead we can only speculate.

What I find fascinating about these brilliant new kids is that our teachers and the educational system found them *defective* when judging this new human race. In the beginning our educational system didn't realize they were so intelligent. They have actually thought they were problematic.

They diagnosed them with attention deficit disorder (ADD) because they thought they could not stay focused. The problem is now becoming clear: It is not the children; it is the educational system itself that is not prepared to educate these gifted children. The children are simply bored with the speed and nature of the delivery and the content of the information. We need to adapt to this exciting new race of children. Give an Indigo child who has been tagged as ADD or ADHD something to study that he or she *is interested in*, and you will see the brilliance unfold before your eyes. There is so much we need to learn in order to allow the great potential of these kids to come to light.

It is clear to people studying these children that they also have very heightened psychic abilities. They can literally read their parents' minds. They know what you are thinking. These and other differences you can read about in *The Indigo Children* have led researchers to realize that a new way of raising these children is mandatory. If you have had a child or are raising a child born after 1984, you need to read this book.

Who the Indigo children are, of course, is in great debate. Many psychics are saying that they are coming from the indigo ray, a very high level of consciousness not of this Earth. I also feel this is true, for when I first met the angels in 1971 they began talking about these new children that would come in the future and change the world. They told me many details about them that are coming true at this time.

Also, many psychics I have discussed this subject with feel that there are actually two different cosmic sources for these children. One is the indigo ray and the other is the deep-blue ray, similar but different. Wherever they come from, it definitely is a diversion from the normal human evolutionary track. And the Indigo children are not the only ones who have changed their DNA.

The Children of AIDS

The children of AIDS are a special grouping of mostly children who have made their DNA change because of a different problem. It was not food (if that *is* a cause) that changed them, but AIDS/HIV.

I recommend that you read a book by Gregg Braden called *Walking between the Worlds: The Science of Compassion*. Mr. Braden was the first one to report this new race in a popular publication. I quote from him: "If we define ourselves genetically, this new species looks different in terms of specific DNA, though their bodies may appear as the familiar bodies of friends and loved ones. On a molecular level, beyond the seeing of the naked eye, they have allowed themselves to become genetic possibilities that were not available just a few short years ago. In the open literature there are reports of a phenomenon that scientists have named *spontaneous genetic mutation*. They are called spontaneous because they appear to have developed during the course of an individual's lifetime in response to a life challenge rather than appear as a new form of the code detected at birth. In these instances, the genetic code has learned to express itself in a new way that serves the individual's survival."

There is a report of a young boy in kindergarten who was born with HIV. As quoted from Mr. Braden's book [page 81], "'Researchers at the University of California, Los Angeles, School of Medicine report unambiguous evidence of a boy who tested positive for HIV twice—at 19 days of age and one month later. Yet by every measure, this kindergartner appears to have been HIV-free for at least 4 years' [in a quote from an article in the April 1995 *Science News*]. The study was reported by Yvonne J. Bryson and her colleagues in the March 30, 1996, *New England Journal of Medicine*. . . . The virus is not lying dormant within the body, opportunistically awaiting an external cue to become active; it is eradicated from the body!"

This new resistance to HIV infection is so strong that in a few of the cases it was 3000 times more resistant than what it would take to infect a normal person. In all cases their resistance to HIV is noticeably higher. If this were just one small boy showing these changes, it would simply be an interesting phenomenon, but this is not the case. From *Walking between the Worlds*: "A study released in the August 17, 1996, issue of *Science News* reports that about 1 percent of the population tested now have developed genetic mutations that make them resistant to HIV infection!" In October 1999, the United Nations reported that the six-billionth person was born, which means that 1 percent of the population (60,000,000 children and adults worldwide) have altered their DNA to become resistant to HIV.

Exactly what has changed in the DNA of these children is known. It has to do with codons*. In the human DNA there are four nucleic acids, which combine in sets of three to form 64 codons. Normal human DNA has 20 of these codons turned on, plus three others that act much like the stop-and-start codes in software programming. The rest of these codons are inactive. Science has always thought that these unused codons were from our genetic past, but now that theory is changing. Perhaps they are actually from our future. These children have turned on four more of these "unused" codons, giving them 24, which has completely altered their resistance to HIV infection.

The potential of what this means is staggering. These children appear to have superheightened immune systems. As they are being tested for other diseases, it is becoming clear that they very well may be disease-resistant or even immune to many other, if not all, diseases. Testing in this last area is not yet conclusive.

The Bible Code and AIDS

I would also like to bring your attention to something taking place in another arena of investigation. This one has to do with the Bible code, the

---

* Codon: A sequence of three adjacent nucleotides constituting the genetic code that specifies the insertion of an amino acid in a specific structural position in a polypeptide chain during protein synthesis.

computer code found in the Torah. Some researchers of the Bible code at the Hebrew University in Israel plugged the acronym AIDS into the computer program to see what would happen. You can read in *Cracking the Bible Code* by Jeffrey Satinover, M.D., on page 164, the amazing supportive revelation. "AIDS" brought forth the following words in the matrix: *death, in the blood, from apes, annihilation, in the form of a virus, the HIV, the immunity, destroyed*—all words you would expect from the search term AIDS. But in the matrix was also a phrase that made no sense to the Bible code researchers in Israel, because they didn't know what was happening with AIDS research here in America. In the matrix of AIDS it was clearly stated, "*the end to all diseases*"! I believe this new race of children will eventually make its mark on humanity in a way that will change forever the experience of being alive on Earth.

In the beginning of this section, Mr. Braden mentioned the phrase "spontaneous genetic mutation"—spontaneous because it takes place during a person's lifetime, not before birth. What does this mean to you? When this mutation was first discovered, it was always in children, but over time science has found more and more adults who have followed these children and mutated in exactly the same manner. This is exciting, because it means that you and I, even if we don't have AIDS, might possibly alter our DNA to superstrengthen our immune system just as they have. How is this possible?

You are all aware of the hundredth-monkey theory. (We mentioned this in chapter 4, page 106.) It was first a young female monkey, a child, that began to wash the sand off her potatoes. Then her friends, who were also children, imitated her. Soon the mothers began to imitate their children, and finally the fathers. At one point the potato-washing phenomenon, in a single day, expanded to the other monkey-inhabited islands, even to the mainland of Japan. In the same way, it may be possible that you and I can change our DNA to give us a superstrong immune system.

We are researching this exciting possibility ourselves at this moment, using the Mer-Ka-Ba and meditation. In the same way that attention and intention are the key to psychic abilities, placing your attention on your DNA and having the intention for it to change in the same way as these kids' DNA is a definite possibility for evolutionary change. What is happening with the following third new race of children will present further possibilities.

The Superpsychic Children

The superpsychic children are perhaps the most unusual and charismatic race being born today. Their dramatic abilities distinguish them from the other two races with their sensational demonstrations. These children are able to do things that most people thought could be done only in movies with computer graphics. What is so amazing of all is that it is real. If these children don't change our world, nothing will. Notice how some of the abilities of these children resemble the manifestations of consciousness we talked about in chapter 18, during the dimensional shift. What you think is what you get! These children are able to demonstrate that whatever they think becomes reality.

Paul Dong and Thomas E. Raffill wrote *China's Super Psychics*. It reports what has been transpiring in China around these new psychic children who have begun to emerge since 1974 with the young boy who could see with his ears. Actually, the Chinese government claims that these children, when blindfolded, could see either with their ears, nose, mouth, tongue, armpits, hands or feet. Each child was different and their vision from these unheard-of areas was perfect. These tests were not just a percentage right some of the time; they were flawless.

I first spoke about these children in 1985 when I mentioned the article about them in *Omni* magazine. *Omni* was invited to come to China to observe some of these children and write an article about them. *Omni* assumed that there might be cheating involved, so when they were given some of these children to test, they conducted their examinations in a way that ruled out any possible cheating. They left nothing to chance.

One of the tests began this way: With the children present, *Omni* took a stack of books and at random selected one of them, then opened the book at random and ripped out a page, crumpling it up into a small ball. *Omni* then placed it in the armpit of one of these children—and this child could read every word on the page perfectly! After many varied tests, *Omni* became convinced that the phenomenon was real, but they could not explain how these kids were doing it. Their report was released in their January 1985 issue.

But *Omni* was not the only one to send researchers to observe these children. Several other world magazines and also papers in respected journals such as *Nature,* a prestigious science magazine, have also agreed that this phenomenon is real.

In Mexico City we found exactly the same new human traits emerging in the children there. There may be more, but we found over 1000 children able to see with various parts of their bodies. What is noticeable is that these Mexican children can see with the very same parts of the body as the Chinese children do. It sounds like this DNA mutation has jumped across the ocean just as in the hundredth-monkey phenomenon. Soon I will come back to one of these children, now nineteen, to give my direct experience of the abilities she demonstrated to us.

According to Paul Dong in *China's Super Psychics,* seeing with various parts of the body was the psychic ability that caught the attention of the Chinese government, but this ability was quickly understood to be only the tip of the iceberg. These children began to demonstrate other psychic abilities that are truly difficult to accept inside this "normal" reality.

Mr. Dong reports how several times a large audience of a thousand people or more would enter the auditorium and be handed a live rosebud. When everyone was seated and quiet, the demonstration would begin with a young Chinese girl, about six years old, who would come on stage all by herself and stand in the center facing the audience. Then with a silent wave of her hand, the thousand rosebuds would slowly open into full-blown, beautiful roses before the eyes of the astonished audience.

Mr. Dong also speaks of how over 5000 young children have demonstrated in public another amazing feat. Realize here that the Chinese government has carefully tested these children to see if what I am about to say is real or not. The government is convinced it is true.

One child would take a sealed bottle of pills off a shelf at random, like vitamin pills, for example. The bottle would be sealed with the original plastic wrap and have a tightly screwed metal or plastic top. The bottle would then be placed in the center of a large bare table. Then a video camera would observe what happened next.

The child would say to the audience that he/she was beginning, but nothing was visible to the audience. Suddenly, the pills inside the sealed bottle would pass right through the glass and appear on the table. In many cases, the child would then take another object, such as a coin, set it on the table, and it would pass into the sealed bottle. This demonstration and others like it are definitely approaching what I would call fourth-dimensional consciousness. What you *think* and what *happens* are connected.

There are several other psychic abilities that have been demonstrated in China, according to this book. If you are interested, read what has been reported. You may think that this is just magic tricks, but when you see these things in person, it is very hard to explain. For the first ten years the Chinese government would not believe it either, until the number of these children who could do these things kept growing. By the time *China's Super Psychics* was released in 1997, the Chinese government had identified over 100,000 of these children. In fact, by about 1985, the government and the Chinese scientific community simply had to admit it was true.

Because they realized what this could mean, the government set up training schools to assist these children in their psychic abilities. Whenever a psychic child is found now, he or she is sent to one of these schools. Important is the fact that they have found that they can even take children who are not known to be psychics and in the presence of the naturally psychic kids, the trained children can perform the same wonderful feats.

This brings forth the memory of Uri Geller, the famous psychic from Israel who could bend metal objects just by looking at them. In his book, *Uri Geller, My Story*, he talks about when he demonstrated his psychic abilities on television throughout Europe. He went on TV and asked people to get knives, spoons and forks and place them in front of the television set. With millions of witnesses, he then bent tableware before their eyes *and* tableware in the homes in Europe who were watching the show. This single act had an interesting side effect. From the phone calls immediately after the show and the following days, it was discovered that over 1500 children were able to do the same thing *just by seeing it happen one time*. They could all bend the metal tableware with their minds.

People, especially scientists, were convinced that Mr. Geller was a magician and that everything he did was a trick of some kind. Stanford Research Institute asked if he would submit his magic to scientific scrutiny. Mr. Geller agreed. For a period of time Mr. Geller did whatever Stanford asked him to do to prove once and for all that his psychic ability was not a trick.

Just to give you an idea of how tight the testing at Stanford was, one of the tests placed Mr. Geller in a sealed steel room, which was also a Faraday cage (a room where electromagnetic fields, such as radio waves and even brain waves or thoughts, could not pass through the walls). He was sealed in physically as well as energywise. The Stanford researchers placed outside the test chamber a sealed, hand-blown glass tube that was twisted on each end so that it could not be opened without breaking it. Inside it was a piece of the hardest metal known to man. Then they told Mr. Geller to bend it. With all their scientific instruments recording the test, Stanford scientists watched in total amazement as the piece of superhard metal bent as if it were Jell-O. Mr. Geller could in no way have cheated.

What is so impressive is that besides Mr. Geller, there were about 15 children from Europe who could also do these things, and they were tested along with him. Everything that Stanford did to test Mr. Geller they also did with the children, and these kids could do everything he could do. So if this was a trick, then 15 children were also "advanced magicians," and Stanford Research Institute, with all their scientific magic, could not detect fraud.

This test and the rest of the research from Stanford was printed in *Nature* magazine in its October 1974 issue. The *New York Times* immediately came out with an editorial that said: "The scientific community has been put on notice 'that there is something worthy of their attention and scrutiny' in the possibilities of extrasensory perception." Yet here we are in the next millennium, and science still will not seriously admit that the human potential for psychic abilities is real. I believe that these new children appearing around the world will soon force science into accepting what has always been true. The old paradigm has nowhere to go and must dissolve.

In Denver, Colorado, in July 1999, I spoke about these new children to a large audience. I asked a young woman named Inge Bardor from Mexico to demonstrate directly to this audience her ability to see with her hands and feet. At that time she was eighteen years old. For about an hour, Inge placed a blindfold around her eyes and accepted photographs at random from the audience. She would hold the photograph and lightly touch it with the fingertips of her other hand.

First she would describe the picture perfectly, as though she was looking at it, but then she would become more specific, giving information that would be impossible for her to know even from a photo. She could tell everything about the people or place in the photo. She could tell exactly where the photo was taken and what was around the area outside the view, such as a lake or buildings.

Inge could even describe the person who took the photograph and what he/she was wearing that day. She could tell you what everyone in the photo was thinking at the moment the picture was taken. In one photo of the inside of a house, Inge went into the house psychically and described exactly what was down the hallway. She even described what was on the bedside table.

Finally someone placed a newspaper under Inge's feet, and with her high-heeled shoes on, she was able to read the paper as if it was in her hands and she wasn't blindfolded. (If you are interested in this video, please call Lightworks Video at 1-800-795-TAPE and ask for "Through the Eyes of a Child.")

Under the strict discipline of scientific research, the Chinese government has observed these children changing the human DNA molecule in a petri dish before cameras and scientific equipment necessary to record this supposedly impossible feat. If this is true, which the Chinese government claims, would *we* not be able to change our own DNA with just the right understanding? I think so. Just follow the children.

How is it possible that 60 million people in the world have already changed their DNA to drastically improve their immune systems against HIV infection through spontaneous genetic mutation, if not through a process similar to what our new children of China have demonstrated? This is a grand time in the history of the Earth—and you are alive to experience this extraordinary world change!

I was recently in Russia, in September 1999, and there I spoke with many Russian scientists about these new children. I talked with people who asked me not to print their names, but some were on boards of directors that controlled over 60 Russian scientific communities, including the Russian space program. They told me personally that what was happening in China was also happening in Russia. Thousands of Russian children were exhibiting the same kinds of psychic abilities. I am convinced that these three new races of children are truly a worldwide phenomenon, one that is altering the human experience on Earth forevermore.

The Fourth-Dimensional Shift and the Superkids

The question is, have we actually entered the fourth dimension and recreated it to appear like the third dimension? It does seem this way as I observe these new children. But the truth will come out of its own accord. Now that you know the nature of the original Reality mingled with the Lucifer reality, search your own heart. Is it true? Look inside yourself. Are *you* changing? Are you even remotely the same person you were just a few years ago? And now that you are exploring, or about to explore, your higher consciousness with your lightbody, the Mer-Ka-Ba, will your life ever be the same? Birth has its way of making everything new again.

Life Is Great

We live in a world that exists only in the mind of God. It is only light. Using sacred geometry, the Mother/Father spirit of life has created a universe of light for us to play in and love each other. We are the children of God. Great Spirit expresses through each one of us and speaks of worlds of consciousness far above the ordinary life of humanity. We hold within us a potential so great that if all the adjectives in the dictionary were compressed into one word, it would still not fully describe the innate greatness shining out of the eyes of a single ordinary, everyday child.

You have a choice. You can continue to live life from the normal human perspective, where the only reason for being alive is to become comfortable through material things or to gain control over other human beings through force—or realize that the outer world is not something you appropriate, but rather an opportunity to express joy and love in your life. The outer world and our inner world are one.

Breathe deeply the pure life force into your glowing chakras and let your Mer-Ka-Ba live. Open your heart fearlessly to the unknown and look with the eyes of a child into the eyes of God in each person who stands before you. It is all so simple.

I love you.
Drunvalo

NOTE TO THE READER

The Flower of Life Workshop was presented internationally by Drunvalo from 1985 until 1994. This book is based on a transcript of the third official videotaped version of the Flower of Life Workshop, which was presented in Fairfield, Iowa, in October 1993. Each chapter of this book corresponds more or less to the same-numbered videotape of that workshop. However, we have changed the written format where necessary to make the meaning as clear as possible. Hence, we've shuffled paragraphs and sentences and occasionally even whole sections to their ideal locations so that you, the reader, can glide through this with the greatest of ease.

Please note that we have added current **updates** throughout the book, which are in **boldface**. These updates begin in the margin alongside the old information. Since so much information was presented in the workshop, we have divided the material into two parts, each with its own table of contents. This is volume 2.

For those who wish to locate a facilitator in their area, see the Flower of Life Web site www.floweroflife.org or call the Flower of Life Headquarters in Phoenix, Arizona (English only) at (602) 996-0900 or fax (602) 996-4970. Or call the Latin American division office at 52-5-846-0007 in Mexico City (Spanish and English available).

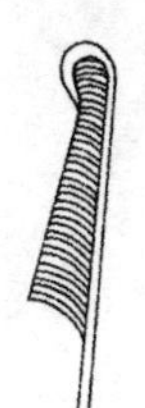

MAAT RESEARCH

The Way of Truth

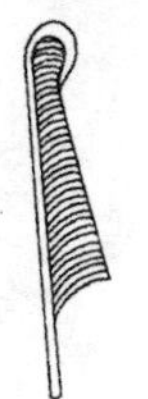

Maat is the ancient Egyptian goddess of Truth. She is still alive in the hearts of those who love the Mother.

In the summer of 2000, a new Web site will open that seeks to find integrity in the world's information. This is important, for we believe that the Internet is forming a global brain and birthing a new type of planetary communication. At the moment, there is so much distortion of information moving through the Web that it is akin to being mentally unbalanced, not knowing what is reality and what is not. The truth would bring clarity. Most important, truth might just find the answer(s) to save ourselves from ourselves. We might even find peace.

How will this be accomplished? This site will report the truth on a specific subject as it is known and give all supporting documentation. It will not merely refer to a specific source, but actually show the documentation whenever possible or tell you how to get it so that everyone can make their own interpretation of what is being claimed.

Once all known documents are released, the site will ask the public to respond with what they personally know. Anything that anyone in the world knows that can be proven will be checked out and posted on the site, providing a data bank of reliable knowledge and a search engine to find what is needed.

Whereas most news agencies report on a subject only once and perhaps never talk about it again, we will maintain the subject and keep building the database until the truth reveals itself.

Nine months in the birthing, Maat Research will soon open just for you and for Mother Earth.

www.maatresearch.com

If you really want to know.

REFERENCES

Chapter 1

Liberman, Jacob, *Light, the Medicine of the Future*, Bear & Co., Santa Fe, NM, 1992.

Temple, Robert K.G., *The Sirius Mystery*, Destiny Books, Rochester, VT (www.gotoit.com).

Satinover, Jeffrey, M.D., *Cracking the Bible Code*, William Morrow, New York, 1997.

West, John Anthony, *Serpent in the Sky*, Julian Press, New York, 1979, 1987.

Cayce, Edgar: many books have been written about him; the Association for Research and Enlightenment in Virginia Beach, VA, is a source of an enormous amount of material. Perhaps the most well-known book is *The Sleeping Prophet* by Jess Stearn.

Chapter 2

Lawlor, Robert, *Sacred Geometry: Philosophy and Practice*, Thames & Hudson, London, 1982.

Hoagland, Richard C.; see www.enterprisemission.com/.

White, John, *Pole Shift*, 3rd ed., ARE Press, Virginia Beach, VA, 1988.

Hapgood, Charles, *Earth's Shifting Crust* and *The Path of the Pole* (out of print).

Braden, Gregg, *Awakening to Zero Point: The Collective Initiation*, Sacred Spaces/Ancient Wisdom Pub., Questa, NM; also on video tape (Lee Productions, Bellevue, WA).

Chapter 3

Hamaker, John and Donald A. Weaver, *The Survival of Civilization*, Hamaker-Weaver Pub., 1982.

Sitchin, Zecharia, *The 12th Planet* (1978), *The Lost Realms* (1996), *Genesis Revisited* (1990), Avon Books.

Begich, Nick and Jeanne Manning, *Angels Don't Play This HAARP*, Earthpulse Press, Anchorage, AK, 1995.

Chapter 4

Keyes, Ken, Jr., *The Hundredth Monkey*, Vision Books, 1982, not copyrighted. Obtainable at www.testament.org/testament/100thmonkey.html and other Web sites.

Watson, Lyall, *Lifetide*, Simon and Schuster, New York, 1979.

Strecker, Robert, M.D., "The Strecker Memorandum" (video), The Strecker Group, 1501 Colorado Blvd., Eagle Rock, CA 90041 (203) 344-8039.

The Emerald Tablets of Thoth the Atlantean, translated by Doreal, Brotherhood of the White Temple, Castle Rock, CO, 1939. Obtainable from Light Technology Publishing.

Chapter 6

Anderson, Richard Feather (labyrinths); see www.gracecom.org/veriditas/.

Penrose, Roger; see http://galaxy.cau.edu/tsmith/KW/goldenpenrose.html http://turing.mathcs.carleton.edu/penroseindex.html; www.nr.infi.net/~drmatrix/progchal.htm.

Adair, David; see www.flyingsaucers.com/adair1.htm.

Winter, Dan, *Heartmath*; see www.danwinter.com.

Sorrell, Charles A., *Rocks and Minerals: A Guide to Field Identification*, Golden Press, 1973.

Vector Flexor toy, available from Source Books (see below).

Langham, Derald, *Circle Gardening: Producing Food by Genesa Principles*, Devin-Adair Pub., 1978.

Chapter 7

Charkovsky, Igor; see www.earthportals.com ; www.vol.it/ ; www.well.com.

Doczi, György, *The Power of Limits: Proportional Harmonies in Nature, Art and Architecture*, Shambhala, Boston, MA, 1981, 1994.

Chapter 8

"Free Energy: The Race to Zero Point" (video), available from Lightworks, (800) 795-8273, $40.45 ppd., www.lightworks.com.

Pai, Anna C. and Helen Marcus Roberts, *Genetics, Its Concepts and Implications*, Prentice Hall, 1981.

Critchlow, Keith, *Order in Space: A Design Source Book*, Viking Press, 1965, 1969 and other books are out of print; see www.wwnorton.com/thames/aut.ttl/at03940.htm.

Chapter 9

Lamy, Lucie, *Egyptian Mysteries: New Light on Ancient Knowledge*, Thames and Hudson, London, 1981.

Albus, James S., *Brains, Behavior and Robotics*, Byte books, 1981 (out of print).

The Unknown Leonardo, Ladislas Reti, ed., Abradale Press, Harry Abrams, Inc., Publishers, New York, 1990 ed.

Blair, Lawrence, *Rhythms of Vision: The Changing Patterns of Myth and Consciousness*, Destiny Books, 1991 (out of print).

Martineau, John, *A Book of Coincidence: New Perspectives on an Old Chestnut*, Wooden Books, Wales, 1995 (out of print).

Chapter 10

Hall, Manley P., *The Secret Teachings of All Ages*, Philosophical Research Society of Los Angeles, 1978.

Chapter 11

Hancock, Graham and Robert Bauval, *The Message of the Sphinx: A Quest for the Hidden Legacy of Mankind*, Crown Publishers, Inc., 1996.

Chapter 12

Puharich, Andrija, *The Sacred Mushroom*, Doubleday, 1959 (out of print).

Cayce, Edgar, *Auras: An Essay on the Meaning of Color*, A.R.E. Press, Virginia Beach, VA, 1989.

Chapter 13

Ramacharaka, Yogi, *Science of Breath: A Complete Manual of the Oriental Breathing Philosophy of Physical, Mental, Psychic and Spiritual Development*, Yoga Publishers Society, 1904.

Chapter 19

Carroll, Lee, and Jan Tober, *The Indigo Children: The New Kids Have Arrived*, Hay House, Carlsbad, CA, 1999.

Braden, Gregg, *Walking between the Worlds: The Science of Compassion*, Radio Bookstore Press, Bellevue, WA, 1997.

Satinover, Jeffrey, M.D., *Cracking the Bible Code*, William Morrow, New York, 1997.

Dong, Paul, and Thomas E. Raffill, *China's Super Psychics*, Marlowe & Co., New York, 1997.

Geller, Uri, *Uri Geller, My Story*, Praeger Press, New York, 1975 (out of print).

"Through the Eyes of a Child," 2-video set from Lightworks, (800) 795-TAPE (795-8273).

Most of the books and sacred geometry tools, in addition to posters, kits, videos, tapes and CDs recommended in this workshop, are available from Source Books, P.O. Box 292231, Nashville, TN 37229-2231, (800) 637-5222 (in U.S.) or (615) 773-7652. Catalog available.

Index

A

Aborigines (Australian) 64, 107, 132, 228-229, 237-238, 252, 279
and the first level of human consciousness 64, 108, 119
Abraham 440
Abu Simbel 120-121, 262
Abydos 30-33, 230, 280-281
See also Osirian temples
Adair, David 165
ADD
See Attention Deficit Disorder
Africa 10, 14-15, 64, 77, 83, 85, 87, 89, 445
Age of Aquarius 58, 304
Age of Pisces 304
AIDS 76-79, 179
and the Bible Code 449-50
children of AIDS 78-79, 448-450
See also DNA
akashic records 20, 135, 144-146, 423
Akhenaten 134-146, 441
Mystery School of, the Law of One 145-146
reign of truth 137-138
See also Left Eye of Horus Mystery School; Right Eye of Horus Mystery School
Akkad 79
Alabama 93
Alaska 445
Albuquerque Zoo 21
Albuquerque, New Mexico 117
Albus, James S. 232
alchemy 25-26, 28, 166-167, 169
alcohol 388
Alpha and Omega Order of Melchizedek 169
Alpha and Omega Order of Melchizedek School 401-402
Alpha Centauri 434
Amanita muscaria mushroom 317
Amazon 394
Amenhotep II 135
Amenhotep III 135-136
Amenhotep IV 135
American Astronomical Society 54
Anderson, Richard Feather 157
angels 168, 403, 412-416, 418
the angels 24-26, 28-29, 164, 190-191, 195, 198-199, 216, 278, 305, 308, 345, 369, 372-374, 376, 381, 385, 391, 394-395, 398, 400, 404-405, 408, 419-422, 448
clear (angel of completion) 406-407
gold angel (next level of higher self) 400-401, 406-407
green angel (Earth/lower self) 24, 400-401, 406
and the octave 407
pure white angel 406
purple angel (Sun/higher self) 24, 400-401, 406
Angels Don't Play This HAARP 76
ankh 21, 128, 137, 257, 260-263, 279, 330-334
and the orgasm 330
See also Egypt; Egyptian tools and symbols for resurrection; resurrection
ankhing 333-334, 360
See also orgasm; sexual energy
Aquarius 58, 304
Araragat 108, 110, 113, 116
archangels 119, 407, 413, 417-418
Archangel Gabriel 418
Archangel Michael 388-390, 407, 412, 414, 417-418
Archangel Raphael 418
A.R.E.
See Association for Research and Enlightenment
Aries 303
Arizona 304
Arizona Gazette 305-306
ascended masters 76, 104-105, 108, 114-116, 119, 123-124, 133-135, 300-301, 304, 336, 419, 423, 426-427, 435, 400
ascension 14, 35, 43, 92, 113-114, 128-130, 134, 146-147, 260, 286, 308, 335-336, 341, 350, 353, 363, 367, 426, 440, 444
and the planetary dimensional shift 430-431
Association for Research and Enlightenment 19, 110
astrological wheel 58, 130, 280, 294-295, 298, 303-304
Atlantean 1, 3, 27-28, 96-97, 100-101, 103-104, 106, 113, 115-116, 123, 131-132, 270, 273, 276, 306
See also Atlantis
Atlantic Ocean 69, 91, 101-102
Atlantis 19-20, 27, 79, 91, 93, 95-96, 99-100, 102-104, 115-116, 119, 122, 130-131, 137, 282, 286, 305, 317, 331, 336, 387, 393, 418, 422, 431, 445
and the Christ consciousness grid 108, 113-114
discovery of 93
and the Fall 1, 3-4, 105, 108, 123, 132-133, 135, 336, 393-394, 422, 431
and Plato 19, 91, 93, 97
Poseidia 97
the sinking of 90, 101-102, 113-114
and the Tree of Life 97-98
and the Troano document 97-98
atomic bomb 75-76, 169
atomic structure 165, 175, 437
in the fourth-dimensional world 437
atoms 8-12, 29, 44-45, 50, 97, 112, 133, 156, 165-166, 172-173, 175-176, 178-180, 182, 185, 320, 355, 371, 379-380, 423, 437, 444
patterns of 166, 170-173
Attention Deficit Disorder 448
aura 337-340, 343
See also energy field, human
Auras: An Essay on the Meanings of Colors 338
See also Cayce, Edgar
Australia 15, 64, 73, 88, 107-108, 119, 132, 194, 237, 302
Australian 11, 54, 107-108
Avalon, island of 157
See also Druid
Awakening to Zero Point: The Collective Initiation 61
See also Braden, Gregg
Ay 92, 119, 122, 131, 135, 144, 285-286
Aztec 117

B

Baba, Neem Karoli 24
Babaji 440
Babylon 79
Babylonians 81
bacterium 178-179
Bar Harbor, Maine 284
bardo
See Void, Great
Bardor, Inge 453-454
Bauval, Robert 302
Beaman, Donald 133
Begich, Dr. Nick 76
belief patterns 5, 10, 367, 381-382, 386
Belize 117
Bell Laboratories 45, 370
Berkeley, California 23, 374
Bermuda 91
Bermuda Triangle 103-104, 305-306
Bible, the 39, 81, 84, 86, 89, 130, 150, 153, 180, 324, 411-412, 444-445
Christian 8, 79, 86, 147
and the creation story 147
Hebrew 8, 16
See also Christianity; Essene Brotherhood; Genesis

Bible code, the 16, 79, 449-450
 and AIDS 79, 449-450
The Bible Code 16
 See also Drosnin, Michael
Bielek, Al 308
Bimini 93, 102, 305
binary sequence 189, 207, 214-219, 283-286, 288
 and mitotic cell division 189, 214-215
bird migratory routes
 and magnetic lines 62, 430
black holes 12
black-light (energy) 255-256, 268
Black Sea 193
Blair, Lawrence 246
Blue Lake 117
Bolivia 116-117, 169
A Book of Coincidence: New Perspectives on an Old Chestnut 250
 See also Martineau, John
Borea 91
Boulder, Colorado 195
Braden, Gregg 61, 264, 431, 448-450
brain, human 44, 95-96, 115, 132, 142, 148, 201, 222, 232, 335, 338, 386, 418, 436, 447, 453
 experiencing component 96, 222
 female brain 8, 95-96
 left brain 8-9, 64, 95-96, 146, 154, 167, 186, 201, 204, 207-208, 222, 255, 287, 310, 348, 357
 left-brain technology 100-101
 logical component 8, 96, 222
 male brain 8, 95-96, 225, 259
 memory and magnetic fields 115
 right brain 8-9, 23, 41, 90, 95-97, 146, 164, 167, 169, 201, 207-208, 222, 230, 255, 260, 287, 292, 326, 348, 357
 right-brain technology 100
 See also corpus callosum
Brains, Behavior and Robotics 232
 See also Albus, James S.
Brazil 181
breathing 3, 5, 15, 25, 39, 55, 212, 241, 261-262, 267, 273, 279, 436
 and the Mer-Ka-Ba meditation 346-348, 350, 352, 355, 360, 365, 382, 408
 spherical breathing 49, 346-347, 350-352
 yogic breathing 49, 337, 350, 352-355
British Columbia 25, 402
British Museum 97, 254-255
Brotherhood of the Seven Rays 169
Brown, Hugh Auchinloss 60
 Brown theory 60
Bryson, Yvonne J. 449
Buddha 137, 200, 440
Burnaby, British Columbia 25, 405
Bush, George 73

C

Cairo Museum 138-139, 260
California 46, 88, 117, 194, 269, 404, 446
Cameron, Duncan 307-308
Canada 23, 372-374, 382, 398, 403-405
Canadian government 405
carbon 12, 52, 182-183, 213, 215, 423, 444
Carroll, Lee 447
Carroll, Peter 306
cartouche 128, 260-261
Catholic Church 373, 387
Cayce, Edgar 19-20, 58-60, 110, 299, 303, 338, 434, 442, 444
CBS's eye 237
Central America 92, 116, 444
Central Sun 278
cetaceans 15, 88
 and magnetic lines 430-431
 See also dolphins
chakras 3, 43, 45, 117, 148, 157, 264, 267, 310-324, 327-330, 332-337, 343-345, 350, 354, 358, 388, 455
 body surface map of 322-323
 Christ chakra 322, 334-335, 346, 349, 353, 355, 380
 crown chakra 148, 191, 323, 336
 external chakras 319
 half-step/wall 314-318
 heart chakra 130, 157, 241, 318, 322, 329, 334, 380, 385-386
 hidden (secret) doorway 315-319
 solar plexus 322, 329, 349, 355
 third eye 29, 148, 257, 323, 335, 349
 See also chakra system, pineal gland, pituitary gland
chakra system 120, 330, 334, 347
 eight-chakra system 310, 314-316, 323-324, 327, 332, 334
 energy moving through 314, 324, 328
 geometry of 310-314
 and the musical scale 311-314
 thirteen-chakra system 310, 320-324, 327, 334
 See also chakras
Charkovsky, Igor 193-194
Charleston, South Carolina 101
Chavín 117
Cheops 18, 109
chi 324
 See also prana
chi field 337
 See also energy field, human; prana
Chichén Itzá 117
children 130, 442-454
 children of AIDS 78-79, 448-450
 Indigo children 446-448
 superpyschic children 450-454
Chile 72
China 40, 75-76, 156, 159, 175, 269, 316, 446, 451-452, 454
China's Super Psychics 451-452
 See also Dong, Paul; Raffill, Thomas E.
Chinese 76, 225, 311, 330, 446
Chinese government 451-452, 454
Chiquetet Arlich Vomalites
 See Thoth
Christ breath 353
Christ consciousness 25, 35, 64, 77, 105-106, 108, 117, 134-135, 145, 147, 168-169, 228-229, 240-241, 244-245, 250, 252-254, 262, 278, 323, 352, 415-416, 423-425, 429
 chromosomes of 64, 146-147
 See also unity consciousness
Christ consciousness grid 35, 76-77, 95, 106, 118, 120, 129-130, 167-168, 362, 420, 422-423, 426
 three aspects of 118
 See also stellated dodecahedron
Christianity 37-39, 81, 134
 and the creation story 81
 and the Greek Orthodox Church 39
 and Lucifer 411
 symbolism of 37-39, 330-331
 understanding of Reality 147
 See also Bible; Copts; Essene Brotherhood
chromatic scale 43-44, 46, 178, 288, 320-322
 See also dimensions; music; octave; sacred geometry
chromosomes, human 4, 64, 118-119, 133-135, 186, 188-189, 237, 252
 of Christ consciousness 64, 146-147
 in conception 284
 and levels of consciousness 237, 252
 See also consciousness, human
Churchward, Colonel James 91
Clarion Call 16
coca leaf 317
coccyx 328
"coin in stone" 302
coincidence 236, 371-373, 400
cold fusion 213
Colombia 445
Colorado 117, 304
colors 25, 50, 116, 164, 214, 398
 in the aura 338-340

and the dimensional shift 430, 432, 435-437
and your higher self 408
in the Mer-Ka-Ba meditation 347, 349, 351, 359-360
computers 4, 13, 16, 18-19, 55, 70, 76, 115, 156, 166, 199, 213-214, 250, 289, 303-304, 338, 368, 375, 446-447
and crystals 370
and knowledge 51, 216
and the Mer-Ka-Ba 370
silicon/carbon 52, 182-183, 215-216, 444
conscious communication 394, 403-404, 409, 440
See also self
consciousness, human 1, 3, 21, 24, 27, 44, 50-51, 67-69, 77, 92, 95-97, 102, 114, 118-122, 127-128, 157, 177, 218, 222, 248, 250, 257, 301, 307, 323, 352-353, 361, 367-368, 393, 423-425, 430, 445
and chromosome levels 64, 118-119, 133-134
the circles and squares of human consciousness 225-248
and creation 412
disharmonic levels of 63-65, 228-229, 234, 324
and Down syndrome 64
fifth level of 64, 120, 324, 415
first level of 64, 108, 118-119, 131-133, 227-230, 232, 235-240, 252, 324, 415
fourth level of 64-65, 119-120, 324, 415
harmonic levels of 63-64, 228-229, 324
and healing 383-384, 388
higher levels of consciousness 4, 6, 9, 104-105, 109, 118, 398
inner world of 368, 379-380, 388, 403, 455
intentions of 382-383, 385
and love 379
and matter 379
and the nine crystal balls beneath the Sphinx 226
outer world of 368, 379-380, 403, 455
and the phi ratio 226
and the precession of the equinoxes 56-57
and sacred geometry 225-226
second level of 64-65, 108, 118-119, 131-133, 228-229, 232, 235, 239-241, 245, 250-252, 255, 324, 415
third-dimensional consciousness 6, 393
third level of 64, 108, 118-121, 131, 227-229, 232, 235, 240, 244-245, 250, 252-253, 256, 324, 415
See also Christ consciousness; duality consciousness; fourth-dimensional consciousness; freewill consciousness; polarity consciousness; unity consciousness
Contact 435
Copernicus 187
Copts 37-39
symbols of 37-39
Cornell University 54
corpus callosum 9, 95-96, 167, 255, 286
See also brain, human
Cousteau, Jacques 69, 75
Crab Nebula 350
Cracking the Bible Code 79, 450
See also Satinover, Jeffrey
creation 30, 130, 148, 153-154, 158, 171, 399, 412-414
and consciousness 379
and love 379
creation story 15, 85, 147-154
Creator, the 411
Critchlow, Keith 219-220
Critias 97
See also Plato
crocodiles 265-267
crystal, beryl 170, 178
crystal, fluorite 174-176
crystal, ice 179
crystal, quasi 165-166, 172
crystals 106, 113, 166, 170, 174-183, 185, 223, 255, 275, 326, 337, 370-371, 381
gender of 181-182
hexagonal 174
isometric 174
monoclinic 174
orthorhombic 174
programming of 370-371
tetragonal 174
and thoughts, emotions and feelings 371
triclinic 174
x-ray diffraction patterns of 170-171
cuboctahedron 177-178, 229
See also Platonic solids; sacred geometry
cuneiform 80
Cuzco, Peru 14-15, 117

D

da Vinci, Leonardo 200, 207, 241-246
canon of 48-49, 197-199, 201, 205, 207, 211, 234, 237-238, 245-247, 299, 319, 334-335, 345, 349, 352
and the Flower of Life 242-244
dark-light (energy) 252-253, 255-256
Dass, Ram 24
Davidson, Doris 381-382
Day of Purification 116, 429, 433
death 79, 129-130, 158, 259-260, 313, 316-317, 330, 350, 430, 440, 450
deep-blue ray 448
de Lubicz, R.A. Schwaller 17-18, 230
Dendera, temple of 130, 280-282, 294-295, 298, 303
Denver, Colorado 453
Desert Storm war 281
diatoms 223
didgeridoo 279
dimensional octave 426
dimensional shift (planetary) 63, 429-442, 444-446, 451
axis shifts 430-431, 442
birth into the fourth dimension 430, 437-438
changing of the Schumann frequency 431
collapse of the Luciferian reality 434
dissolution of civilization 429, 431-432
passing through the Void 129, 430, 434, 436-437
pole shifts 58-61, 63, 90, 113, 431
six hours before 430, 432, 434-436
and the superkids 454
and synthetic objects 433-434
weakening of geomagnetic fields 63, 429-431,434
dimensional window 388-397, 426, 438
dimensions (dimensional levels) 1, 5-7, 23, 28-29, 43, 48-49, 57, 92, 100, 103-104, 106, 109-110, 115-116, 119, 129-130, 135, 146, 156, 166, 225, 263, 278, 282, 284-286, 291, 293, 301, 304-306, 309, 313, 321, 323, 336, 340, 343, 379, 386-389, 399, 407, 409, 415, 422, 426, 429, 435, 442
and the Bermuda Triangle 103-104
and the Great Void 367, 426
humans as multidimensional 78, 393-396
and the musical scale 45-47
and the precession of the equinoxes 57
shift from the third to the fourth dimension 63, 104, 429-442, 451, 454
stargates 47, 350, 360, 440-441
travel between 42, 44-45, 47, 301, 413
and wavelength 44-45, 47

See also fourth dimension(al); third dimension(al)
disease 69, 76-79, 104, 361, 380-383, 385-388, 390, 449-450
divine order 27, 101, 384, 404, 433
DNA, human 4, 54, 56, 84-85, 118-119, 134, 144-145, 167-168, 189, 332, 424, 445-446, 454
and AIDS 78-79, 448-450
alteration of 425
codons 78, 332, 449
cosmic DNA 144, 411-412
DNA mutations 4, 134, 451
in blood type 445-446
in children 78-79, 447-451, 454
Doczi, Gyorgy 201
Dogons 10-15, 39, 80, 417
drawings of 12-14
and the number 23 14
and Sirius A and B 11-13
dolphins 10, 13, 15, 39, 69, 88, 278, 417, 445
homodolphinus 194
and magnetic lines 62, 430-431
as midwives 193-194
Oceanea 88
Dong, Paul 451-452
Donner Lake 117
Doreal 112
Doryphoros the Spear-Bearer 201
Down syndrome 64
dowsing rods 100, 401
Dratch, Bob 370
dreams 379, 435, 437, 444
Dreamtime 132
Drosnin, Michael 16
drugs 317, 388-389
crack 317
heroin 317
opium 317
psychedelics 317-318
See also LSD
Druids 37, 157, 298, 400
duality consciousness 396, 411, 416, 418, 427
transcending of 411
See also good and evil; polarity consciousness; self, middle
duat
See Void, Great
Du Val, Aaron 93
dysfunctional thought forms 386-387
healing of 386-390

E

Earth 1, 3-4, 6-8, 10-14, 19, 27-29, 35, 41, 45-65, 80-84, 86-88, 90, 99-103, 119, 122, 125, 127, 129-130, 146-147, 160, 169, 182-183, 186-187, 190, 206, 249-250, 252-254, 256, 263, 269, 274-275, 278-280, 283, 285-286, 295-296, 299, 301-305, 309-310, 314-315, 318-319, 326, 332-333, 335-336, 343, 346, 348-350, 355-357, 368, 377, 383-385, 393, 395, 400, 409, 411, 417-425, 427, 443-446, 454
ancient Earth (Tiamat) 81-82
and consciousness 168, 226, 228, 237, 308, 344, 352-353, 415, 422, 448
crust of 61, 182-183
fields around 107-108, 114, 168, 252, 362, 376, 420, 422, 424-425
geomagnetic field of 61-63, 114, 193
geometry of 171, 246-248, 253
and the green angel 400
lightbody of 424
and the lower self 396-397, 399
octahedral field of 252
and the planetary grid 104-118, 168, 362, 420, 422
planetary shift of 123, 130, 429-442, 444
Earth, pollution of 67-78, 308, 398
atomic bombs 75-76, 169
CFCs 70, 72, 75
greenhouse effect 60, 73-74
ozone layer 70-74, 82-83
red tide 69
Earth's Shifting Crust 61
See also Hapgood, Charles
Earth-Sky Workshop 73, 367, 375, 407
Earth Summit 67
Easter Island 90-91, 117
Egg of Life 158, 160, 190-191, 198, 238, 247-248, 343-344, 414-416
and the eight-chakra system 311-312
and Luciferian geometry 414-416
original eight cells 87, 190-193, 195, 198-199, 206, 209, 211, 238, 245-246, 311, 332, 343-344, 354, 358, 361, 414, 424
See also Flower of Life; sacred geometry
Egg of Metamorphosis 43, 260-261, 293, 441
See also Egyptian archaeology; immortality
ego 346, 367, 369, 372, 374, 384, 395, 405, 410, 439
Egypt 14, 17-18, 21-22, 27-28, 31-33, 39, 58, 64, 76, 109-111, 113-114, 116, 118-120, 122-125, 127, 131-132, 134-137, 141-145, 157, 170, 180, 209, 220, 249, 259, 262, 264-265, 267-276, 279, 290, 292-304, 307, 316-317, 330, 357, 440
astrological chart/wheel 58, 130, 280, 294-295, 298, 303-304
Eighteenth Dynasty 5, 134, 137-138
First Dynasty 18, 22, 133
and the Flower of Life 30, 40-42, 287-296
and the Four Corners 304-307
Fourth Dynasty 18, 304
Lower Egypt 130, 133-134
mummification 254-255
Nineteenth Dynasty 144
pyramids of 18, 22, 87, 93, 111, 125-126, 128, 209, 260, 277-278, 297-299, 302-304, 434
and resurrection 127-130, 211, 261-262
temples of 14, 28, 30-37, 47, 116, 123, 130, 146, 230-233, 263-265, 267, 269, 270-271, 273, 279-282, 294, 298, 302-303
Upper Egypt 130, 133-134
and the zodiac 130
See also Egyptian archaeology; Egyptian tools and symbols of resurrection; Egyptians; Giza Plateau; Great Pyramid; Osirian temples; Saqqara; Solar Cross; Sphinx
Egyptian Antiquities Minister 249
Egyptian archaeology 17-19, 31-32, 122-123, 125, 230-231, 250, 301-302
burial ceilings 42, 290-296, 441
cartouche 128, 260-261
Egg of Metamorphosis 43, 260-261, 293, 441
Egyptian wheels 42-43, 47, 290, 290-296, 303
red oval of metamorphosis 128, 262
time bands 32, 281
See also Egypt; sacred geometry
Egyptian government 126, 240, 271, 300-302
Egyptian initiations 146, 240-257, 262-269, 279
Egyptian mummies 139, 305
Egyptian tools and symbols of resurrection 127-129, 261-262
ankh 21, 128, 137, 257, 260-263, 279, 330-334
the hook and flail 128, 261
tuning fork 128, 261-262, 331
See also Egypt; resurrection
Egyptian window 301, 304
Egyptians 4, 17-18, 20-21, 26, 28, 31-33, 37-38, 40-42, 47, 80, 86, 110-111, 119,

121-125, 130-135, 137, 139, 144-146, 150, 197, 201, 203, 211, 230, 232, 250, 252-256, 259, 262-263, 267-268, 274-275, 285-287, 290, 292-294, 296-300, 302, 304-305, 307, 309, 329, 335, 441
and chakras 310, 314-316, 320, 322-324, 327, 329
and consciousness 230-232, 234-235
philosophy of 221, 236, 287
religion of 131, 133-134, 144, 147, 281, 303, 331
and sacred geometry 209, 230-231, 327
and seeing into the future 32, 280-281
sexual practices of 262, 330-334, 360
understanding of Reality 147-148
Egyptology Society in Miami 93
Einstein, Albert 61, 75, 443
electromagnetic 44, 55, 103, 106-107, 178-179, 340, 343, 365, 370, 379, 453
electron 10, 50, 87, 167, 172, 247, 355
electron cloud 172
elohim 89
The Emerald Tablets 27, 111-112, 114, 121, 248, 250
See also Thoth
emotions, human 7, 62, 99, 104, 152, 164, 214, 222, 307-308, 314, 370-371, 379, 386, 410, 431, 440
and auras 338-340, 343
fear 63, 67, 71, 101, 103, 262-263, 265-267, 270, 274-276, 286, 357, 373-375, 386, 388-389, 407, 410, 422, 432, 436, 438-439
and the Left Eye of Horus 260, 262-263, 286
and the Mer-Ka-Ba experience 355, 357-358, 360
and sacred geometry 225
Encyclopedia Britannica 51
"end of time" 16, 144
See also dimensional shift
energy field, human 4-5, 167, 177, 181, 188, 200, 247, 250, 252, 286, 290, 310, 331, 337-341, 343, 361-365, 367, 382
Alpha and Omega of 363, 365
auric field 338-340, 343
and the dodecahedron 362-363
electromagnetic energy field (EMF) 3, 8, 21, 152, 225, 338, 340, 343, 362, 379
external chakras 319
as compared to galactic energy spheres 55
geometry of 340-341, 344-345, 361-365
prana field 137, 337-338, 343
sphere of consciousness 241
spirals around the body 204-206, 211, 213-214
star tetrahedral field 48-49, 178, 223, 319, 332, 343, 361
See also auras; human grid; Mer-Ka-Ba
England 40, 107, 156-157, 169, 213, 298
entities
ET spirit 386
good entity 387
healing of 386-390
human spirit 386
Environmental Protection Agency 71
EPA
See Environmental Protection Agency
Erech 79
Eskimos 445
Essene Brotherhood 146
Jesus and 146
Joseph and 146
Mary and 146
Essenes 37
etheric field 337
See also energy field, human; prana
ETs 83, 98, 104, 226, 305, 424, 432, 434
See also Grays; Hathors; Hebrews; Martians; Nefilim
Europe 157, 166, 238, 316, 389, 452-453
evolution 4, 21, 51, 54, 65, 87, 90-92, 98-100, 112-113, 285, 301, 314, 318, 343-344, 376, 408, 424-425, 448, 450
stair-step evolution 122-124, 133
exorcism 387
eye, human 324-327

F

faith 225, 310, 349, 372-374, 382, 391, 402, 404
Fall, the 1, 3-4, 105, 108, 123, 132-133, 135, 336, 393-394, 422, 431
Faraday cage 453
Fayhed, Ahmed 122, 271-273, 275, 278
Fayhed, Mohammed 271
FBI 376
Fibonacci, Leonardo 207
Fibonacci sequence 86, 199, 207-209, 211, 213-214, 216-218, 227, 239, 283-284, 286, 297, 327, 354
in nature 207-208, 210
Fibonacci spiral 110, 117, 204, 206, 209-211, 213, 237-239, 254
black-light spirals 221
dark-light spirals 252-253, 255-256
and the Giza Plateau 297, 299
and the King's Chamber 211
male and female 209
in nature 210
and the polar graph 218
and sacred sites 110-111, 116-118, 206
white-light spirals 221, 252, 268
fifth dimension 43, 437-438, 441
fission 169
Florida 93, 194
Flower of Life 28-30, 38, 118, 128, 139, 147, 170, 179, 181, 186, 198, 204, 268, 414, 416
and Egypt 30, 40-42, 287-296
geometry of 29-31, 40-41, 159-160
and the Halls of Amenti 29, 86
and Leonardo da Vinci 207, 242-244
as compared to Luciferian geometry 416-417
and the Osirian temples in Abydos 31, 33, 36-37
and Pythagoras 244
See also Egg of Life; Fruit of Life; Genesis Pattern; sacred geometry; Seed of Life; Tree of Life
Flower of Life facilitator 346
Flower of Life workshop 268, 347, 361, 367, 375, 382
flying (astral-projection and remote-viewing) 383
The Forty-Two Books of Thoth 132-133
Four Corners area 304-307
fourth dimension(al) 43, 46-48, 86-87, 104, 110, 118, 129, 225, 267-268, 278, 285, 336, 343, 355-356, 385, 424, 429-430, 432-433, 436, 446, 454
birth into 437-438
parents in 439-440
preparing for 440-441
survival in 438-440
thought manifestation in 438-439
transition into 429-442
fourth-dimensional consciousness 352, 452
France 20, 76, 91, 194
free-energy machine 213
"Free Energy: The Race to Zero Point" (video) 213
See also Lightworks Video
freewill consciousness 412-414, 416, 425-426
French 97, 371
Freud, Sigmund 357
Fruit of Life 159-162, 166, 177, 193, 222-223, 288-291, 293-294
and the circles and squares of human consciousness 225, 230, 232-234
See also Flower of Life; informational systems; sacred geometry
Fuller, Buckminster 177, 229
fusion 11-12, 169, 423

G

Galactic Command 98, 104-105, 422-424
galactic consciousness 423
galactic law 88, 104
galactic law of noninterference 434
galaxy 4, 55-57, 88, 114, 204, 252-253, 316, 423, 426, 429
    spiral model of 53-54, 221-222
Garden of Eden 413-414
Gantenbrink, Rudolf 250
Gazes, Diana 383-384, 390-391
"Gazes into the Future" 384
Geller, Uri 452-453
gender 181, 332
    female (energies) 8, 29, 49-50, 77, 87, 90, 92, 95-96, 99-100, 110-111, 116-117, 146, 150, 160, 164, 167-168, 180-182, 186-190, 200, 205, 209, 212-214, 216-217, 220, 223, 225-226, 234, 237, 239, 244-245, 248, 253, 259-260, 274, 283-284, 287, 295, 310, 312-314, 324, 328-329, 332-333, 345, 348, 350, 353, 356-357, 360, 375, 377, 380, 382, 441
    male (energies) 8, 29, 49-50, 77, 87, 90, 95-96, 99-100, 108, 111, 116-117, 130, 146, 150, 160, 167-168, 180-182, 186-190, 200-201, 205, 209, 211-214, 216-217, 220, 223, 225-226, 234, 237, 244-245, 248, 253, 259-260, 283-284, 287, 310, 312-314, 327-330, 332-334, 345, 347-348, 353, 356-357, 360, 375-377, 380, 382, 441
    See also sacred geometry
Genesa 177
    See also Langham, Derald
Genesis 81, 86, 89, 119, 147, 150-153, 158, 187, 190, 324, 326, 416
    Adam and Eve 81, 85, 88-90, 150, 285-286
    Enlil and Enki 89
    See also Genesis pattern
Genesis pattern 86, 152-153, 155, 157-158, 190, 223, 285, 287, 312, 414
    fifth motion/day 153
    first motion/day 150-153, 187, 416
    fourth motion/day 153, 417
    second motion/day 152, 416
    sixth motion/day 153
    third motion/day 153, 417
    See also reproductive system; sacred geometry
Genesis Revisited 79
    See also Sitchin, Zecharia
genetics, human 189
    changes in 445-449
Genetics, Its Concepts and Implications 215
    See also Pai, Anna C.; Roberts, Helen Marcus
Geological Society of America 59
Geology 59
geomagnetic field 62, 429-431, 434
    and the human mind 431, 434
    and memory 431
    See also dimensional shift
geomagnetics 60-61, 431
geometric progression 46, 178, 227, 241, 289, 296, 325
Georgia 93
Germany 213, 431, 446
Gestalt therapy 358
Giza Plateau (complex) 109, 270-271, 297, 307
    and Orion's Belt 302
    sacred geometry of 297-300, 303
    underground city 116, 300-302
    and the unity consciousness grid 109
    See also Egypt; Egyptian archaeology; Great Pyramid; Sphinx
Giza Survey: 1984 297
    See also McCollum, Rocky
Glastonbury, England 298
Global Positioning System
    See GPS
God 1, 4, 7-9, 16, 24, 30, 46-47, 76, 86, 89, 92, 99, 109, 115, 130, 134, 136, 144, 147-149, 151-152, 168-169, 180, 189, 208, 210-211, 229, 276, 300, 302, 309-310, 315, 318, 322, 324, 326, 329, 335, 340-341, 346-347, 353, 360, 368-369, 372-374, 377, 388, 391, 393-394, 401, 403, 411-414, 416-419, 421, 426-427, 432-437, 439-442, 455
Godhead 314
Golden Mean logarithmic spiral 50, 110, 204-205, 207-210, 213-214, 217-218, 223, 254, 327
    black-light spirals 54, 221
    dark-light spirals 252-253, 255-256
    and the Giza Plateau 109-110, 297, 303
    male and female 205
    phi ratio 205-206, 208
    and the polar graph 217-218, 223
    white-light spirals 54, 221, 252, 268
    See also Fibonacci spirals; sacred geometry
Golden Mean ratio 41, 164, 205, 208, 289, 327
    and the circles and squares of human consciousness 227-230
    and Metatron's Cube 164-166
    See also informational systems; sacred geometry
Golden Mean rectangle 211, 250
    and the Giza Plateau 279-299, 303-304
    and Metatron's Cube 164-165
    and the Sphinx 14, 303
    and spirals around the body 204-206
    See also energy field, human; informational systems; sacred geometry
Gondwanaland 85, 87-88, 90
good and evil 4, 411-412, 414, 418, 427
    See also duality consciousness
Goodman, Sandy 358
Gorbachev, Mikhail 73
GPS system 302, 348
Grand Canyon 305-307
    See also Four Corners; Temple of Isis
Grays 14, 104, 112-113, 305-306, 418
Great Flood, the 90, 123
    and pole shifts 90
Great Pyramid 18, 27-28, 76-77, 86, 97, 109, 111, 114, 116, 123, 146-147, 196, 199, 204, 209, 229, 240-259, 264, 267-269, 271-274, 277, 279, 298, 301-304, 331
    building of 109
    Grand Gallery 248-249, 251, 255
    and initiation 240-257
    King's Chamber 211, 240-241, 248-256, 268, 277, 318, 333-334
    the Pit or Grotto 248-251
    purpose of 147
    Queen's Chamber 248-251, 255-256
    sarcophagus 145, 249, 251, 253-255, 268, 318
    and the second level of consciousness 229, 240, 248, 251
    the tunnel 116, 118, 249-250, 254-256, 267-268, 272, 274-277
    the Well 248-251, 255-256, 267-268, 272-273
Great Spirit 308, 394, 444, 455
Great White Brotherhood 168-169, 301, 423, 426
Greece 25, 27, 40, 93, 166, 170, 187, 193, 201-202, 248, 446
Greek Orthodox Church 39
    See also Christianity
Greek Parthenon 204
Greeks 91, 201, 204
grids 105-108, 116-118
    Christ consciousness 35, 76-77, 95, 106, 118, 120, 129-130, 167-168, 362, 420, 422-423, 426

human 108, 211-212, 420, 433-434
planetary 105-108
unity consciousness 108-111, 116-118
Guam 108
Guatemala 117, 445
Gurdjieff 312, 317

H

HAARP
See High-Frequency Active Auroral Research Project
Haiti 77, 145
Haleakala Crater 117
Hall, Manley P. 269
Hall of Records 111, 146-147, 335
and Edgar Cayce 19-20, 229
and the Sphinx 19-20, 301-302
See also Egypt; Egyptian archaeology; Giza Plateau; Sphinx
Halls of Amenti 86-87, 115-116, 145, 256, 275-276
and the Flower of Life 29, 86
and our Sirian "fathers" 87, 115-116
Hamaker, John 73-74
Hancock, Graham 302
Hapgood, Charles 61
harmonics 43-44, 47, 102, 178-179, 240, 247, 321, 360
geometrical progression 46, 178, 227, 241, 289, 296, 325
in geometry 288, 290-292
musical scale 45-46, 311-312, 314, 320
and the polar graph 219-223, 225
See also music
Harvard University 16
Hathors 120, 278-280
Hawaii 59-60, 90-91, 117, 369, 390, 393-394, 396-397, 445
healers 380, 384-386
Chi Gong masters 385
hands-on healers 380
medicine men and women 354, 356, 380
practitioners of witchcraft 380
prana healers 380, 385
psychic healers 380
psychic surgeons 380
Reiki masters 380
shamans 354, 356, 380
See also healing
healing 279, 379-391
and belief patterns 381-382
and consciousness 382-384
emotional healing 357-358
healing others 382, 384-390
healing yourself 382-384
and intention 385-387
and love 380-382, 386-387, 391
and the Mer-Ka-Ba meditation 352, 354, 356, 382
permission for 381, 384-385, 387, 389
and prana 352, 382, 385-386
with sound 279
techniques 380, 387
Heartmath 168
See also Winter, Dan
Hebrews 40, 64, 98, 100, 119, 168
Hebrew University 450
Hermes 25, 27, 248
See also Thoth
Heston, Charlton 10
hieroglyphics 20-21, 32-33, 80, 128, 271, 275-276, 281-282, 293, 299
higher consciousness 10, 78, 109, 118, 353, 361, 398, 454
See also self, higher
higher knowledge 393, 422
See also self, higher
higher self
See self, higher
High-Frequency Active Auroral Research Project (HAARP) 75, 77
Himalayan mountains 116, 118
Hindi 314
Hindu 1, 24-25, 45, 57-58, 92, 150, 321, 330, 348, 369, 433
Hitler, Adolf 79
HIV
See AIDS
Hoagland, Richard 48, 98, 110, 223
Holland 331
holographic 46, 288
holographic field 424-425
holographic images 29, 111, 195
holographic memory 132-133
Holy Trinity 49-50, 286
homodolphinus
See dolphins
Hook 400
Hopi Indians 304
Hoppe, Peter C. 284
Horus 197, 262, 264, 282
Hotel San Agustin 14-15
Hudson, David 25
Human Dimensions Institute 337, 340
human grid 108, 211-212, 420, 433-434
and zero-point technology 167, 211-214
The Hundredth Monkey 106
hundredth monkey theory 106-108, 450-451
See also planetary grid
Hunt, Dr. Valorie 338
Hunter, Larry 302
hypnotherapists 358, 387
hypnotism 382-383
See also healing

I

ibis 21, 260
Iceland 40
I Ching 404
Illmenser, Karl 284
immaculate conception 282-286
See also interdimensional conception; parthenogenesis
immortality 28, 33, 92, 95, 105, 113, 119, 123, 131, 135, 145-146, 211, 261, 285-286, 300, 313, 341
and memory 143-144
and tantra 92, 119, 131, 330-333
Incas 117, 267, 317
libraries of 421
temples of 421
Inca Trail 14
India 137, 170, 316
Indian Ocean 75
indigenous (populations) 393, 397, 424, 429, 444-445
Indigo children 446-448
and the educational system 447-448
See also children
The Indigo Children: The New Kids Have Arrived 447
See also Carroll, Lee; Tober, Jan
indigo ray 448
informational systems of the Fruit of Life 160, 225
the circles and squares of human consciousness (third) 225-248
Metatron's Cube (first) 160-170, 177, 193, 195, 197-198, 223, 225
polar graph (second) 216-223, 225, 295
See also Fibonacci spiral; Golden Mean logarithmic spiral; Platonic solids
initiate 128, 134, 253, 255-257, 262, 266-267, 275-277, 318
initiation 28, 146, 240-257, 268-270, 272-273, 275-278, 317-319
crocodile 262-267
sound of the ankh 279
inner child 24, 397-398, 403
inner guidance 394-395
See also self
intention, human 354, 359, 364, 369-371, 382, 385-387, 412, 444, 450
interdimensional conception 282, 284-286

See also immaculate conception; parthenogenesis
interdimensional lovemaking 92, 119, 135, 146, 282
See also tantra
ions 172, 175
Iowa 106
Iraq 83, 89, 301
Ireland 40, 156
Isis 116, 131, 134, 261-263, 281-282
Island of the Sun 15, 116-117
Israel 40, 450, 452
Italian Renaissance 170

J

Japan 40, 69, 106-107, 204, 213, 402, 445, 450
Japanese 106, 204, 402-403, 446
and the Sphinx 248-249, 299, 301
Japanese pagoda 204
Jesus 8, 39, 124, 144, 146, 186-187, 256, 283, 285, 372, 382, 397, 416-417, 430, 438-440, 442
Joseph 146, 282, 285
Jung, Carl 396
Jupiter 81-82

K

Kabah 117
Kabala 149
kabbalah 40
See also Tree of Life
kahunas 393-394, 397-399, 408, 445
Kalu Rinpoche 143
Karnak, temple of 40, 230-233
Kepler, Johannes 250
Keyes, Ken 106
Khem 108, 114
See also Egypt; Giza Plateau
kinetic energy 148, 150, 379
King Menes 133-134
King Tutankhamun (King Tut) 142, 261, 302
King Zoser 33
See also Saqqara
Kirlian photography 337
Kogi 444-445
Kohunlich 117
Kom Ombo 262, 264-267
Kootenay Lake 23-24
Koran 8, 84
and Egyptian archaeology 18
Koshima, Japan 106
Krishna 16, 283, 285, 440
kundalini energy 261, 379

L

Labna 117
labyrinth 156-157
Lake Tahoe 117
Lake Titicaca 15, 92, 116-117
Lama Foundation 130
Lamy, Lucie 17, 203-204, 230-234
Lucie's ladder 231-234
and the "second" Osirian temple 35
Land of Khem
See Giza Plateau
Langham, Derald 177-178
Language of Light 40
See also Flower of Life
Language of Silence 40
See also Flower of Life
Lao-tsu 440
Lapland 40
Lawlor, Robert K.G. 34-35
Law of One
See Akhenaten
Left Eye of Horus 146, 259-260, 281-282
Left Eye of Horus Mystery School 145, 253, 259-296, 357
The Legend of the Golden Dolphin 88
See also Shenstone, Peter
Lehirit 125, 128
Lemuria 90-93, 100-101, 105, 113-114, 286
Ay and Tiya 92, 119, 131
beginning of tantra 92-93
explorations of 91
Naacal Mystery School 92, 96-97, 131
sinking of 90, 92-93, 97, 101
and Udal 95-97, 122, 131
Leo 58, 303
Le Plongeon, Augustus 91, 97
Liberman, Jacob 3
Life 20, 91
Lifetide: The Biology of the Unconscious 106
See also Watson, Lyall
light 3, 5, 8, 11, 28, 44, 53, 55-56, 70, 72, 86-87, 108, 116, 129, 134, 147, 151-152, 171, 176, 178, 214, 221, 223, 251, 264-266, 277, 301, 309-311, 328-329, 337, 347, 349, 350-352, 379-380, 385, 394, 412, 417, 419, 423, 426, 443-444, 448
and the dimensional shift 432, 436-437, 439-440
electromagnetic spectrum 44, 53, 326
and the Reality 383, 387, 400, 407, 410
sacred geometry of 187, 324-327, 343, 415
and the vesica pisces 151-152, 324-327
See also sine waves
light field 171, 301-302
Light, the Medicine of the Future 3
See also Liberman, Janet
lightbody 9, 49, 166, 241, 286, 308-310, 330, 334, 340, 343, 358-359, 363, 365, 367, 418, 424, 454
See also Mer-Ka-Ba
Lightworks Video 212-213, 454
See also "Free Energy: The Race to Zero Point"; "Through the Eyes of a Child"
Lima, Peru 143
limitation 381-382, 384, 390, 395, 407, 434
Livingstone, David 401-403
Long Island, New York 306
The Lost Realms 79
See also Sitchin, Zecharia
Louisiana 93
love 5-6, 24, 47, 64, 99, 103, 105, 228, 262-263, 278-279, 286, 307-308, 317, 340, 370, 374, 398, 400, 406, 419, 423, 430, 435, 440-442, 455
in the fourth dimension 439-440
and healing 379-382, 386-391
and the heart chakra 322-323, 329
and light technology 418
and Lucifer's experiment 413, 416, 418-419
and the Mer-Ka-Ba 310, 347-348, 350-353, 355, 360, 380, 413
vibration of 379-380
LSD 307, 317
LSD-25 317
Lucifer 99, 368, 371, 407, 411-419, 422, 424, 426, 433
Lucifer experiment 411-419, 424, 433
Lucifer rebellion 98-99, 411
See also Lucifer experiment
Luciferian geometry 414
Luxor, temple of 40, 230-232, 271, 273, 275

M

Machu Picchu 14, 110-111, 117
magnetar 12
magnetic field
and memory 62, 115, 431
See also geomagnetic field
magnetic flow 62-63
magnetic poles 59-60, 90, 130
Manhattan Project 75
Manning, Jeanne 76
Maori 445
Marduk 81-83, 260, 281-282
Mars 68, 81-82, 98-99, 102, 223, 305, 413, 418

See also Martians
Martians 98-101, 105-106, 132, 418
and the Mars experiment 102, 305
and failed Mer-Ka-Ba attempt 102-104, 305, 387, 418, 422
rebellion of 99
Martineau, John 250
Martin-Marietta 326
Mary 146, 282, 285
Masada, Israel 146
Masons 195-198, 200, 233
mastabas 125
See also stepped pyramids
matter 11-12, 50, 61, 112, 169, 212, 225, 360, 415
and consciousness 379-380
and energy 379-380
in the fifth dimension 437-438
in the fourth dimension 437
maya 78, 150
Maya 393, 437, 443-445,
ball games 268
calendar 16, 61, 444
records of 97-98
McCollum, Rocky 110
McCollum survey 110, 297-298, 303-304
meditation 24-26, 28-29, 44, 78, 91, 149, 255, 266, 270, 278, 305, 318-319, 368-369, 373, 375, 399-403, 405, 408-409, 450
Kriya Yoga 368
Taoist 368
Tibetan 368
Vapasana 368
Mediterranean 15
Mediterranean Sea 69, 75
Melchizedek, Machiventa 169
Melchizedeks 80, 85, 122, 143, 157, 429
Melchizedek transition 440-441
memory 4, 7, 63, 77, 101, 129, 135, 145, 255, 317, 367, 395, 434
and the geomagnetic field 431
holographic, 132-133
and immortality 143-144
and magnetic fields 62, 115
photographic 132
transpersonal 132-133
Memphis 271, 279
Men, Hunbatz 443
meridian 311, 343
merkaba
See Mer-Ka-Ba
Mer-Ka-Ba 4-7, 9, 48-49, 54-55, 112, 114-115, 119, 126, 129, 166, 186, 191, 241, 250, 277, 286-287, 307-330, 334, 336, 341, 343-347, 367-371, 380, 382, 385, 387, 413, 418, 454-455
and ascension 353-356, 367
conscious breather 346-347
and the failed Martian attempt 102-104, 305, 387, 418, 422
compared to the galactic heat envelope 4-5, 55, 114
and healing 352, 354, 356, 382, 388
and love 348, 350-353, 355, 380, 413
Mer-Ka-Ba meditation 9, 29, 49, 55, 191, 241, 272, 276, 309, 343, 346-361, 365, 367, 378, 382, 420, 436, 450
programming of 369-371, 375-378
sacred geometry of 307, 310, 337, 343-345, 361-365
science of 306, 308
surrogate Mer-Ka-Ba 376, 378
synthetic Mer-Ka-Ba 99, 102-104, 115, 305-308, 413
Tri-Phased Mer-Ka-Ba 375-376
See also energy field, human; mudra; star tetrahedron
merkabah
See Mer-Ka-Ba
merkavah
See Mer-Ka-Ba
MES
See molecular emissions scanner
The Message of the Sphinx 302
See also Bauval, Robert; Hancock, Graham
metallurgical scientist 165
metamorphosis 40, 47, 128, 261-262
Metatron 64, 119
Metatron's Cube 160-170, 177, 193, 195, 197-198, 223, 225
See also informational systems; Platonic solids
Mexico 92, 116-117, 389, 445-446, 453
Mexico City 451
Middle Eye of Horus Mystery School 259-260, 278
See also Third Eye of Horus Mystery School
Mitchell, Edgar 443-444
mitosis 188, 214-215, 284, 343, 416
Mohammed 440
molecular emissions scanner (MES) 319, 321, 370
Mona Lisa, the 198, 262
Montauk Experiment 102, 306-307
Moon 50, 53-54, 171, 246-248, 400, 420, 422, 443
the full moon and geomagnetics 62, 431
and the lower self 397
Mooréa Island 76, 110-111, 117-118
Morgan, J.P. 212
Mormon 430
morphogenetic 107, 158
Moses 81
Mother Earth 49, 68-69, 73, 76, 116, 308, 315, 349, 376, 385, 396-400, 404, 407-408, 445
Mother Mary 440, 444
Mount Shasta 92
mudra 49, 347-350, 352, 354, 359
mummification 254-255
Murshid Sam Lewis (Sufi Sam) 130
music 6, 24, 29, 43-44, 46-47, 117, 178, 219-223, 225, 311-314, 398
and the angels 407
and the chakras 317-318
and the Mer-Ka-Ba meditation 356, 360
musical notes 43, 291
musical scale 45-46, 311-312, 314, 320
and sacred geometry 178, 219-223, 288, 291-292, 321
See also chromatic scale; harmonics; octave
Muslim 18, 25, 248
Mutwa, Credo 302
"The Mysterious Origins of Man" (video) 10
"The Mystery of the Sphinx" (video) 10
Mystery Schools 119, 132, 145-146, 148-149, 153, 267, 309, 357
the Law of One 145-146
Left Eye of Horus 145, 253, 259-296, 357
Middle Eye of Horus 259-260, 278
Naacal 92, 96-97, 113, 131, 137
Right Eye of Horus 145-146, 253, 259-260, 335, 357

N

Naacal Mystery School 92, 96-97, 113, 131, 137
and Ay and Tiya 92, 131
See also Atlantis; Lemuria
nanotechnology 166
Napoleon 111
NASA 6, 48, 51, 81-82, 165, 250, 431, 443-445
National Geographic 55
Native American Indians 25, 100, 117, 127, 149, 156, 317, 429, 432
Nature 453
navel 199-201, 205, 321-322, 329, 350-352, 388
Near Earth Asteroid Rendezvous spacecraft 12

NEAR spacecraft
See Near Earth Asteroid Rendezvous spacecraft
Nefertiti 135-140, 142, 441
Nefilim (Nephilim) 80, 82, 86-90, 115, 124, 279, 281, 336, 417, 423
and Adam and Eve 88-90
Elders 336
Els 336
Enki 89
Enlil 83, 87-89
gold mines of 83-85, 88-90
as "mothers" of Homo sapiens 84-88
rebellion of 83-85, 88
Nephthys 131, 282
Neptune 12
neters 43, 133-135, 138
Anubis 133-134
Maat 138
neutron 50, 87, 167
New England Journal of Medicine 449
New Guinea 73
"New Light of the Sun" 443
New Mexico 117, 130, 304
New York 383
New York City 69, 242
New York Jets 306
New York Times 72, 453
New Zealand 194, 445
Nibiru 81-83
See also Marduk
Nichols, Preston 307-308
Nile River 34, 117, 130-131, 146, 263-265, 273, 282
Noah 123
Nobel Prize 68
Nommo 11
See also Dogon tribe
North America 97, 445
North Carolina 93
North Pole 72, 90, 304
North Star 55
Nostradamus 444
Nubian sorcerers 145

O

occiput 388
octave 6, 28, 43, 46-47, 178, 182, 219-220, 288, 304, 312-314, 320-321, 367, 407
in the Great Pyramid 374
overtones 1, 46-47, 113, 129, 278, 441
and sacred sites 117
void between 46-47, 320, 367
and the Wall 46-47, 367
See also harmonics; Void, Great
Old Kingdom 128
Olympia, Washington 396
Om 45, 279
See also wavelength
Omni magazine 451
Orcas Island 401
orgasm, human 194, 262, 284, 330, 332-334, 389
See also ankhing; sexual energy
original eight cells 87, 190-193, 195, 198-199, 206, 209, 211, 238, 245-246, 311, 332, 343-344, 354, 358, 361, 414, 424
See also Egg of Life
Orion 350
Orion's Belt 11
and the Giza complex 302
Osborn, David 16
Osirian temples 31
"second" temple 31, 33-37
Seti I temple 31-33, 280-281
"third" temple 31, 33
See also Flower of Life; sacred geometry
Osiris 31, 33-35, 128, 131-135, 261-263, 275-276, 281-282
and immortality 131
ozone layer 70-74, 82-83

P

Pacific islands 283
Pacific Ocean 69, 90
Page, Nita 269-272
Pai, Anna C. 215
Palenque 117
papyrus 20-21
Paramount Studios 302
parthenogenesis 284-285
See also immaculate conception; interdimensional conception
The Path of the Pole 61
See also Hapgood, Charles
pendulums 401
Penrose, Roger 165
Penrose patterns 165-166
Pentagon, the 16, 51
pentatonic scale 178, 320, 407
perineum 190-191, 322, 328, 358
See also chakras
Periodic Table of the Elements 179
Perl, Fritz 358
Perona, Bernard 422
Peru 14-15, 39, 110-111, 113, 116-118, 127, 143, 156, 169, 176, 286, 421
peyote 317
pharaoh 33, 122, 136, 144, 180, 254, 441
See also Egypt
Philadelphia Experiment 91, 102, 305-308
The Philadelphia Experiment 306
Philippines 385
phi ratio 156, 164, 170, 197-198, 202-205, 208, 210, 250
in architecture 204
in butterflies 202
and the circles and squares of human consciousness 226-228, 230, 232, 235-236, 239, 241, 245-247
in fish 203
in a frog skeleton 202-203
and the Giza complex 297-298, 303
and the Golden Mean logarithmic spiral 204-206, 208
in the human body 199-202, 204, 232, 245-246, 250
Phoenix, Arizona 346
Physical Review Letters 55
pi 227, 247
and Sanskrit writings 16
piano 43, 45, 312, 320
pineal gland 3, 9, 148, 157, 253, 314, 323, 335-336
and the six sensing rays 148-149
Pisces 58, 304
pituitary gland 157, 255, 314, 323, 336
planetary grid 105-108
See also hundredth monkey theory
Plato 19, 91, 93, 97, 167
Platonic solids 161-164, 166-168, 170, 173-174, 176-178, 180, 185, 189, 193, 223, 225, 229, 250, 324
characteristics of 161
cube 14, 86, 96, 150, 158, 161-162, 164, 166-168, 170-171, 173-181, 187, 190-191, 193, 195, 197-199, 226, 311, 344-345, 414
and the cuboctahedron 177-178, 229
icosahedron 35, 96, 161-163, 166-168, 173, 176, 180, 362
and Metatron's Cube 161-166
octahedron 149-151, 161-162, 166-167, 173, 175-178, 180, 306, 345, 363, 388
pentagonal dodecahedron 35, 96, 161, 163-168, 173, 176, 178, 180, 362-363
and the six elements 166-167
and the star tetrahedron 162, 168, 178, 180-181, 190-191, 193, 223
tetrahedron 3, 49, 96, 103, 161-162, 166-168, 170, 173, 176, 180-181, 189-190, 193, 219-223, 312-313, 321, 324-325, 332, 344-345, 347-350, 353-354, 356-359, 378
See also informational systems; sacred geometry, sphere
Pleiades 11, 286

Pluto 12
polar graph 216-223, 225, 295
See also informational systems; polar grid; sacred geometry
polar grid 290-291
See also polar graph
polarity 4, 8, 49-50, 77, 100, 116, 130, 207, 213, 216, 264, 312-313, 352-353, 357, 372, 375, 377, 411
polarity consciousness 4, 49, 154
Pole Shift 60
See also White, John
pole shifts 58-61, 63, 90, 100-101, 130, 431
and Atlantis 90, 113-114, 123, 130
and the Great Flood 90, 123
and the Great Void 114
and Lemuria 90
polytheism 133
possession
See entities
The Power of Limits 201
See also Doczi, Georgy
prana 1, 3, 49, 86, 137, 166-167, 241, 272, 324, 330, 334, 337-338, 343, 347, 350, 352, 359-360, 363, 382, 385-386, 408, 436
See also chi
prana sphere 350-351, 385
See also Mer-Ka-Ba, Mer-Ka-Ba meditation
precession of the equinoxes 55-58, 81, 101, 106, 109, 113-114, 123-124
celestial equator 56
Earth's ecliptic 56
See also yugas
proton 50, 87, 167, 172
psychic energy 355, 364, 371-372, 390
psychic powers 369, 390, 450
in children 450-454
See also siddhis
psychotronic instruments 100, 401
psychotronics 421
Puharich, Andrija 317
Purcell, William 54
pyramids 18, 22, 87, 93, 98-99, 109-111, 117-118, 125-126, 128, 149, 209, 260, 277-278, 297-299, 302-304, 434
Pyramid Lake 117
Pythagoras 27, 166, 236
and the Flower of Life 244
Pythagorean school 27, 167, 244

Q

quantum mechanics 44
quantum physics 10, 44, 320, 443
quasar (quasi-stellar radio source) 52

R

Ra 108, 110, 113, 116, 123
radiocarbon dating 59
Raffill, Thomas E. 451
Ralston, John 55
Raphaell, Katrina 30-31, 33, 36, 181, 264, 267, 270, 272-273, 280, 381
Reagan, Ronald 73
Reality, the 1, 3-4, 7, 10, 25, 27, 44, 46, 53, 64, 99, 102-104, 106, 118, 132-133, 144, 150-151, 153-154, 159-160, 171-172, 178, 180, 187, 226, 228-229, 235, 237, 239, 309, 316-317, 320, 322, 324, 361, 365, 377, 379, 383, 387, 403, 406, 410, 413-414, 433, 444
in the fourth dimension 438-439
holographic 424-426, 444
Lucifer's synthetic Reality 413-414, 416-419, 424, 433-434, 454
multidimensional 413
the original Reality 414, 416-419, 425-427, 433-434, 454
and sine waves 44
third, integrated Reality 419
Reich, Wilhelm 357-358
reincarnation 34, 39, 129-130
reproduction 92, 283
of bees 283
of mourning geckos 283
See also immaculate conception
reproductive system
fallopian tubes 329
morula 192, 287
ovum 87, 186-187, 193
pronucleus 186-188, 214
sacred geometry of 189-193, 238, 245
sperm 84, 87-88, 186-187, 284, 330
womb 88
zona pellucida 186-189, 191-192, 198, 245-247, 284, 287
zygote 188, 227
See also Egg of Life; Genesis pattern
resurrection 33, 35, 38, 43, 47, 92, 127-131, 146-147, 211, 250, 261-262, 264, 267, 293, 331, 350, 430
Rhode Island 101
rhombic dodecahedron 178
Rhythms of Vision 246
See also Blair, Lawrence
Rife, Royal 178-179
Right Eye of Horus 127, 146, 259-260
Right Eye of Horus Mystery School 145-146, 253, 259-260, 335, 357
Rio de Janeiro 67-68
Rips, Dr. Eli 16
Roberts, Helen Marcus 215
Rocks and Minerals 177
See also Sorrell, Charles A.
Rolfe, Ida P. 358
Rolfing 358
Romans 201-202, 279
Russell, Walter 180
Russia 194, 431, 446, 454
Russian government 107-108

S

The Sacred Balance: Rediscovering Our Place in Nature 72
See also Suzuki, David
sacred geometry 3, 17, 27, 29, 35, 41, 44, 119, 126, 150-151, 154-155, 161, 164, 166, 168, 173, 179-180, 198, 200-201, 204, 210-212, 219-220, 222, 225, 229-231, 233, 244, 296, 310, 314, 412, 414, 416, 455
7.23 centimeters 45, 203, 314
in architecture 204, 238
binary sequence 189, 207, 214-219, 283-286, 288
concentric circles 159, 217, 223, 225-226, 230, 233, 244
and the cuboctahedron 177-178, 229
curved lines 150-151, 209, 212-214, 217, 220
diamond view 149, 177, 228-229, 414-416
of the Earth and the Moon 246-248
and Egypt 230, 287-296
female (energies) 49, 95, 150, 160, 205, 209, 211-214, 216-217, 220, 226, 237, 239, 244-245, 253, 283, 310, 312-314, 328
Fibonacci sequence 86, 199, 207-211, 213-214, 216-218, 227, 239, 283-284, 286, 297, 327, 354
of the Flower of Life 29-31, 40-41, 159-160
heart-shaped relationship 214
of the human body 48-49, 167, 185-206, 211-212, 216, 238, 245-248, 250-251, 311, 345, 361
of the human chakra system 314-315, 319-321
and human consciousness 225-257
innermost circle point 152-153
and language 28, 40, 126, 156
of light 309, 324-327, 343
and Lucie Lamy 35, 203-204, 230-234
and the Lucifer experiment 414-419
male (energies) 49, 150, 160, 205, 209, 211-214, 216-217, 220, 225-226, 237, 244-245, 253, 283, 310,

312-314, 328
ratcheting 155-157
and sacred sites 47, 110-111, 116-118, 206
and the "second" Osirian temple 33-36
spheres 55, 86, 151-153, 156, 158-160, 166, 171-172, 186-187, 189, 198, 222, 225, 246, 292, 311, 319, 343, 414-416
spirals 53-54, 108-110, 117-118, 151, 182, 204-206, 209-214, 218, 221, 223, 237, 244, 253, 298, 314, 327-328, 334
square-and-circle sacred ratios 226
squaring the circle 195-196, 225
straight lines 150-151, 168, 198, 205, 209, 212-214, 217, 220, 225
and Thoth 27, 225
and thoughts and emotions 225
transcendental number 156, 200
transcendental pattern 156
truncating 175-177
zero point 62, 211-212, 214, 237, 244-245, 252-253, 255
See also crystals; Egg of Life; Fibonacci spiral; Flower of Life; Fruit of Life; Genesis pattern; Golden Mean logarithmic spiral; Golden Mean ratio; Golden Mean rectangle; human grid; informational systems; phi ratio; Platonic solids; reproductive system; Star of David; star tetrahedron; torus; vesica piscis
Sacred Geometry: Philosophy and Practice 34-35
See also Lawlor, Robert K.G.
The Sacred Mushroom 317
See also Puharich, Andrija
sacred sites 47, 110-111, 116-118, 206
Sacsayhuaman 117
Sananda Ra 270, 272
San Francisco, California 181
San Juans 401
San Pedro cactus 317
Sanskrit 16-17, 56-57, 63, 137
Saqqara 18, 22, 33, 125-126, 128, 271
See also Egypt; Egyptian archaeology
sarcophagus 145, 249, 251, 253-255, 268, 318
Satinover, Jeffrey 79, 450
Schinfield, Mary Ann 6-7
Schoch, Robert 18
Schumann Frequency 431
See also dimensional shift
Science 283
Science News 449
Science of Breath: A Complete Manual of the Oriental Breathing Philosophy of Physical, Mental, Psychic and Spiritual Development 348
See also Yogi Ramacharaka
Scientific American 165
secret government 68, 76-77, 98, 108
The Secret Teachings of All Ages 269
See also Hall, Manley P.
Sedona, Arizona 376
Seed of Life 36-37, 40-41
See also Flower of Life
self
higher self 6-7, 344, 346, 353, 355-356, 359-360, 367-368, 372, 377-378, 384-385, 387-390, 393-396, 398-399, 401-402, 406-410
lower (unconscious mind) 396-399, 400-401, 407-408
middle (duality consciousness) 396, 399, 422
multidimensional 393
reconnecting with the higher self 7, 395, 401, 407
self-realization 368, 378
Serpent in the Sky 18
See also West, John Anthony
Set 131, 282
Seti I 31-33, 144, 280-281
See also Osirian temples
seven-color map 155
See also Torus
sexual energy 131, 260, 262, 267, 284, 307, 311, 330-334, 379, 389
and the Mer-Ka-Ba 360
and resurrection 92, 128, 262, 267
See also ankhing; orgasm, human; tantra
shadow form 217, 312
shamans 354, 356
Shenstone, Peter 88
Shesat 28, 286, 301, 336, 426
See also Thoth
Shintos 400, 445
Shiva 16, 375
Shroud of Turin 256
siddhis 367-369, 372, 374-376, 378
See also psychic powers
silicon 52, 181-183, 215, 444
See also computers
Silverado, Colorado 176
Simply Living 11, 15
sine waves 169, 288, 370-371
and the Reality 44
sine-wave signature 44, 370-371, 380
Sirian Experiment 419-427
Sirians 87, 105, 115, 142, 417, 420-421, 423-426
as our "fathers" 86-88, 115, 124, 419, 423, 441
sculptures of 420
See also Sirian Experiment
Sirius 10-12, 14, 52-54, 87-88, 128, 142, 260-261, 286, 303, 417
Earth's gravitational connection with 53-54
heliacal rising of 14, 298, 303
solar system of 12-13, 53-54
See also Sirius A; Sirius B
Sirius A 11-13, 54, 128, 142
See also Dogon tribe
Sirius B 10-13, 54, 87-88, 128, 142, 417
See also Dogon tribe
The Sirius Mystery 10
See also Temple, Robert
Sister Teresa 440
Sitchin, Zecharia 78-81, 84-85, 87, 260
skulls, elongated 122, 140-143, 232
Sky People 15
"the sleeping prophet"
See Cayce, Edgar
Smithsonian Institute 305
snake 89, 127, 261, 274-276
Snead, Rodman E. 217
snowflakes 179
Sobek, the crocodile god 264
Solar Cross 110, 297
See also Giza Plateau
Sombrero galaxy 5, 307, 365
Sorrell, Charles A. 177
Sothic calendar 14, 303
soul 394
sound 16, 44-45, 156, 204, 217, 222-223, 225, 252, 278-279, 292, 300, 311, 314, 316-317, 323, 360, 370
sound-of-the-ankh initiation ceremony 279
Source 210, 356, 440
South America 64, 97, 116, 177
South Carolina 93
South Pacific 110, 118
South Pole 60, 70, 72, 217
spaceship 12-13, 15, 44-45, 55, 83, 99, 413, 417-419, 422, 434
Sphere 435
sphere of consciousness 86, 241
Sphinx 14, 19-20, 80, 111, 249, 271, 301-304
age of 17-19
and the nine crystal balls 226
placement of 298-300
and the warship 111-113, 115-116, 199
See also Egypt; Egyptian archaeology; Giza Plateau; Hall of Records
Spiritual Hierarchy 394, 423, 426

Spock, Mr. 99
spontaneous genetic mutation 448-450, 454
Sri Yukteswar 24, 57-58
stair-step evolution 122-124, 133
Stanford Research Institute 453
Star of David 3, 125-126, 231, 353
    See also sacred geometry
star tetrahedron 3, 48-49, 152, 162, 168, 178, 180-181, 190-191, 193, 223, 225, 241, 245-246, 290-291, 306, 311-313, 319-320, 323-324, 344-345, 347-348, 350, 353-354, 356, 359, 361, 363-364
    Earth tetrahedron 48, 345, 348-350, 353, 356-357, 366
    emotional tetrahedron 353-354, 358-359
    and the Mer-Ka-Ba 241, 306, 344-345, 347, 350, 353-354, 356-357
    mind tetrahedron 353-354, 358-359
    and the polar graph 225
    Sun tetrahedron 48, 345, 347, 350, 353, 356-357, 361
Star Trek 83, 99, 424, 435
Stargate 108
stargate 47, 350, 360
    patterns of 360, 440-441
stars 7, 10-12, 20, 45, 53-55, 142, 156, 170-171, 294, 302, 304, 399
stele 301
stellated dodecahedron 168, 363
    and the Christ consciousness grid 35
    See also informational systems; Platonic solids
stepped pyramids 125
Step Pyramid 33
    See also Saqqara
Stonehenge 110
Strait of Gibraltar 91
Strecker Memorandum 76-77
    See also AIDS
Sufism 25, 130
Sumer 79-80, 84, 116, 123-125
    Sumerian records 80-89, 119
Sumeria
    See Sumer
Sumerians 19, 51, 80-82, 85, 122-125
Sun 14, 48-50, 52, 54, 56, 74, 81-83, 112, 130, 136-137, 171, 277-278, 303, 345-347, 350-351, 353, 356-357, 385, 400, 443-444
    expansion into a helium sun 423-425
    and the purple angel 400-401
The Survival of Civilization 74
    See also Hamaker, John
Suzuki, David 72
Sweden 40

T

Tacoma, Washington 283
Tahiti 91
Tahitian Islands 76, 110
Takasakiyama, Japan 107
tantra 92, 119, 131, 241, 267, 330-333, 360
    See also Ay; immortality; Lemuria; Naacal Mystery School; Tiya
Taoist 25, 78, 330, 377
Taos Indians 117, 432-433
Taos, New Mexico 30, 117, 382
tarot 404
Tat 123, 286
Tat Brotherhood 123-124, 134, 146, 300-301, 331
technology 1, 101, 109, 165, 216, 420-422, 434
    Luciferian 417-419, 422, 433
Tel el Amarna 136, 138-139
telepathy 29, 142, 388, 421
Temple, Robert 10, 13
Temple of Isis 305-307
    See also Four Corners; Grand Canyon
Tesla, Nicola 212, 305
Texas 93
Thebes 136
third dimension(al) 1, 43, 45-47, 48, 50, 86-87, 104-105, 116, 118, 130, 137, 267, 278, 315, 354-356, 384, 386, 394, 429-430, 433, 438, 446, 454
    transition into fourth 429-442, 446
third eye 29, 148, 257, 323, 335, 349
Third Eye of Horus Mystery School
    See Middle Eye of Horus Mystery School
Thoth 20, 23, 27-30, 43, 64, 78-80, 85-88, 90, 93, 95-98, 104, 118-119, 123, 128, 130-131, 134-135, 138-139, 142-143, 145-146, 225-230, 235, 237-239, 242-243, 245, 248, 250, 252-253, 255-257, 261, 264-266, 269-277, 281-282, 299-302, 324, 326, 332, 335-336, 369, 420, 423, 426
    and the Christ consciousness grid 108-114, 116
    and *The Emerald Tablets* 27, 111
    family tree of 285-286
    Hermes 25, 27
    hieroglyph for 20-21, 282
    Sekutet (mother) 285-286
    Tat (son) 123, 286
    Thome (father) 96, 286
    and writing 21-22
    See also Shesat
thought, human 7, 29, 87, 91, 96, 109, 112, 225, 263, 349, 370-371, 386-387, 389-390, 396, 410, 425, 433, 440, 444, 453
    and auras 338-340, 343
    manifestation in the fourth dimension 263, 438-439
    and the Mer-Ka-Ba experience 112, 349, 352, 355
    and sacred geometry 225
three-dimensional reality 318
three missing atoms 26
"Through the Eyes of a Child" (video) 454
    See also Lightworks Video
Tiamat 81-82
Tibet 40, 118, 127, 143, 156, 170, 316
Tibetan lama 143
Tibetan 25, 47, 57, 143, 330, 335, 348, 368
Tikal 117
Timbuktu 10
time 14, 16, 43, 50, 56-58, 61, 99-100, 102, 104, 132, 152, 225, 303, 305, 379, 413, 434-435, 437
    foretelling the future 404-406
    the present (the Now) 397-398
    spherical 395
    See also precession of the equinoxes; yugas
Time magazine 54, 68-69, 74, 186
Tiya 92, 119, 122, 131, 135, 144, 285-286
Tober, Jan 447
Torah 450
torus (tube torus) 62, 116, 155-157, 160, 191-193, 343
    seven-color map 155
    See also sacred geometry
tree of the knowledge of good and evil 89, 193, 414
Tree of Life 40-41, 414
    and Atlantis 97-98
    geometry of 40-41
    and the six primal shapes 167
    and the vesica pisces 41
    See also Flower of Life; sacred geometry
trinity 49-50, 286, 379, 396
Tri-Phase Mer-Ka-Ba workshop 375-377
Troano document 97-98, 114
Trombly, Adam 75
Tulum 117
Turkey 40
The Twelfth Planet 79
    See also Sitchin, Zecharia

U

Udal 95-97, 114, 122, 131, 286
    See also Atlantis; Lemuria
UFOs 44
    sightings of 10
unconscious mind 396
    See self, lower

underwater birthing 193-194
See also dolphins
unified field theory 443-444
United Nations 48, 76-77, 223, 449
United States 23, 45, 60, 67, 76-77, 91, 93, 113, 117, 126, 144-145, 174, 194, 304, 316-318, 357, 446
United States Geological Survey 63
United States government 107-108, 431
unity consciousness 64, 108-109, 168, 228-229, 324, 411, 429
See also Christ consciousness
unity consciousness grid 108-111, 116-118
University of California, Los Angeles (UCLA) 78-79, 449
University of Kansas 55
University of Rochester 55
The Unknown Leonardo 242-243
Uranus 12
Uri Geller, My Story 452
See also Geller, Uri
Uros Indians 15
USGS
See United States Geological Survey
U.S. Navy 305
Utah 304
Ute Mountain 117
Uxmal 117

V

Vancouver, Canada 24, 401-402
vector equilibrium
See cuboctahedron
Venus 82, 278, 285-286
See also Hathors
Venusian consciousness 285
Venusians 120
See also Hathors
vesica piscis 41, 151-152, 187-188, 235-236, 238, 324-327, 329, 335
See also Genesis pattern; light; sacred geometry
vibration 20, 44, 113, 128, 225, 262, 274, 320, 379-380
Vietnam 23
violet light 70, 385
virgin births
See immaculate conception
Virgo 58, 304
virtual reality 413
virus 76-77, 170, 178-179, 449-450
Vitruvius 238-242
canon of *frontispiece*, 238-241, 244-245, 349
Vogel, Marcel 370
Void, Great 41, 44, 114-115, 129, 132, 147-151, 154, 166-167, 169, 187, 221-222, 255, 312, 324, 367, 372, 413-414, 416, 426, 429-430, 434, 436-438, 440
bardo 47
duat 47
and pole shifts 114
See also octave
volcanoes 60, 98
von Neumann, John 305
voodoo 358
vortex 97-99, 109, 117, 153, 158-160, 268, 288, 297, 414

W

Walking between the Worlds: The Science of Compassion 448-449
See also Braden, Gregg
Wall Street Journal 72
Washington Post 72
Watson, Lyall 106
waveform 29, 43-45, 179, 212, 320, 370, 393
See also dimensions; wavelength; sine-wave signature
wavelength 6, 44-45, 47, 291
significance of 7.23 cm 45, 203
and Om 45
of the universe 45, 203
See also dimensions
Wayna Picchu 110-111
Wayne, John 276
West, John Anthony 18, 80, 111-112, 297
whales 15, 88
and magnetic lines 62, 430-431
wheels, Egyptian
See Egyptian archaeology
white dwarf 11-12, 87
White, John 60
white-light (energy) 252-253, 256, 268
WHO
See World Health Organization
Williams, Robin 400
Winter, Dan 168
witchcraft 358, 380
World Atlas of Geomorphic Features 217
See also Snead, Rodman E.
World Health Organization 77-78
"World Scientists' Warning to Humanity" 67
World War I 91, 306
World War II 75, 79, 108, 177, 305-306
writing, ancient 16-17, 20, 23, 27, 39, 56-58, 80, 118, 122, 126, 137, 238, 249, 301
introduction of 21-22, 132-133
Wulfing, Sulamith 163

X

x-ray diffraction pattern 165, 170-171

Y

Y2K 432, 443
Yale University 16
yoga 92
Yogananda, Paramahansa 24, 57, 444
Yogi Bhajan 322-323
yogic pranayama 212
Yogi Ramacharaka 348
Young, Arthur 155
Yucatan 40, 112, 117-118, 443
yugas 57-58
dwapara yuga 57
kali yuga 57-58, 124
satya yuga 57
treta yuga 57
See also precession of the equinoxes

Z

Zaghouan 110
zero-point technology 167, 211-214
See also human grid
zodiac 58, 130, 167
Zulus 85, 309, 445

Template for a STAR TETRAHEDRON

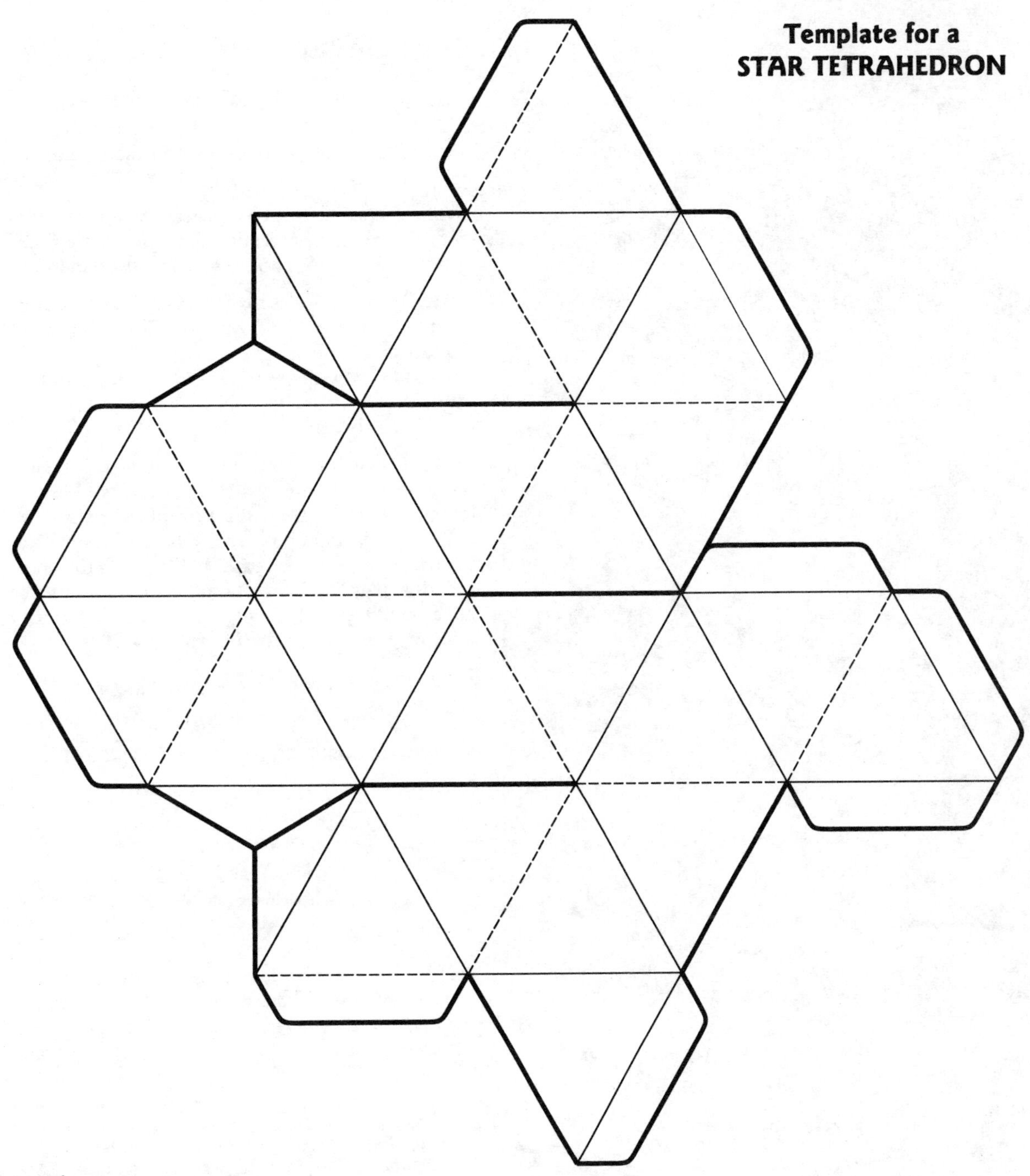

Instructions:

1. Cut out the outline.
2. Cut along all heavy lines.
3. Score plain lines on the front.
4. Score dotted lines on the back.
5. Fold triangles upward along plain lines.
6. Fold triangles downward along dotted lines.
7. Glue or tape tabs to form small tetrahedrons.
8. Continue until you have a star tetrahedron.

Note: This will take concentration, so don't be discouraged. (It might be helpful to make several copies.)

LIGHT TECHNOLOGY PUBLISHING PRESENTS

THE EXPLORER RACE SERIES

Zoosh through Robert Shapiro

The Origin . . .
The Purpose . . .
The Future of Humanity

"After all the words that we put out, ultimately the intention is to persuade people's minds, otherwise known as giving their minds the answers that their minds hunger for so that their minds can get out of the way and let their hearts take them to where they would naturally go anyway."

— Zoosh/Robert Shapiro

THE SERIES

Humans — creators in training — have a purpose and destiny so heartwarmingly, profoundly glorious that it is almost unbelievable from our present dimensional perspective. Humans are great lightbeings from beyond this creation, gaining experience in dense physicality. This truth about the great human genetic experiment of the Explorer Race and the mechanics of creation is being revealed for the first time by Zoosh and his friends through superchannel Robert Shapiro. These books read like adventure stories as we follow the clues from this creation that we live in out to the Council of Creators and beyond.

❶ the EXPLORER RACE

This book presents humanity in a new light, as the explorers and problem-solvers of the universe, admired by the other galactic beings for their courage and creativity. Some topics are: The Genetic Experiment on Earth; The ET in You: Physical Body, Emotion, Thought and Spirit; The Joy, the Glory and the Challenge of Sex; ET Perspectives; The Order: Its Origin and Resolution; Coming of Age in the Fourth Dimension and much more! 574p $25.00

❷ ETs and the EXPLORER RACE

In this book Robert channels Joopah, a Zeta Reticulan now in the ninth dimension, who continues the story of the great experiment — the Explorer Race — from the perspective of his race. The Zetas would have been humanity's future selves had not humanity re-created the past and changed the future. 237p $14.95

❸ EXPLORER RACE: Origins and the Next 50 Years

Some chapters are: THE ORIGINS OF EARTH RACES: Our Creator and Its Creation, The White Race and the Andromedan Linear Mind, The Asian Race, The African Race, The Fairy Race and the Native Peoples of the North, The Australian Aborigines, The Origin of Souls. THE NEXT 50 YEARS: The New Corporate Model, The Practice of Feeling, Benevolent Magic, Future Politics, A Visit to the Creator of All Creators. ORIGINS OF THE CREATOR: Creating with Core Resonances; Jesus, the Master Teacher; Recent Events in Explorer Race History; On Zoosh, Creator and the Explorer Race. 339p $14.95

❹ EXPLORER RACE: Creators and Friends — the Mechanics of Creation

As we explore the greater reality beyond our planet, our galaxy, our dimension, our creation, we meet prototypes, designers, shapemakers, creators, creators of creators and friends of our Creator, who explain their roles in this creation and their experiences before and beyond this creation. As our awareness expands about the way creation works, our awareness of who we are expands and we realize that a part of ourselves is in that vast creation — and that we are much greater and more magnificent than even science fiction had led us to believe. Join us in the adventure of discovery. It's mind-stretching! 435p $19.95

❺ EXPLORER RACE: Particle Personalities

All around you in every moment you are surrounded by the most magical and mystical beings. They are too small for you to see as single individuals, but in groups you know them as the physical matter of your daily life. Particles who might be considered either atoms or portions of atoms consciously view the vast spectrum of reality, yet also have a sense of personal memory like your own linear memory. These particles remember where they have been and what they have done in their infinitely long lives. Some of the particles we hear from are Gold, Mountain Lion, Liquid Light, Uranium, the Great Pyramid's Capstone, This Orb's Boundary, Ice and Ninth-Dimensional Fire. 237p $14.95

❻ EXPLORER RACE: EXPLORER RACE and BEYOND

In our continuing exploration of how creation works, we talk to Creator of Pure Feelings and Thoughts, the Liquid Domain, the Double-Diamond Portal, and the other 93% of the Explorer Race. We revisit the Friends of the Creator to discuss their origin and how they see the beyond; we finally reach the root seeds of the Explorer Race (us!) and find we are from a different source than our Creator and have a different goal; and we end up talking to All That Is! 360p $14.95

❼ EXPLORER RACE and ISIS (COMING SOON!)

Isis, caregiver to the Creator and the Earth goddess prototype, has had long and loving interactions with humanity — some even before the Explorer Race came to Earth to continue the experiment. She explains the beginning of the Isis Egyptian myths and chronicles some of her adventures with humans. Her love and caring come through the words, and her sense of humor is exquisite.. $14.95

Ⓐ EXPLORER RACE: Material Mastery Series

Secret shamanic techniques to heal particular energy points on Earth, which then feed healing energy back to humans. The reader will begin the joyous process of connecting on an intimate feeling level with Earth and all of its parts and all sentient beings on Earth — people, animals, plants, minerals, water and so forth. Physical people — spiritual masters on other dimensions — are here to learn material mastery. This book is a textbook on the subject. $19.95

AVAILABLE FROM LIGHT TECHNOLOGY PUBLISHING

CALL (800) 450-0985 or Fax (800) 393-7017

✦ BOOK MARKET ORDER FORM ✦

BOOKS PUBLISHED BY LIGHT TECHNOLOGY PUBLISHING

Title	Price	No. Copies	Total
1-800-God-Help-Me	$15.95		$
Acupressure for the Soul	$11.95		$
Ancient Secret of the Flower of Life	$25.00		$
Arcturus Probe	$14.95		$
Auras 101	$ 6.95		$
Behold a Pale Horse	$25.00		$
Cactus Eddie	$11.95		$
Channelling: Evolutionary . . .	$ 9.95		$
Color Medicine	$11.95		$
Forever Young	$ 9.95		$
Guardians of The Flame	$14.95		$
Great Kachina	$11.95		$
I'm OK, I'm Just Mutating	$ 6.00		$
Keys to the Kingdom	$14.95		$
Living Rainbows	$14.95		$
Mahatma I & II	$19.95		$
Millennium Tablets	$14.95		$
New Age Primer	$11.95		$
Path of the Mystic	$11.95		$
Poisons That Heal	$14.95		$
Prisoners of Earth	$11.95		$
Sedona Vortex Guide Book	$14.95		$
Shadow of San Francisco Peaks	$ 9.95		$
Shifting Frequencies	$14.95		$
The Soul Remembers	$14.95		$
Story of the People	$11.95		$
This World and the Next One	$ 9.95		$
Welcome to Planet Earth	$14.95		$
Robert Shapiro/Arthur Fanning			
Shining the Light	$12.95		$
Shining the Light — Book II	$14.95		$
Shining the Light — Book III	$14.95		$
Shining the Light — Book IV	$14.95		$
Shining the Light — Book V	$14.95		$
Shining the Light — Book VI	$14.95		$
Robert Shapiro			
The Explorer Race	$25.00		$
ETs and the Explorer Race	$14.95		$
Explorer Race: Origins . . .	$14.95		$
Explorer Race: Particle . . .	$14.95		$
Explorer Race: Creator . . .	$19.95		$
Explorer Race and Beyond	$14.95		$
Explorer Race and Isis	$14.95		$
Shamanic Secrets/Material Mastery	$19.95		$
Shamanic Secrets/Physical Mastery	$19.95		$
Arthur Fanning			
Soul, Evolution, Father	$12.95		$
Simon	$ 9.95		$
Wesley H. Bateman			
Dragons & Chariots	$ 9.95		$
Knowledge From the Stars	$11.95		$
Lynn Buess			
Children of Light, Children . . .	$ 8.95		$
Numerology: Nuances . . .	$13.75		$
Numerology for the New Age	$11.00		$
Ruth Ryden			
The Golden Path	$11.95		$
Living The Golden Path	$11.95		$
Dorothy Roeder			
Crystal Co-Creators	$14.95		$
Next Dimension is Love	$11.95		$
Reach For Us	$14.95		$
Hallie Deering			
Light From the Angels	$15.00		$
Do-It-Yourself Power Tools	$25.00		$
Joshua David Stone, Ph.D.			
Complete Ascension Manual	$14.95		$
Hidden Mysteries	$14.95		$
Beyond Ascension	$14.95		$
Soul Psychology	$14.95		$
Ascended Masters Light the Way	$14.95		$
Cosmic Ascension	$14.95		$
Beginners Guide to Ascension	$14.95		$
Golden Keys to Ascension	$14.95		$
Manual for Planetary Leadership	$14.95		$
Your Ascension Mission	$14.95		$
Revelations of a Melchizedek . . .	$14.95		$
How to Teach Ascension Classes	$14.95		$
Asc. & Romantic Relationships	$14.95		$
Vywamus/Janet McClure			
AHA! The Realization Book	$11.95		$
Light Techniques	$11.95		$
Sanat Kumara	$11.95		$
Scopes of Dimensions	$11.95		$
The Source Adventure	$11.95		$
Prelude to Ascension	$29.95		$
StarChild Press ★ ★ ★ ★ ★ ★ ★ ★ ★ ★ ★ ★ ★ ★			
Leia Stinnett			
A Circle of Angels	$18.95		$
The Twelve Universal Laws	$18.95		$
All My Angel Friends	$10.95		$
Animal Tales	$ 7.95		$
Where Is God?	$ 6.95		$
Just Lighten Up!	$ 9.95		$
Happy Feet	$ 6.95		$
When the Earth Was New	$ 6.95		$
The Angel Told Me . . .	$ 6.95		$
Color Me One	$ 6.95		$
One Red Rose	$ 6.95		$
Exploring the Chakras	$ 6.95		$
Crystals R For Kids	$ 6.95		$
Who's Afraid of the Dark	$ 6.95		$
Bridge Between Two Worlds	$ 6.95		$

BOOKS PRINTED OR MARKETED BY LIGHT TECHNOLOGY PUBLISHING

Title	Price	No. Copies	Total
Access Your Brain's Joy Center	$14.95		$
Alien Bases on the Moon II	$19.95		$
Atlantis Connection	$14.95		$
Awaken to the Healer Within	$16.50		$
Earth in Ascension	$14.95		$
God This is a Good Book	$16.50		$
The Humorous Herbalist	$14.95		$
I Want To Know	$ 7.00		$
Jane Roberts A View from the . . .	$14.95		$
Life Is The Father Within	$19.75		$
Life On the Cutting Edge	$14.95		$
M.A.S.S. 101	$ 9.95		$
Mayan Calendar Birthday Book	$12.95		$
Mayan Calendar Coloring Book	$ 8.95		$
Mayan Calendar: Voice of the Galaxy	$13.00		$
Medical Astrology	$29.95		$
Miracles & Other Ordinary Things	$19.95		$
Our Cosmic Ancestors	$ 9.95		$
Perfect Health	$15.95		$
Plant Power	$19.95		$
Reclaiming the Shadow Self	$15.95		$
Reflections on Ascension	$12.95		$
Sedona Starseed	$14.95		$
Sedona Vortex Experience	$ 4.95		$
Song of Sirius	$ 8.00		$
Soul Recovery and Extraction	$ 9.95		$
Stalking the Wild Pendulum	$12.95		$
Temple of The Living Earth	$16.00		$
Touched by Love	$9.95		$
The Armstrong Report	$11.95		$
The Emerald Tablets of Thoth . . .	$15.95		$
The Humorous Herbalist	$14.95		$
The Transformative Vision	$14.95		$
We Are One	$14.95		$
Lee Carroll			
Kryon–Book I, The End Times	$12.00		$
Kryon–Book II, Don't Think Like .	$12.00		$
Kryon–Book III, Alchemy of . . .	$14.00		$
Kryon–The Parables of Kryon	$17.00		$
Kryon–The Journey Home	$14.95		$
Kryon–Partnering with God	$14.00		$
The Indigo Children–with Jan Tober	$13.95		$
Tom Dongo			
Mysteries of Sedona — Book I	$ 6.95		$
Alien Tide — Book II	$ 7.95		$
Quest — Book III	$ 9.95		$
Unseen Beings, Unseen Worlds	$ 9.95		$
Merging Dimensions	$14.95		$
Sedona in a Nutshell	$ 4.95		$
Richard Dannelley			
Sedona Power Spot/Guide	$11.00		$
Sedona: Beyond The Vortex	$12.00		$
Jani King			
P'taah–The Gift	$19.95		$
P'taah–An Act of Faith	$15.50		$
P'taah–Transformation of the Species	$15.50		$
MSI			
Second Thunder	$17.95		$
Preston B. Nichols with Peter Moon			
Montauk Project	$15.95		$
Montauk Revisited	$19.95		$
Pyramids of Montauk	$19.95		$
Encounter in the Pleiades . . .	$19.95		$
The Black Sun	$19.95		$
Montauk: The Alien Connection	$19.95		$
Lyssa Royal and Keith Priest			
Preparing For Contact	$12.95		$
Prism of Lyra	$11.95		$
Visitors From Within	$12.95		$
Millennium	$13.95		$

ASCENSION MEDITATION TAPES

Title	Code	Price	No. Copies	Total
Joshua David Stone, Ph.D.				
Ascension Activation Meditation	S101	$12.00		$
Tree of Life Ascension Meditation	S102	$12.00		$
Mt. Shasta Ascension Activation Meditation	S103	$12.00		$
Kabbalistic Ascension Activation	S104	$12.00		$
Complete Ascension Manual Meditation	S105	$12.00		$
Set of all 5 tapes		$49.95		$
Vywamus/Barbara Burns				
The Quantum Mechanical You (6 tapes)	B101-6	$40.00		$
Taka				
Magical Sedona through the Didgeridoo	T101	$12.00		$
Brian Grattan				
Seattle Seminar Resurrection 1994 (12 tapes)	M102	$79.95		$
Easter Seminar 1994 (7 tapes - translated)	M103	$35.00		$
YHWH/Arthur Fanning				
On Becoming	F101	$10.00		$
Healing Meditations/Knowing Self	F102	$10.00		$
Manifestation & Alignment w/ Poles	F103	$10.00		$
The Art of Shutting Up	F104	$10.00		$
Continuity of Consciousness	F105	$25.00		$
Merging the Golden Light Replicas of You	F107	$10.00		$
Kryon/Lee Carroll				
Seven Responsibilities of the New Age	K101	$10.00		$
Co-Creation in the New age	K102	$10.00		$
Ascension and the New Age	K103	$10.00		$
Nine Ways to Raise the Planet's Vibration	K104	$10.00		$
Gifts and Tools of the New Age	K105	$10.00		$

❑ CHECK ❑ MONEY ORDER

CREDIT CARD: ❑ MC ❑ VISA

\# ______________________

Exp. date: ______________________

Signature: ______________________

(U.S. FUNDS ONLY) PAYABLE TO:

LIGHT TECHNOLOGY PUBLISHING

P.O. BOX 3540 • FLAGSTAFF • AZ 86003

(520) 526-1345 FAX: (520) 714-1132

1-800-450-0985

Fax 1-800-393-7017

BOOKSTORE DISCOUNTS HONORED — SHIPPING 15% OF RETAIL

NAME/COMPANY ______________________

ADDRESS ______________________

CITY/STATE/ZIP ______________________

PHONE ______________ FAX ______________

E-MAIL ______________________

SUBTOTAL: $ ________

SALES TAX: $ ________
(8.5% – AZ residents only)

SHIPPING/HANDLING: $ ________
($4 Min.; 15% of orders over $30)

CANADA S/H: $ ________
(20% of order)

TOTAL AMOUNT ENCLOSED: $ ________

All prices in US$. Higher in Canada and Europe. Books are available at all national distributors as well as the following international distributors:

CANADA: Dempsey (604) 683-5541 Fax (604) 683-5521 • ENGLAND/EUROPE: Windrush Press Ltd. 0608 652012/652025 Fax 0608 652125
AUSTRALIA: Gemcraft Books (03) 888-0111 Fax (03) 888-0044 • NEW ZEALAND: Peaceful Living Pub. (07) 571-8105 Fax (07) 571-8513